THE SMITHS

Songs That Saved Your Life

THE SMITHS

Songs That Saved Your Life

SIMON GODDARD

Reynolds & Hearn Ltd
London

To Sylv. 'Crivens!'

Front cover image © Stephen Wright (www.smithsphotos.com)/Redferns
Back cover image © Pete Cronin/Redferns

Picture pages 1, 3 (bottom), 4 (bottom) – Redferns
Picture pages 2, 3 (top), 4 (top) – Retna Pictures
Picture pages 6, 7 – The Joel Finler Collection
Picture page 8 (top) – Rex Features
Picture page 8 (bottom) – Thames Television

First published in 2002 by
Reynolds & Hearn Ltd
61a Priory Road
Kew Gardens
Richmond
Surrey
TW9 3DH

A CIP catalogue record for this book is available from the British Library.

ISBN 1 903111 84 6

Designed by Peri Godbold

Printed and bound in Great Britain by Biddles Ltd, King's Lynn, Norfolk.

Contents

Acknowledgements

Thanks... Johnny Marr, Joe Moss, Mike Joyce, Andy Rourke, Stephen Street, John Porter, Craig Gannon, James Maker, Grant Showbiz, Dale Hibbert, Amanda Hallay, John Peel, Andrew McGibbon, Kevin Armstrong, Gail Colson, Audrey Riley, Linder Sterling, Stephen Wright, Stuart Batsford, Pete Shelley, Julie Snelling, the Granada Television team of Kieron Collins, David Nolan and Tom Smetham, James Nice, Tom Sheehan, Jake Kennedy, Marcus Hearn, Richard Reynolds, Matthew Harvey and, for his part in the extraordinary tapes adventure, Dominic Whiteland.

RIP, Ian MacDonald (1948-2003): during my introduction to the first edition I made no secret of the fact that its format was explicitly modelled upon *Revolution in the Head*, Ian's scholarly account of The Beatles' recording career first published in 1994. Just as without T.Rex's 'Metal Guru' there'd have been no 'Panic', without Ian's *Revolution in the Head* there'd be no *Songs That Saved Your Life*.

Lastly, for their ceaseless support I thank Pippa Hall, Dan Drage and Sylvia Patterson.

Preface

Stop me if you think you've read this one before. If you *didn't* see the previous (pale blue) edition of *The Smiths: Songs That Saved Your Life*, then skip the next paragraph.

If you *did*, then you'd be forgiven for approaching this new (redbrick) edition with scepticism. Trust me, there are umpteen reasons for removing the old version from your shelf, lobbing it onto the fire and replacing it with this. If you don't then you may still believe, as I misinformed you in the old version, that 'How Soon Is Now?' was inspired by an old Elvis song and that Johnny Marr listens to James Taylor. You'll also be oblivious to such delights as the 'lift shaft' in 'Rubber Ring' and – perish the thought – run the risk of ending your days never having found out from whence the brass band at the beginning of 'Sheila Take A Bow' originates. In comparative Smiths-speak, if that pale blue antecedent was an equivalent *The Smiths* (a first major work with flawed production) then this redbrick replacement is *The Queen Is Dead* (the definitive document, I hope).

Proud as I was of *Songs That Saved Your Life* when it was first published in 2002, I'd be the first to admit its flaws. Even so, I never imagined tackling a revised edition and couldn't have entertained the idea without there being a sufficient wealth of new material to justify such a venture. An ever-expanding list of details I'd omitted or subsequently discovered after publication wasn't enough. A handful of new interviews with some of those I'd been unable to secure last time around made me reconsider and start redrafting. But it wasn't until Johnny Marr agreed to cooperate that the need to validate a full textual revision was finally eradicated. His voice is the obvious fundamental difference between this book and the old one, though there are enough nips and tucks elsewhere to easily distinguish the two versions at a glance. Essentially it's the same book, the same story, but one which I'd like to think of as having a bigger cast, a tighter script and improved cinematography. All this, and not a penny extra.

The objective I set out in the original introduction remains the same: to rejoice in the beauty of The Smiths and the music they created by burrowing beneath the surface of the songs. Not to demystify or deflate the Morrissey/Marr repertoire, but to unashamedly marvel at their ingenuity, audacity and innovation; to try and comprehend how and why the group's career evolved with such intensity in so short a time scale; and to examine how these songs were presented utilising the available media of the time.

The actual musical history of The Smiths was an area that had never been fully examined until this book. As the first explorer in this field, I soon discovered why. Piecing together the where and when of The Smiths' recording sessions was far from easy. Although I was granted access to studio out-takes and home demos, the actual chronology had to be painstakingly double and treble checked from hastily scribbled inlays, diaries, the conflicting recollections of producers and musicians and a long process of investigative deduction. Without being privy to any official studio log, I throw my hands up and freely confess there may be a slim margin of error on some of the chronological ordering (where early album tracks are concerned) and a handful of dates. Even so, if according to Marr the last one as it stood was 'really close', then this version is, to the best of my knowledge and diligent research, correct.

During my preface to that first edition, I also expressed concern that The Smiths' legacy had been so tainted by the 1996 court case and so marginalized by critics who preferred to dismiss them as an abnormality of Eighties pop culture that the magnificence of the art they created was in danger of being forgotten. In that respect, the tide definitely *has* shifted in the two years since this book was first published, during which time their profile (as measured by the extent to which they've soaked into the fabric of contemporary print media, TV and radio) has been raised considerably. It's difficult for me, personally, to speculate on what part this book has played in their gradual 'reacceptance'. It would, however, seem the days when authors pitching ideas to publishing directors are told 'well the thing is, The Smiths aren't really *that* popular anymore' (I speak from experience) are a thing of the past.

I remember, about a year after the first version came out, being introduced to a fellow music journalist and dyed-in-the-wool Smiths nut who, I was charmed to learn, had read my book in one sitting. 'I could write about that band forever,' he said. 'Me too,' I replied. And that's the problem. The word 'obsessional' doesn't fully do justice to the past four to five years spent writing and researching both old and new versions of *Songs That Saved Your Life* (the word 'dysfunctional' might). So those concerned that they'll be forced to invest in a further revised edition of this book in a few years time can rest assured that a third version is about as likely a prospect as a fully fledged Smiths reunion. There are probably dozens of lyrical steals, untold anecdotes and I daresay more lost recordings waiting to be discovered. But my work here really is done.

In finishing, I'm still struck by a comment Johnny Marr made to me at the end of our interview as I gathered my things to leave. 'When it was just the four of us in 1982, *never* did we think the day would come when somebody would be writing like this about the music we were banging out in some tiny rehearsal room.' Back in 1985, when I returned home from seeing The Smiths and stuck a poster on my bedroom wall of Marr sat posing beside his Gretsch guitar, *never* did I think the day would come 20 years later when he would personally thank me for 'caring' enough to write this book. 'Caring'? When it comes to The Smiths I'm incapable of anything less.

For the music they made, the wisdom they imparted and the emotional refuge they provided, The Smiths will forever be 'the band of my life'. So *obviously* I'm going to insist they're the greatest band ever to exist. I genuinely believe it. By reading this book, I don't necessarily expect you to agree. Simply to understand.

Simon Goddard,
London,
July 2004

Finally, a brief word on how to 'use' this book. *Songs That Saved Your Life* is the story of The Smiths through their music. It can be read from beginning to end as a narrative biography or used as a reference text with the aid of the Song Index. Adapting the chronological model of Ian MacDonald's Beatles study *Revolution in the Head*, recordings are numbered with relevant studio, producer and release details. Tracks are also cross referenced where appropriate (eg **[see 21]**).

Each individual entry also carries its own separate set of appendices: *'In Concert'* (a brief synopsis of that song's concert shelf-life from first to last performance, noting any unusual absences or relevant anecdotes), *'Radio'* (details of any alternate BBC session or concert recording broadcast in the UK) and *'Television'* (a record of any mimed or live studio performances on UK television only). All the above elements can also be viewed in relation to the group's official Rough Trade discography using the Timeline appendix.

Unless otherwise indicated in brackets beside the title, all songs are written by Morrissey and Marr.

Part 1

'Take me back to dear old Blighty...'

Origins & Recordings 1982-1983

Four years before they formed The Smiths, the actual first meeting between Morrissey and Johnny Marr took place on the night of Thursday, 31 August, 1978.

At the time, Morrissey was 19 years old and unemployed. His future partner was two months shy of 15 and still at school. Both were nevertheless compelled to spend that evening under the same roof at Manchester's Apollo Theatre to witness a concert by New York 'godmother of punk' and self-styled 'Field Marshal of rock 'n' roll', Patti Smith.

It was here, thanks to Billy Duffy and Howard Bates, mutual acquaintances from Marr's native Wythenshawe, that he and Morrissey were briefly introduced. As was perhaps to be expected considering the significant age gap, conversation began and ended with 'a quick hullo' Instead, both concentrated on the mesmerising stage presence of Smith herself. Little could these two relative strangers have imagined that four years hence they would together remodel one of the songs from her set that night, 'Kimberly', as their own 'The Hand That Rocks The Cradle'. Yet the differing lives, locales, families and friends of the young Morrissey and Marr were such that they could so very easily not have crossed paths ever again.

Born 22 May 1959, Steven Patrick Morrissey's ambition to become a singer had already been half-realised prior to that Patti Smith gig. Some months earlier, he'd made his stage debut after forming a brief alliance with the man responsible for the initial introduction to Marr, future Cult guitarist Billy Duffy. At the time, Duffy was involved with local punk troop The Nosebleeds (formerly Ed Banger & The Nosebleeds). Yet, although Morrissey co-wrote a handful of songs[1] and made it as far as two aimless support slots – sharing the bill with Jilted John, then Magazine – the association with Duffy fragmented soon after.

1 These, the earliest known Morrissey lyrics, include 'I Get Nervous', 'Peppermint Heaven', 'The Living Juke-Box' and '(I Think) I'm Ready For The Electric Chair'. Morrissey would also be briefly linked with Duffy's next group, Slaughter & The Dogs, though has since denied any such involvement.

Struggling to find a suitable outlet for his vocal urges, by the early Eighties Morrissey had surrendered to his more hermitical impulses as a writer and would-be journalist. He continued the bombardment of the music weeklies' letters pages that he'd begun as far back as 1974, as well as furiously scribbling plays, fantasy *Coronation Street* storylines and fictional prose. Still living at home with his mother and older sister (his parents had separated in 1976), he would later mythologize his youth as one crippled by insecurity, ineptness and a stifling sense of isolation from his peers. Instead, he sought solace in books – from Oscar Wilde to pro-feminist rhetoric such as Warren Farrell's *The Liberated Man*; in films – from classic Hollywood melodramas starring Bette Davis and Katharine Hepburn to the British 'kitchen sink dramas' of the early Sixties; and most pertinently in music.

Prior to punk, Morrissey's tastes were chiefly moulded by glam rock, from populist, home-grown chart fare like T.Rex, Bowie and Roxy Music to Sparks, Jobriath and glam-drag proto-punks The New York Dolls. Though he would famously declare Marianne Faithfull's 1964 hit 'Come and Stay With Me' as the first record he bought, it was really through The Dolls that Morrissey developed his renowned fascination with girl singers of the 1960s, from American teen screamers like The Shangri-Las and The Marvelettes to Britain's own Sandie Shaw (Dolls frontman David Johansen would cover Shaw's 1964 hit 'Girl Don't Come' in his late-Seventies solo shows and occasionally mentioned her in press interviews[2]).

The Dolls dominated Morrissey's adolescence enough for him to try and organise a UK fan club, corresponding with other fanatics across the country through small ads in the back pages of the music press (among them future Clash guitarist Mick Jones). In 1981, he finally got to champion them properly in a short biographical essay issued as a 24-page booklet, *The New York Dolls*, through local publishers Babylon Books. Though a small-scale affair with a modest print run (Morrissey himself was only entitled to two complimentary author copies), alongside his subsequent James Dean volume for Babylon (*James Dean Is Not Dead*) and his sporadic freelance reviews for *Record Mirror*, the Dolls book whetted his appetite for an alternate career in music journalism, which, had The Smiths never formed, he would certainly have pursued further.

The myth of Morrissey's pre-Smiths early adulthood, one largely self-propagated in press interviews, is that of a 'boy out of time', cocooned in his bedroom, listening to antiquated sixties girl pop and forgotten B-sides by

2 As a case in point, Shaw crops up in 'Whatever Happened To Davie Doll?', Tony Parsons' interview with Johansen in the 30 September 1978 edition of the *NME* The same feature also finds Johansen singing the praises of another Morrissey favourite, The Foundations' 'Build Me Up Buttercup'.

early British rock 'n' rollers like Billy Fury. Though his fascination with such vinyl obscurities was genuine, at the same time Morrissey was also a regular concertgoer who still maintained an interest in the alternative/post-punk music scene: from recent works by Lou Reed (1979's *The Bells*) and Brian Eno (*Before and After Science*) to Magazine, The B-52s, The Fall and even the synthesizer gloom of Simple Minds' third album, *Empires and Dance*.

Also among his favourite contemporary groups was The Monochrome Set, a lyrically arch, musically whimsical ex-art school quartet from London. The extent of Morrissey's preoccupation with the band became evident when he sent a Clark Gable postcard to Scottish pen pal Robert Mackie, the reverse of which he emblazoned with the last verse of 'Ici, Les Enfants' from their 1980 debut LP, *Strange Boutique.*[3] It's even fair to speculate that the song's sexually risqué content ('the face of a woman and the body of a child', 'I know you're only 12 so I'll keep it pretty tame') might have encouraged the similarly contentious lyrics of early Smiths compositions such as 'Handsome Devil'.

Equally influential, but much closer to home, were the arty punk-jazz ensemble Ludus. Their frontwoman was the enigmatic Linder Sterling, the renowned collage artist and sleeve designer responsible for the iconic iron-headed nude adorning the 1977 Buzzcocks single 'Orgasm Addict' and the painting featured on Magazine's 1978 debut album *Real Life.* Linder would have a profound effect on the young Morrissey who by 1981 had made a rapid transition from devoted fan to doting friend.[4] Consequently, Morrissey took much from Linder's lyrics, which were heavily informed by gender politics and feminist literature ('Anatomy Is Not Destiny', 'You Open My Legs Like a Book') as well as her unorthodox vocal technique which would often leap into a wailing, high-pitched primal falsetto. At the age of 21, the besotted Morrissey would even go as far as to mimic Linder's visual art by slavishly reproducing the geometric caricatures from Ludus' record sleeves onto his own correspondence.

It was through Linder and her intellectual clique that Morrissey would also befriend her ex-boyfriend, Buzzcocks' founder and Magazine singer Howard Devoto, as well as the head of Ludus' New Hormones label, Richard Boon. Even Factory Records' boss Tony Wilson knew of Morrissey as a minor

3 Could the depressed and disillusioned 21-year-old Morrissey have ever imagined that, 20 years after sending that postcard of Gable to Mackie, he'd actually be living in the Hollywood legend's house? In 1998, Morrissey settled in LA, moving into the Spanish villa Gable built in 1931 for his wife, actress Carole Lombard, who, as the singer explained, 'was killed in a plane crash before she'd had time to pick out the curtains.'

4 Conflicting rumours speculate on whether or not Morrissey actually spent a brief spell cohabiting with Linder and Ludus guitarist Ian Devine at their flat on Mayfield Road in Whalley Range. He was, at the very least, a frequent visitor there.

character on the fringes of Manchester's punk community (or as journalist Paul Morley sardonically put it, 'the village idiot'). Yet despite such apparently healthy connections in the local music scene, by 1982 Morrissey was becoming increasingly desperate that his singing talents had yet to be realised, combating his resultant depression 'on a diet of sleeping pills' and dulling his anxiety 'in barbiturate dreams'. Linder Sterling still recalls his evident frustration: 'There was always that sense around Morrissey that he was about to go somewhere, but then it seemed like a long, long time before, in his own words, the world *would* listen. I think it tried his patience beyond any human endurance.'

In the meantime, Johnny Marr's patience would be equally tested in the years following that Patti Smith show at the Apollo.

Back then, John Martin Maher (born 31 October 1963, later changing the spelling of his surname so as not to be confused with the identically christened drummer from the Buzzcocks) was only just discovering American punk pioneers like Smith and The New York Dolls, both of whom would eventually lead him to Morrissey. Only a few months earlier, in April 1978, Marr had read an interview with ex-Dolls vocalist David Johansen in *Melody Maker* that left a lasting impression: 'It was a massively important article, 'The Last Doll Comes In From The Cold' Almost a life-changing moment. Same as the day I bought [Iggy & The Stooges'] *Raw Power* and the day I bought [Johnny Thunders & The Heartbreakers'] *L.A.M.F.*'[5]

Though inspired by the example of the Dolls' Johnny Thunders and The Patti Smith Group's Ivan Kraal, Marr's reputation as the school guitar virtuoso rested on more mainstream American rock influences such as Tom Petty, Nils Lofgren and Neil Young. It was because of Young, specifically a button badge bearing the title of his 1975 album *Tonight's the Night,* that Marr first struck up a conversation with fellow classmate and future Smiths member Andy Rourke (born 17 January 1964). 'Originally we were in different classes,' explains Rourke. 'I was in the bad lads' class and basically I got a bit too bad so they switched me and Phil Powell – who later became Johnny's guitar roadie in The Smiths – into Johnny's class, the good lads' class, to sort us out. He saw this Neil Young badge I was wearing and we started talking.'

In fact it was Rourke, himself a guitar player, who originally helped his new friend master the basics. 'He was dead keen,' Rourke elaborates when reminiscing about their late-Seventies schooldays at St Augustine's Grammar

5 'The Last Doll Comes In From The Cold' ran in the 15 April 1978 edition of *Melody Maker.* Written by Stanley Mieses, it offered a fascinating primer in the background of The New York Dolls' rise and fall.

where his and Marr's form room fortuitously doubled as the music class. 'There was a piano in the corner which we used to muck around on and we both used to bring our guitars in. I'd show him something and a week later he could play it better than me. That's how keen he was.' Such was Marr's proficiency on the instrument that Rourke graciously volunteered to switch to bass when forming their first proper band, The Paris Valentinos. Since they practised in a school hall that was regularly used for jumble sales, it was not uncommon for Marr and Rourke to rummage through the vinyl stock of the next charity fête and pilfer the richest pickings: old seven-inches by The Rolling Stones, The Kinks and The Beatles.

After leaving school in 1980, their joint adolescent rock 'n' roll fantasies would be cruelly taunted when, after sending a homemade demo tape in response to an *NME* ad, Marr and Rourke's next group, White Dice, was invited to audition for the London-based record label F-Beat. Beyond the temporary excitement of a trip down South and their first time in a proper recording studio, it proved an ultimately disappointing experience. In the wake of their rejection, Marr and Rourke changed tack with their own side project, which saw them make the transition from rock to funk as the short-lived Freak Party. Augmented by drummer Simon Wolstencroft, by the end of 1981 the trio were practising on average three nights a week at Decibel, a local studio and rehearsal space in Ancoats. It was here, with the assistance of trainee engineer Dale Hibbert, that they recorded their only demo, 'Crak Therapy' (a Marr original).

While Rourke and Wolstencroft were content to pursue the instrumental funk route, Freak Party didn't satisfy Marr's own musical needs for long. He eventually quit, in part due to their frustrating inability to find a suitable vocalist. 'He was a bit more hungry for it,' reflects Rourke, 'so he eventually left. I didn't hear from him then for about a year.' Already employed at X-Clothes, an alternative fashion outlet in Manchester city centre, Marr admits to cutting himself off from his past in a conscious effort to change his social and musical circles. 'I decided to get a whole new life, one away from the suburbs that Andy and I were stuck in. I finally came into my own when I got *out* of the suburbs and *into* Manchester. I was a townie. A definite line was drawn from when I'd stopped playing with Andy and Si. I just dived into a load of new influences.'

Being in the city centre meant Marr resumed an old friendship with Andrew Berry, hairdresser by day and DJ by night. Soon Marr became a temporary lodger at Berry's house on Palantine Road where he'd be turned on to early electro and hip hop (J Walter Negro & The Loose Jointz's 'Shoot The Pump' and Lovebug Starski's 'Live At The Fever Disco'), as well as keeping tabs on current guitar music, from the savage punk-blues of LA's The Gun

Club to the scratching indie-funk of Scotland's Josef K (in particular their February 1982 swansong single, 'The Missionary').

He was also fortunate enough to inherit an entire record collection from Altrincham record shop manager Pete Hunt, who entrusted Marr to baby-sit his entire vinyl archive while he went travelling in Europe. Ecstatic over his new bequest, Marr spent weeks flicking through Hunt's encyclopaedic collection, which now lined the walls of his latest abode, an attic room in the house of Granada Television presenter Shelley Rohde, several miles out of town in Bowden, Cheshire. Hunt would also throw Marr a possible career lifeline by introducing him to Matt Johnson, then in the process of forming The The. Johnson was duly taken with Marr's talent, though in the event Johnny declined the offer to relocate down South and join Johnson's group.

However, neither Hunt nor Berry would have as big an impact on Marr and the eventual genesis of The Smiths as Joe Moss. It now seems divine destiny that X-Clothes was situated on Manchester's Chapel Walks, next door to Crazy Face, a second branch of the rag trade business Moss operated from his Portland Street headquarters. Marr was particularly captivated by the vintage publicity stills of Fifties rock 'n' roll idols that adorned Crazy Face's walls and the in-store rotation of old blues and R&B records. In turn, Moss, an avid vinyl collector and nominal guitar player, was greatly impressed by the young Johnny's energy, enthusiasm and his insatiable desire to form a group of his own.

By this time, Marr's self-aggrandising gift of the gab was local legend. Even Pete Shelley, having just gone solo after the demise of the Buzzcocks, remembers a brief encounter illustrative of the guitarist's fearless precocity: 'He just came up to me one night, I didn't know who he was, this kid, and said "If you're looking for a guitar player, I'm your man". I think he approached practically every band in Manchester at that time saying exactly the same thing. They all ignored him.'

All, that is, except Joe Moss, who actively encouraged Marr's musical apprenticeship. Their convivial lunch hours at Crazy Face listening to LPs by John Lee Hooker, Moby Grape, Jefferson Airplane and Van Morrison's Them progressed to evenings at Moss's home watching Stones videos and rock 'n' roll documentaries. It was through this sage-like tuition that Marr finally stumbled upon his road to Damascus – in the form of a programme Moss insisted he should see; a documentary taped off ITV's *South Bank Show* arts series focussing on the life and work of Jerry Leiber and Mike Stoller, the American song writing team who'd penned umpteen classic rock 'n' roll hits, most famously Elvis Presley's 'Hound Dog'. Watching the programme, Marr was struck by the fact that their partnership had been formed after Leiber allegedly turned up one day at Stoller's front door unannounced, suggesting they collaborate. This was Marr's epiphany.

'I wanted someone who was just a singer and wasn't playing an instrument,' says Marr. 'I didn't want a musical co-writer. I wanted someone who looked good and who was serious about words. But most important of all, I wanted somebody who was as serious about it as a life option as I was.'

Speculating on who his respective Stoller might be, Marr remembered Steven Morrissey, the older lad he'd met just briefly at that Patti Smith gig nearly four years ago through ex-Nosebleed Billy Duffy. As if Duffy's glowing recommendation of Morrissey's lyrical abilities wasn't enticement enough, Marr's sense of intrigue was further fuelled by the local knowledge that this 'Morrissey character' had recently had a book published on one of his favourite bands, The New York Dolls. 'It was because of The Dolls that I was first told about Morrissey,' Marr confirms, 'that's really what brought me to him.'

It would be another Wythenshawe guitarist, Steve Pomfret, who'd provide the final bridge. Forewarned that Pomfret could arrange a formal introduction, Marr made a point of befriending him with the promise of a place in the new group he was forming. Pomfret duly obliged one summer's day in May 1982, taking Marr to the door of 384 Kings Road in Stretford where, in a direct re-enactment of Jerry Leiber's doorstepping of Mike Stoller, he barged his way back into the life of Steven Patrick Morrissey.

'It's still really clear,' reminisces Marr. 'It was a sunny day, about one o'clock. There was no advance phone call or anything. I just knocked and he opened the door. As soon as the door opened, Pommy [Pomfret] took two very firm steps back. Which is one of the things that got me to talk so fast, it was just plain exuberance.'

However absurd and potentially awkward it might have seemed, once Marr calmed down sufficiently so they could discuss one another's musical reference points – The Dolls, Patti Smith, the Brill Building, Sixties girl groups – their symbiotic connection was obvious, right down to their shared retro-Fifties dress sense and mutual quiffed haircuts. 'When I came across Morrissey, in terms of influences it was pretty phenomenal that we were so in synch. Because the influences that we had individually were pretty obscure. So it was absolutely like fucking lightning bolts to the two of us. This wasn't stuff we liked. This was stuff we lived for really.'

That one visit was enough for Morrissey to agree to Marr's proposition that they begin working together as respective wordsmith and composer. Marr left elated, if somewhat cautious. 'My feeling, as I left him, was "well, yeah, okay. But I'll wait to see if he calls me tomorrow."'

The next day, Marr was back at work in X-Clothes when he received the phone call from Morrissey he'd been hoping for. 'And that was it,' says Marr. 'I thought "Right. Okay. We're on."'

The crucial compatibility test came a few days later when Morrissey arrived for their very first practice in Marr's rented attic room in Bowden. Proceedings got off to a clumsy start with Marr trying to make the best of a tune he hoped would fit some lyrics Morrissey had already given him, 'Don't Blow Your Own Horn'. 'We were kind of half doing it,' says Marr, 'but neither of us liked it very much. It was quite a jaunty, strummy thing. It didn't cut it and I don't think Morrissey really liked it either. We lived with it for about a week then decided not to bother with it.'

Thankfully their next effort, 'The Hand That Rocks The Cradle' **[see 11]**, was a far more auspicious omen of what was to come. 'When I saw the words, I just thought it scanned over the metre, the tempo, of 'Kimberly' by Patti Smith. Also it was terra firma, that was a real big touchstone for us. Remember we didn't know each other then so it was really important to the two of us that it worked. So I played this chord progression for 'The Hand That Rocks The Cradle' and we decided that it sounded good. So good that we recorded it on my legendary TEAC three-track cassette recorder, which enabled me to put down two guitar tracks then a vocal on top. So after trying 'Don't Blow Your Own Horn', that was the first song we actually wrote.'[6]

Morrissey had also prepared another sheet of lyrics entitled 'Suffer Little Children' **[see 19]**. 'I was sat on the floor with these words that he'd typed out. As I was looking at them I just started to play this chord progression, this figure I'd been fiddling around with for a couple of weeks. Straight away Morrissey said "Is that it? Keep going". So as I was looking at the lyrics, I didn't know how the vocal melody went, but I was getting a feeling from the words and just sticking with it. I thought it felt right.'

By the time the singer returned to Stretford, the first two Morrissey/Marr originals, both later immortalised on their debut album barely two years later, were done and dusted. 'After that first meeting we really couldn't get together often enough,' says Marr. 'It was a few times a week. We got a hell of a lot done in that first month.'

They were, Marr admits, in awe of one another's potential. 'He and I almost had this unspoken relationship where we were both able to be ourselves but we both knew how important we were to each other. What shouldn't be forgotten is that we really, *really* liked each other. It wasn't some

6 Marr's idea to apply Morrissey's 'The Hand That Rocks The Cradle' to the tune of 'Kimberly' from 1975's *Horses* seems a subconscious recognition of thematic lyrical parallels between the two songs. 'Kimberly' was Smith's ode to her baby sister in which she reminisces 'so with one hand I rocked you'.

business arrangement or relationship of convenience. There was intrigue and understanding because as different as we were, the thing that was paramount inside each of us was pop records and that absolute promise of escape. And he understood that without us ever having to talk about it.'

When not writing songs of their own, the pair strengthened their partnership, absorbing each other's tastes. 'We'd do each other tapes,' says Marr, 'as you do when you first meet a friend. I can remember when he gave me Marianne Faithfull's 'The Sha La La Song'.[7] It was like, wow! That song really hit the jackpot for about two weeks. But we didn't have to be absolutely magnetically joined by everything. If you live and work so closely together you just observe the things you don't share like peaking over the garden fence. Eyebrows were often raised from both sides! So the stuff he liked that I didn't, like Jobriath for example, I didn't have any violent objection to it. I thought it was kind of intriguing, it just didn't touch me.'

Steve Pomfret, meantime, had realised his superfluity to Morrissey and Marr's already impenetrable dynamic after a handful of token rehearsals. His exit, however bitter, was therefore inevitable. While the songs continued to flow (Marr names 'These Things Take Time', 'Handsome Devil', 'What Difference Does It Make?' and 'Miserable Lie' as 'that first bunch'), the hunt for adequate musicians to bring them to life gathered speed. As local face and boy-about-town, it was left to Marr to find the suitable candidates.

'I was inspired by Andrew Loog Oldham and his example,' explains Marr. 'I thought that was really noble, someone who was able to make things happen. In my head I thought I was running around the Brill Building. But that's how I was. I wore hyperactivity as a badge of honour. With Morrissey, he didn't actually need to physically get involved in that side. I was happy finding group members, places to rehearse, places to record, clothes, haircuts, managers and record companies. All he had to do was be brilliant and be with me, for us to be next to each other. That's what it was about. However, he was by no means sat in his front room with the telly on. What connections he was able to draw on, he could. There was a guy in Stretford he'd known for a number of years who was a drummer. He got us all together one evening. This guy was really amiable and chatty but he just didn't seem like a living breathing musician to me, just a nice guy with a drum kit, so obviously he wasn't in. But whatever could be done we both did.'

They may not have had a full working band, but by the end of the summer at least they finally had an agreed name of Morrissey's choosing: The Smiths. His stock answer in future interviews was that it was a

7 *The Face*'s Nick Kent later suggested that The Smiths toyed with covering Faithfull's 'The Sha La La Song', a 1965 B-side, and its flip 'Summer Nights'. According to Andy Rourke neither amounted to more than a passing rehearsal experiment.

celebration of ordinariness ('It was the most ordinary name and I thought it was time the ordinary folk of the world showed their faces') as well as a deliberate reaction against preposterous early-Eighties monikers like Orchestral Manoeuvres In The Dark. It may even have been a subconscious reference to Moors Murderers Ian Brady and Myra Hindley, the subject of their second earliest collaboration, 'Suffer Little Children'. In 1966, the notorious child-killers were only caught through the testimony of Hindley's sister Maureen, and her husband David Smith, frequently referred to in passing as 'the Smiths' in books such as Emlyn Williams' *Beyond Belief*, Morrissey's primary source for the song's lyrics **[see 19]**.

'I seem to remember them saying it was to do with Patti Smith,' recalls Dale Hibbert, the next musician to be drafted in by Marr as the band's first bass player. 'Because they were fans of hers, I seem to remember that it came from that. But it was discussed that the one thing they didn't want was to be referred to as "Johnny Smith", "Steven Smith" etc. They wanted to make it clear that was never going to happen.'

A sound engineer by day who'd previously fronted a succession of local bands, Hibbert was already acquainted with Marr, having recorded Freak Party's one demo at Decibel Studios barely a year earlier. After accepting Marr's invitation to join The Smiths, Hibbert was taken to meet Morrissey – but not before Marr had imparted a bizarre word of warning. 'The first thing Johnny said as I was going to meet him was "whatever you do, don't call him Steve. He absolutely hates it. Always refer to him as Steven". I thought that was a really odd thing to say, but I just went along with it.'

Morrissey had never been fond of the common colloquial abbreviations of his Christian name, already reprimanding those pen pals who took such liberties. 'Please don't call me "Steve". It reminds me of the Bionic Man, to whom I bear little resemblance.[8] It's almost worse than being called "Stephen" which reminds me of somebody with a snotty nose. So please call me "Steven". Am I being unreasonable? Actually, I hate the name Steven, but I won't go into THAT.'

Years later, Morrissey revealed that he was christened after American actor Steve Cochran (star of the 1956 small-town melodrama *Come Next Spring*), though by the time The Smiths signed to Rough Trade in the summer of 1983, he would forbid the use of his forename altogether. 'There was a definite moment when it happened,' smiles Marr. 'A directive went out. A verbal directive, which went out by a "representative". But it was fine, it made absolute sense. I wouldn't really have addressed him as anything other than

8 Steve Austin, (aka 'The Bionic Man') as played by Lee Majors in the 1970s US TV series *The Six Myillion Dollar Man*.

'Mozzer'. I'd already started to call him 'Moz' because of the absurdity of it. It's so ill suited.'

Like Pomfret before him, Dale Hibbert would attend a handful of practices at Marr's digs in Bowden. 'We both had semi-acoustic guitars. I had a Hofner and Johnny had a Gretsch, so we didn't even need amplifiers. I used to have to pick Steven up from his mum's house on Kings Road in Stretford and take him to band practices on my motorbike, with him clinging on to the back of me. So I got to know him quite well. He certainly didn't appear shy or retiring. I was told he had a history of journalism and had a lot of contacts in the music business which is why they were gonna take a shortcut to getting signed.'

It was here in Marr's attic room, after recruiting Hibbert, that the earliest surviving audio evidence of The Smiths was recorded. And so, this is where our chronology begins.

1 a

'I Want A Boy For My Birthday' *(Sylvester Bradford)*

Recorded **Manchester, August 1982**

Informal home recording

1 b

The Decibel Demo

Recorded **Decibel Studios, Manchester, August 1982**

First studio recording: **'The Hand That Rocks The Cradle', 'Suffer Little Children'**

Alongside the handful of originals they'd already written, Morrissey suggested they cover 'I Want A Boy For My Birthday', a song by early-Sixties black American girl group trio The Cookies.[9] 'I'd never heard it before,' says Marr, 'but I thought "Great, this'll really freak 'em out!" I was really happy to encourage it.'

Together, Morrissey and Marr recorded a stripped-down demo of the song on the guitarist's TEAC three-track machine, featuring just vocal and guitar, specifically intended for Hibbert to familiarise himself with. An ascending major-key dollop of girlish angst in which the protagonist forlornly hopes to be granted the birthday gift of a male companion who'll 'hug me, kiss me, squeeze me day and night', The Smiths' own interpretation was brave in its surprising lack of irony. Though of murky quality – Morrissey's vocal is at times almost inaudible beneath Marr's chorus pedal electric wash – their reading of the song as captured on tape is both faithful in arrangement and earnest in sentiment.

The decision to tackle 'I Want A Boy For My Birthday' was an obvious overspill from Morrissey's New York Dolls fixation. The Dolls had covered the likes of The Shangri-Las' 'Give Him A Great Big Kiss' in concert and pilfered its opening line – 'when I say I'm in love you'd best believe I'm in love, L-U-V!' – on their own 'Looking for a Kiss'. Shadow Morton, The Shangri-Las' original producer, was even drafted in to record their second

9 The original 'I Want A Boy For My Birthday' was the B-side of The Cookies' 1963 single 'Will Power'. Led by Earl-Jean McCree (who as 'Earl-Jean' enjoyed moderate solo success with the first recording of Goffin/King's 'I'm Into Something Good', later popularised by another of Morrissey's favourites, Herman's Hermits) the group's biggest hit was the previous year's 'Chains'; a further Goffin/King R&B classic, which inspired The Beatles to attempt an ill-advised cover on their 1963 debut album, *Please Please Me*. Coincidentally, after The Smiths, Andy Rourke co-wrote a handful of songs with Morrissey during the early stages of his solo career. One of these, 'Girl Least Likely To' (originally the 12-inch B-side to 1990's 'November Spawned a Monster') borrowed the melody of another little known Cookies track, 'Only To Other People'.

album, 1974's *Too Much Too Soon*. It's clear Morrissey's objective was to emulate the trans-gender subversion that the Dolls touched upon in relocating the female adolescent kitsch of Sixties transistor pop into an all-male, seventies rock 'n' roll environment. Marr was in total agreement. 'I knew about Phil Spector through Patti Smith, I knew about Shadow Morton through The Dolls. That's the context 'I Want A Boy For My Birthday' was done in.'

According to Hibbert, the Cookies cover was among the tracks considered for the first real studio demo, which, as engineer at Decibel, he himself was in a position to instigate. 'If there were any local bands that I liked then we used to do these overnight sessions', he recalls. 'I was left to lock up so I used to let these bands in. Nobody ever paid. I used to justify it by saying that I was learning a skill.'

The accepted story of Hibbert's involvement in The Smiths is that the free studio time he promised was the only reason he was roped into the band to begin with. Dale refutes this, keen to reiterate that he was asked to join them long before their first demo session. 'I always maintained that it wasn't because of free session time', he stresses, 'because as a friend of Johnny's I would've given them that anyway whether I was in the band or not.'

Whatever their motives for recruiting Hibbert, it was thanks to him that in August 1982 Morrissey and Marr entered Decibel to cut The Smiths' historic first demo. Over an insomniac marathon seven-hour session between 11.00 pm at night and 6.00 am the next morning, two tracks were recorded and mixed down, aided by former Freak Party drummer Simon Wolstencroft who'd been coerced by Marr to provide a necessary rhythmic backbeat at the eleventh hour.

It figured that the two songs recorded were the first two songs they'd written together. 'The Hand That Rocks The Cradle' **[see 11]** featured a characteristically low Morrissey vocal, typical of the group's formative recordings, while Marr soaked his sketchy, central riff in a shallow flange-pedal wash. Surprisingly, the surviving demo also reveals Marr's shaky attempt at a backing vocal harmony. Though Hibbert played bass (following Marr's direction), come the next track, the controversial Moors Murders elegy 'Suffer Little Children' **[see 19]**, he was banished to the control room, leaving Marr himself to overdub a crude bass line of his own.

At seven minutes plus, the Decibel 'Suffer Little Children' is a much longer prototype than that which was finally to appear on 1984's *The Smiths*. Though Wolstencroft's pattering rhythm was discernibly different from that later applied by Mike Joyce, Marr's basic melody was intact, if less pithy. So too was Morrissey's stirring baritone, utilising wraithlike reverb for added drama (the only lyrical difference being the surplus lament from Myra Hindley's conscience 'oh, what have you done?'). The mock Hindley voiceover was also more explicit, cackling haughtily and audibly crying out the victims' Christian names: 'Lesley! Edward! John!'. 'That was a girl, a friend of Steve's,' says Dale. 'She just turned up towards the end and did this weird laughing.'

'Never saw her before, never saw her afterwards,' laughs Marr. 'She was nice. Very kind of studenty. From what I remember she had an archetypal Sixties vibe – a bob haircut and a duffle coat. Morrissey never being one to miss a sartorial angle!'

The mystery girl was one Annalisa Jablonska, whom Morrissey had previously named as being his actual 'girlfriend' in correspondence with his pen pal Robert Mackie. 'Do you have a girlfriend?' he teased in a letter dated 4 December 1980. 'Do you like girls? I have a girlfriend called Annalisa.' In view of his later cat-and-mouse game with the press regarding his sexual preference, the 21 year-old Morrissey's next flippant confession in the same paragraph seems uncharacteristically frank: 'We're both bisexual. Real hip, huh?' he quipped, hastening to add 'I hate sex.'

In preparation for 'Suffer Little Children', Marr brought in a cassette of a piano part, which, despite being a separate melody unconnected to its main chord sequence, he decided to tack onto the end of the studio take. Grinding to a halt on a slovenly strummed A-minor, the song finally segues into this fittingly maudlin piano coda. Its grief-stricken tone would be amplified by the distant sound effects of children playing (a device they would repeat on 'What Difference Does It Make?' **[see 20]**) and a chiming music box.

'I'd recorded that on this little piano in Shelley Rohde's house. I stuck a microphone out of the window as there were children coming out of school. So I had this music box going, kids playing outside and me playing this piano part all at the same time. I can remember it clearly, a beautiful summer's day, because when me and Morrissey met it was the start of summer so our relationship, our writing relationship, just bloomed all the way through that summer of '82. I was living in the attic of this groovy bohemian house with an inherited record collection and an amazing girlfriend, having just met 'the other guy'. So, y'know, no wonder I was happy. It was a fantastic time and that's how I remember that whole first demo.'

Morrissey and Marr were more than satisfied with the finished recording, especially the latter, who would play it on repeat to oblivious customers in X-Clothes as often as he could ('I seem to remember it being on whenever I went in' laughs Hibbert). Unfortunately, their enthusiasm failed to rub off on Simon Wolstencroft, who refused to commit himself to The Smiths full time. With a debut gig already pencilled in for the first week of October, the search for a permanent drummer accelerated. Thankfully, the urgent vacancy would be filled through another of Marr's friends, Pete Hope, who informed the guitarist about the 'Buzzcocks freak' he lived with who was already drumming in local punk band Victim.

Enter Mike Joyce (born 1 June 1963), who, like Morrissey and Marr, shared an Irish ancestry that, while not strictly prerequisite, inevitably played its part in establishing The Smiths' inter-group chemistry. 'I used to go in X-Clothes,' recalls Joyce, 'so I knew Johnny as a face around town. I was into punk so used to buy these fluffy mohair jumpers whereas Johnny was more into the biker gear they were selling. He used to have a quiff, his three-quarter-length Johnson's leather coat and biker boots. So I knew him but not necessarily to talk to.'

Prior to arriving for his audition at Spirit Studios, Joyce had made the not altogether advisable decision to ingest some magic mushrooms. Though 'tripping his head off', his hallucinogenic feast did little to hamper his performance. Marr was impressed, as much by his nerve as his playing, and offered Joyce a place in The Smiths. He readily accepted, quitting Victim in the same breath. 'I remember saying to some of my friends at the time that they could be the next Psychedelic Furs', laughs Joyce. 'That's as big as I could see it. But there was something instant about the music, Johnny's tunes and Morrissey's words, that wasn't like anything I'd heard before. I thought "yeah, I want to be a part of this."'

The rhythm section seemingly complete, Hibbert was beginning to feel the chill of an unspoken separatism already evident in the band. 'I used to socialise with Johnny so we'd talk about the group and where it was going. But even then there was always an air of isolation where anything important happened. For instance, they went to meet Tony Wilson at some point to discuss the possibility of signing to Factory. Neither me nor Mike were invited.'

It was actually Morrissey alone who confronted Wilson about the possibility of Factory signing The Smiths. 'Like I said, whatever contacts Morrissey could draw on, he did,' explains Marr. 'He physically brought the tape to Tony Wilson to play him. I can remember I was working in X-Clothes that day when he rang me up and told me the news that Tony wasn't into it.' In fact, neither Wilson nor New Order manager Rob Gretton were taken with their Decibel demo, though Marr contends that Factory's legendary 'failure' to sign The Smiths has been somewhat exaggerated in hindsight (not least at the finale of the Factory biopic *24 Hour Party People*, in which Wilson receives a visitation from God who chastises him that 'you probably should have signed The Smiths').

Whatever Morrissey's motives for gauging Wilson's response, Marr would always insist it was 'absolutely crucial' they didn't sign to Factory in a conscious effort to break from the obvious traditions of Manchester's past.

'Even though we'd been to see Factory,' explains Marr, 'around that time myself and Morrissey had already discussed in private Rough Trade being a really good label. Because of The Monochrome Set, who started out on Rough Trade, and certainly The Fall.'[10]

His exclusion from the Factory discussions aside, Hibbert's trepidation increased as the band's debut gig approached, particularly when he was subjected to an emergency makeover. 'It sounds like I was a sheep,' laughs Hibbert, 'but basically it was like "There's a hairdresser here and this is how you're gonna have your hair, and these are your clothes." It was really bizarre. I had to get a flat top because they were into this Fifties thing. At one point we all went down to this Army & Navy store where they'd got hold of these Fifties bowling shirts with different names embroidered on the front. Initially, that's what we were gonna wear. But there was never really a band feeling. It was always just those two. I was always under the impression that's the way it was, right from the start. It wasn't something that needed to be vocalised, it was just fairly obvious those were the conditions they were forming the band under. It's about control. Two people can control an image a lot better than four.'

An even bigger shock was in store for Hibbert on the day of the debut gig itself. On 4 October 1982, The Smiths were booked to open for Blue Rondo A La Turk as part of a music/fashion event, 'An Evening of Pure Pleasure', at Manchester's Ritz. 'We knew we were gonna wipe the floor with them,' Marr later remarked of the headline act who, as he put it, epitomised 'the 80s Hard Time/Demob scene' and who had stolen their preposterous moniker from Dave Brubeck's jazz standard. 'We actually played on the floor in front of the stage', recalls Hibbert. 'But there was this other guy that came out with us, wearing stilettos *(sic)* and a leather jacket.'

The combination of their guest's footwear and that night's inclusion of The Cookies' 'I Want A Boy For My Birthday'[11] was enough for Hibbert to misinterpret Morrissey and Marr's vision of The Smiths as being angled towards an overtly gay aesthetic. 'They actually came out and said it,' alleges Hibbert. 'It was Steven's idea. It wasn't something that was mentioned and then dropped, it was something they wanted to follow through. I mean that tape of 'I Want A Boy…' was intended to be on the first demo, so obviously a song like that would go hand in hand with that image. Steven said "We're

10 Rough Trade grew out of the West London record shop founded by Geoff Travis in the mid-Seventies at the outset of punk. Among its earliest signings were Stiff Little Fingers, Swell Maps, The Raincoats, Cabaret Voltaire and The Monochrome Set. When The Smiths finally approached Rough Trade in early 1983, the label's most prominent acts at the time were Scritti Politti and Aztec Camera.

11 The Smiths played just four songs that night: 'The Hand That Rocks The Cradle'; 'Suffer Little Children'; 'Handsome Devil'; and 'I Want A Boy For My Birthday'.

going to be a gay band, but not in a Tom Robinson, effeminate kind of way but more in an underlying kind of macho type way." It was a very strongly manufactured image that was being prepared.'

'Well I'm guessing if I was Dale,' Marr coolly responds, 'and you're stood on the stage with a guy in woman's shoes, playing 'I Want A Boy For My Birthday', around a very effete little guitar player and an unfathomable singer, then he's probably on the money isn't he. But we didn't sit down with Dale and say "Hey Dale – get with the programme!" We hardly knew him for a start. I think that's a bit clumsy that whole area and we just weren't and aren't that clumsy. Us doing that Cookies song was absolutely echoing The New York Dolls who everyone had forgotten about but Morrissey hadn't and I hadn't. We wanted to bring something to our audience that The Dolls and Patti Smith had brought to us. That was it.'

It fitted that the high-heeled gatecrasher in question was the dedicatee of Morrissey's New York Dolls book, James Maker, whom the singer affectionately referred to as 'Jimmy' on account of his resemblance to Morrissey's idol, James Dean. 'I was living in London and travelled to Manchester to attend a couple of the early rehearsals,' recalls Maker. 'I'd heard the songs on cassette. I wasn't there to rehearse. The idea of me going through dance steps whilst Morrissey sang 'I Want A Boy For My Birthday' would have been just a little *too* Diana Ross & The Supremes. I was there to drink red wine, make extraneous hand gestures and keep well within the tight, chalked circle that Morrissey had drawn around me. There was no discussion on how I would fit into the stage show. My involvement was not part of any long-term plan.'

Maker does, however, strongly refute Hibbert's allegation that his stage props included white stilettos: 'They were black court shoes! I wouldn't be seen – on a kidney machine – in white stilettos. And they were not props, I assure you. I was given a pair of maracas – an optional extra – and carte blanche. There were no instructions – I think it was generally accepted that I would *improvise*.'

Even at this, their debut gig, Morrissey had decided upon dramatic entrance music. As Klaus Nomi's rendition of Henry Purcell's 'The Cold Song' played through the venue's sound system, Maker stepped up to the mic and announced the band in French: 'J'ai l'honneur de vous introduire The Smiths. Je crois qu'ils vont faire BOUM ici – et je suis certain que leur musique vous sera fascinant!'[12]

'It was great,' says Marr. 'When we walked out on stage that first time I really knew there'd be a lot of people who'd never heard anything like it

12 'In English it sounds awful,' says Maker. '"I'm honoured to introduce you to The Smiths. I believe that they are going to make a huge impact – and I know that you'll be enthralled by their music." See? Awful!'

before, or wouldn't get us, especially with James Maker stood next to us. Because I was out all the time seeing whatever groups there were. So I knew we absolutely did not fit in.'

In the aftermath of the Ritz show, it became evident to Morrissey and Marr that Dale Hibbert was unsuited to life as a full-time Smith. His incongruity within the overall group aesthetic aside, Joyce also insists that Hibbert's musicianship was lacking in substance. 'Dale wasn't a bass player, just a guy who owned a bass, and that was the problem.'

Marr chose his moment at a rehearsal session in Spirit Studios to hand Hibbert his marching orders. 'I can remember it well,' says Dale. 'It was on the stairs as I was going out. Johnny said something like "We need a parting of the waves" and I thought they meant they wanted to rehearse somewhere else. So I said "Yeah, alright. So where d'you wanna rehearse then?" Johnny went "Er, no. I mean we don't need you!" It fell to him to tell me because he was the one that introduced me to the band. But there was no way I would have made it with them. There was no way I'd have gone on tour and done all that stuff because I was married with kids. I just didn't suit the image that was being prepared.'[13]

Hibbert's void would be amply filled before the year was out by the prodigal return of Andy Rourke. Nearly 12 months had elapsed since Marr quit Freak Party and purposely isolated himself from his former school friend. 'We hadn't seen each other for about a year,' says Marr. 'So I asked him round to mine and it was good to see him again. But he was a bit confused, I think, because he had to put up with me playing The Drifters whereas a year and a half before me and him were listening to David Bowie's *Low* and A Certain Ratio!'

Their friendship rekindled, Rourke agreed to help Marr by accepting his offer to join the new group. With Morrissey ('Voice'), Johnny Marr ('Guitar'), Andy Rourke ('The Bass Guitar') and Mike Joyce ('The Drums'), the final Smiths line-up was at last complete.

13 Popular myth has it that Hibbert only realised he had been ousted from the group after turning up at their next demo session at Drone Studios **[see 2]** to find Rourke already setting up his own bass and amplifier. 'We could see Dale giving us quizzical looks through the glass from the control booth,' Joyce recalls, 'so Johnny went in and had a word with him, because he obviously didn't know what was going on. Dale was got rid and that was that.' Hibbert himself strongly denies this version of events. 'That story's absolute rubbish. It's true I did see them at Drone, but only because I was an engineer and a partner in Spirit Studios, so I was there checking out the competition. I already knew Andy because I'd recorded the demo of Freak Party and he was far, far superior to me as a bass player. I honestly didn't mind.'

2a

The Drone Demo

Recorded Drone Studios, Manchester, December 1982

Second studio recording: 'What Difference Does It Make?', 'Handsome Devil', 'Miserable Lie'

2b

'A Matter Of Opinion'

Recorded Crazy Face, Manchester, December 1982

Informal recording

Rourke's inauguration into The Smiths coincided with their next recording session at Drone Studios in Chorlton. Intended as an audition tape for EMI, the Drone demo commenced with a primitive version of 'What Difference Does It Make?' **[see 20]** containing an uncomfortably low vocal from Morrissey. Even more unusual were Marr's backing harmony vocals during the final verse and the sound of the entire group applauding in unison over the 'no more apologies' refrain.[14] Morrissey's voice was just as audibly stretched during the second track, 'Handsome Devil' **[see 3]**, where his straining baritone evoked the ghoulish timbre of Bobby 'Boris' Pickett's novelty disc 'The Monster Mash'. Stranger still was the added saxophone of guest Andy Gill, who mimicked Marr's riff in abrupt alto blasts in a failed effort to assimilate his given brief of a Stax-like R&B horn sound.

Most peculiar of all was the third track; an epic seven-minute blueprint for 'Miserable Lie' **[see 17]**. Though its slow introductory passage was intact, the remainder became an almost unrecognisable sub-funk workout dominated by Rourke's unwarranted slap-bass improvisation and Marr's erratic chops evoking the post-punk abrasiveness of the Gang Of Four. Morrissey's lyrics were also much more repetitive, dwelling upon the 'criminal world' exhortation and swimming in reverb. Only after three and a half minutes did he switch into falsetto mode (trilling 'what did I do to deserve this?') while Joyce charged towards a chaotic fade-out finish of bombarding tom-tom rumbles pursued by Marr's separated left-and-right channel screeches.

Though the end product was unsuccessful in its intended objective to impress EMI (ironic considering that they'd later sign The Smiths in 1986 – a year prior to their split), the three tracks completed proved an invaluable learning curve. By the beginning of 1983, Marr and Rourke overcame the obstacle of Morrissey's depressed vocals, so painfully vivid on the Drone

14 They would reprise the clapping effect over four years later on 'Paint A Vulgar Picture' **[see 72]**.

demos, by employing guitar capos in order to play in a higher key better suited to his natural range. Most important of all, though, was Rourke's successful induction, and with it the consolidation of that final Smiths line-up after months of trial, firing and error.

The rest of December was spent honing their ever-expanding repertoire in the new permanent rehearsal home that Joe Moss, now the band's official manager, had recently provided; the upstairs of his Portland Street Crazy Face Clothing Co warehouse where The Smiths would spend their intensive incubation period over the winter months. By Christmas, four more songs were ready to add to their live set: 'These Things Take Time' **[see 13]**, 'What Do You See In Him?' (rewritten in the new year as 'Wonderful Woman' **[see 10]**), 'Jeane' **[see 5]** and the rarest Smiths song of all, 'A Matter Of Opinion'.

As the only original Morrissey/Marr composition after the recruitment of Andy Rourke never to be released or even played in concert, 'A Matter Of Opinion' would avoid detection from biographers and fans for the best part of 20 years. Thankfully, one lone practice tape survives, captured on a domestic ghetto blaster that remained permanently to hand at Crazy Face and retained by Mike Joyce.

Modelled in the same twanging R&B vein as other early Marr rockers ('Handsome Devil', 'What Difference Does It Make?'), just as 'The Hand That Rocks The Cradle' was a generous steal from Patti Smith's 'Kimberly' **[see 11]**, so 'A Matter Of Opinion' owed much to Buffalo Springfield's 'Mr Soul'. In essence, 'A Matter Of Opinion' *is* 'Mr Soul', powered by Marr's identical dirty blues growl.[15]

Morrissey's words are suitably bitter and accusatory; the first of its monotone verses appears to sneer at politicised intellectuals ('sit by the fire with your books and pretend that you're active'), while the second (and repeated third) already pitches him on the outside of pedestrian society, looking in at 'the boys on the factory floor', each cycle ending in the caustic pay-off, 'oh, it's all a matter of opinion'. The most uncharacteristic passage comes after the second chorus, where Marr draws out a squealing one note guitar solo and Morrissey shrieks staccato cries of what sounds like 'Any!' At the time, Joyce interpreted the same short, sharp vocal hollers as 'Ollie!', in reference to their friend Ollie May who would later form part of The Smiths' road crew. When Joyce asked Morrissey if he was indeed screaming a homage to May, the singer mischievously avoided comment.

Though a sure-fire feisty crowd pleaser, and no more impudent a carbon copy of 'Mr Soul' than 'Panic' would be of T.Rex's 'Metal Guru' **[see 58]**, 'A

15 Featured on 1967's *Buffalo Springfield Again*, 'Mr Soul' was Neil Young's overt steal of Keith Richards' riff from The Rolling Stones' '(I Can't Get No) Satisfaction'.

Matter Of Opinion' would be discarded shortly before their next gig on 25 January 1983 at Manchester's Manhattan. In their decision to jettison the song, it seems The Smiths were already showing a commendably ruthless ambition to up the ante of their own creative capabilities, rather than lapse into safe rock parody. 'It didn't sound like us,' confirms Marr. 'It wasn't that we were bothered about copying a tune, but it was too blatant, almost so blatant that if it had worked I wouldn't have had a problem with it. For me, at that time, it was such a cool association to do a Buffalo Springfield tune, but it just didn't have our heart or spirit in it. Besides, it's never satisfying to just lift a riff lock, stock and barrel.'

The Manhattan gig itself would be both Rourke's first gig as Smiths bassist and James Maker's last as their additional 'go-go dancer'. 'Morrissey telephoned me,' explains Maker, 'and related a conversation that Joe, their manager at the time, had had with the group. It went along the lines of: "There can't be two lead singers in one band." Which, retrospectively, was true. My guest appearances with them were quite superfluous, really. And I would have been the first to agree with that sentiment. It was not a problem. It was a good decision.'

'I never belonged with The Smiths,' he continues, 'and I didn't wish for it. I was 21. The maracas-shaking go-go dancing was just a silly and enjoyable, temporary diversion. I very much had my own plans – and went on to formulate them.' Indeed, Maker was to savour 15 minutes of fame as singer with his own group, Raymonde, who famously made the cover of *Melody Maker* in January 1986 before ever releasing a record. To his detriment, Maker was hostile to any critical comparisons between the two groups, while his defensive statement in that same *Melody Maker* feature – 'I think we're better and far more exciting than The Smiths and what's more we'll prove it in the next year' – was as ridiculous at the time as it now seems with hindsight.

Nevertheless, Raymonde finally attracted the interest of Chrysalis, releasing just one album, *Babelogue*, in 1987.[16] That it shared its title with that of a track on Patti Smith's *Easter* echoed a ripping yarn Morrissey had previously spun to *Melody Maker*'s Frank Owen about a teenage experience from hell in which he and Maker were chased by thugs, found themselves lost in the countryside, returned home days later and 'listened to *Horses* by Patti Smith and wept on the bed'. 'Never tamper with embellishment for the sake of a good story,' says Maker, 'actually, it was terrifyingly true!'

16 Raymonde, named after Dusty Springfield producer Ivor Raymonde, split within two years of *Babelogue*'s release. Maker later returned in the early Nineties under the heavier (metal) guise of RPLA. In 2004, Morrissey would perform a cover version of *Babelogue*'s opening track, 'No One Can Hold A Candle To You', in concert, also signing Maker to his Sanctuary imprint, Attack Records.

3

'Handsome Devil'

Recorded **4 February 1983, Live at the Hacienda, Manchester**

Produced by **The Smiths**

B-side to **'Hand In Glove', May 1983**

'I repeat, the only thing to be in 1983 is handsome!' With these words, Morrissey introduced 'Handsome Devil'[17] on stage at Manchester's Hacienda club on 4 February; The Smiths' second gig that year and only the third of their entire career. It also marked the first occasion flowers were properly introduced into the group's milieu, symbolising Morrissey's professed love of nature (the direct influence of Oscar Wilde), as well as a conscious attempt to combat the industrial 'sterility' of the venue itself.

Still unsigned, this concert allowed them the opportunity to record their set through the venue's mixing desk with the aim of creating a possible demo tape. Of the eight tracks played, 'Handsome Devil' was singled out as the best performance and subsequently coupled with the studio recording of 'Hand In Glove' **[see 4]** as a two-track tape concocted to win the approval of Rough Trade's Geoff Travis. As it happened, the Hacienda recording of 'Handsome Devil' was deemed good enough to be officially released as their debut single's B-side.

Bristling with the nervous energy one might expect from such an early live document, 'Handsome Devil' hinted that far from being wilting violets, The Smiths were a band capable of delivering a more violent musical kick, spurred by Joyce's breathless pace and Marr's nagging riff with its menacing back drone. 'To me, 'Handsome Devil' always felt like a Mancunian anaemic Patti Smith group,' says Marr. 'I think subconsciously, the chords probably came from 'Ask The Angels' off *Radio Ethiopia*. The same A-minor to F. Although it doesn't really sound like it.'

Morrissey's lyrics were similarly savage; the gratuitous entreaty of a sexual predator intent on corrupting bookish novices (paraphrasing a line from Kurt Vonnegut's *Slaughterhouse 5* that 'There's more to life than what you read in books') sharing something of the whip-cracking sado-masochism of The Velvet Underground's 'Venus In Furs'. 'The message of the song is to forget the cultivation of the brain,' explained Morrissey, 'and to concentrate on the cultivation of the body.'

17 Though of course not unique to its dialogue, Morrissey might have taken the phrase 'Handsome Devil' from a remark by Jon Voigt in 1969's *Midnight Cowboy*; a wild premise, but also a rational one considering the film's story of homoerotic metropolitan loneliness and the track record of its director John Schlesinger (*A Kind of Loving, Billy Liar, Far From the Madding Crowd*).

That certain critics would find 'Handsome Devil' thematically objectionable was to be expected, but not the tabloid hysteria inflamed by its repeat broadcast when rerecorded for their debut BBC John Peel session. At the heart of this lamentable affair was a vicious enmity between two *Sounds* journalists, Dave McCullough and Garry Bushell. Both represented rival musical, ideological and political factions: McCullough the pretentious pop intellectual, Bushell the Luddite advocate of Oi!, a punk sub-genre with dubious right-wing undertones. Neither could agree on the time of day, let alone matters of popular music, so when McCullough seized upon The Smiths early on as his pet favourites, it was mandatory for Bushell to want to cut them down to size at any given opportunity.

We can trace Bushell's discontent back to The Smiths' debut *Sounds* feature in June 1983, in which McCullough mischievously provoked Morrissey into slandering his colleague. 'The British press is an art form,' said the singer, before commenting that Bushell was 'an exception to the rule'. Unfortunately for The Smiths, though he may indeed have been the scourge of the music weeklies, Bushell could avenge such insults via colleagues at *The Sun* newspaper, arming them with all the misinformation they needed to concoct the allegations in question.

Even more unfortunate was that the story should appear in the week they'd recorded a new BBC session for David Jensen. On Monday 5 September in a '*Sun* Exclusive' headed "Ban Child-Sex Pop Song' Plea To Beeb', the paper erroneously claimed that 'Handsome Devil' was one of the four new Jensen tracks to be broadcast that evening, proudly announcing how 'after *The Sun* drew the attention of Radio 1 chiefs to its sleazy lyrics, it could be taken off the air for good.'

It was typical tabloid sensationalism; roping in the 'grave disquiet' of Tory MP Geoffrey Dickens[18] and dangerously misquoting Morrissey as having protested 'I don't feel immoral singing about molesting children… it makes a change.' The charges against The Smiths couldn't have come at a more sensitive time, with the press still reeling from the scandal of *Coronation Street* actor Peter Adamson[19] and with Tory Home Secretary Leon Brittan announcing 'tough new action to control child-molesters' the same week. 'That report in *The Sun*,' recalls Rourke with visible unease, 'that killed me when that came out, but it was worse for our parents, just because of the

18 Dickens was more prominent as an anti-witchcraft campaigner targeting occult and pagan groups, though was equally active in the public denunciation of controversial pop music. The Smiths would become his regular foil, even going so far as to call Morrissey 'exceptionally evil' for his comments against the Queen and Margaret Thatcher.

19 Adamson (who played *Coronation Street*'s Len Fairclough) had been arrested for indecently assaulting two girls in a swimming pool. He was subsequently cleared of the charges.

implications of it. We all had to warn our families, I had to tell my grandparents and try and explain it to them. It was mortifying.'

The irony was that 'Handsome Devil' hadn't even been recorded for Jensen, though in the event the BBC decided not to broadcast that session's version of 'Reel Around The Fountain' **[see 14]**. All the same, The Smiths were forced into a position where they had to defend the song publicly. 'I can't understand why anybody should write such a thing about us,' said Morrissey. 'We must stress that 'Handsome Devil' is aimed entirely towards adults and has nothing to do with children, and certainly nothing to do with child molesting. It's an adult understanding of quite intimate matters.'

Though Rough Trade considered legal action against *The Sun*, in reality they lacked the financial muscle to instigate such proceedings. 'Quite obviously we don't condone child molesting or anything that vaguely resembles it,' concluded Morrissey. 'What more can be said?'

In Concert

One of four songs performed at their debut concert at Manchester's Ritz (4/10/82), 'Handsome Devil' was a favourite rabble-rouser integral to their early gigs. Used as a regular set opener at the tail end of 1983, the song was absent from the opening dates of their first major UK tour in spring 1984, only to be re-introduced after the first half dozen shows as an encore. It remained in the standard set-list well into the *Meat Is Murder* era, before being finally dropped midway through their first comprehensive American tour in the summer of '85. 'Handsome Devil' was last played at the Tower Theater, Philadelphia (12/6/85).

Television

Despite the tabloid furore over its lyrical content, 'Handsome Devil' was broadcast uncensored by BBC2 on 9 December 1983 as the opening number of a gig recorded at Derby Assembly Rooms two days earlier for *Whistle Test – On The Road*.

Afterwards, Marr would famously denounce the show as one of the most regrettable instances in their career, listing it in 1985's *Meat Is Murder* tour booklet as his 'greatest embarrassment'. Though not a bad performance by any means, Marr's main gripe seems to have been the audience, many of whom appeared to have only been there because of the BBC cameras eager to grab their 15 minutes of fame.

Radio

The version of 'Handsome Devil' most commonly referred to is that taped at BBC Maida Vale Studio 5 on 18 May 1983 for The Smith's debut John Peel session. Widely considered the song's definitive interpretation, especially following its inclusion on 1984's *Hatful Of Hollow* compilation, the Peel 'Handsome Devil' is a cleaner recording than the actual live Hacienda B-side, but no less ferocious.

4

'Hand In Glove'

Recorded **February 1983, Strawberry Studios, Stockport, Manchester**
Produced by **The Smiths**
Single A-side, May 1983
Re-mixed by **John Porter** for the album ***The Smiths*, February 1984**

On a typically dark, drizzly Sunday night in January 1983, Marr and his girlfriend Angie paid a visit to his parents' home in Wythenshawe. 'I went round to visit me little brother,' recalls Marr. 'There was a crappy old acoustic that I'd left there and I started to play these chords. I was playing it quite clipped, almost funky. I thought "I'm really onto something here". Angie said to me "That sounds pretty good". So I looked round for something to record it on, but there wasn't anything.'

The nearest tape recorder Marr knew he could lay his hands on was six miles away; 384 Kings Road, Stretford to be precise. 'I had to get to a tape recorder,' says Marr, 'so I needed to get to Morrissey's, even though I didn't know if he was gonna be home or not.' Luckily for Marr, Angie had the loan of her parents' Volkswagen Beetle. 'We used to drive around in it when we had nowhere to go. More often than not it was where I used to practise me harmonica playing as she was driving which, looking back on it now, was probably really irritating!' Not wanting to lose his new riff, Marr persuaded Angie to ferry him in the car to Stretford.

As they drove north, Marr continued to jam the same 'clipped' chords. 'I was trying not to change or forget it, when Angie suddenly says to me "Make it sound more like Iggy". So because of the car journey, and her screaming, I started to bring it more in line with something off *Raw Power*. Finally, we get to Morrissey's. And he's like "Oh... hullo?" He wasn't expecting me. It was a bit, y'know, "On a Sunday night! Without an appointment!" But anyway, we made a cassette of the riff. So the genesis of 'Hand In Glove' metamorphosised somewhere down the M56!'

Morrissey would later claim that he wrote the lyrics at home in just two hours, conscious of the fact that his handiwork was destined to be the first record. Explaining its theme of 'complete loneliness', Morrissey elaborated:

'It was important to me that there'd be something searingly poetic in it, in a lyrical sense, and yet jubilant at the same time. Being searingly poetic and jubilant was, I always thought, quite difficult because they're two extreme emotions and I wanted to blend them together.'

In his carefully concocted juxtaposition of triumph and tragedy, Morrissey would source inspiration from his own bookshelf and record collection. As his most explicitly referenced muse in subsequent works, it comes as no surprise to discover echoes of Salford playwright Shelagh Delaney. Here, the otherwise unobtrusive final cry 'I'll probably never see you again', appears in both Delaney's 1959 *A Taste of Honey* and its lesser-known 1962 successor, *The Lion in Love.* A more conspicuous steal is the paraphrase of 'everything depends upon how near you sleep to me' from 'Bells', a Leonard Cohen song first written for and recorded by Canadian protest singer Buffy Sainte-Marie.[20] Morrissey would confess his admiration for Sainte-Marie to *Q* magazine many years later. 'In 1964 she was singing about drugs in a very exciting way. "My mother, my father, said whiskey's a curse, but the fate of their baby's a million times worse". This was 1964. The Beatles were singing "She loves you, yeah yeah". It didn't catch on and I can't imagine why. A very underrated artist.'[21]

Even the sentiment of being 'hidden by rags', a lyric Morrissey would single out as being 'most precious to me', may have been a nod to Sandie Shaw, another principal reference point in the early days of The Smiths. On her 1967 hit 'You've Not Changed', Shaw sings 'I do like your hair and the clothes you wear – but if you wore rags you'd still look good to me.' A fairly tenuous link, were it not for the fact that Morrissey quoted these very lines when pinpointing the highlights of Sandie's career in an article for *Sounds* from December 1983. Nonetheless, Morrissey later referred to these same lyrics as being wholly autobiographical. '[They're about] how I felt when I couldn't afford to buy clothes, and used to dress in rags but I didn't really feel mentally impoverished. The inspiration? Just the very idea of people putting enormous importance on what they had and how they dressed and this very materialistic sense of value, which is completely redundant. It goes back to the old cliché of what one has inside is really what one is.'

Five days after Marr's impromptu Sunday night visit, Morrissey unveiled the song during a group rehearsal at Crazy Face. As Marr recalls, 'When we heard the vocals, we were all like "Wow!" From then on it was always going

20 Cohen would later record his own version of 'Bells' in 1974 under the revised title of 'Take This Longing'. Given Morrissey's professed love of Buffy Sainte-Marie, it's more likely he would have been influenced by her original (featured on 1971's *She Used to Wanna Be a Ballerina*) than Cohen's rewrite.

21 Morrissey was quoting 'Cod'Ine', Sainte-Marie's grim portrait of a codeine addict from 1964's *It's My Way*.

to be the first single.' Even before its live debut at the Hacienda in early February, opinion that 'Hand In Glove' was their strongest track to date was unanimous within the group ('it was as if these four people had to play that song' Morrissey later proclaimed). Still without a deal but with Rough Trade now topping their list of candidates after recent rejections from Factory and EMI, it was decided that they should record the song themselves before trying to gain the label's interest.

On Sunday 27 February, The Smiths entered Strawberry Studios in Stockport, famed as the home of 10cc (where they cut their 1975 number one 'I'm Not In Love') and where local luminaries Buzzcocks and Joy Division had also previously recorded. Other than a quick edit of 'Handsome Devil' from the Hacienda mixing desk master tapes **[see 3]**, the one day session was devoted to 'Hand In Glove'. Funded by Joe Moss at a cost of just under £250, this recording would later become their debut single.

'Hand In Glove' creeps in slowly, wailing like a ghost train approaching out of the mist courtesy of Marr's harmonica, symbolic of the very same 'blunt vitality of working-class northernness' Ian MacDonald attributes to The Beatles' 1962 debut single 'Love Me Do'. It's on this same opening bridge section that Angie's Iggy Pop influence is most explicit, strongly resembling the acoustic hook underpinning *Raw Power*'s 'Gimme Danger' as Marr readily admits. "Gimme Danger' was one of the most important tracks in my guitar education. You've just got to listen to the start of that song to hear it.'

What were to be Morrissey's first words on vinyl are those of the song's title; his arrestingly odd yet inimitable Northern timbre trembling upon each syllable, exorcising a lifetime's frustrated ambition with each and every breath (those resonant background murmurs of 'kiss my shades' included). Rhythmically, 'Hand In Glove' is matchless in its peculiar structure, punctuated by Joyce's cymbal stutters, jumpstarting Marr's melancholic minor-chord backwash every eight bars. Rourke, too, contributes one of his most inspired bass patterns, which successfully lends the song its essential swaggering weight. A bleak proclamation of doomed happiness, 'Hand In Glove' is a shattering left-hook of self-loathing, loss and desperation, skilfully enhanced by its irregular, fatalistic melody.

The prospective debut single in the can, The Smiths upped their campaign to lure Rough Trade the following week. On Friday 4 March, Marr and Rourke made the momentous pilgrimage down from Manchester to London. Barging their way into the label's Blenheim Crescent offices, they cornered Travis in the kitchen while he was making a mug of coffee. Forcing a cassette into his hand containing both 'Hand In Glove' and the live edit of

'Handsome Devil', Marr insisted 'listen to this, it's not just another tape.' Impressed by their gall, Travis promised he would. Over the weekend, The Smiths stewed in Manchester awaiting Rough Trade's response. Monday morning, Marr received a phone call from Travis, who was so impressed by the tape that he agreed to cut 'Hand In Glove' as a single; not a contract, as such, but a one-off deal for both parties to test the water before making any long-term commitments.[22]

The pedantic fanaticism with which Morrissey gleefully approached The Smiths' long-awaited immortalisation on 7-inch vinyl was apparent in the fastidious instructions given to Rough Trade's art department. He instructed that the single should have a paper label centre with four vents encircling the middle, a homage to the similar model popular in the Sixties, which was designed to be played domestically while making it easier to snap out the centre to fit American-style jukeboxes. Morrissey's specifications may well have had personal significance in that Marianne Faithfull's 1965 Decca single 'Come and Stay with Me' (the first record he'd bought), contained this same four-vent centre. Marr was equally besotted with the idea of seeing his name on a navy blue label, 'like The Stones or Marianne Faithfull.'

If his designs on the actual record were retro, the sleeve itself was provocatively modern with its Jim French photograph sourced from Margaret Walters' history of *The Nude Male* **[see Appendix II]**, which reinforced the single's 'sun shines out of our behinds' refrain in its three-quarter length portrait of a man's naked rear. When the single was finally issued in May, the overt homoerotic overtones, coupled with the lyrics of its B-side 'Handsome Devil', struck exactly the kind of perplexed, outraged and uneasy response that Morrissey had intended. Such unease stretched to the families of The Smiths themselves. 'I remember showing a copy to my Dad,' Rourke reminisces, 'saying "this is my first record". He was mortified. He said to me "that's a bloke's bum" and I said "yeah" but when he asked me why I just didn't have an answer for him.' One can only imagine the reaction of the rest of the band had they browsed through Walters' book and found the page upon which French's photo appears – directly opposite a pornographic cartoon by the infamous Fifties gay artist 'Tom O' Finland'.

The eventual release of 'Hand In Glove' coincided with a landmark performance at the University of London Union on 6 May. The audience at

22 Morrissey would later offer a suspiciously embellished account of the making of 'Hand In Glove' to *The Catalogue* in 1988, stating he'd returned to Strawberry a week later to redo his vocal and that the very next day he personally travelled to London to hand the tape to Geoff Travis. Neither claim corroborates with the testimonies of the other Smiths. Similarly, Morrissey's later gripe that Travis refused to issue an accompanying 12-inch of 'Hand In Glove' seems dubious. His own preference for the classic 7-inch 45 rpm pop single notwithstanding, in May 1983 The Smiths had no other releasable tracks in the can to justify such a venture.

this, their second gig in the capital, included Rough Trade plugger Scott Piering, who brought along BBC producer and John Peel session scout, John Walters. 'It was Walters who heard The Smiths before I did,' confirms Peel. 'He went to see them at ULU and it was as a result of his enthusiasm that the band were initially booked for the programme.' Recorded and broadcast that same month, The Smiths' debut Peel session, along with others recorded for David Jensen between May and September 1983, proved as influential in sewing the roots of their early fan base as the 'Hand In Glove' single itself. 'I was impressed because unlike most bands, and I've said this before because it remains true, you couldn't immediately tell what records they'd been listening to,' enthuses Peel. 'That's fairly unusual, very rare indeed. It made you think "how have they got to where they are?" and "where have they come from?". It was that aspect of The Smiths that I found most impressive.' With Peel leading the charge, the music press soon followed as glowing live reviews and the first tentative interviews appeared in the pages of the *NME* and *Sounds*.

'Hand In Glove' would sell consistently well for the next 18 months, although, outside of the independent singles chart,[23] the record failed to impact upon the national Top 40. 'It should have been a massive hit,' Morrissey would bemoan, 'it was so urgent. To me, it was a complete cry in every direction. It really was a landmark.' Just as Morrissey would repeatedly inform the press that he felt as if his entire life had been leading up to the release of 'Hand In Glove', so Mike Joyce also informed *Record Mirror* that his 'life began' with that first single, believing its lyrics to be autobiographical of the spirit within the group.

The Smiths would attempt further studio versions of 'Hand In Glove' over the next 12 months; during the ill-fated Troy Tate sessions in July **[see 5]** and again with John Porter during the October session at Pluto Studios in Manchester. The latter, more spirited arrangement, which Marr would later revive for their Sandie Shaw collaboration **[see 21]**, was ultimately rejected. Instead, with time already against their finishing on schedule, the version that finally appeared on *The Smiths* was a remix of the original Strawberry demo with Joyce's drums to the fore, Rourke's bass pushed back and clearer separation between vocal and guitar. Porter also opted for a more dramatic start (exploding with a piercing snare beat) and finish (a brooding G-minor ring out). Though a sharper mix, this album version's filtering process loses the ambience of 'Hand In Glove' as it first appeared and for which, to savour The Smiths' first footing in all its precious naivety, there is still no substitute.

23 In January 1984, 'Hand In Glove' would aid The Smiths in gaining a *Guinness Book of Records* entry when they became the first group to occupy the top three positions of the UK Independent charts with 1. 'What Difference Does It Make?', 2. 'Hand In Glove', 3. 'This Charming Man'.

In Concert

Debuted at the band's third gig (Manchester Hacienda 4/2/83), by the winter of 1983 'Hand In Glove' was The Smiths' standard set closer/expected encore, played twice the same night on several occasions by popular demand. Switched to the routine opening fanfare of 1984's spring UK tour, it remained a stalwart of Smiths shows henceforth with few exceptions. By July 1986, it was once again the obligatory final encore, though come their British tour that October The Smiths broke with tradition and dropped it altogether. There was, however, to be an uncanny recompense when what turned out to be their very last concert at London's Brixton Academy on 12 December 1986 climaxed with a farewell encore of 'Hand In Glove', its last chord savagely pulverized for a full 40 seconds by way of a grand finale. Fate decreed that this, their anthemic debut single, should effectively blot a full stop to the Smiths' concert career with supernatural poignancy.

Television

Filmed at Derby Assembly Rooms (7/12/83), a live version of 'Hand In Glove' was first broadcast on 9 December 1983 as part of BBC2's *Whistle Test – On The Road* special **[see 3]**. Three months later, when promoting the first album, another live rendition was recorded in the Newcastle studios of Channel 4's *The Tube* on Friday 16 March 1984 along with 'Still Ill' and the yet to be recorded 'Barbarism Begins At Home' **[see 9 and 34]**.

The third, and best, televised performance of the song was again on *The Tube*. Filmed in concert at Glasgow Barrowlands (25/9/85) as part of a lengthy feature on The Smiths' autumn Scottish tour broadcast the following month, 'Hand In Glove' was shown in its entirety, capturing the audience hysteria (impulsive stage invaders and swarthy bouncers dragging asphyxiated fans out of the scrum) and on-stage electricity to a tee.

Radio

The Smiths never cut a BBC session version of 'Hand In Glove', although the fact that the single was broadcast on 4 July 1983 in conjunction with the first airing of three tracks recorded for David Jensen has led many to misinterpret this was the case (Morrissey himself was present at Radio 1 that evening for his premiere national radio interview).

It's also been incorrectly suggested that this alleged Jensen version of 'Hand In Glove' was a live recording taped at London's Brixton Ace (29/6/83). Never broadcast by the BBC, the origin of this live take stems from a Rough Trade promo cassette distributed in the late summer of 1983. It contained the seven tracks from the first Peel and Jensen sessions, excerpts from the latter's accompanying interview and the new live recording purely as a promotional extra. This Rough Trade-sanctioned BBC compilation was subsequently adapted by bootleggers, prolonging the falsehood that 'Hand In Glove' had indeed been recorded especially for the BBC.[24] The only live version of 'Hand In Glove' the BBC actually broadcast was recorded at the Oxford Apollo (18/3/85), and aired on Janice Long's *Evening Show* on 9 May 1985.

5a

The Troy Tate Album

Recorded **July-August 1983, Elephant Studios, London**

Produced by **Troy Tate**

First draft of debut album

5b

'Pretty Girls Make Graves' (Troy Tate Version)

Recorded **July-August 1983, Elephant Studios, London**

Produced by **Troy Tate**

B-side to **'I Started Something I Couldn't Finish', October 1987**

5c

'Jeane'

Recorded **July-August 1983, Elephant Studios, London**

Produced by **Troy Tate**

B-side to **'This Charming Man' (7-inch format only), November 1983**

After the success of 'Hand In Glove' in the independent charts, in June 1983 The Smiths decided to cautiously steer clear of major offers and stick with Rough Trade. Their admiration for the label's back catalogue aside, it helped that its associates included Richard Boon, whom Morrissey already knew through Linder Sterling. 'That connection was really important,' stresses Marr. 'Morrissey was closer to Richard than I was, but he was an interesting character. He was almost like our 'man on the inside' in a way because everyone else at Rough Trade was a stranger to us. We respected Geoff Travis and everything that he'd done, but we were so adamant about having

24 The Brixton Ace live version of 'Hand In Glove' was finally granted an official release as the B-side to WEA's posthumous 'There Is A Light That Never Goes Out' single in December 1992.

control. Not because of megalomania but because we knew how we were gonna bring up our baby.'

Geoff Travis duly travelled up from London to Manchester to officially sign The Smiths at their Crazy Face base. Prior to his trip, Travis allegedly received specific instruction for there to be space for just two signatures on the contract. Marr denies any such responsibility: 'I didn't make any phone calls to Rough Trade saying "make sure there's only two names on the contract". It wasn't in my sphere of consciousness. It's not something I would have thought of. But somebody did.' Though Travis would conflictingly reflect how he was 'fully expecting it to be signed by all four members', as has now become music and legal legend, it was Morrissey and Marr alone who scribbled their names upon the Rough Trade deal.

Bitterly, their failure, for whatever reasons, to specify the agreed share of band earnings with Rourke and Joyce in writing would famously result in the High Court dispute of 1996. 'Somebody thought they were being clever by not getting it down [on paper], and it ended up blowing up in everyone's faces,' Marr later admitted, also confessing that if he could have changed anything he 'would have got a signed agreement from the word go, so we were all aware of the financial situation.'[25] Unknown to all concerned at the time, as the ink dried on the Rough Trade contract, so the depressing inevitability of The Smiths' eventual undoing was irreversibly set in motion.

Meantime, having demonstrated the size, scope and depth of their repertoire over two rapturously received BBC sessions, as well as in concert (the Morrissey/Marr songbook now swelling beyond a dozen sturdy originals), it seemed perfectly reasonable for Travis to suggest that The Smiths' first studio session as Rough Trade signings be a full album. Upon Travis's recommendation, former Teardrop Explodes guitarist Troy Tate (who'd recently released his own 'Love Is' solo single on Rough Trade) was handed the historic task of producing The Smiths' debut long player. Recorded between mid-July and early August in the sweltering London heat at Elephant Studios in Wapping, Tate bonded well with the group, successfully capturing them in their eager, if callow, infancy in the process.

The 14 tracks completed would include: a pristine 'The Hand That Rocks The Cradle' **[see 11]** illustrating Marr's original, more linear riff; a creditable 'You've Got Everything Now' **[see 18]** with an unusual slide-guitar overdub during its finish; 'These Things Take Time' **[see 13]** heralded by an

25 Morrissey and Marr maintain, to this day, that Rourke and Joyce were aware, and had verbally agreed, to the following percentage split in performance earnings: Morrissey (40 per cent), Marr (40 per cent), Rourke (10 per cent) and Joyce (10 per cent). On their part, Rourke and Joyce uphold that the reason they never signed the Rough Trade contract was because they were told only two signatures were needed, and that as the group songwriters Morrissey and Marr were the obvious candidates.

elongated thunderous drum intro; two alternate takes of 'What Difference Does It Make?' **[see 20]** – the first a sturdy guitar assault utilising devilish arcs of sustained feedback and additional haunting background falsettos from Morrissey, the second underpinning its governing guitar riff with a high piano vamp; a rerecording of 'Hand In Glove' **[see 4]** experimenting with a shorter intro, more vocal reverb and imbuing Marr's harmonica finale with a haunted, distant quality reminiscent of Ennio Morricone's score for *Once Upon a Time in the West*; and another stab at 'Handsome Devil' **[see 3]** admittedly lacking in the song's usual sadistic intent.

There was also a triumphant take on 'Wonderful Woman' **[see 10]**; 'I Don't Owe You Anything', in which Morrissey's phrasing was more horizontal, lacking the subtle vocal inflexion in its opening line that he'd add when rerecording the song with John Porter **[see 12]**; a polished six-and-a-half minute 'Suffer Little Children' **[see 19]** – complete with haunting piano coda and featuring a much crisper guitar melody than on its previous Decibel demo **[see 1]**; a superb 'Miserable Lie' **[see 17]** placing greater emphasis on Marr's mesmerising *mêlée* of aggressive guitar overdubs; and two different attempts at 'Accept Yourself' **[see 8]**, the second version being particularly impressive with its staccato rock 'n' roll piano punches during the pre-chorus breakdowns, Morrissey's doubled vocal and some enlivening falsetto shrieks.

Best of all was Tate's 'Reel Around The Fountain' **[see 14]**, probably its most satisfying and moving incarnation. Opening with an effervescent, echoing guitar prologue, the song builds for a full six minutes to a superb crescendo of cascading guitar hail-stoning between Joyce's heart-skipping tom-tom hammers; good enough to be earmarked as The Smiths' next single in fact.

Equally spectacular was a markedly different translation of 'Pretty Girls Make Graves' **[see 16]**, featuring an unusual clip-clopping traditional folk tempo accentuating the tune's possible debt to late-Sixties 'folk super group' The Pentangle; similar in style and ambience to what Marr refers to as their 'woozy riffy stuff' such as 1969's 'Light Flight', and with a decidedly Bert Jansch/John Renbourn-like coda of soft arpeggios, glockenspiel and backwards guitar. Its combination of Marr's multiple acoustic overdubs with the mournful cello of guest Audrey Riley gave the song a haunting austerity the band would never quite recapture again. 'I'd been playing with Virginia Astley and The Ravishing Beauties who were signed to Rough Trade,' explains Riley. 'She probably recommended me to Geoff Travis. One day he just rang me and said "Come down to Elephant Studios, there's a session going off." I hadn't a clue who The Smiths were at that time as they hadn't really taken off, but I was still terribly nervous. They sat me down and played the track and said "Can you think of something that goes along with this?". So I noodled around until I found the right notes.'

'But I really wasn't very clued up,' adds Riley, 'because when the album eventually came out I had no idea they'd rerecorded it. I even bought it expecting to see my name on the sleeve and hear my cello on that track so afterwards I rang up Geoff thinking they hadn't liked what I'd done. He said "I promise you that version will see the light of day eventually", and of course it did. He put it out as that B-side years later and even included my name on the label, which was really nice of him.'[26]

Once the sessions wrapped, Morrissey would boast to *Melody Maker* that the album they had in the can, provisionally titled *The Hand That Rocks The Cradle*, was perfect.[27] 'We've done everything exactly right and it'll show.' Unfortunately for Tate, such enthusiasm was to wane considerably over the coming weeks as doubts over the quality of his production began to fester in the corridors of Rough Trade. With hindsight, Andy Rourke now philosophically suggests Tate was made a scapegoat for the band's lack of experience; that Morrissey and Marr 'wanted to make this big sounding album that we just weren't capable of doing'. He and Joyce also acknowledge the plausible suggestion that Tate's good working relationship with Johnny Marr was another key factor; that Morrissey, whose green-eyed repulsion of those who got too close to his song-writing partner would deteriorate considerably over the years that followed, wanted him out of the frame.

It didn't help Tate that two weeks after completing the album, the BBC chose not to broadcast a version of 'Reel Around The Fountain' recorded for David Jensen's show because of alleged paedophilic references **[see 3 and 14]**. Consequently, Rough Trade were forced to scrap plans to issue Tate's version of the track as The Smiths' next single. More significantly, that same Jensen session had brought the group into contact with producer John Porter, best known for his work with Roxy Music in the Seventies.[28] Concerned by the quality of the Tate album and tempted by Porter's reputation as a 'good clean-up guy', Geoff Travis had already invited the

26 The Tate version of 'Pretty Girls Make Graves' would be posthumously released as the B-side to 'I Started Something I Couldn't Finish' in October 1987, featured on all formats.

27 Surviving album master reels show the running order as follows. Side 1: 'The Hand That Rocks The Cradle'/'You've Got Everything Now'/'These Things Take Time'/'What Difference Does It Make?'/'Reel Around The Fountain'/'Hand In Glove'/'Handsome Devil'. Side 2: 'Wonderful Woman'/'I Don't Owe You Anything'/'Suffer Little Children'/'Miserable Lie'/'Accept Yourself'/'Pretty Girls Make Graves'. It appears the only other Tate track, 'Jeane', was always intended as a non-album B-side.

28 Porter's Roxy CV covered 1973's *For Your Pleasure*, Bryan Ferry's first four solo albums and Andy MacKay's 1974 LP *In Search of Eddie Riff*. Coincidentally, 'Eddie Riff' would become Morrissey's regular pseudonym when booking into hotels well into the mid-Nineties.

producer to a playback at Regent Sound Studios where, as he feared, Porter concurred that the album The Smiths had recorded with Tate was 'out of tune and out of time'.

'Geoff wanted an honest opinion of what could make it good,' says Porter, 'and sadly my opinion was that it would be easier, cheaper and quicker to do it again rather than try and fix it. That is no slight against Troy Tate, that was just the state of the game at that time.' It followed that Porter volunteered to remake it from scratch himself. Travis agreed, as did Morrissey. By October, after a more hesitant Johnny Marr had finally been persuaded, the Tate sessions had officially been consigned to the vaults as a failed first draft. Whether their career would have followed the same trajectory had it been released is doubtful. It would only be through the indispensable John Porter that Marr would grasp the art of multi-layered production, pushing the group into a whole new stratosphere of studio innovation. Even so, Tate's rough and ready blueprint admittedly captured something of the thrilling rawness of the early Smiths in a way that their eventual eponymous debut perhaps failed to grasp.[29]

Speaking to the *NME* about the album's fate the following year, Tate would confess 'disappointment is not strong enough a word' On his part, Morrissey proffered something of a belated olive branch when asked to stand in as a guest singles reviewer for *Melody Maker* in August 1984, allowing him the chance to praise Tate's own 'Thomas' 45 as 'the best record he has ever appeared on ... This should be a sizeable hit should justice prevail. However, we know that it very rarely does.'

The only consolation for Tate was that his recording of 'Jeane', originally scheduled as the B-side to the withdrawn 'Reel Around The Fountain', would be retained for that of its replacement, 'This Charming Man'. Recorded towards the end of the Elephant sessions, the Kinks-like 'Jeane' was one of Morrissey and Marr's oldest – and simplest – songs, dating back to the winter of 1982. 'It didn't have any strong design behind it,' says Marr, 'it wasn't like I was necessarily trying to play a Kinks track. That staccato, block chord thing was just me trying to get away from the other jangly riffs I was playing at the time, just to get a bit of variety really. I always thought 'Jeane' was quite original.' Marr's two-chord vamp between D and A, bashed out to a persistent football-terrace rhythm over Joyce's bouncing Motown pulse, inspired Tate at first to experiment with some slapback echo overdubs, which gave it a distinct Buddy Holly/Fifties feel. These delightful guitar parts were sadly buried in the final mix, which, for those unacquainted with the

29 Widely available on bootleg, caution should be heeded by those seeking copies of the abandoned Troy Tate album. Many of the most popular versions in circulation stem from unfinished mixes missing their final overdubs and are a great disservice to the finished album master.

full Troy Tate bootleg, still offers a fair taster of the uncluttered directness of that aborted first album.

Morrissey's desperate tale of failed romance against a backdrop of domestic squalor was a variation on the 'rented room in Whalley Range' scenario detailed in 'Miserable Lie' **[see 17]**. The fact that Morrissey was rumoured to have briefly shared such a flat with his friend Linder Sterling was enough for *The Face*'s Nick Kent to suggest that 'Jeane' was one of a handful of Smiths lyrics based upon Morrissey and Linder's relationship. Whether autobiographical or not, the song's narrative was already anchored in Morrissey's love of the classic Sixties 'kitchen-sink' aesthetic, particularly the dire lodgings Jo and her mother flit between in Shelagh Delaney's *A Taste of Honey* (it's probably no coincidence either that the phrase 'paid cash on the nail' appears in Act I of Delaney's *The Lion in Love*).

Author Johnny Rogan has also reasoned that the name itself could have been a reference to the illegitimate child of Oscar Wilde's 'friend and possible lover' Lillie Langtry or Morrissey's own auntie, Jeane Dwyer. Regardless, 'Jeane' remains an ambiguously androgynous handle, highlighted in the cover versions by Billy Bragg and Sandie Shaw **[see 21]**, which offer the same heterosexual interpretation from conflicting gender perspectives.

'Jeane' in Concert

Routinely dropped from their set time and time again, 'Jeane' would somehow survive within The Smiths' concert repertoire for two and a half years. Debuted at their third gig at Manchester's Hacienda (4/2/83), by the spring it had been axed and, in spite of its vinyl release that winter, wasn't performed again for over a year. Reinstated at Dublin's SFX Centre (19/5/84), 'Jeane' stayed in their standard set for the rest of 1984 up until the end of their November Irish jaunt. At these later gigs, Marr was often prone to using the breakdown prior to the song's climax to incorporate the riff of The Beatles' 'Day Tripper'.

In all likelihood, The Smiths would never have performed the song again had it not been for Billy Bragg. Invited to join their first American tour in June 1985, Bragg was already covering 'Jeane' in his own set (he would later record it for a BBC John Peel session and finally release it as a B-side in 1986). On hearing Bragg's version, by the second week of the tour The Smiths resumed playing 'Jeane' themselves, having never even released the track in America. The final show at the Irving Meadows Amphitheater in Laguna Hills (29/6/85) should have been its last outing. However, come the autumn Scottish tour, 'Jeane' was resuscitated one final time for the ecstatic audience of Aberdeen's Capital Theatre on 30 September 1985.

'Jeane' on Television

Never played on television by The Smiths, Johnny Marr did perform an acoustic version with Sandie Shaw on the Charlie's Bus segment of TVam's Saturday morning children's programme *SPLAT* on 16 June 1984 **[see 21]**.

6

'This Night Has Opened My Eyes'

Recorded **September 1983, BBC Maida Vale Studio 4, London**

Produced by **Roger Pusey**

Album track from the compilation ***Hatful Of Hollow***, **November 1984**

While the fate of the Troy Tate album was still being decided, Marr had spent the end of August and early September writing the first new material since its completion. A fourth BBC session for John Peel that month (a consolatory booking after the corporation's decision not to broadcast 'Reel Around The Fountain' recorded for David Jensen a few weeks earlier) provided a timely opportunity to showcase this fresh batch, none of which had yet been played in concert.

Because of the tabloid furore over 'Handsome Devil' **[see 3]**, producer Roger Pusey was under strict orders to vet any lyrics to avoid further media outrage. Two lines into the session's opener, 'This Night Has Opened My Eyes', Pusey ground proceedings to a halt at the graphic reference to drowning a newborn baby. Only after Morrissey explained the song's meaning and assured Pusey of his honourable intentions were they allowed to continue.

Lyrically, it would be the most overt instance of borrowing in their entire canon, even though Morrissey made no attempt to conceal his source. 'I've never made any secret of the fact that at least 50 per cent of my reason for writing can be blamed on Shelagh Delaney, who wrote *A Taste of Honey*,' he later confessed to the *NME*, 'and 'This Night Has Opened My Eyes' is a *Taste of Honey* song – putting the entire play to words.' Which, in a nutshell, is precisely what it does: distilling Jo's dilemma over her unwanted pregnancy as delineated in Act II of Delaney's play into a moribund pop ballad, cut-and-pasting entire quotes wholesale. The song also contained a slender appropriation from Janis Ian with the phrase 'a grown man of 25' plucked

30 Morrissey would later refer to 'Stars' in his 1997 interview with Joni Mitchell for *Rolling Stone*. Thematically, 'Stars' shares Morrissey's fascination with fleeting fame and the tragedy within celebrity lives. In fact, Ian's full lyric – 'You never saw the eyes of grown men of 25, that followed you as you walked and asked for autographs' – is heavily reminiscent of The Smiths' later 'Paint A Vulgar Picture' **[see 72]**.

from 1972's 'Stars'.[30] Marr's complementary score heaves with obligatory sorrow over Joyce's subtly complex drum pattern with its soft pauses and delicate hi-hat fills; cheerless, yet strangely beautiful.

It wasn't until the summer of 1984, during the 'William, It Was Really Nothing' session at Jam Studios in North London **[see 25]**, that The Smiths got round to tackling a new version of 'This Night Has Opened My Eyes.' Though a competent re-recording, it was never used as an official flipside at the time. Instead, when collating 1984's *Hatful Of Hollow*, a superlative compilation of B-sides and BBC tracks originally retailing at a fan-friendly £3.99, the Peel version was finally made available to the public.

Essentially a stopgap between *The Smiths* and *Meat Is Murder* released in time for Christmas 1984, *Hatful Of Hollow* outstripped their debut proper on virtually every level. 'A good portion of our mail contains imploring demands that we release versions of our songs that we recorded for Radio One sessions,' explained Morrissey. 'As far as we're concerned, those were the sessions that got us excited in the first place, and apparently it was how a lot of other people discovered us also.' Although American audiences had to wait until 1987's *Louder Than Bombs* to hear the song, in 1985 journalist Dave Di Martino teasingly informed readers of US magazine *Creem* that 'This Night Has Opened My Eyes' was 'likely the best Smiths track there is'.

The dazzling heights/plagiarised depths of Morrissey's 'Shelagh Delaney period' prompted mixed reactions in the press. Though he was chastised for his lyrical looting by some quarters, it was rarely mentioned in his defence that the critically-immune Beatles had hitherto not only covered the 'theme song' inspired by (but not actually featured in) the 1961 film version of *A Taste of Honey* on their debut album *Please Please Me*, McCartney too had taken the title of 'Your Mother Should Know' on 1967's *Magical Mystery Tour* EP from its dialogue. It was amusing nevertheless to hear Morrissey finally concede in 1994 that 'I mean, even I – *even I* – went a little bit too far with *A Taste of Honey*.'

In Concert

A month after its BBC recording, 'This Night Has Opened My Eyes' was first played at Sheffield University (17/10/83), staying in their set for the rest of 1983. A standard of the spring '84 UK tour and the European and Irish dates that followed, it was eventually dropped after the Provinssi Rock Festival in Finland (2/6/84).

The song would reappear in concert only twice more; first at Galway Leisureland (17/11/84), coinciding with its inclusion on *Hatful Of Hollow*, and more significantly at Brixton Academy over two years later (12/12/86) at what would be The Smiths' final concert. Of all the songs featured during that last historic performance, 'This Night Has Opened My Eyes' was by far the most surprising and emotionally loaded blast from the past.

Television

First shown as part of BBC2's *Whistle Test – On The Road* Derby Assembly Rooms concert in December 1983 **[see 3]**, it was also performed live in the Manchester studio of BBC North West's *YES* programme on 6 February 1984 along with 'What Difference Does It Make?'. At a time when it was still unavailable on vinyl (and absent from the debut album they were currently promoting), 'This Night Has Opened My Eyes' was a markedly esoteric choice.

Of more trivial interest, this song was the equally unlikely first Smiths track featured as background music in the Queen Vic pub on *EastEnders* shortly after the soap began on BBC1 in spring 1985. At the time, Morrissey seemed unimpressed with the programme ('It can be witty but I find it a little bit "how's your father" and "stone the crows"'), although he later used its Elstree Studios' Albert Square set for a solo 1991 photo session.

7

'This Charming Man'

Recorded **September-October 1983, Matrix Studios, London/Strawberry Studios, Stockport, Manchester**

Produced by **John Porter**

Single A-side, November 1983 (Highest UK Chart Position #25)

The record that was finally to shove The Smiths above the parapet of being just another John Peel-championed, music-press cult and into the mainstream pop arena remains not only one of their greatest achievements but a fair contender for the most life-enhancing piece of seven-inch vinyl ever pressed.

The *NME*'s Danny Kelly would accurately describe the impact of first hearing 'This Charming Man' as 'one of those moments when a vivid, electric awareness of the power of music is born or renewed'. Reviewing the single in the same paper, Paul Morley praised its 'accessible bliss' nominating it as one of the greatest singles of that year at the very least. More so than the emotionally fraught gravitas of its predecessor, 'Hand In Glove', 'This Charming Man' was a knowingly exuberant 'pop' construction. By eventually bringing them into living rooms nationwide via *Top of the Pops*, for legions of future fans (this author included) it imparted the first glimpse into the unknown dominion of Smithdom. The prelude now over, 'This Charming Man' felt like The Smiths' concrete *beginning*.

On Friday 8 July, with a fortnight off between gig commitments, Morrissey relaxed by staying in and watching the late-night movie on BBC1. *Sleuth*, starring Laurence Olivier and Michael Caine, boasted a furiously witty script by Anthony Shaffer, based upon his own stage play. Morrissey was impressed enough to take note of a heated exchange in which Olivier has Caine at gunpoint and accuses him of being 'a jumped-up pantry boy who doesn't know his place'. When exacting his revenge towards the film's finale, Caine himself repeats the phrase (absent from Shaffer's original play). As the crux of 'This Charming Man', Morrissey would later have to account for the expression to overseas journalists. 'It [refers to] a low-life street character. I'm sure there are worse things that you could be rather than a jumped-up pantry boy, but it just seemed very rhythmical at the time.' It would be a year or two before the press finally rumbled its *Sleuth* origins.

Nor was it the only appropriated dialogue used in the song. The ubiquitous Shelagh Delaney makes her mark during the second verse, though this time it's the script of the 1961 film version of *A Taste of Honey* that is looted. During its pre-credit prologue, after the school netball game, one of Rita Tushingham's classmates asks 'Are you going dancing tonight?'. 'I can't,' she sulkily replies, 'I haven't got any clothes to wear for one thing'. However, Morrissey still claimed this scenario to be based upon his own experiences when quizzed by the *NME* in 1984: 'I found that on those very rare occasions when I did get invited anywhere, I would constantly sit down and say, "Good heavens, I couldn't possibly go to this place tonight because I don't have any clothes... I don't have any shoes." So I'd miss out on all those foul parties. It was really quite a blessing in disguise.'

Jumbled together with its snatches of Shaffer and Delaney, 'This Charming Man' is one of Morrissey's more opaque lyrics. Even Johnny Marr called it 'flummoxing' when pressed as to the song's meaning. From the implicit erotic overtones of the opening hillside rendezvous to the protagonist's empty wardrobe, its innocent veneer masks a subtext open to infinite interpretations. Consider the fetishistic details of leather upholstery, the anxiety of holding out for a sexual awakening and the calculated vocabulary of 'gruesome' against 'handsome'. Above all, 'This Charming Man' is loaded with designs that invite a specifically homosexual reading. Stepping into a stranger's car on an isolated country road, is the star-crossed cyclist intentionally consenting to an illicit fumble in the nearest lay-by? Or does he just want his puncture fixed? 'Really it was just a collection of lines that were very important,' came Morrissey's ultimate explanation. 'They seemed to stitch themselves perfectly under the umbrella of 'This Charming Man'.'

Incredibly, the melody was written by Marr 'in 20 minutes' one early September morning in preparation for their second John Peel session.[31] When Geoff Travis attended the recording at BBC's Maida Vale studios and heard that first rudimentary version of 'This Charming Man', he immediately recognised its potential as a substitute single in place of their more controversial 'Reel Around The Fountain' **[see 14]**. It was, according to Travis, 'a happy, casual but serious decision. I remember saying, "That's a fantastic track, it'd make a great single," and the band said, "That sounds OK by us".'

Intent on maintaining the label's release programme, barely a week later The Smiths had cancelled a handful of live bookings up North in order to remain in London for their first proper studio session with John Porter at London's Matrix, a subterranean studio located near The British Museum. It was Porter who would supply the song with its dramatic tension, recommending they adopt its signature start-stop pauses similar to the glam punctuations employed in Roxy Music's 'Virginia Plain'. Yet, as with the Troy Tate album, their initial efforts fell below par. The Matrix master – which as 'This Charming Man (London)' would finally feature on the single's 12-inch format as an alternate bonus – lacked the vital emphasis the track deserved, its rhythm too soft, its introduction not nearly robust enough. 'We worked like maniacs recording those tracks for the single over one weekend,' Porter recalls. 'I think when we played it to Geoff he dug it but he didn't think it was clean enough. He suggested we go and do it again in Manchester. I think Geoff wanted us to re-do it up there because he wanted it to be more raw and more "Smiths-like" I suppose.'

At least this time all parties were in agreement as to the Matrix version's shortcomings, and instigated a reparative second attempt the following week back at Strawberry Studios in Stockport (distinguished on the 12-inch as 'This Charming Man (Manchester)'). Unusually, Joyce's 'live' drums were added last having been substituted by a synthetic Linn drum track for the majority of the recording. As would become customary during all sessions with Porter, Marr's guitar parts took priority over everything else. 'This Charming Man' allegedly contains in excess of a dozen guitar tracks including three acoustic, a backwards melody with added reverb and Marr's lead played on a Telecaster. The echoing treble clangs heard at the end of each chorus were also achieved by dropping a standard metal-handled household knife onto the strings. 'Early on they made it clear they didn't want any other instruments on their records,' says Porter. 'They wouldn't allow backing

31 As if this weren't remarkable enough, Marr has stated on several occasions that he'd sketched 'Still Ill' **[see 9]** the previous evening – a miraculous 24 hours' work by any composer's standards.

vocals or whatever. Mozzer was clear about that so it was a case of "okay, any sound we need we'll do it with guitars". So me and Johnny would be dropping spanners on them, taping bits up, just having fun smoking a lot of dope while staying up all night and making silly noises.'

The necessary re-recording process paid off a treat. 'This Charming Man', as finally released in early November, positively sparkled. Beginning with Marr's godlike tinkling preface, the song erupts in unrelenting Motown ricochets, sustained by Rourke's complementary Tamla bass tremors. Equally enchanting was its revitalised chorus; a revolving chord run of near jazz-like complexity secured by Rourke's ascending/descending blues scales. Twenty years on, 'This Charming Man' still sounds an immaculate pop single, two minutes and fifty-three seconds of sheer genius and, in Marr's own words, 'the start of Morrissey being a true, wonderful vocalist.'

Their first single to warrant both 7- and 12-inch formats (shrewdly pressed with separate B-sides ensuring completists would be forced to buy it twice), Rough Trade made their first major breech of The Smiths' trust when, in December 1983, they released a second 12-inch single containing two dance-floor-orientated remixes by New York DJ Francois Kervorkian. Both rather crude by today's sophisticated sampling standards, the 'New York Vocal' and 'New York Instrumental' cuts were too benign to be considered sacrilegious, swamping vocals and drums with reverb and accentuating Rourke's bouncing bass pattern. Yet its release – supposedly against the group's consent though Travis strongly refutes such accusations – prompted Morrissey to scold Rough Trade in ensuing interviews. 'I'm still very upset about that,' he brooded to *Record Mirror* the following February, 'it was entirely against our principles, the whole thing, it didn't seem to belong with us. There was even a question of a fourth version, which would have bordered on pantomime. It was called the Acton version, which isn't even funny.'[32] Marr, though critical, was slightly more forgiving when speaking to *Sounds* the same month, admitting 'we didn't like the dance mix of 'This Charming Man' which they put out as a 12-inch and we told them so, but we're certainly not going around saying Rough Trade have screwed us up.'

However, the New York remix debacle was one of the prime catalysts for Morrissey, and soon the rest of the group, to relocate to London by the beginning of 1984 in order to 'keep an eye on the record company'. Relations between the two parties would worsen considerably in the years ahead, though for the time being the thrill of their first UK Top 30 hit

32 Whether this is true or not, the reference to 'Acton' tallied with the West London locale of Eden Studios where *The Smiths* LP was completed.

single was an achievement both were justly proud of. Nine years later, 'This Charming Man' would go on to reward The Smiths with their highest ever singles chart placing, albeit posthumous, after WEA's reissue to promote the *Best* compilation reached number 8 in August 1992.

In Concert

Introduced into their set the day after recording it for John Peel (London The Venue 15/9/83), 'This Charming Man' became a mandatory standard for the next 12 months. An obvious choice of encore perhaps, unusually it was more often than not played early on or mid-performance. Towards the end of 1984, it had even been incorporated into a short-lived medley, coming out of 'Rusholme Ruffians' with an effective drum and bass bridge (uncannily reminiscent of the New York remix 12-inch they professed to despise) before launching into the song proper.

By the *Meat Is Murder* tour in early 1985, they made the brave (if rash) step of dropping it altogether (with the exception of Northampton Derngate 29/3/85, where it became an impromptu encore), though saw fit to restore it thereafter. It was last played at Inverness Eden Court Theatre (1/10/85), their final show that year and just four weeks before Marr's 22nd birthday. True to his word, the guitarist had prophetically informed the *NME* a few months earlier that 'I don't want to be playing 'This Charming Man' when I'm 22.'

Television

The esteem with which their first generation of fans still hold 'This Charming Man' has much to do with the TV exposure the single instigated at the time. *Uncut*'s David Stubbs described The Smiths' historic entry into the medium, and their debut *Top of the Pops* performance in particular, as 'an unexpectedly pivotal cultural event in the lives of a million serious English boys.' And, indeed, boys and girls of all British denominations from Dundee to Derry.

Their first UK TV appearance was Friday 4 November on Channel 4's *The Tube*. A short, specially commissioned film showed the group miming to the Matrix 'London' version of the track in their Crazy Face rehearsal room (its floor carpeted with flowers for the occasion). Poorly filmed in soft focus, this clip was made available on the *NME*'s *Video Bongo* collection in September 1984 and would also be used posthumously as an official promo by WEA to accompany its 1992 reissue. It would be a similar flower strewn affair on BBC2's *Riverside* the following Monday (7/11/83), where a second mimed performance in a disused Shepherd's Bush power station saw them obscured by rogue spurts of dry ice.

Their momentous entrance onto *Top of the Pops* finally occurred a fortnight later, on Thursday 24 November. With Billy Joel's 'Uptown Girl' at number one, The Smiths had the dubious honour of following Marilyn, the latest contender for Boy George's gender-bending crown, and preceding the monstrous Thompson Twins. 'It was live, and you're expecting to slip and fall over,' Marr later reminisced, admitting to his hazardous choice of moccasin shoes. 'My feet were rooted to one spot and I was trying to move around without moving my legs.' With his three cohorts in matching Marks & Spencers polo-neck jumpers and black jeans from Moss's Crazy Face line, Morrissey held court, swivelling on one foot in a lank, oversized cardigan, his sallow chest strewn with beads. Most eye-catching of all was the sword of gladioli he spun around his head like helicopter blades; less a bouquet than an offensive weapon to keep the world at a permanent arm's length. As Andy Rourke also notes, 'Morrissey was one of the first people to refuse to use a microphone on *Top of the Pops* and pretend he was actually singing. He just sang it without one because obviously he was miming. Nobody's really credited The Smiths for that.'

Later that same evening, the band sped back to Manchester where they were given a heroes' welcome at the Hacienda (their stage entrance preceded by a crowd-teasing live video link-up to the dressing room with Morrissey blowing kisses to the camera). *Melody Maker*'s Frank Worrall was there to witness this euphoric champions' homecoming performance: 'Even before they took the stage, girls were being pulled aside for treatment after fainting and too much screaming. Talk about The Beatles! Clearly, The Smiths will go a long way.'

They would perform the song twice more on UK television: as part of their *Whistle Test – On The Road* Derby Assembly Rooms concert shown on BBC2 in December **[see 3]** and, in farcical acoustic form on TVam's Saturday morning children's show *Datarun* the following April. The latter was, alongside their equally hysterical Charlie's Bus appearance in June **[see 21]**, the most ridiculous venture of their TV career. Aimed at pre-teens, *Datarun* was presented by Edwina Lawrie, sister of Lulu, and her make-believe computerised sidekick 'Edwyn'. One would be hard pushed to imagine a more surreal platform for The Smiths, yet Morrissey and Marr were good humoured enough to indulge in a bizarre question and answer session from the pupils of the former's old primary, St Wilfred's in Manchester. It was indicative of the producer's shoddy research that the singer himself was captioned on screen as 'Paul Morresey', not only misspelling his surname but obviously confusing his Christian name with the director of Andy Warhol's *Flesh* credited on the reverse of *The Smiths* LP.

Between enlightening their juvenile inquisitors as to why they chose their name and why they liked flowers ('it's better than waving socks about'),

Morrissey, with Johnny on acoustic guitar, offered a snatch of 'This Charming Man' sabotaged by a comically out-of-sync chorus from the kids themselves. This ludicrous affair – which also incorporated brief sound-check footage from their Manchester Free Trade Hall show ('Still Ill' and 'Hand In Glove' witnessed by an attentive Sandie Shaw) – ended with two puppets dancing to 'What Difference Does It Make?' while reading a copy of *Melody Maker*.

Radio

The John Peel version of 'This Charming Man', recorded 14 September 1983 at Maida Vale Studio 4, was later included on 1984's *Hatful Of Hollow* compilation. Rough around the edges, Rourke's bass line hadn't fully evolved while Joyce's beat remained a uniform pacesetter without the dramatic pauses later concocted for the single (against which this chipper blueprint seems laidback by comparison).

8

'Accept Yourself'

Recorded **September 1983, Matrix Studios, London**

Produced by **John Porter**

B-side to ***'This Charming Man'*** **(12-inch format only), November 1983**

Written and rehearsed in April 1983 alongside 'You've Got Everything Now' and 'I Don't Owe You Anything', 'Accept Yourself' was a more sophisticated take on the stomping Motown template The Smiths had hitherto experimented with on 'Jeane' and the short-lived 'A Matter Of Opinion'. With a signature riff possibly inspired by that of The Four Tops' 1965 Tamla Motown single 'Something About You', Marr's vivacious arrangement of brusque chops based around C-major, laced with descending arpeggios and sudden tempo changes, was among his most ambitious yet. 'That was just in the air at the time,' admits Marr, 'I was buying a lot of Motown singles'. At early practices, Morrissey was so over-excited by the song's inexorable energy that he found himself incapable of listening to its twanging pre-chorus bridge without manically hooting falsetto barks.

'Accept Yourself' also saw Morrissey move away from the darker, self-critical desperation of earlier material towards a more fanciful celebration of his outsider ideal. Here, it's almost as if the Morrissey of spring 1983 is talking to the pre-Smiths Morrissey of 12 months before, exorcising the isolation and resignation he must have felt in an Agony Aunt's address to stop snivelling and start living. It also snuck in a gracious nod towards his friend Howard Devoto, the Buzzcocks founder who left in 1977 to form Magazine. The latter's 1980 single 'A Song from Under the Floorboards' opens with the phrase 'I am angry, I am ill and I'm as ugly as sin', mirroring the similarly self-piteous concerns in 'Accept Yourself' of being 'sick', 'dull' and 'plain'.

Recorded at Matrix alongside the original 'London' mix of 'This Charming Man', to the song's detriment Porter flattened out Joyce's original irregular if effective drum configuration (as displayed on previous versions for Troy Tate [**see 5**] and the BBC) to a more even keel. Even so, when released as a B-side, the finished 'Accept Yourself' provoked an influx of fan mail from those touched by its inverted triumphalism. 'We received so many letters by people utterly affected by this song,' exclaimed Morrissey, 'people who'd let their shoes and their past completely dominate their lives.' A rallying cry to the dispossessed, 'Accept Yourself' was upheld by its author as 'the fundamental request of Smithdom. Simply accept yourself, be yourself, relax, don't worry about anything as there's no point.'

In Concert

Introduced in May 1983, by the summer's end 'Accept Yourself' had become a favourite set closer, only ever played among the final few numbers or the last encore itself. Regardless of its popularity and pseudo-anthemic lyrical qualities integral to Morrissey's underdog principle, following their last gig of the year at London's Electric Ballroom (19/12/83) the track was sadly never played again.

Radio

A much stronger version produced by John Porter for their second David Jensen session at Maida Vale Studio 4 on 25 August 1983 later surfaced on 1984's *Hatful Of Hollow* collection.

9

'Still Ill'

Recorded **September-October 1983, Matrix Studios, London/Pluto Studios, Manchester**

Produced by **John Porter**

Album track from ***The Smiths***, **February 1984**

Of the four tracks recorded during the September Matrix session, only 'Still Ill' would be reserved for inclusion on their eventual debut album,[33] while the others formed the basis of the 'This Charming Man' 12-inch single. Marr composed the tune shortly after completing the doomed Troy Tate album in preparation for their second John Peel session. As the most recent song to be included on *The Smiths* at the time of its recording, it fitted that The Smiths tackled 'Still Ill' with a verve that still shines through in the finished master when compared to its more tired neighbours suffering from inevitable fatigue after their, in some cases, fourth studio incarnation.

By the autumn of 1983, Marr's arrangements were becoming increasingly bolder. Compared to his earlier melodies, some based around only three or four chords though deceivingly intricate with it, 'Still Ill' was a much sharper configuration. From its very first instrumental rehearsal with Joyce and Rourke at Crazy Face in early September the song seemed destined for prominence within The Smiths' repertoire. A surviving practice tape bursts with keyed-up vigour, revealing that originally Marr had foreseen a very effective two-bar bridge (coming out of what would become the 'old days anymore' section) that gave its eventual chorus even greater impact (since it didn't coordinate with Morrissey's words, added afterwards, this passage was later axed). Throughout 'Still Ill', Marr and Rourke play off against one another magnificently, one rising in scale as the other descends; the bassist pummelling the root notes that allow Marr free reign to unfurl its celestial, tingling hook-line as Joyce underscores the buoyant optimism of the chorus itself with triumphant cymbal splashes.

Although, as on the rest of *The Smiths*, Porter's drum sounds have dated badly, on 'Still Ill' he ensured that its distinct 'scratching' intro (Marr and Rourke gyrating plectrums over their deadened strings thus forming a percussive unity with Joyce's backbeat) was milked for supreme impact. A powerful opener for *The Smiths*' second half, it was released by Rough Trade as a supplementary promotional single for radio only (coupled with 'You've Got Everything Now') and in different circumstances would have easily justified an exceptional A-side in itself.

It was definitely of great importance to its author and provided *The Smiths* with some of its most memorable sound bites. Its disparate verses cover much of Morrissey's fundamental lyrical ideals: droll ennui, comical hypochondria, the anti-work ethic, thorny patriotism and the lamentation over lost loves and times past. From here on also, his references would become more subtle as opposed to the wholesale bricolage of the early Delaney patchwork songs. True, there's a hint of *The Lion in Love* ('I'd sooner

33 After recording the backing track of 'Still Ill' at Matrix, final overdubs were added later during the main first album session at Pluto Studios in Manchester.

spit in everybody's eye' cries Kit in Act III), but the sentiments seem authentic rather than appropriated regurgitation. Only in its infamous 'iron bridge' stanza does Morrissey draw from second-hand experience by integrating a passage from *Spend, Spend, Spend*, the tragic autobiography of Viv Nicholson **[see Appendix II]**. 'We walked for miles,' she writes, describing her early courtship with her second husband, 'right over the iron bridge and down underneath it on the towpath ... we were kissing away and touching and getting really sore lips from biting one another.' In spite of this steal, the coincidental location of a real life iron bridge near Morrissey's former home on Kings Road in Stretford would make it a place of pilgrimage for fans during future Smiths sightseeing tours of Manchester.

In many ways, the pivotal track on *The Smiths* (as its prolonged concert shelf-life would suggest), its every sentence – that 'England is mine and it owes me a living' – reads like a laconic, hymnal rallying cry. An indispensable fragment of Morrissey's lyrical psyche, 'Still Ill' remains a quintessential representation of The Smiths' musical manifesto.

In Concert

Introduced at London's The Venue (15/9/83), 'Still Ill' would prove one of the most durable songs throughout The Smiths' live career. A favourite opener or second-to-opener by the end of the year, it remained a permanent bastion throughout 1984 and 1985 with only a handful of exceptions. Performing the song in Eire, Morrissey acknowledged The Smiths' Irish ancestry by altering the lyrics to protest that 'Ireland is mine and it owes me a living'.

The song's first noticeable continued absence occurred in the summer of '86 for the first UK dates with additional guitarist Craig Gannon, though it was soon reinstated for their lengthy Canadian/US tour, used as an opener on the majority of American shows. Come the final UK October tour, 'Still Ill' returned as the penultimate encore and the only track from the first album featured in that tour's set list. It was last played at the final Brixton Academy concert (12/12/86).

Television

First featured on BBC2's *Whistle Test – On The Road* Derby Assembly Rooms broadcast in December 1983 **[see 3]**, The Smiths also performed 'Still Ill' as one of three live songs in the studio of Channel 4's *The Tube* on 16 March 1984 **[see 9 and 34]**. This same *Tube* clip – in which Morrissey squirmed on the floor in foetal spasms and shook the hands of a few besotted worshippers in the front row with papal grace – was also shown during a lengthy Morrissey interview with Muriel Gray for ITV's *Studio One* on 24 May 1985.

Radio

Recorded for their second John Peel booking at Maida Vale Studio 4 on 14 September 1983, a great BBC session version of 'Still Ill' featuring a never-to-be-repeated bluesy harmonica intro and coda was subsequently included on 1984's *Hatful Of Hollow*.

A live rendition taped at the Oxford Apollo (18/3/85) was also aired by Radio 1 on Janice Long's *Evening Show* on 9 May 1985. Although another version was recorded by the BBC at Kilburn National Ballroom (23/10/86) and included on 1988's live album *Rank*, 'Still Ill' wasn't actually broadcast during the original April 1987 *In Concert* programme edited from the Kilburn show.

10

'Wonderful Woman'

Recorded **September 1983, Matrix Studios, London**

Produced by **John Porter**

B-side to **'This Charming Man' (12-inch format only), November 1983**

The last track completed at Matrix was the curious 'Wonderful Woman'. Written in the winter of 1982, it was the only Morrissey/Marr song to change its title between concert debut and actual studio recording. Originally christened 'What Do You See In Him?', its first draft was a fairly basic expression of bitter, unrequited love. Early rehearsal tapes reveal that Morrissey had problems with scanning, his words clumsily trying to pin themselves to Marr's melancholic backdrop as its verses constantly evolved. Come their third gig at the Hacienda in February 1983 (from which all popular bootleg versions of 'What Do You See In Him?' stem) he'd already reshaped its lyrics to omit phrases such as 'when will you ever learn?' and 'ice water for blood' (though the latter would be reinstated during its re-write as 'Wonderful Woman'). As the title suggests, the gist of 'What Do You See In Him?' is the age-old incomprehension of seeing the object of one's desires arm in arm with an unworthy partner who will ultimately bring them heartache.

Though the music and vocal arrangement stayed intact, as 'Wonderful Woman' – remodelled in May 1983 – its new lyrics offered a very different interpretation. Morrissey was now a victim ensnared by a heartless femme fatale who trips and robs the disabled, yet whom he feels powerless to escape. Considering its sarcastic title and wholly unflattering portrait of a malicious witch, it was less than cordial of *The Face*'s Nick Kent to suggest that Morrissey's friend Linder Sterling might have been the eponymous lady in question.[34] 'In a monotonous way it's quite tongue in cheek' Morrissey would later clarify, in doing so admitting that – whoever the subject – the song *was* autobiographical. 'The wonderful woman is actually an incredibly vicious person, but still at the end of the day she had this incredible magnetic ray to me. All the things that she wanted to do, nasty as they were, were completely forgivable due to whatever reason. It's all metaphysical.'

Previously tackled with Troy Tate for the scrapped debut album **[see 5]**, the version of 'Wonderful Woman' recorded with John Porter at Matrix (which would be resigned to the 12-inch of 'This Charming Man' alongside 'Accept Yourself') remains one of his more satisfying early Smiths productions; both Morrissey's troubled vocals and Marr's arpeggio minor chords quake with ethereal reverb, while its chorus fills of lonesome harmonica are another inspired addition to the mix, cut from the same cloth of glum ambience as 'Hand In Glove'.

'I loved that song,' enthuses Marr, 'I really, really loved it. That's a good example of John Porter bringing out the essence of the band and a certain kind of sadness and putting it on the record. I always saw 'Wonderful Woman' as this thick, melancholic, dense atmosphere. It needed to drip with atmosphere and John had the patience to pour over it and do that. It all started to come together at about half four in the morning. I was thrashed through sheer tiredness because we'd been working three days non-stop. Those schedules that Rough Trade put John Porter under were unbelievable by anyone's standards. But I was dying on me knees and John was going "let's put a vibrato on that bit, let's do a high string thing here." We were restringing guitars at five in the morning, just for one little bit, but he helped me through it.'

In Concert

Debuted at Manchester's Manhattan (25/1/83) under its working title of 'What Do You See In Him?', by their seventh gig at the Cannock Chase Miner's Gala (2/6/83), it had re-emerged as 'Wonderful Woman', in which guise it would remain a regular set fixture throughout the summer. Oddly, after appearing on vinyl at the end of the year it was rarely played, squeezed out by their increasingly superior newer material. Last performed at Liverpool's Edge Hill College (18/11/83), there is evidence to suggest that The Smiths were thinking about bringing it back since it was occasionally tried at sound checks as late as spring 1985.

34 Though possibly an innocuous slip of the tongue, it was intriguing that in September 2002 Morrissey should decide to introduce Sterling on stage at the second of two concerts at London's Royal Albert Hall (where she was taking official photographs) as 'Linder Sterling – a wonderful woman'.

Radio

A powerful take of 'Wonderful Woman' was recorded for their first BBC David Jensen session at Maida Vale Studio 4 on 26 June 1983.

11

'The Hand That Rocks The Cradle'

Recorded October 1983, Pluto Studios, Manchester
Produced by John Porter
Album track from *The Smiths*, February 1984

With 'This Charming Man' in the can, The Smiths could now concentrate on the arduous re-recording of the debut album. Having already committed themselves to clusters of promotional live dates across the country in anticipation of the single's release, the prospect of a repeat long-term studio residency similar to that which they'd spent with Troy Tate at Wapping was immediately ruled out for their second attempt with John Porter.

Consequently, what eventually became *The Smiths* was recorded piecemeal fashion. If the general consensus is that their John Porter produced debut isn't the album it should have been, we ought to at least give it some leeway when considering the unorthodox and hasty circumstances under which it was made. Having already cut a usable take of 'Still Ill' at Matrix, the remaining tracks were recorded in one week at Manchester's Pluto studios in mid-October (prior to a final overdub session back in London at Eden studios in early November where the composites of all three sessions were spliced together). The frequent interruptions of sporadic concert obligations, time constraints and Rough Trade's watertight budget increased their trepidation. 'We had very little money,' confirms Porter. 'Seriously, I think there was something like £500 left.' Add to this John Porter's comprehensive manipulation of the music, which created further strife, and Morrissey's own unease over the group dynamics **[see 20]** and, by all accounts, the making of *The Smiths* was a far from comfortable experience for all concerned.

'Poor old John gets so much criticism for that first album,' says Marr, 'but I always took the view that a few of those songs we'd tried to get right for the third time so it wasn't a case of John putting a gun to our heads and saying "now you must change your arrangements fellas". By that time we were desperate to get the record finished, so I think having done those Peel sessions, the amount of times we'd played them live and having gone through that very intensive recording that we did with Troy, we took our hands off the wheel. John came in and steered it as best he could. He was put up in some really crummy little place in Manchester, having to remake a record with now famously strange vibes. Technically, obviously, it didn't suit what the band was about but the experience of working with John was amazing for us and quite difficult for him.'

'I think the band were realistic,' reflects Porter. 'I mean, yeah, at first they probably thought "Who is this guy and what the fuck is this?" but then I think they got used to trying new ideas out to see if they worked, and after a while they *did* work. As for Morrissey, I wouldn't say he was the easiest of people to work with, in fact he didn't seem very interested in the studio process particularly. I remember trying to get him interested in recording, like Johnny was interested and learned very quickly. But not Mozzer. I can remember showing him the mixing desk one time with all the faders explaining what everything did, showing him reverb and asking him "Would you like your voice to sound like this?" He just wouldn't touch it, he wasn't bothered.'

Though even Porter would later confess to having 'actively butchered' some of the songs in question, his nurturing of Johnny Marr was an epiphany in the group's musical maturity that more than compensated for any disquiet. 'I always felt as though John was there for Johnny,' Joyce reflects. 'They worked together like a dream and when Johnny was happy that contentment and inspiration filtered through to the rest of us. Johnny learnt so much which he stored up for later years. There were loads of tiny, subtle things we'd have never have done without John Porter's guidance.'

'I actually felt like we were kindred spirits,' agrees Porter. 'I'd originally come down to London from the North. I was pretty green, I didn't have much of a clue when I was younger. I recognised them as being very similar. Just down from the North and they hadn't got a fucking clue. But I was immediately impressed with Johnny's playing. He became like a younger brother to me.'

The first track completed with Porter at the main Pluto session would be 'The Hand That Rocks The Cradle', Marr's canny modification of Patti Smith's 'Kimberly' previously attempted a year earlier at that very first Decibel demo session **[see 1]** and more recently with Troy Tate **[see 5]**. Though it was the first song Morrissey and Marr wrote together in the summer of 1982 (discounting the abandoned 'Don't Blow Your Own Horn'), its lyrics actually predate The Smiths. Future Rough Trade associate Richard Boon remembers hearing a very strange home demo of an unaccompanied and inaudible Morrissey (taped while his mother was asleep in the next room) singing 'The Hand That Rocks The Cradle' to a different melody circa 1980. On the same tape was a weirdly prophetic cover of an obscure Bessie Smith tune, 'Wake Up Johnny'.

According to Morrissey, the song came 'from a relationship I had that didn't really involve romance'. Lyrically, it's unlike anything else in The Smiths' canon and is arguably the only song that reads like a prose poem forcibly put to music; heavy on alliteration ('ceiling shadows shimmy by') and lacking Morrissey's usual candour. The ubiquitous spectre of Shelagh Delaney reappears with a line lifted from *The Lion in Love* ('That's it – that's right – rattle her bones over the stones, she's only a beggar whom nobody owns') though moreover one is forced to question some of the more prickly inferences to paedophilia, which cannot be avoided. The quotation from the 1920s Al Jolson standard 'Sonny Boy' notwithstanding (a citation the singer would have to acknowledge by crediting writers De Sylva, Henderson, Brown and Jolson on the finished album's inner sleeve), Morrissey can be plainly heard intoning 'your mother she need never know'. Even so, tabloid suggestions during the 'Handsome Devil' scandal **[see 3]** that 'The Hand That Rocks The Cradle' was merely a twisted cover of 'Sonny Boy' advocating the corruption of 'a seven-year-old in a park' were dangerously off the mark (this was partly the fault of journalist Dave McCullough who'd already misconstrued such a reading in an early live review printed in *Sounds*).

Under John Porter's direction, the song's central looping guitar riff would be deconstructed into a gossamer jigsaw of indistinct, chinking arpeggios. According to Joyce, Morrissey was particularly unhappy with the producer's interference in Marr's original melodic hook. 'I remember in the studio Morrissey giving me the "over here" look, so I went to see what was up,' recalls Joyce. 'He was concerned that the original guitar line, which was why we'd chosen to record it in the first place, was pretty much gone. Morrissey was saying that he'd written a melody around that guitar, and that's why everyone loved it. But it had been buried completely amongst all the other guitars that got put on. That's what John Porter was into. It'd be drums, bass, vocals out of the way and then "Right! Guitars!" and him and Johnny would then spend the rest of the time putting about 15 guitar parts down.'

Regardless of Joyce's misgivings, and largely due to its new myriad guitar pattern, 'The Hand That Rocks The Cradle' would age better than most other tracks on their debut and stands as one of Porter's best early Smiths productions.

In Concert

As the opening number of their stage debut supporting Blue Rondo A La Turk at the Manchester Ritz on 4 October 1982, 'The Hand That Rocks The Cradle' was the very first song The Smiths ever played live (with Hibbert on bass, prior to Rourke's recruitment). Joyce accidentally split the skin of his snare halfway through and had to finish the rest of the gig with the drum turned upside down. Thereafter it was performed at the next half dozen gigs in early 1983 up to and including the Electric Ballroom in Camden, London (21/5/83) after which it was permanently dropped.

12

'I Don't Owe You Anything'

Recorded **October-November 1983, Pluto Studios, Manchester/Eden Studios, London**
Produced by **John Porter**
Album track from ***The Smiths*, February 1984**

After scrapping a first take with Porter for being too fast, a second stab at the tender ballad 'I Don't Owe You Anything' would be one of the first tracks completed on *The Smiths* and one of the few to really do its composition justice. Surpassing their previous version for Troy Tate **[see 5]**, Porter's rousing mix profits from the background Hammond organ whirr provided by guest musician Paul Carrack (formerly of Ace, Roxy Music and Squeeze, and later to enjoy greater success with Mike and the Mechanics) added during a later overdub session at Eden Studios in West London.[35] Carrack would also contribute keys to 'Reel Around The Fountain' and 'You've Got Everything Now' **[see 14 and 18]**. 'A lot of those songs seemed to meander a bit,' says Porter, 'there was no real dynamic, they were very linear. So my getting Paul Carrack in was just trying to get a bit of colour into those songs that I thought was lacking.' Morrissey complimented Carrack that his organ melodies were 'like Reginald Dixon on acid' and seemed pleased with the end product.

Written in late April 1983, it would appear that Morrissey and Marr romantically conceived 'I Don't Owe You Anything' as an imaginary vehicle for legendary Sixties chanteuse Sandie Shaw. Their fantasy was later realised a year after its composition when Sandie finally recorded it after months of intense cajoling **[see 21]**. Melodically, it was one of Marr's breezier works to date, not dissimilar to some of Sandie's more heart-rending torch songs penned by Chris Andrews during her mid-Sixties heyday. Even the title – 'I Don't Owe You Anything' – could have plausibly been that of a classic

35 The extra overdub session at Eden was only made possible after Geoff Travis secured an American deal with Sire Records which, as Porter puts it, 'meant there was a little bit of extra money in the pot.' A horrid alternate take also cut at Eden in which Carrack echoes Morrissey's vocal melody with a crass high-pitched, bontempi shrill was thankfully binned.

Sandie single. It's surely more than coincidence that in one of several fan letters to Shaw sent by Morrissey and Marr as part of their campaign to gain her trust they praised 1967's 'Keep In Touch', the B-side of one of Sandie's lesser known near-misses, 'I Don't Need Anything'.

Rehearsed with 'You've Got Everything Now' and 'Accept Yourself' that spring, early arrangements stretched to an epic seven minutes, partially due to an extra end verse that was eventually discarded. Graphically spelling out what will make the lyric's addressee smile that night, Morrissey reveals it's 'the rude girl that you have known' before concluding 'how I want to forget tonight, and I will, as will you.' Even without this explicit postscript, the words hinted at a sordid and regrettable liaison while the constant beseeching to 'go out tonight' was an amusing inversion of the 'This Charming Man' scenario. More tenuously, allowing for Morrissey's systematic ransacking of Shelagh Delaney's *A Taste of Honey*, a line at the very beginning of Act I where Jo protests to her mother 'I don't owe you a thing' ought to be noted as well.

In Concert

Brought into the set list in May 1983 (its first recorded performance being at London's Electric Ballroom 21/5/83), 'I Don't Owe You Anything' was played throughout the summer (including London Dingwalls (9/8/83) where its sentiment proved too much for Mike Joyce who was moved to tears halfway through playing) and early autumn until being dropped midway through their October university dates.

Though performed at the opening Sheffield gig of the '84 spring tour to promote the first album (31/1/84), it was only played at three of the remaining 31 shows; namely the final night at Birmingham Tower Ballroom (20/3/84) and more prominently a week earlier at London's Hammersmith Palais (12/3/84) and Manchester Free Trade Hall (13/3/84) where both nights they were joined on stage by Sandie Shaw – who sang lead instead of Morrissey **[see 21]**. Come the release of 'Heaven Knows I'm Miserable Now', it was back in the main set for the duration of their May/June mini-tour of Ireland and mainland UK, last played at Cornwall's St Austell Coliseum (22/6/84).

Radio

The Smiths recorded a solid BBC rendition of 'I Don't Owe You Anything' for their second David Jensen session at BBC Maida Vale Studio 4 on 25 August 1983.

13

'These Things Take Time'

Recorded **October 1983, Pluto Studios, Manchester**

Produced by **John Porter**

B-side to **'What Difference Does It Make?' (12-inch format only), January 1984**

Considered an obvious album candidate when previously recorded by Troy Tate **[see 5]**, 'These Things Take Time' would instead be commandeered as a B-side to 'What Difference Does It Make?'. An early composition dating back to the late summer of 1982, the track was central to the canon of fairly bleak, failed and unconsummated relationship songs Morrissey produced during this period (eg 'Miserable Lie', 'What Do You See In Him?'). Sharing its title, yet again, with a line of dialogue from Shelagh Delaney's *The Lion in Love* (Act I:1), its lyrics went through several drafts during early rehearsals. The first verse originally concluded with the histrionic flourish 'I'm saved, I'm saved, you took my hand' while similarly verse two suggested Morrissey was 'useless' (later changed to 'ill').

Its opening line, a paraphrase of the first line from the American 'Battle Hymn of the Republic', may well have been inspired by a similar pun in 'Psychotherapy' by late-Sixties folk heroine Melanie ('Mine eyes have seen the glory of the theories of Freud'). 'These Things Take Time' also contains a skilful example of Morrissey's wordplay in its subversion of the overture from *The Sound of Music*, the hills now being alive 'with celibate cries'. As an open glorification of carnal abstinence (seemingly born out of physical ineptitude like the later 'Pretty Girls Make Graves' **[see 16]**), it was one of Morrissey's most explicit statements yet on sexual politics and the notion of celibacy; a subject which would dominate the majority of the press's gratuitously intrusive interviews with the singer.

When compared to earlier versions of the song for Tate and the BBC, Porter's arrangement tightens the rhythm section to a faster, more consistent beat while Marr's growling guitar is administered a lighter pop gloss. An obvious A-side candidate to less prolific groups, The Smiths could relegate treasures such as 'These Things Take Time' to 12-inch extra tracks with cavalier confidence.

In Concert

Debuted at The Smiths' second gig at Manchester's Manhattan (25/1/83), 'These Things Take Time' was played live throughout 1983 almost without fail. Despite coinciding with its vinyl release on the 12-inch of 'What Difference Does It Make?', it was omitted from the bulk of 1984's spring UK tour, although public demand instigated its necessary re-introduction as an impromptu curtain call on a handful of latter dates.

For the rest of the year it remained an unshakeable encore despite numerous attempts to drop it. Seemingly axed by the beginning of 1985, when closing an acutely euphoric show at London's Brixton Academy (1/3/85), the song was revived one last time as a final farewell.

Television

A live version was featured as part of BBC2's *Whistle Test – On The Road* Derby Assembly Rooms concert (7/12/83), televised 9 December 1983 [**see** 3].

Radio

Recorded by Dale Griffin for their first David Jensen session at Maida Vale Studio 4 on 26 June 1983, a magnificent BBC version of 'These Things Take Time' – easily its most satisfactory incarnation – was later included on 1984's *Hatful Of Hollow* compilation.

14

'Reel Around The Fountain'

Recorded **October-November 1983, Pluto Studios, Manchester/Eden Studios, London**
Produced by **John Porter**
Album track from **The Smiths, February 1984**

Hailed upon its release as 'the greatest love song written since the Buzzcocks' by the *NME*, Marr composed 'Reel Around The Fountain' in early 1983, having purposely set out to write what he described as a 'classic melodic pop tune'. His specific foundation model was Jimmy Jones' 1960 R&B hit 'Handy Man'.[36] 'It came from one of mine and Joe Moss's marathon R&B record sessions one morning at Crazy Face,' says Marr. 'We went from listening to The Platters, who I wasn't really getting behind, to Jimmy Jones. I remembered hearing the track from when I was a kid, 'cos one of me aunties or somebody used to play it. So I remembered the melody of 'Handy

36 The original edition of this book reiterated the suggestion by Johnny Rogan in *Morrissey & Marr: The Severed Alliance* that it was James Taylor's cover of Jones' 'Handy Man', as featured on 1977's *JT*, that inspired the tune. Marr is eager to dispel this myth. 'I'd never even heard James Taylor's version until I read that 'Reel Around The Fountain' was copied off it. I mean Neil Young's one thing but I draw the fucking line at James Taylor! Absolutely no way.'

Man' but then when I tried to play it myself I got it all wrong, which was useful really.'

Like the later 'This Night Has Opened My Eyes', 'Reel Around The Fountain' was another of Morrissey's more concentrated tributes to Salford playwright Shelagh Delaney. 'Obviously most people who write do borrow from other sources,' he told the *NME* in 1986. 'They steal from other's clothes lines. I mentioned the line "I dreamt about you last night and I fell out of bed twice" in 'Reel Around The Fountain', which comes directly from *A Taste of Honey*, and to this day I'm whipped persistently for the use of that line. Just because there's one line that's a direct lift people will now say to me that 'Reel Around The Fountain' is worthless, ignoring the rest of it which almost certainly comes from my brain.'

Actually, 'the rest of it' also bears the thumbprints of 'other sources'. There are traces of feminist critic Molly Haskell – whose compelling Seventies study of women in the movies *From Reverence to Rape* refers to Samantha Eggar in *The Collector* being 'pinned and mounted like one of [Stamp's] butterflies' – and more Delaney still. Its opening line was derived from Jesse's song at the end of *The Lion in Love*; 'Winter's coming in my lass, The north wind's blowing cold, I think we've courted long enough, It's time our tale was told.'

Because of its emotive major-key melody's commercial potential, 'Reel Around The Fountain' seemed the obvious follow up to 'Hand In Glove'. Regrettably, the proposed single as recorded by Troy Tate **[see 5]** was scuppered as a result of the tabloid controversy in September 1983 accusing the band of condoning paedophilia **[see 3]**. Although it was 'Handsome Devil' that had created the furore, the fact that the papers mistakenly suggested the BBC were having doubts about broadcasting a version of 'Reel Around The Fountain' recorded for David Jensen (which they hadn't) resulted in the corporation nervously withdrawing a session version of the song. Defending the track to *Melody Maker* that same month, Morrissey explained 'on our David Jensen session, one song, 'Reel Around The Fountain' was chopped simply because the word 'child' was mentioned and they were frightened people might put the wrong interpretation on it. But at the end of the day, the BBC turned out to be allies.'[37] All the same, rather than exacerbate the witch-hunt gathering pace, Rough Trade cautiously reconsidered the move to issue it as the next Smiths 45 (even though approximately 50 white labels had already been pressed up and a small teaser advert had been published in anticipation).

37 By 'allies', Morrissey was referring to the fact that as compensation for pulling the Jensen version of 'Reel Around The Fountain', BBC producer John Walters immediately booked them for another John Peel session the following week.

Given the task of rerecording 'Reel Around The Fountain' at Pluto, John Porter at first provided a subtle country sheen with some beautifully expressive Nashville style guitar glimmers. Rourke's original bass line – a constant oscillating pulse behind the verses – was also reconstructed into a series of hesitant couplets; less insistent and therefore less effective than before. Similarly, Morrissey's vocal was markedly reserved in contrast to the unbridled passion of previous versions for the BBC and Troy Tate. At least in his suggested use of piano, Porter managed to bestow the song with a novel texture, thanks to Paul Carrack's organ backwash and sensual ivory glaze.

Even in the far from perfect state that finally appeared as the lead track on *The Smiths*, 'Reel Around The Fountain' still bore all the hallmarks of an early masterpiece. Together, Marr's sweetly appealing melody and Morrissey's literary assemblage coalesce to make it a ballad of acute beauty. Far from being a sordid anecdote of juvenile abuse, at the heart of the song is an extremely moving divulgence of physical desire spiked with tremendous humour. While it thumps with erotic intent ('shove me on the patio') the main thrust of the song is still, on a basic emotional level, one of unexpurgated love (Morrissey's final *cri de cœur* – 'I do' – trembles with desperate yearning). The first truly magnificent Smiths weepie, 'Reel Around The Fountain' has that unnerving, unique quality to makes the listener laugh and cry simultaneously. 'The greatest love song since the Buzzcocks' then? Absolutely. A monumentally powerful work and among The Smiths' very best.

In Concert

Introduced in May 1983, 'Reel Around The Fountain' became an audience favourite well before its eventual vinyl release almost a year later. While the media controversy following its BBC session ban raged, The Smiths continued to play it live for virtually every date that year and the majority of shows on the 1984 spring UK tour. By the summer however, having grown wary of the track they omitted it from all European fixtures, only to reinstate it for their four Irish shows in May before, once again, dropping it from their summer UK concerts.

Resurrected for that year's autumn dates, it stayed within their regular set well into the new year and the *Meat Is Murder* tour, where it was dropped in favour of 'Stretch Out And Wait' following Margate Winter Gardens (8/3/85) and never played in Britain again. The Smiths did however resurrect the song a few more times during their first US itinerary later that year, its last performance being the Laguna Hills Irving Meadows Amphitheater (29/6/85).

Television

The fact that the BBC had chosen not to air 'Reel Around The Fountain' when recorded for Radio 1's David Jensen show earlier in the year didn't prevent them from broadcasting the same potentially offensive track when televising the Derby Assembly Rooms concert on BBC2's *Whistle Test – On The Road* in December 1983 **[see 3]**.

Radio

When it came to recording their first ever BBC session for John Peel in May 1983, The Smiths chose to perform all three tracks previously attempted during the Drone demo in December 1982 **[see 2]** alongside the more recent 'Reel Around The Fountain'. Produced by Roger Pusey at Maida Vale Studio 5 on 18 May, the Peel recording (as later included on 1984's *Hatful Of Hollow*) is sublime, possessing a stainless purity that even the Tate remake never quite surpassed. Set in the slightly higher key of B major, each instrument cuts through with diamond precision, from Joyce's double snare commas to Marr's solitary guitar shimmers and Rourke's unencumbered throbbing root notes. Morrissey's reverb-soaked vocal, too, is overwhelmingly plaintive, perfectly focussed at the eye of the storm and delivered with arrestingly precise diction.

It was their second BBC session version recorded at Maida Vale Studio 4 on 25 August 1983 for David Jensen that was subject to the notorious 'ban'. While the other three tracks ('Accept Yourself', 'I Don't Owe You Anything' and 'Pretty Girls Make Graves') were all aired as planned on 5 September, the Jensen 'Reel Around The Fountain' wasn't actually broadcast until two years later on 12 August 1986, when the full session was repeated on Janice Long's programme for the first time in its uncensored entirety. The Jensen version is easily distinguishable by its prominent acoustic guitar track, which John Porter raises high in the mix as a textural counterpoint to Marr's complementary electric picking.

15

'Back To The Old House'

Recorded **October 1983, Pluto Studios, Manchester**

Produced by **John Porter**

B-side to **'What Difference Does It Make?', January 1984**

Recorded during *The Smiths* sessions, but, like 'These Things Take Time', eventually relegated to a non-album B-side for its mandatory spin-off single, 'Back To The Old House' was written prior to their second John Peel session in September 1983. 'That session was the first time we'd recorded it,' says Marr. 'It just poured out.'

Thankfully, it is this magnificent 'unplugged' version, taped for the BBC and later immortalised on *Hatful Of Hollow*, that is most commonly referred to over its B-side counterpart. A paean to an unrealised lost love while struggling to resist the nostalgic temptation to revisit one's past locale (a theme Morrissey would later explore in even greater depth on the epic 'Late Night, Maudlin Street' from his 1988 solo debut *Viva Hate*), when stripped down to the basics of Morrissey's forlorn echo against Marr's string-squeaking acoustic picking, the song achieves a rare beauty as poignant as anything The Smiths' canon has to offer. It's especially mesmerising in Marr's adept display of unaccompanied folk guitar, revealing the influence of his musical heroes beyond the rock norm such as Bert Jansch. The tenderness and technique evident in this one track alone positioned the 19-year-old Marr in a different class from his peers.

Having yet to tackle the song in concert as a four piece, it was perhaps no fault of John Porter's that when they came to record 'Back To The Old House' at Pluto as a full-band arrangement with bass and drums, the finished track lacked the ambience of that simplistic Peel adaptation. Though sufficiently pretty, it was much less moving and an ultimately inferior adaptation of the tune when compared with the expressive intensity of Morrissey and Marr minus their rhythm section as captured at the BBC.

In Concert

Only introduced live at the tail end of that year (London Electric Ballroom, 19/12/83), 'Back To The Old House' was subsequently played throughout the spring 1984 UK tour, normally as a precursor to its sibling A-side, 'What Difference Does It Make?' It was last performed on the penultimate date at Sheffield City Hall (19/3/84). Though The Smiths never played the track again in concert, Johnny Marr would on rare occasions pick the melody unaccompanied between songs or during technical difficulties at later gigs to keep the crowd amused (eg Inverness Eden Court 1/10/85).

Radio

The aforementioned John Peel acoustic take of 'Back To The Old House' featured on *Hatful Of Hollow* was recorded at BBC Maida Vale Studio 4 on 14 September 1983.

16

'Pretty Girls Make Graves'

Recorded **October 1983, Pluto Studios, Manchester**
Produced by **John Porter**
Album track from ***The Smiths*, February 1984**

Morrissey took the title of this painfully frank admission of sexual incompetence from Jack Kerouac's 1959 beat novel *The Dharma Bums.* Explaining his voluntary celibacy because he'd 'come to a point where I regarded lust as offensive and even cruel', the protagonist Ray Smith (co-incidentally) tells us '"Pretty girls make graves" was my saying, whenever I'd had to turn my head around involuntarily to stare at the incomparable pretties of Indian Mexico.'

Repeatedly probed about his sex life by the media, Morrissey never shied away from discussing his ostensible lack of one. 'I could tell you of years of celibacy when I just couldn't cope with physical commitment because it always failed,' he told *Sounds* in 1983, though he'd tell *i-D* magazine four years later that he'd lost his virginity at the age of 13. 'But it was an isolated incident, an accident,' Morrissey reiterated. 'After that it was downhill. I've got no pleasant memories from it whatsoever.' Frank but circumspect, his admissions of sexual failure were never short on humour, while Marr even disclosed to *The Face*'s Nick Kent that 'when [Morrissey] gets really upset, frankly I think it's just because he needs a good humping!'

In any case, 'Pretty Girls Make Graves' takes Kerouac's hymn to celibacy and adopts it as a more sobering drama of male impotency. Unable to respond to the gauche advances of his female partner, Morrissey laments that 'nature played this trick on me'; a likely paraphrase of 'nature played me a dirty trick' from the 1961 film *Victim* starring Dirk Bogarde as a homosexual barrister being targeted by a blackmail ring. By the final verse, abandoned in favour of another more ready, able and willing beau, the central femme fatale is bitterly scolded for her 'stupid face'. As the song climaxes, Morrissey wispily croons the opening lines of 'Hand In Glove', a possible indication that 'Pretty Girls Make Graves' may indeed be a correlated sequel, drawing the relationship narrative begun in that earlier composition to its bleak conclusion.

The song contains another more obvious requisition in the line – 'I'm not the man you think I am' – swiped from 'I've Been A Bad, Bad Boy', a 1967 UK Top Five hit by former Manfred Mann singer Paul Jones, which Morrissey would revealingly nominate in a list of 'Singles to be cremated with' for the *NME* in 1989. Jones' disc originated from his starring role in the cult British semi-musical movie *Privilege*, an Orwellian allegory about a pop star (called Steve) manipulated by the State and the Church to control the country's youth via mass media propaganda and sado-masochistic, ritualistic concerts. As described in John Burke's paperback adaptation of Norman Bogner's original screenplay, there's more than a passing resemblance between the fictitious deification of Jones's screen alter-ego, Steve Shorter, and the very real veneration of Steven Morrissey by The Smiths' more extreme fanatics: 'Steve still has to speak for all of us, all of you, all those men and women and kids tied up in the bond of a drab life, a drab country, a dismal daily drudgery.' Morrissey's own interest in *Privilege* was doubtlessly encouraged by Patti Smith's cover of another song from the film, 'Free Me', included on her 1978 album *Easter* (where it was re-titled 'Privilege (Set Me Free)' also incorporating her reading of the 23rd psalm).

A radically different, overtly folky prototype of 'Pretty Girls Make Graves' had been recorded with Troy Tate a few months earlier **[see 5]**, though come its final album version produced by John Porter at Pluto, the tune's original jerky rhythm had been straightened, while its previously unfocussed end section was now fashioned into a more coherent melody. Even so, 'Pretty Girls Make Graves' was far from single material, not that this prevented Morrissey from suggesting it should be their next 45. Thankfully, commercial catastrophe was avoided with 'What Difference Does It Make?' being issued instead **[see 20]**.

In Concert

Premiered at London Dingwalls (30/8/83), 'Pretty Girls Make Graves' stayed in The Smiths set for the rest of the year, (once as the opener supporting Gang Of Four at London Lyceum, 25/9/83) and throughout the following spring's UK tour. Dropped from a couple of foreign dates in Holland and Belgium thereafter, it returned to the main set until being phased out during that winter's Irish tour save Waterford Savoy (11/11/84) and Galway Leisureland (17/11/84), where it was last played.

Television

'Pretty Things Make Graves' was featured as part of BBC2's *Whistle Test – On The Road* Derby Assembly Rooms concert first televised in December 1983 [see 3].

Radio

Among the many potential BBC session tracks that failed to make it on to 1984's *Hatful Of Hollow* compilation was the rendition of 'Pretty Girls Make Graves' taped at BBC Maida Vale Studio 4 for their second David Jensen session on 25 August 1983. Missing the 'oh, really?' insert, Morrissey's chorus wailing benefited from some added reverb, while the outro remained a woolly improvisation lacking the form of the final album version.

17

'Miserable Lie'

Recorded **October 1983, Pluto Studios, Manchester**
Produced by **John Porter**
Album track from ***The Smiths*, February 1984**

Among their earliest songs, Morrissey and Marr wrote the bitter tempo-changing tirade 'Miserable Lie' together in the guitarist's rented attic room in Bowden during the late summer of 1982. 'It came out exactly as it was,' remembers Marr. 'I just had some bananas idea that I gave to Morrissey while he was there. I think as a guitar composition it was kind of caught between two stools, but I was trying to do something original. It was an odd, quirky little thing. Used to confuse the hell out of people at our early gigs.'

Of all the early Morrissey lyrics that may, possibly, have been an address of his relationship with Linder Sterling, 'Miserable Lie' would seem the most overt contender. As Nick Kent speculated, 'one could read more than enough about the nature of Morrissey's relationship with Linder in the song's complete lyric', his calculation predominantly based upon its specific naming of Manchester's Whalley Range district where, Kent claimed, he and Linder temporarily cohabited sometime in the early Eighties.

'It's this little suburb of Manchester bedsit land and everyone who lives there is an unrecognised poet or a failed artist,' Morrissey would inform those interviewers genuinely mystified as to whether Whalley Range actually existed. 'Anyone who wishes to pursue their destiny ends up there and never gets out. I lived in Whalley Range a miraculously short time and it was nice to be immersed in the low life, living the life of pained immaculate beauty, walking around the park inhaling the riches of the poor as it were,[38] but the sense of being entrapped by the DHSS was worrying.' In late 1984, Morrissey even confessed to having revisited the area out of curiosity and still feeling 'great sorrow for the people who were still nailed to the place.'

Besides Whalley Range, 'Miserable Lie' contains another more covert link with Sterling. Earlier that year, Morrissey had written 'Let's Look At Ludus', a detailed press biog for Linder's band. In it, he refers to them as being

38 'The riches of the poor' would later reappear as a lyric in 'I Want The One I Can't Have' **[See 36]**.

'flower-like', a figurative simile borrowed from Oscar Wilde which he'd keep in his poetic vocabulary to use again when composing 'Miserable Lie' a few months later, this time in describing his own 'flower-like life'.[39]

Opening with a deceptively submissive farewell, Morrissey's words suddenly flinch in synch with Marr's schizophrenic score to become an unremittingly pessimistic discourse on romantic nihilism. 'I just don't really have a tremendously strong belief that relationships can work,' he told *Melody Maker*'s Allan Jones, 'I'm really quite convinced that they don't. And if they do, it's really quite terribly brief and sporadic. It's just something that I eradicated from my life quite a few years ago and I saw things more clearly afterwards.' In its protagonist's ruthless self-loathing, 'Miserable Lie' is taxingly graphic. 'I look at yours, you laugh at mine' wails Morrissey (he himself would later tease the press that 'I always thought my genitals were the result of some crude practical joke').

Following its awkward funk blueprint cut at The Smiths' second demo session in December 1982 **[see 2]**, 'Miserable Lie' would be wisely remodelled into its familiar metamorphosis from Byrdsian folk ballad into double-timed punk thrash for subsequent versions recorded for John Peel and the Troy Tate album **[see 5]**.

Unfortunately, the final John Porter take, as recorded during the October 1983 Pluto session, is by far the least satisfying. Despite Porter's main bequest to Marr being the process of 'layering' guitars (whereby up to a dozen or more separate guitar tracks are painstakingly slotted together to form an overall more complex melody) it's ironic that the weakest links within *The Smiths* are its actual guitar lines, which occupy a tinny, indistinct middle ground.[40] 'Miserable Lie' is one of the worst culprits. The changeover from slow to fast is given sufficient oomph, yet Marr's picking is lost. 'Basically the guitar sound wasn't rocky enough to pull that song off properly,' admits Marr. 'Had we played it like 'Sweet And Tender Hooligan' or had I used a Les Paul and a couple of overdrive pedals, it would have been better.'

Marr's sonically subdued delivery on 'Miserable Lie' would be further sabotaged in the finished mix by Joyce's inexplicably pronounced hissing cymbal crashes. The track's odd flashes of brilliance make its multiple shortcomings all the more disappointing; Marr's bending twang to herald his

39 The phrase originates from *De Profundis*, Oscar Wilde's famous address to his former lover Lord Alfred Douglas, written from his cell in Reading prison. Wilde comments about Christ: 'He was the first person who ever said to people that they should live "flower-like" lives.'

40 Porter's production aside, Marr mainly blames the album's colourless guitar sound on his choice of amplifier, the Roland Jazz Chorus: 'Hey man, it was the Eighties! They sounded fine to the player, but I think they failed out front. There seemed to be a big hole in the sound.'

(admittedly pasty) instrumental break, Joyce's tom-tom rolls and not least Morrissey's suitably aggrieved vocal.

Those who witnessed 'Miserable Lie' in concert will verify that no studio cut of the song ever captured the mania The Smiths tore out of it on stage. Still, *The Smiths* version is a diluted travesty of its maximum potential.

In Concert

From its first outing at Manchester's Manhattan on 25 January 1983 (during which Morrissey produced confetti from his pockets and scattered it over his head), 'Miserable Lie' was the obvious set closer of their early stage shows. It wasn't until July that year that it slowly slipped back into the body of the set, played at every date for the rest of 1983. Consequently, when it came to the first full UK tour to promote *The Smiths*, the absence of 'Miserable Lie' from all but two shows (Sheffield University 31/1/84 and Hammersmith Palais 12/3/84, the latter as set opener) was rather surprising (though since Morrissey had contracted bronchitis during the first week, its howling falsetto may have been both physically impossible and medically inadvisable).

On their European dates that April it returned with a vengeance, Marr making a subtle addition to the first half by incorporating a new, descending arpeggio opening riff. Seemingly unshakeable for the next 18 months, it was more often than not the final encore during which the stage would be invaded by as many fans as it took to overwhelm the venue security. Last played in its original format at Dublin National Stadium (10/2/86), thereafter it was dropped until the final concert at Brixton Academy (12/12/86), where it was performed as a medley with the yet to be released 'London'. As the latter reached its climax, the band segued straight into the erratic second half of 'Miserable Lie' with masterful aplomb.

Early live recordings of the song also reveal lyrical variations absent from all studio recordings; expressly where Morrissey screeches 'I'd run a hundred miles away from you'. It's curious to note that over three years later at that final Brixton gig, he was still singing this same line in spite of its non-inclusion on the record.

Television

Perhaps the most comical incident captured by BBC2's *Whistle Test – On The Road* recording of the December 1983 Derby Assembly Rooms concert **[see 3]** was that in which Morrissey was hit in the eye with a rebounding flower stalk, forcing him to stagger off into the wings half-blinded while 'Miserable Lie' continued as an instrumental.

Radio

Of the four songs recorded for their debut BBC John Peel session in May 1983, 'Miserable Lie' was the only one not to be included on *Hatful Of Hollow*. This version, easily distinguishable by Marr's brief use of harmonica during the frantic end section, was finally made available in 1988 on a 12-inch EP released on the Strange Fruit label (part of a generic series of classic Peel sessions)

A fantastic live version recorded at the Oxford Apollo (18/3/85) was also broadcast by BBC Radio 1 on Janice Long's *Evening Show* on 9 May 1985. Originally one of five tracks chosen for the unreleased *Meat Is Murder* live EP **[see 37]**, the Oxford 'Miserable Lie' was instead featured on the import album *Rough Trade*, a label showcase compilation issued in Canada and Holland only.

18

'You've Got Everything Now'

Recorded October-November 1983, Pluto Studios, Manchester/Eden Studios London

Produced by John Porter

Album track from *The Smiths*, February 1984

Prior to 'Heaven Knows I'm Miserable Now' and 'Frankly, Mr Shankly', 'You've Got Everything Now' was the earliest illustration of Morrissey's anti-work ethic. At the height of Thatcherism, unemployment had reached record levels while Tory party chairman Norman Tebbit had the audacity to insist that the nation's three million jobless get on their bikes and look for work as his father had done. Without resorting to party dictated dogma, on a basic social and humanitarian level Morrissey's address of the work issue – in this instance that he'd never had a job because he 'never wanted one' – was an incredibly daring political statement for its day, which he would return to with increasing bravado in the aforementioned later songs.

'Jobs reduce people to absolute stupidity,' he told *Sounds* in June 1983, 'they forget to think about themselves. There's something so positive about unemployment. It's like, Now We Can Think About Ourselves. You don't get trapped into materialism, you won't buy things you don't really want.' If his idealised concept of life on the dole seemed more than a little naïve, it must be said Morrissey's own employment history was hardly that of a long-suffering working-class hero. Cosseted by his mother and still living at home, in early interviews he'd inconsistently maintain that, in keeping with 'You've Got Everything Now', he'd never held down a proper job. In fact, after leaving school Morrissey worked for the Inland Revenue in order to save up money to visit relatives in America.

Written during the same period as 'I Don't Owe You Anything' and 'Accept Yourself' in spring 1983, the earliest surviving rehearsal tape finds 'You've Got Everything Now' much longer (over six minutes) and laden with extraneous lyrics, which were later jettisoned. Principally the same bitter discourse ruminating on the reversal of fortunes affecting a past friendship, a whole extra verse witnesses Morrissey lamenting that 'when you lost the will to go on, I gave you some' while he later conveys that 'you never really wanted the truth and so I never gave it to you.' By the final chorus, he informs us 'I've never had a friend because I've never wanted one', imploring the object of his remorse to 'please make your move'. It should be no surprise that traces of Shelagh Delaney also filter through Morrissey's prose. Namely Banner's jeer 'Shall I tell you something? I don't like your face' from *The Lion in Love* and Shakespeare's 'As merry as the day is long' (from *Much Ado About Nothing* Act II:1) as recited by Helen in *A Taste of Honey* (Act II:2).

Having already recorded a passable version with Troy Tate **[see 5]**, it was a shame that John Porter's obligatory remake at Pluto never managed to seize the drive of Marr's feisty arrangement. Though Rourke's securing bass, crucial to the savage momentum of its verses, is perceptible, Marr's own strident chops are disappointingly diluted. Joyce's clamant tom-tom fills are also dormant under Porter's influence, the only positive addition being Paul Carrack's pre-chorus Hammond swells. Released as a double-sided radio promo with 'Still Ill' to publicise *The Smiths*, although Porter's 'You've Got Everything Now' falls short of its potential, at least its deadpan absurdity – particularly Morrissey's concluding desire to be 'tied to the back of your car' – offered a welcome touch of black humour amid the album's otherwise solemn first half.

In Concert

One of the key songs in The Smiths' early live history, 'You've Got Everything Now' was introduced in May 1983 (the first recorded bootleg being London's Electric Ballroom 21/5/83) and opened their standard set lists throughout that summer. By the end of the year it moved to the show's finale, where it remained for the following spring's first major UK tour, customarily the last encore alongside 'Handsome Devil'.

Its first notable absence from regular set lists was the mini Irish tour at the close of 1984, where it was played only once at Letterkenny Leisure Centre (20/11/84). By 1985's *Meat Is Murder* excursion, they seemed intent on leaving 'You've Got Everything Now' behind, reserving it exclusively for encores when the occasion suited; specifically Oxford, Sheffield, Middlesbrough and

Manchester. Last played on home soil at that tour's epic London Royal Albert Hall finale (6/4/85), it would be the final rapturous encore yet again at the ensuing Rome and Madrid dates. The latter Paseo De Cameons performance on 18 May 1985 (filmed for Spanish TV) marked its fond farewell.

Television

The closing number of BBC2's *Whistle Test – On The Road* Derby Assembly Rooms show in December 1983 **[see 3]**, the song had been the third to last played at the gig itself, yet the farcical stage invasion it inspired forced the programme makers to re-edit the running order placing 'You've Got Everything Now' as the grand finale. The unkempt teenage throng – some looking no older than 12 – enjoyed their one moment of televised glory, punching the air in clumsy pogos beside an amused Marr and a severely strangulated Morrissey, whose lank frame was pulled in every conceivable direction by the excitable mob.

Radio

A wonderfully assertive version of 'You've Got Everything Now' recorded at BBC Maida Vale Studio 4 on 26 June 1983 for their first of two BBC David Jensen sessions was later included on 1984's *Hatful Of Hollow* compilation.

An equally fiery rendition, captured at the Oxford Apollo concert (18/3/85), was also broadcast by BBC Radio 1 on Janice Long's *Evening Show* on 9 May 1985. This is worth hearing as an example of Morrissey's amusing penchant for changing words in concert, declaring that he's never had a job because 'I've never had an interview' and 'because I'm too sensible'.

19

'Suffer Little Children'

Recorded **October 1983, Pluto Studios, Manchester/Eden Studios London**

Produced by **John Porter**

Album track from ***The Smiths*, February 1984**

Subsequently issued as B-side to **'Heaven Knows I'm Miserable Now', May 1984**

One of the first songs to cement the partnership of Morrissey and Marr, the dreadful yet captivating 'Suffer Little Children' was the former's highly controversial elegy to the victims of the 'Moors Murderers', Ian Brady and Myra Hindley.

Morrissey's primary resource in moulding its lyrics was Emlyn Williams' sensationalist biography *Beyond Belief*, which described with chilling matter-of-factness the fate of the three victims the couple were originally convicted of. First published in 1967 (barely a year after their imprisonment), Williams' book tells the Moors Murderers' story in vicarious, narrative prose that chooses fictitious supposition over clinical analysis. 'Suffer Little Children' itself was one of Williams' chapter titles,[41] as was 'Hindley Wakes', a pun on Stanley Houghton's Thirties Lancashire drama *Hindle Wakes* Furthermore, Williams draws explicit attention to Lesley Ann Downey's 'white beads' and cites Hindley's confession during police interrogation that 'wherever he has gone, I have gone.' And at his most objectionably harrowing, Williams further describes the buried bodies upon Saddleworth Moor screaming out 'find me, find me.' All these phrases would of course be appropriated by Morrissey within the song's finished verses.

That any art form – be it fiction, song or painting (eg Marcus Harvey's contentious 1997 'Sensation' exhibition at London's Royal Academy) – on the topic of the Moors Murderers is destined for controversy goes without saying. Five years prior to The Smiths' formation, in 1977 a pre-Pretenders Chrissie Hynde and pre-Visage Steve Strange had played their shameful part in a press sting that overstepped the mark even by punk's inflammatory agenda of swastika sensationalism. Calling themselves 'The Moors Murderers', they masqueraded anonymously in black-bin-bag masks and teased the media with the lyrics of their appalling 'Free Myra Hindley'. The tabloids' justifiable disgust presaged the aggro The Smiths would also endure for treating the same subject with far greater intelligence and sensitivity.

In understanding 'Suffer Little Children', we have to place it, and its author, into the context of time and location. In 1966, Ian Brady and Myra Hindley were sentenced to life imprisonment for the murder of 17-year-old Edward Evans, 10-year-old Lesley Anne Downey and 12-year-old John Kilbride. The latter two victims had been buried in shallow graves on Saddleworth Moor just outside of Manchester, a gory detail that was to bestow the condemned culprits with their reviled epithet. The killings took place between July 1963 and October 1965, in and around Manchester and its surrounding market towns. Born in May 1959, Morrissey would have been a six-year-old child living in the city at the time of their arrest when they were still on the lookout for potential prey. 'I happened to live on the streets where, close by, some of the victims had been picked up,' he told *The Face* in 1985. 'Within that community, news of the crimes totally dominated all attempts at conversation for quite a few years. It was like the worst thing

41 It's either coincidence or doubly significant that 'Suffer Little Children' is also the title of a song by another of Morrissey's favourite singers, Buffy Sainte-Marie, featured on her 1968 LP *Illuminations*.

that had ever happened, and I was very, very aware of everything that occurred. Aware as a child who could have been a victim.'

Therefore 'Suffer Little Children' is an account of the Moors Murders as written by somebody who, but for the grace of God, could so easily have become another statistic in this foulest of crimes; a personal memorial intended to highlight the diabolical enormity of what Brady and Hindley had committed. But we must also consider this: at the time of its composition, and release on *The Smiths*, the couple had only ever been convicted of the three murders Morrissey describes (those of Kilbride, Downey and Evans as detailed in Williams' book) while Hindley had continually protested her innocence as a mere love-struck accomplice. Finally, in 1987, three years after 'Suffer Little Children' first appeared on vinyl, Brady confessed to a journalist interviewing him in prison that, as suspected, they were also responsible for the deaths of 16-year-old Pauline Reade and 12-year-old Keith Bennett, who had vanished during the same period between 1963-65. After a cordoned search of the moor, remains of Reade's body were found. Tragically, those of Bennett have yet to be located to this day.

Consequently, the song's grim refrain usurped from Williams – 'find me, find me' – now assumes an unbearable weight in the context of the Bennett case. In a sense, the subsequent admission from Brady (and by proxy the exposure of Hindley as a calculated manipulator who'd hitherto endeared herself to the sympathy of penal reform groups) now renders 'Suffer Little Children' not so much redundant as deficient. Only in its merciless attack on Hindley's hollow pleas of innocence was Morrissey to be deeply prophetic. In an interview with *Record Mirror* at the time of Brady's confession in 1987, journalist Stuart Bailie commented that 'on the subject of the Moors Murderers, and the recent turn of events [Morrissey] is genuinely concerned about the parents of the dead children, and is upset that the public attitude to Myra Hindley has become 'dangerously civil'.'

Like 'The Hand That Rocks The Cradle', Morrissey had already written the lyrics to 'Suffer Little Children' before forming The Smiths, while Marr had also been tinkering with the chords for some time, even playing a rough arrangement to Matt Johnson when previously considering joining The The. As with the version taped for their first demo at Decibel studios **[see 1]** and that recorded for the Troy Tate album **[see 5]**, originally Marr conceived the track with a separate melancholy piano epilogue tacked onto the end. Though axed from the final John Porter remake,[42] this proposed outro

42 A two-minute take of Marr's 'Suffer Little Children' piano epilogue has survived on the studio reels from the John Porter sessions, suggesting that its removal was very much a last minute decision during the final mixing stages.

wouldn't go to waste, since Marr later adapted this same piano part as the basis of 1985's 'Asleep' **[see 45]**.

Whatever their misgivings about the quality of their debut album after the event, Marr always expressed contentment that with Porter, 'Suffer Little Children' had come out exactly as they'd intended. Beautifully arranged (Joyce's rhythm unleashed in full only after the first verse), Morrissey's delivery is impeccable, accentuating the 'stolid stench of death' with thespian stateliness over Marr's tender yet lachrymose score. The Hindley vocal, again courtesy of Morrissey's friend Annalisa Jablonska **[see 1]** was also denser and less vaudevillian than the Decibel original.

Unnoticed on the original album, it was only when 'Suffer Little Children' was given a second lease of life as the B-side to 'Heaven Knows I'm Miserable Now' in May 1984 that The Smiths found themselves in a fresh tabloid controversy (aggravated by the cover still of a peroxide Viv Nicholson **[see Appendix II]**, which bore an unsettling resemblance to Hindley herself). The story didn't break until September that year, long after the single was out of the charts though it still resulted in high-street chains such as Woolworths and Boots temporarily refusing to stock either *The Smiths* or the offending single. Their troubles began when the grandfather of one of the victims, John Kilbride, heard it on a pub jukebox and immediately sparked a protest in the local Manchester press. 'He said he was going to kill us if he ever saw us,' Joyce warily confirms. 'As far as I'm aware 'Suffer Little Children' was Morrissey saying that he didn't think such a heinous crime should be put under the carpet. But in the Sixties people couldn't really understand it. That's what they did.'

When the outrage stretched to the national tabloids, as with the previous 'Handsome Devil' paedophilia debacle **[see 3]**, The Smiths found themselves the target of impassioned moral ire. 'I had to ring round my family,' explains Joyce, 'as the papers gave out all our names and ages. It was awful having to explain it to my parents, because they wouldn't really understand that kind of thing. They're simple folk from Ireland, it was terrible even having to talk about it.'

An official press statement from Rough Trade reiterated their innocence. 'The song was written out of a profound emotion by Morrissey, a Mancunian who feels that the particularly horrendous crime it describes must be borne by the conscience of Manchester and that it must never happen again.' The scandal was only placated when Morrissey arranged a meeting with Ann West, the mother of Lesley Ann Downey, to express his concerns over the media misunderstanding and explain to her the song's honest intent. He succeeded, both in mollifying the witch-hunt and sustaining a friendship with West for several years. 'Veiling the Moors Murders is wrong,' Morrissey explained to America's *Spin* magazine. 'We must bring it to the fore. If we don't overstate things, they'll continue to happen. We don't forget the atrocities of Hitler, do we? In the North, I was painted as a hideous Satanic monster, and the word was that I had upset Ann West. In fact, I had not, and have since become great friends with her. She is a formidable figure.'

In Concert

Played just once at The Smiths' very first gig at Manchester Ritz on 4 October 1982, 'Suffer Little Children' would never be performed in public again. Marr would later confirm that all along he and Morrissey had regarded it as an album track not suited to their regular concert repertoire.

20

'What Difference Does It Make?'

Recorded **October-November 1983, Pluto Studios, Manchester/Eden Studios, London**

Produced by **John Porter**

Single A-side, January 1984 (Highest UK Chart Position #12)

Subsequently featured on the album ***The Smiths*, February 1984**

Another very early composition, 'What Difference Does It Make?' depicted a doomed relationship involving a morally disreputable partner similar to that featured in 'Miserable Lie', written around the same time, and the slightly later 'Wonderful Woman'. Morrissey's lyric would also allude to the inspiration for another early song, 'Suffer Little Children', in its citation from Emlyn Williams's Moors Murderers study *Beyond Belief* (the 18th-century religious proverb 'the devil found work for idle hands' – 'Idle Hands' also being one of Williams' chapter headings).[43] Later pressed to explain the song's meaning, Morrissey's reply was characteristically opaque: 'I just wanted to have a very easy attitude, and that's what the lyrics imply. People get so neurotic about themselves. Their lives, their hair, their teeth. What difference does anything make, really?'

Having already recorded it for their second 1982 demo tape **[see 2]**, their debut Peel session, and the Troy Tate album **[see 5]**, by the time they began work on a new version with John Porter at Pluto, The Smiths were more familiar with 'What Difference Does It Make?' than any other song in their repertoire. Inevitably, when Porter then began dramatically re-arranging the

43 Of equal significance, Shelagh Delaney had also mused 'It's true I suppose that the devil does find work for idle hands' in her 1964 short story *Sweetly Sings the Donkey*.

song to his own specifications, his interference split the band into two opposing factions. On one side were Morrissey, Rourke and Mike Joyce whose original rolling, almost tribal, drumbeat Porter decided to even out in mechanical 'straight fours' On the other, Porter himself and Marr, who shared the producer's vision of a more linear rhythm at the expense of Rourke and Joyce's hard-practised handiwork. 'I thought the drums were a bit bumbling,' reflects Porter, 'but I really liked its groove.'

Porter of course won the argument, though as it transpired the recording of 'What Difference Does It Make?' was further hindered by matters of far more gravity than the music itself. For weeks, Morrissey had been stewing over the group's financial arrangements, which had yet to be finalised to his satisfaction. Rather than vocalise his concerns, he expressed himself by dramatically absconding from the session at Manchester's Pluto Studios until the matter was settled. Presuming he'd merely 'popped out for a bag of chips', Porter and the rest of The Smiths hung around awaiting his imminent return. As one hour became five, it was obvious Morrissey wasn't coming back. Finally, a phone call came from Geoff Travis at Rough Trade's London offices. Morrissey had walked out of Pluto, caught the next train south and gone straight to Travis expressing his concerns over the financial nitty-gritty; specifically the split of band earnings later contested during the 1996 High Court case. Once the matter was 'sorted' (Rourke and Joyce claimed they verbally acquiesced to the singer's demands for Marr's sake, so as not to split the group on the cusp of success) Morrissey returned to the fold, completing his vocal in time for the album's final mixing session at London's Eden Studios in early November.

For all his reservations as to Porter's transformation of the song, when chosen as The Smiths' third UK 45 the following January,[44] 'What Difference Does It Make?' proved their biggest hit to date (vindication in itself for the producer's meddling). With its polished, dance-floor, pendulum beat and Marr's gut-stirring twang – an instantaneous blues riff resonating with the sleazy eroticism of The Stones' 'Paint It, Black' or 'Jumpin' Jack Flash'[45] – Porter had transformed a potentially uncommercial R&B rocker into an abnormally powerful pop record. It was afforded an even more sinister edge courtesy of Morrissey's added playground noises sourced from one of his own sound effects LPs (the end result coming in at 2.09 is actually two different recordings of children overdubbed simultaneously).

44 The 7-inch single of 'What Difference Does It Make?' featured an edited guitar outro shorter than that which appears on *The Smiths*.

45 Contrary to Johnny Rogan's *Morrissey & Marr: The Severed Alliance*, Marr firmly denies the riff has any connection with 'Run Run Run', a 1972 roadhouse boogie by Spirit off-shoot Jo Jo Gunne.

Nevertheless, the singer would later confess to thinking the single 'absolutely awful the day after the record was pressed', a grim disposition perhaps only consoled by the band's doggedness to retain their original arrangement of the song (with Joyce's preferred drum pattern) in concert. That said, within a year The Smiths would cease playing 'What Difference Does It Make?' altogether.

In Concert

Debuted at their second gig at Manchester's Manhattan (25/1/83) though played throughout 1983 and 1984, the song's commercial popularity didn't prevent it being brutally axed by the latter year's end. Last played at the Paris Versailles (1/12/84) Marr in particular seemed unrepentant in the unorthodox practice of scrapping one of their biggest hits not just to date, but of their entire career to come. 'There was one stage where I was playing 'What Difference Does It Make?' seven or eight gigs on the trot,' he told *Melody Maker*, 'and I didn't like the feeling.' Morrissey's own boredom of the song was evident in his droll lyrical changes, singing that he had 'only got two heads' during a show taped in Amsterdam for Dutch radio (21/4/84).

Television

Prior to its release as a single, 'What Difference Does It Make?' was first aired as part of the *Whistle Test – On The Road* Derby Assembly Rooms show broadcast on BBC2 in December 1983 **[see 3]**.

On 26 January 1984, after it charted at number 26, The Smiths made the second visit of their career to *Top of the Pops*. Morrissey cut an even more eccentric figure than during their previous performance in November; a solitary gladioli drooping out of his back pocket and a hearing-aid wire visibly dangling from his right ear. The device in question was a display model acquired by Rough Trade 'press lackey' (and eventual Smiths chauffeur) Dave Harper from a West End depository. In convincing the establishment to let him borrow the hearing aid (which was never returned), Harper made reference to partially deaf Fifties crooner Johnnie Ray. Although Morrissey later revealed his use of the prop was in response to a letter from a deaf fan, Ray was just as easily the catalyst for what he would term 'the disability-chic movement that I created.' A precursor to the kind of rock 'n' roll hysteria Elvis would later wreak, Johnnie Ray was best remembered for self-pitying powerhouse ballads such as 1951's 'Cry' and his outlandish stage contortions. A bobbysox icon, in private Ray was a tormented, bisexual alcoholic who suffered from extreme depression, eventually dying in 1990 of liver failure induced by a lifetime of binge drinking.

Twelve days after *Top of the Pops*, on 6 February The Smiths performed a live version of the song in the studios of BBC North's *YES* (along with 'This Night Has Opened My Eyes'), the first time Morrissey wore his equally infamous NHS glasses on TV along with the same hearing aid. 'It wasn't a stab at hipdom, more like a tongue-in-cheek chicdom,' Morrissey acknowledged. 'It was a complete accident – I wore NHS spectacles, which I still do so it wasn't a mantle or a badge – and suddenly I saw all these people who didn't need to wear spectacles doing so in imitation of The Smiths and bumping into an awful lot of walls. Other bands have tours sponsored by Levi's – maybe we should find a large firm of opticians.'

In the meantime, The Smiths' first major UK tour to promote the debut album had run aground after a handful of dates, beset by all manner of administrative problems, on top of which Morrissey had come down with bronchitis. 'I remember looking at him at about 10.30 in the morning and thinking he seemed a very strange colour,' said Marr of their next *Top of the Pops* appearance that same week (9 February) which they managed to fulfil in spite of their singer's ill health. With the song now at number 13, this second appearance to promote 'What Difference Does It Make?' was even more enigmatic, with Morrissey stood in the round, arms outstretched like a gaunt, crucified Buddy Holly.

The next day (10 February), The Smiths gave one final mimed performance of 'What Difference Does It Make?' on BBC2's *Oxford Road Show* (its name taken from the address of the Manchester studios from which it was broadcast). Before a noticeably rapturous audience – this being home territory – the show was noteworthy for a solitary stage invader who momentarily interrupted Morrissey's impeccable lip-syncing by clinging to his chest like a limpet. Such intense displays of spontaneous worship and uninhibited affection would in time become par for the course within The Smiths' concert ritual.

'It seemed like a natural thing,' reflects Joyce, 'it wasn't like "what the hell are these people doing?", it seemed like a natural progression. At gigs you could see that there was this kind of momentum and people wanted to join in. I mean nobody's gonna get up and hug Mark King out of Level 42 are they?'. Rourke was equally touched: 'The first few times people got on the stage, it was a massive compliment to us because people literally couldn't help themselves. When they got up there, past the security, they didn't know what to do and they felt really embarrassed so they'd just sort of hug you for a second then think "Shit, what am I doing up here?" and scuttle off. It was nice, they were obviously that into it they couldn't help themselves.'

Radio

Featured on 1984's *Hatful Of Hollow,* the version produced by Roger Pusey for their debut John Peel session at BBC Maida Vale Studio 5 on 18 May 1983 is quite different to the finished single arrangement. Showcasing Joyce's original rumbling drum rhythm and Rourke's more expressive bass configuration – both of which John Porter later deconstructed – Morrissey admitted that this is the version of 'What Difference Does It Make?' that he himself always preferred.

Part 2

'... Put me on the train for London town...'

Recordings 1984

Between completing their debut album in November 1983 and its eventual release, The Smiths were dealt an unexpected blow in the departure of their original benefactor, Joe Moss.

Though a 'father figure' to Marr, Moss's relationship with Morrissey was much less paternal. When it became evident that the singer was unhappy with Joe as group manager, to Marr's dismay Moss stood down, quietly exiting The Smiths' camp so as not to place unnecessary strain on Johnny's sense of loyalty to both parties. His gracious, self-sacrificing resignation successfully prevented the disruption in Morrissey and Marr's relationship Moss had feared, even if his regrettable ousting cast the die for the revolving-door management policy that was to prove instrumental in their dissolution four years hence.

Their severance from Moss was reinforced by a group decision to shift base from Manchester to London, ostensibly to maintain closer contact with Rough Trade. Morrissey took up the lease on a flat off Kensington High Street (previously occupied by former Skids vocalist Richard Jobson), Marr found a flat a stone's throw away in Earls Court while Rourke, Joyce and guitar technician Phil Powell took a shared house several miles north in Willesden.

With a new single scheduled for January in anticipation of the following month's long-awaited debut album, there was little time to grieve for Moss as 1984 began. Though Morrissey repeatedly declared *The Smiths* 'a complete signal post in the history of popular music', his bravado masked a grim realisation that, however formidable its content, John Porter's album was a sonically impaired seven rather than the perfect ten it ought to have been. Listening to a finished mix on a Walkman while travelling from London to their *Whistle Test – On The Road* Derby Assembly Rooms gig in December 1983, Morrissey dolefully informed Porter and Geoff Travis that it wasn't good enough. 'They said it cost £60,000,' he later joked, '[they said] it has to be released, there's no going back.' Marr, who also declared it 'phenomenal' at the time, humbly back-pedalled a year later that 'a lot of the fire was missing on it and most of our supporters realise that as well.'

Critically adored at the time and by no means a failure (it entered the UK album charts at number 2), *The Smiths* was a necessary coming of age that effectively closed the door on the first epoch of their career. By the beginning of 1984 Morrissey and Marr had now progressed to a successful writing routine of composing in regular batches of three. 'I often wrote in threes because of the single and B-sides scenario I guess,' says Marr. 'Occasionally we would get together and write face to face, but most of the songs would be instrumental demos that I'd give to Morrissey on tape, then he'd add the words.' With the bulk of their repertoire from their first formative year now finally recorded for posterity, from hereon the band's discography would take on a fresher, more stimulating trajectory in keeping with Morrissey and Marr's quickening work rate. The best was definitely yet to come.

21

The Sandie Shaw Single

a. 'Hand In Glove'

Single A-side (Highest UK Chart Position #27)

b. 'I Don't Owe You Anything'

B-side

c. 'Jeane'

B-side (12-inch format only)

Recorded February-March 1984, Matrix Studios, London/'Fallout Shelter' (Island Studios), London

Produced by John Porter

Released as Sandie Shaw solo single, April 1984

Amid high expectations of their imminent debut album, 1984 began with the *NME* announcing the surprising news that The Smiths were about to collaborate with Sixties pop icon Sandie Shaw, backing her on a version of 'I Don't Owe You Anything' **[see 12]** to be issued on Rough Trade.

Long after they'd established themselves as a band, Morrissey and Marr still harboured romantic ambitions for recognition as songwriters by having other artistes cover their work. Top of their wish list was Shaw – the svelte, bob-haired and barefooted[46] Essex siren born Sandra Goodrich. Although Morrissey's hyperbolic approbation that she was 'the most prolific figure in

46 As Morrissey himself explained in his excellent appraisal of Sandie in the 24 December 1983 edition of *Sounds*, Shaw's aversion to footwear was a necessary consequence of her refusal to wear glasses; 'due to virtual blindness she had frequently tripped over camera wires whilst performing, therefore, without shoes she could feel her way along and avoid catastrophe.'

the entire history of British popular music' was a tad over-generous,[47] from her first UK number 1 in October 1964 with Bacharach/David's '(There's) Always Something There to Remind Me' through to her banal 1967 Eurovision winner 'Puppet on a String' (which she famously denounced as 'sexist drivel to a cuckoo-clock tune') Shaw was one of the premiere British female vocalists of her era. Sadly, as with the majority of her peers, her singing career effectively ended at the close of the decade she'd been instrumental in characterising. Despite an unsatisfactory cameo on 1982's British Electro Foundation *Music of Quality and Distinction* album (a side project of Sheffield synth-poppers Heaven 17), by the early Eighties Shaw was largely considered a pop has-been from a bygone era.

Whilst recording the Troy Tate album in London during the summer of 1983, Morrissey and Marr began badgering Shaw to record the song she'd provisionally inspired, 'I Don't Owe You Anything' Despatching a cassette of the track with an accompanying fan letter, Morrissey informed Shaw 'Obviously the song was written with you in mind ... The Sandie Shaw legend cannot be over yet – there is more to be done!' Sandie herself was initially sceptical since their pleas coincided with the 'Handsome Devil' tabloid furore **[see 3]**, which immediately discouraged her. When Morrissey next sent her a copy of their debut single 'Hand In Glove', Shaw apparently took one look at its sleeve and exclaimed in horror to her husband 'he's started sending me pictures of naked men with their bums showing!'

With Geoff Travis' intervention and Morrissey's constant ingratiating plaudits in the press (most prominently an extraordinarily insightful career retrospective printed in *Sounds* that December), Shaw was eventually won over, agreeing 'on the proviso that if I didn't like the result we'd scrap it.' For Morrissey it was a dream come true; 'I've worshipped her for so long, and then to work with her is just the highest thrill that I can think possible.'

Contrary to that initial *NME* report, Shaw eventually selected an upbeat arrangement of the anthemic 'Hand In Glove' as the single's A-side, later enthusiastically describing it as 'real Joan of Arc stuff' (a quote Morrissey may have had in mind when penning 'Bigmouth Strikes Again' the following year **[see 46]**). A more vibrant rendition than The Smiths' original, its introductory passage put the accent on a breezier, major-scale riff, while producer John Porter suffused Joyce's beat with added bounce. 'I remember John and I going bananas on that track,' says Marr, 'because it had about 15 or 16 guitar tracks on it and it only sounded like eight! But I loved it because playing in a different key meant I could play some different riffs, different

47 As mentioned during the introduction of *Part 1*, Marr maintains 'maybe wrongly' that Morrissey's fixation with Shaw was inherited via The New York Dolls' David Johansen.

pitches.' Rourke agrees: 'It was nice just playing the songs in a lower, more naturalistic key. When you've got the strings tuned up to F# they're like cheese wire, so it was great playing in normal tuning for a change.' A remixed version later featured on Shaw's 1988 *Hello Angel* LP also exposed some morale boosting studio chatback from an energized Marr demanding 'can you turn everything now overall, up!' To some fans' displeasure, Shaw even tailored the song to her own specifications with the subtle variation 'so I'll stay on your arm, 'cos you're so charming'.

'I Don't Owe You Anything' (now the B-side) was more in keeping with The Smiths' own version, bar a swift but complementary and tender guitar prelude. That it was every bit as affecting as their original interpretation more than validated Morrissey and Marr's foresight that Shaw should record the track in the first place. Though behind the scenes, The Smiths' were troubled with administrative problems over their first major UK tour as well as Morrissey's bronchial ill-health, by all accounts the Shaw session at Matrix was high spirited and hassle free with frequent visits to a local vegetarian café across the road from the studio (near the British Museum in Bloomsbury), where Sandie happily mothered her smitten young accomplices and tried, not altogether successfully, to engage them in conversation about the benefits of Buddhism. 'Sandie was lovely,' recollects Joyce, 'she was this big kind of blustering character and very exciting to be around. I remember the first time we ran through the songs with her it was fantastic because she could *sing*. Technically, she had a much better voice than Morrissey.'

To justify a full 12-inch release, Rough Trade reasoned that a third track was called for. Consequently, during The Smiths' next session at Island Records' basement 'Fallout Shelter' studio to record 'Heaven Knows I'm Miserable Now' **[see 22]**, Shaw was brought in to cut a beautifully sparse version of 'Jeane' **[see 5]**, featuring just Marr on acoustic guitar and guest backing vocals from Morrissey. 'I remember once asking Johnny who ['Jeane'] was about,' she later remarked. 'He replied "Morrissey's mum probably!" Quite naturally I sang it word for word as written – that was how it was presented to me, and the song seemed perfect as it was.' The simplest, and best, of the three Shaw tracks, 'Jeane' was completed in only a couple of takes.[48]

Released in April, this innovative alliance rewarded Shaw with her first hit in over a decade and was also a belated consolation to The Smiths, who'd failed to take 'Hand In Glove' into the charts first time around. The template they created – hip young pop group teaming up with Sixties diva – would later be repeated time and again; the Pet Shop Boys with Dusty Springfield, Take That with Lulu, Blur with Françoise Hardy, the list goes on. But back in

48 Marr warmed up for Shaw's version of 'Jeane' by running through The Beatles' 'In My Life'.

spring 1984, the union of Sandie Shaw and The Smiths was a daring and unorthodox *coup de grâce* for both parties. 'I loved the fact that the group's identity had expanded,' Marr reflects. 'It was a thing that couldn't be pigeon-holed. People like *Smash Hits* and Radio 1 suddenly had to view us in a slightly different way.'

Upon its release, Sandie optimistically informed *Melody Maker* there was 'talk of an album, so we'll see. Knowing Morrissey he won't give me a moment's peace until we're back in the studio.' In the initial aftermath however, Morrissey expressed mixed feelings over its virtues. Though he considered their endeavour 'the envy of the entire industry', Shaw's thornier press comments about the singer reduced Morrissey to 'a quivering jelly'. Nevertheless, the project reinvigorated Shaw's career to the extent where future projects inevitably arced back to The Smiths in some form or other. Subsequently, she covered the work of Morrissey's favourite contemporary singers such as Patti Smith ('Frederick') and Lloyd Cole ('Are You Ready To Be Heartbroken?'), composed the trite tribute odes 'Steven, You Don't Eat Meat', 'Go Johnny Go' and eventually christened her 1988 solo album *Hello Angel* after the inscription on the back of one of his postcards to her (the same LP also contained the Morrissey/Street throwaway 'Please Help The Cause Against Loneliness' and the dizzy 'Take Him' about dragging his nibs to the local disco).

Although they invited her to participate in the recording of 'Sheila Take A Bow' in December 1986 **[see 68]**, the 'Hand In Glove' single would be Shaw's only full collaboration with The Smiths. 'She kind of fell in love with Morrissey in a way,' reflects Joyce. 'I think it happened to a lot of people who got near Morrissey. That enigmatic side of him. And the mystery. It was easily done. So I think with Sandie she just went in a little bit too deep.'

'I'm not really sure what happened there with Morrissey and Sandie,' comments Marr, 'some sort of estrangement.' Speaking of their collaboration in 1998, Morrissey himself concluded 'it was so great for me personally that I don't actually remember it happening.'

Sandie Shaw & The Smiths in Concert

Prior to the single's release, Sandie Shaw joined The Smiths on stage at two dates of their 1984 spring UK tour, singing lead vocal on 'I Don't Owe You Anything' on both occasions. The first time, at London's Hammersmith Palais (12/3/84), Shaw was so wracked with nerves she went AWOL. Marr later referred to her performance, when finally coaxed out on stage that is, as the only enjoyable incident of the whole gig. Sandie would also divulge that Morrissey rang her at 3.00 am the following morning to see if she had enjoyed it. 'I could have done an hour, one song wasn't enough' she replied.

The next night at Manchester Free Trade Hall (13/3/84), Shaw was only slightly less manic, having locked herself in a cupboard where, as a practising Buddhist, she chanted herself into composure. Amusingly, as the song finished, The Smiths' elated home crowd regaled her with chants of 'Sandie Shaw! Sandie Shaw! Sandie Shaw!' to the time-honoured 'here we go' terrace chant.

Sandie would also perform 'Jeane' when supporting The Smiths at Manchester's G-Mex 'Festival Of The Tenth Summer' on 19 July, 1986 (sharing the bill with, among others, The Fall and New Order).

Sandie Shaw & The Smiths on Television

Their collaboration with Sandie Shaw was first unveiled on Channel 4's *Earsay* on 31 March 1984. After a preview of The Smiths' next single, 'Heaven Knows I'm Miserable Now', Sandie and Morrissey were interviewed together before watching a clip of Shaw in her prime singing 'Girl Don't Come' on *Ready, Steady, Go!* in 1965. As a finale, Sandie then gave a full, mimed performance of 'Hand In Glove' backed by a smirking Marr, Rourke and Joyce. Dancing with excessive zest, she later admitted that she 'looked like a demented housewife.'

On 26 April, just one week after she'd told *Melody Maker* of her hopes to return to *Top of the Pops* 'to prove to my teenage daughter that there's some life in the old bat yet!', Sandie made her first visit to the show in 14 years. Histrionically writhing on the studio floor in a leather skirt, Shaw was flanked by the three Smiths who all performed barefoot as a good-humoured homage.

Two months later, on 16 June, Sandie made one last TV cameo during their notoriously silly Charlie's Bus appearance. The feature in question was a regular segment of TVam's Saturday morning children's show *SPLAT*,[49] in which they joined a group of schoolchildren (including Elvis Costello's son who they were specifically, if perplexingly, instructed not to make a fuss over) for an open-top bus ride to Kew Gardens in South London. Asked by one child where they got their name from, Johnny sardonically replied 'Morrissey the singer thought of the name The Smiths. I wanted to be called The Rolling Stones but it was much too much of a mouthful.' When another youngster inquired 'Where are we going?', Morrissey dryly exclaimed 'We're all going mad!'

After a wander through the botanical gardens to the strains of 'Heaven Knows I'm Miserable Now', The Smiths and their pre-pubescent entourage

49 *SPLAT* (an abbreviation of 'Soap, Puzzles, Laughter and Talent') replaced TVam's previous 8.40 Saturday kids slot *Datarun* (on which The Smiths also appeared). Other pop acts to take a ride on Charlie's Bus included A Flock Of Seagulls, Captain Sensible, Imagination and Yip Yip Coyote.

settled down on the lawn, where, as if by magic, they 'bumped into' Sandie Shaw.[50] 'Well, it just so happens Johnny's brought his guitar with him,' she guffawed before both recreated the acoustic version of 'Jeane'. Though another superb rendition, its sentiments were surely much too adult for their infantile audience to fully appreciate. After filming, The Smiths were each presented with a special limited edition Charlie's Bus Corgi toy replica as a souvenir by the show's producer. 'I loved that day in Kew Gardens,' laughs Marr. 'It was great, but it was mad. I'd been spending all my time in the studio and rehearsal rooms so it wasn't very often that I got out to interact with other humans, let alone little humans!'

Also worthy of note is Sandie's 10 June 1986 performance on *Whistle Test* to promote her cover of Lloyd Cole's 'Are You Ready To Be Heartbroken?' and its Morrissey tribute B-side, 'Steven, You Don't Eat Meat' ('He'll kill me when he knows it's only a B-side', Shaw told *Smash Hits*). As the latter song finished, the studio camera focussed in on Sandie's dress, which bore the unmistakable childlike scrawl of Morrissey: 'I've heard it. Thank you XXX. Love for a lifetime, Steven.'

Sandie Shaw & The Smiths on Radio

On 14 April 1984, Sandie joined The Smiths on BBC Radio 1's *Saturday Live* afternoon programme. The whole band were present, with Marr taking part in a feature sampling various guitar models with Bert Weedon (including Dave Hill of Slade's notorious 'Super Yob'), before Sandie performed two outstanding, stripped-down versions of the single's B-sides; 'I Don't Owe You Anything' backed by Marr and Rourke and 'Jeane' backed by just Marr's solo acoustic.

22

'Heaven Knows I'm Miserable Now'

Recorded **March 1984, 'Fallout Shelter' (Island Studios), London**

Produced by **John Porter**

Single A-side, May 1984 (Highest UK Chart Placing #10)

At the end of December 1983, The Smiths made their first visit to America. Booked to play New York's Danceteria on New Year's Eve, the trip was to prove an unmitigated disaster. Being a James Dean devotee,

50 It was either cryptic coincidence or The Smiths' own black humour that they should choose to rest beside the Kew pagoda; a notorious London suicide point.

Morrissey was initially ecstatic to find that they were to stay at the infamous Iroquois Hotel where Dean himself had lodged during his Broadway period. His enthusiasm was to wane, however, on discovering that the Iroquois was actually a cockroach-infested slum where he found it impossible to sleep. Jet-lagged and undernourished, during the Danceteria show itself Morrissey fell off the stage. The final straw came when Mike Joyce contracted a serious bout of chicken pox. With another New York date to fulfil, the plague-ridden Smiths wisely cancelled and jumped the next flight home.

Surrounded by disease, lice and misery, before they left the Big Apple Morrissey and Marr took solace in composing a cathartic celebration of their abiding discontent in their hotel room. The imminent Sandie Shaw collaboration still very much on his mind, Morrissey's acerbic penchant for puns resulted in his twist of Shaw's 1969 chart failure 'Heaven Knows I'm Missing Him Now' into what became 'Heaven Knows I'm Miserable Now'.

Recorded along with 'Girl Afraid' at the 'Fallout Shelter', the basement studio at Island Records on St Peter's Square in Chiswick, the session proved a fortuitous twist of fate for Island's in-house engineer, Stephen Street. Already a fan of the group, his obvious enthusiasm endeared him to both Johnny and Morrissey who, much to John Porter's unease, asked for his contact details once the recordings were finished. 'I saw the writing on the wall then,' says Porter. 'I think Mozzer was starting to resent that me and Johnny had become good pals. But the thing was, *we* made the records. I had tried to get him involved in the process, but he wasn't interested. He just came in when he needed to do his thing and would do it very quickly and then get out. So obviously me and Johnny would be there 24 hours and he'd only come in for two of those, so the rest of that time we were working together and built up a good relationship. I don't think he liked it. So I could also see that in Stephen Street he saw somebody that could be, like, "his guy", which was fair enough.'

In later years, Marr would admit to disliking 'Heaven Knows I'm Miserable Now'. Although its surface prettiness often veers towards saccharine sentimentality, overall it's a superb arrangement, displaying a masterful grasp of classic pop-song-writing traditions. The introductory passage of *laissez faire* jazzy guitar strums was especially dazzling, if a touch convoluted to start with; early rehearsals and concert performances on the spring '84 UK tour contained a subtly different chord run which John Porter helped tweak into a snappier prologue come its recording in March. The drum pattern was also adapted with Joyce restraining his full rhythm until the main verses, filling the interim pauses with soft cymbal washes (an early test acetate with his original drum fills was used to accompany their first TV preview of the song on Channel 4's *Earsay* in late March).

Given any other lyric and admittedly Marr's offhand, vivacious melody would be an unbearably syrupy confection. But the brilliance of 'Heaven Knows I'm Miserable Now' was its deft juxtaposition against Morrissey's comically disparaging litany of woes. Single-handedly, this song is more responsible than any other for the lazy 'miserablist' tag that still haunts The Smiths' legacy, despite the fact that its lyrics are among the most uplifting, frivolous and funniest Morrissey has ever sung. Here was a single (their first Top 10 hit at that) overflowing with humour, rife with coy vaudeville wit (the music hall ribaldry of 'Caligula would have blushed' for instance) and openly rebellious in its anti-work ethic. 'When I wrote an ineffectual line such as "I was looking for a job, and then I found a job, and heaven knows I'm miserable now", that outraged people,' he told the press later that year. 'All the daily tabloids treat me as a dangerous figure and that pleases me. At least it means that I'm a strong person and I'm not Andrew Ridgeley.'

The Ridgeley comparison was timely, since the single's release coincided with that of Wham's 'Wake Me Up Before You Go Go'; the epitome of hedonistic Thatcherite pop, which this, Morrissey's anthem for what he would later term 'the dole age', opposed so effectively. 'On the very brief spasms of employment that I had in the past,' the singer explained, 'it always seemed to me that there were moments of the day when I'd realise I was working with these people that I despised. I had to talk to these horrible people about what they did yesterday and I would have to report to a boss that I couldn't stand. When you're in that position, which was the absolute basis of 'Heaven Knows I'm Miserable Now', you realise that you're actually spending your entire life living with people you do not like and doing something you do not like, which is incredibly distressing. So that was the basis of the song.'

After the trauma of the debut album and its unspoken shortcomings, Morrissey would speak glowingly of 'Heaven Knows I'm Miserable Now' and its chart success as The Smiths' halcyon days. The biggest hit of their career (and their only Top 10 entry until 'Sheila Take A Bow' three years later), he was nevertheless adamant that it still should have climbed higher, protesting somewhat theatrically that the week it charted at number 10 it had no airplay on national radio.

Sadly, the single was inadvertently tainted by controversy when its B-side, 'Suffer Little Children' became the centre of another press scandal long after the record itself had fallen out of the Top 40 **[see 19]**. By no means their greatest single, 'Heaven Knows I'm Miserable Now' was still a celebratory step forward after the debut album. Brilliantly performed and skilfully produced to extract its utmost pop potential, in the '84 summer of Duran Duran's 'The Reflex', Frankie's 'Two Tribes' and Queen's 'I Want To Break Free', this – The Smiths' anthemic address of a tacit yet widespread Eighties ennui – was simply ingenious.

In Concert

Five months before its release, 'Heaven Knows I'm Miserable Now' debuted at Sheffield University (31/1/84). A set regular throughout that first major UK tour, it stayed for the rest of the year and the majority of 1985 (bar only a handful of dates on the *Meat Is Murder* tour).

An encore during the February 1986 Irish concerts, it was dropped from the set of their July UK dates, but returned during the opening Canadian shows of the lengthy North American tour. Thereafter it was revived with discerning irregularity during encores in the US itself, last played at the Phoenix MESA Amphitheater, Arizona (31/8/86).

Television

'Heaven Knows I'm Miserable Now' was previewed nearly two months in advance alongside the Sandie Shaw version of 'Hand In Glove' on Channel 4's *Earsay* on 31 March 1984. A mimed studio performance accompanied by some outside footage of a particularly scrawny Morrissey plucking flowers from a patch of derelict wasteland beside a busy road, as mentioned earlier the soundtrack itself was a rough mix featuring a slightly different drum track.

When finally issued in May, Rough Trade's TV campaign to promote the single instigated Morrissey's short-lived career as a pop pundit for hire, with his appearance on BBC2's arts forum *Eight Days a Week* on Friday 25 May and the following day's BBC1 prime-time *Pop Quiz.* Typically, he would bitterly regret both experiences. The former saw him sandwiched between George Michael and Tony Blackburn, discussing Everything But The Girl, Paul Morley's Joy Division biography and *Breakdance – The Movie* ('three individuals talking about films and books they hadn't read or watched'). *Pop Quiz* was even more painful ('I realised it was a terrible mistake the moment the cameras began to roll') though both surely aided The Smiths' public profile and partially contributed to the new record's success.

As with 'What Difference Does It Make?', the prolonged chart life of 'Heaven Knows I'm Miserable Now' warranted two separate visits to *Top of the Pops.* The first, on 31 May, witnessed the addition of Morrissey's giant back-pocket bush, which seemed liable to blind the audience with the slightest involuntary twitch. As he humorously recollected to *Jamming!* magazine some months afterwards, 'People stop me in the street and say, "Where's your bush?", which is an embarrassing question at any time of the day. I mean, what do you say to people? "I've left it behind on the mantelpiece"? I don't even mind if people remember me for my bush or my hearing aid – as long as it's for artistic reasons. It was all done to bring some life into *Top of the Pops*.'

The bush was back again on 14 June,[51] when they returned to celebrate their first entry into the hallowed Top 10, as was one of Marr's more ostentatious items of jewellery: a tiara-like necklace previously worn on an earlier visit to *Top of the Pops* when backing Sandie Shaw's 'Hand In Glove' (indeed the same decoration had been hanging from the belt of Morrissey's jeans on the 31 May appearance).

23

'Girl Afraid'

Recorded **March 1984, 'Fallout Shelter' (Island Studios), London**

Produced by **John Porter**

B-side to 'Heaven Knows I'm Miserable Now' (12-inch format only), May 1984

Written the day after The Smiths returned from their disaster-prone New York new year's eve sojourn in early January **[see 22]**, 'Girl Afraid' itself was a delightfully intricate construction on Marr's part, driven by a powerful and persistent minor-key twang in a similar vein to 'What Difference Does It Make?' but faster, tighter and altogether meaner. The tune was actually inspired by Little Richard, with Marr originally composing this key riff as a potential piano hook. 'I'd just got back from New York and was obsessed with Little Richard. I just kept thinking "what'd sound like Little Richard on guitar?", which is how I came up with it.'

Far more intricate was the song's ephemeral intro; as stupefying a display of Marr's lightning-fingered six-string expertise as has ever been recorded (though curiously one of Porter's original test mixes eliminated this passage altogether, replacing it with Morrissey's isolated wail of 'I'll never make that mistake again' pre-empting Joyce's first beat).

Its brooding, pessimistic lyrics and the girl/boy scenario bore subtle similarities with 'Upstairs Downstairs', an obscure Herman's Hermits track from their 1967 album *Blaze*, which, as an aficionado of Manchester's famous sons of the Sixties, Morrissey was probably familiar with. 'I think 'Girl Afraid' simply implied that even within relationships there's no real certainty and nobody knows how anybody feels,' he later divulged. 'People feel that just simply because they're having this cemented communion with another person that the two of you will become whole, which is

51 On the day of broadcast, The Smiths were actually on tour in Scotland. That edition of *Top of the Pops* had been pre-recorded on Wednesday 13 June. Even so, this gruelling itinerary meant them returning to London after the previous night's gig in Carlisle, filming at the BBC and then hurtling back up North for that night's concert at Glasgow Barrowlands.

something I detested. I hate that, that implication. It's not true, anyway. Ultimately, you're on your own, whatever happens in life, however you go through life. You die on your own. You have to go to the dentist on your own. It's like all the serious things in life are things that you feel on your own.'

In Concert

Introduced at Sheffield University (31/1/84), 'Girl Afraid' was road tested on their spring '84 UK tour prior to its release, invariably played back to back with its corresponding A-side 'Heaven Knows I'm Miserable Now'.

Played on their handful of European dates in late April/early May, the song was temporarily dropped for a couple of shows until the London GLC 'Jobs for a Change' Festival at London's Jubilee Gardens (10/6/84), remaining in the set for the June tour and their three mainland UK dates in September. The last of these, Swansea Mayfair (26/9/84), marked its final performance. Its live arrangement was captured for posterity on the *NME*'s cassette compilation *Department of Enjoyment*, available via mail order only in August 1984.

24

The Amanda Malone Single

a. 'This Charming Man'
b. 'Girl Afraid'

Recorded **April 1984, Powerhouse Studios, London**

Produced by **Geoff Travis**

Studio out-takes

In the wake of their Sandie Shaw collaboration, Morrissey toyed with the idea of another satellite Smiths project featuring a female vocalist, only this time using a complete unknown. So began the most ludicrous recording experiment of The Smiths' career.

Morrissey had first met 18-year-old, self-confessed 'Sixties freak' Amanda Malone during their calamitous trip to New York's Danceteria at the end of 1983. Malone was working in the club's office alongside promoter Ruth Polsky,[52] though admits she would sometimes brave the stage and sing. 'Ruth

52 Polsky was killed in an accident in September 1986. The sleeve of The Smiths' 1987 'Shoplifters Of The World Unite' single carried a dedication in her memory **[see Appendix II]**.

said "there's a band coming over called The Smiths",' recalls Malone. 'I'd never heard of them but nobody in the States had much notion of them then. She said "I think you'll really like them because they're really into Sixties stuff too", so I thought they sounded cool.'

Possibly on account of a shared birthday (22 May), Morrissey and Malone bonded during a special 'Welcome to New York' dinner party organised by Polsky. By the time the group headed home a few days later, their singer would entice Malone with a rash if irresistible proposition. 'It was Morrissey's idea really. He said "why don't you come over to England and make a record with us". I was just a kid, I wanted to be a pop star so I thought "Wow! This is brilliant!". So a few months later I went to England to do just that.'

Morrissey's band mates were oblivious to his pet project until the spring of 1984 when Malone, now living on the dole in London anticipating her big break, was thrust upon The Smiths at an abortive session at London's Powerhouse Studios with a bemused Geoff Travis acting as producer. 'It all happened very quickly,' she explains. 'I'd been hanging around, signing on for weeks when suddenly Morrissey just called me up and said "okay, we're doing it tomorrow". I have a feeling that maybe Geoff Travis wasn't really so into the idea. I'd never done any studio recording before so I'd stayed up all night because I was so nervous. I was tired, it was awful!'

'It was comical,' laughs Marr. 'Morrissey knew more about her than we did, even though we had to endure playing behind it! She was very odd. She sang like Cicely Courtneidge, in a 16-year-old Barbara Windsor's body!' 'I was a very freaky looking kid,' admits Malone, 'I was enormously fat and I had a big bouffant hair-do, all done up in Sixties clothes. I looked a lot like Rickie Lake in *Hairspray*!'

As she confesses, the first take, a version of 'This Charming Man' with Morrissey on backing vocals, was excruciating. 'Aw, it was terrible! I'd been singing in the bathroom and then suddenly I found myself in this really intimidating studio. I couldn't find my note because I hadn't sung that way before. So Morrissey came into the recording booth and sang along with me the first time through to get my nerves at bay and to give me my starting note. I was *that* lame!'

Next up was a new arrangement of 'Girl Afraid'. 'That was a little better,' says Malone, 'but I still knew it wasn't going to be great. After we'd finished it I kind of knew it wasn't going to happen, probably because I sounded dreadful so I didn't want it to.' Sure enough, a few weeks later Morrissey finally put Malone out of her misery. 'I went to see him and he said "listen, I've got bad news for you. Rough Trade have decided not to bring this single out." But I was secretly a bit relieved.' The Amanda Malone single that almost was would never be mentioned again, nor Morrissey's imprudent and thankfully short-lived ambition to create a new pop idol under the umbrella of The Smiths. 'I've got nothing but lovely memories,' concludes Malone. 'I was young and shy and they were just too charming. It's one of those stories where someone could have made it big – had they had any talent!'

25

'William, It Was Really Nothing'

Recorded **July 1984, Jam Studios, London**

Produced by **John Porter**

Single A-side, August 1984 (Highest UK Chart Placing #17)

By the summer of 1984, Marr was entering his prime as a composer, relishing the challenge of surpassing the Top 10 success of 'Heaven Knows I'm Miserable Now' by honing an even stronger follow up. Over four days in early June, the guitarist remained at home in his Earls Court flat where he created 'William, It Was Really Nothing' and its two B-sides 'Please Please Please Let Me Get What I Want' and 'How Soon Is Now?' on a 4-track portastudio; an astounding triptych by any measure.

Their shortest 45 up to that point, with 'William, It Was Really Nothing' Marr would later boast that he purposely set out to mould a pop single under three minutes long; 'I thought it was amazing to say what you have to say in two-and-a-half minutes. 'William, It Was Really Nothing' was the first thing I wrote with a real emphasis on keeping it under that.' The finished product only just passed the two minute mark; a courageously snappy 129 seconds. The song's structure was equally unorthodox; 'To start with a short verse and then follow it with three choruses is quite good' he later bragged. That it follows so eccentric a pattern, yet still manages to hold the listener's attention with its catchy consistency says much for Marr's gift as a composer.

Equally concise were Morrissey's lyrics. Though the opening line bore similarities with that of Sparks' 1974 glam masterpiece 'This Town Ain't Big Enough For Both Of Us' ('the rain is falling on the foreign town, the bullets cannot cut you down'),[53] Morrissey's genius in 'William… ' was to distil an entire 90-minute Sixties kitchen-sink drama into less than 20 lines of pop

53 At the age of 15, Morrissey had written to the *NME* praising Sparks' 1974 LP *Kimono My House* (on which the song featured) as 'the album of the year'.

prose. In particular, the small town frustration of the eponymous William, bogged down by his dreary environment and a noxious marriage proposal from a local 'fat girl', had much in common with John Schlesinger's 1963 film adaptation of Keith Waterhouse's *Billy Liar* starring Tom Courtenay and Julie Christie.

However, if the 'William' of the title wasn't Courtenay's fictional portrayal of the hapless Billy Fisher, then it may have been a coy reference to the late Billy MacKenzie of The Associates. Significantly, the song was first mentioned in July 1984 by *The Face.* During the same article, Morrissey was asked about his 'dream date' with MacKenzie, replying that the Scottish singer had visited his Kensington flat only to disappear with one of his James Dean books ('it wasn't my favourite book but these things are sacrosanct').[54] If this wasn't enough to arouse suspicions, then The Associates' eventual rejoinder 'Stephen, You Were Really Something' (a glam-rock pastiche recorded in 1993 but unreleased until 2000) was more than food for thought.

'Billy was very erratic, quite indescribable,' Morrissey later told *Melody Maker.* 'We spent hours and hours searching for some common ground but ultimately I don't believe there was any!' When asked by *Record Mirror* soon afterwards if he thought the lyrics were 'overtly gay', Marr was warily indecisive; 'I haven't managed to work out [Morrissey's] exact angle on that one yet. Usually his lyrics are very much black and white to me, but this one is taking a little bit longer.' Morrissey would never mention the Associates' singer again, though, tragically, after eventually bowing out of the pop spotlight and returning to his native Dundee, the indescribably erratic Billy MacKenzie revealed the full extent of his tortured genius when he took his own life in 1997.

Their first recording session in over four months after extensive touring at home and in northern Europe, The Smiths' residency at London's Finsbury Park Jam Studios in July would be their last with John Porter for over a year. 'William, It Was Really Nothing' was the first and immediate priority as the next single, needing little arranging having already been tested in concert. Rather, Marr and Porter showered the mix in a joyous downpour of guitar overdubs, from its quasi-flamenco acoustic background flutter to its pin-sharp treble electric top-line. The pair also formulated an effectively abrupt intro, swelling into life from out of nowhere, and a corresponding nine-second epilogue drifting into oblivion on an unusual backwards guitar riff.[55] Marr

54 Morrissey's chastisement of MacKenzie's book theft was possibly somewhat hypocritical. At about the same time, a photographer working for a major music weekly leant Morrissey several rare Oscar Wilde books. The gullible smudge claims he hasn't seen them since.

55 The backwards outro was achieved by spinning Marr's B-minor scale down to E (during the 'I don't dream about anyone' section) in reverse.

also experimented with a Hawaiian-style slide on the choruses similar to the classic Santo and Johnny 1959 instrumental 'Sleep Walk', which was eventually scrapped (though he would recycle it on 'How Soon Is Now?' and 'Shakespeare's Sister').

'We eventually came up with a formula for singles,' says Porter, 'this thing of putting guitar intros on because I was crazy about them. As a kid I'd buy a record on the strength of a guitar intro. People had stopped doing that so this was another idea I suggested to Johnny. We had a lot of other musical conventions, for instance we wouldn't allow any musical note to be higher than the voice during the verses so there was some kind of payback in the choruses by bringing in all these high jangly things. By 'William…' we'd gotten really good at this formula, putting in all these backwards guitar bits, backwards cymbals, all these things that we'd use in every record at some point which became trademarks. Sometimes they were almost peripheral, you could barely hear them.'

'William… ' may not have followed its predecessor into the Top 10 – it would be their last hit inside the Top 20 for nearly two years as it happened – but its capricious sentiment and melodic cunning made it one of the most imaginative singles of their career. 'To me, the two minute, ten second single was power,' Morrissey would afterwards insist, 'it was blunt, to the point.'

Blunt and to the point, 'William… ' exemplified the then-forgotten art of the two minute, ten second pop single beautifully.

In Concert

Premiered at the GLC 'Jobs for a Change' festival at Jubilee Gardens on London's South Bank (10/6/84), 'William… ' was played throughout their summer UK tour up to and including their only Glastonbury appearance (23/6/84). Following its vinyl release, it then became the set opener for their three UK shows that September (Gloucester, Cardiff and Swansea) and would likewise begin proceedings on the majority of their concerts the following year; every date of the *Meat Is Murder* tour (bar Margate 8/3/85) and most of the summer's Canadian/US performances.

By the autumn '85 Scottish tour, 'William… ' had become a popular encore, staying as such for their Irish dates in February 1986 and the opening Glasgow Barrowlands gig of their summer UK tour (16/7/86). Thereafter it was dropped from the remaining British shows, only to return for the opening Canadian leg of their gruelling North American expedition from late July to early September. Strangely, with the sole exception of Houston Cullen Auditorium (5/9/86), the song was only played at the first three Canadian concerts. Even when returning to the UK, the ever popular 'William… was conspicuous by its absence on the final autumn *Queen Is*

Dead tour. It would, however, be reprised one last time as the penultimate song played at The Smiths' final Brixton Academy concert (12/12/86).

Television

In one of the most memorable *Top of the Pops* performances of their career, when miming to 'William... ' on 30 August 1984, Morrissey ripped open his shirt during the song's climax to reveal the words 'MARRY ME' daubed across his chest. In doing so, his face could barely contain the perverse delight in aggravating the BBC watchdogs (who'd been inundated with complaints when Echo & The Bunnymen's Ian McCulloch exposed his naked torso earlier that year), swirling his shirt around like a windmill before hurling it into the whooping audience. Marr had also borrowed a guitar for the occasion from Elvis Costello, whose name was visibly embossed across the fretboard.

Radio

To promote its imminent release, a version of 'William, It Was Really Nothing' was recorded for their third John Peel session at BBC Maida Vale Studio 5 on 1 August 1984 (broadcast eight days later). A faithful remake of its single counterpart, without the backwards guitar coda it was even shorter, just scraping the two-minute mark. In December 1987, this BBC 'William... ' was granted an official release as a CD-only extra track on their final Rough Trade single, 'Last Night I Dreamt That Somebody Loved Me'. A live version recorded at the Oxford Apollo (18/3/85) was also broadcast by BBC Radio 1 on Janice Long's *Evening Show* on 9 May 1985. This was one of five tracks scheduled for the unreleased *Meat Is Murder* live EP **[see 37]**.

26

'Please Please Please Let Me Get What I Want'

Recorded July 1984, Jam Studios London

Produced by John Porter

B-side to 'William, It Was Really Nothing', August 1984

The shortest Smiths song of all, 'Please Please Please Let Me Get What I Want' is over and out in one minute and fifty seconds – the last forty of those being purely instrumental. 'When we first played it to Rough Trade,' recalled Morrissey, 'they kept asking, "where's the rest of the song?". But to me, it's like a very brief punch in the face. Lengthening the song would, to my mind, have simply been explaining the blindingly obvious.'

However brief, its undemanding melancholic splendour leaves nothing more to be said. Marr's relatively simple yet persuasive chord combination, carefully spiked with flinching minors lending an emphatically Irish air, is heartbreaking in itself. Accompanied by Morrissey's humbling, soul-baring plea for a better life, the effect is overwhelming. Yet the *pièce de résistance* comes with the vacillating mandolin coda (played not by Marr but by John Porter). Its final note, trembling into oblivion, is the cruellest of cliff-hangers; the end of an illusory middle eight that instinctively begs for the final verse which never arrives. Marr later revealed his muse to be an obscure Burt Bacharach tune, 'The Answer To Everything', as originally recorded by Del Shannon in 1962. 'It was something my parents used to play, and it struck a chord in me because it sounded so familiar. I tried to capture the essence of that tune; its spookiness and sense of yearning.'[56]

That its words were written together with its A-side, 'William, It Was Really Nothing', is perhaps evident in the nonchalant repetition of 'Lord knows' and 'God knows' that crop up in each (significantly Marr gave the music of both tracks to Morrissey simultaneously). In interviews of the period, the singer would speak of The Smiths' recent chart achievements in the aftermath of 'Heaven Knows I'm Miserable Now' as 'good times' (a phrase he'd also etch into the matrix of the 'Barbarism Begins At Home' promo a few months later **[see Appendix II]**). Consequently, 'Please Please Please… ' can be read as a directly autobiographical prayer to sustain Morrissey's ambition, which in the summer of 1984 had only just been fully realised.

Although the coupling of 'William… ' and 'Please Please Please… ' on one seven-inch single was a thrilling ploy (and yet another contender for the perfect pop single), Morrissey later criticised its 'sinful' relegation to a B-side, though consoled himself that they'd included it on *Hatful Of Hollow* 'by way of semi-repentance.' The track was particularly popular in the US where it featured on two Hollywood soundtracks from Brat Pack impresario John Hughes; *Pretty In Pink* and, as covered by The Smiths' maudlin UK peers The Dream Academy, *Ferris Bueller's Day Off*, both released in 1986. Two decades on it is still one of the best-loved and most frequently covered Smiths compositions.

In Concert

First introduced at Gloucester Leisure Centre (24/9/84)[57] – the only time it

56 There is indeed a similarity between the pre-chorus bridge of 'The Answer To Everything' (a US B-side featured on the UK album *Hats Off To Del Shannon*) and Marr's chord run between the fifth and tenth bars of the verse in 'Please Please Please…' (the 'so for once in my life… ' section).

57 The Gloucester concert was the first time The Smiths used their dramatic signature walk-on music from Prokofiev's ballet *Romeo & Juliet*, 'Dance of the Knights'. This replaced their earlier walk-on theme, Cilla Black's 'Love of the Loved', and would be used for the remainder of their concert career.

was ever performed in England, incidentally – 'Please Please Please...' was played as an encore for their three mainland UK shows that autumn to coincide with its release as the current single B-side. A rather shaky arrangement with scant percussion, it merely looped the second verse twice omitting the instrumental finale altogether.

By November, in a more accomplished take on the same three verse arrangement with a more considered rhythm section, 'Please Please Please... ' provided an unlikely set opener on their short Irish tour circa *Hatful Of Hollow*, before being temporarily dropped. The song didn't appear again in concert until Chicago Aragon Ballroom (7/6/85), where it was routinely played as an encore on that summer's 13-date US tour, apart from the final three concerts.

Absent from UK and European shows thereafter, it was only resurrected again for the following year's North American tour, where it was played on the first three Canadian dates and again as set opener at both the Los Angeles' Universal Amphitheater shows (25-26/8/86). On these latter shows with Craig Gannon, the song adhered to its original vinyl arrangement with Marr mimicking the closing mandolin solo on lead guitar against Gannon's rhythm.

27

'How Soon Is Now?'

Recorded **July 1984, Jam Studios London**

Produced by **John Porter**

B-side to **'William, It Was Really Nothing' (12-inch format only), August 1984**

Subsequently issued as a **Single A-side, February 1985 (Highest UK Chart Placing #24)**

The song that would later be hailed as 'the 'Stairway To Heaven' of the Eighties' by Seymour Stein, the enigmatic music mogul behind The Smiths' American label Sire, began life as 'Swamp' – one of Marr's home portastudio demos concocted during the early summer of 1984 at his flat in Earls Court.

The basis of the tune was the guitarist's attempt to capture the spirit of Creedence Clearwater Revival; no mean feat considering at the time Marr had heard almost nothing of the group. Rather, his starting point was a cover of their 'Run Through The Jungle' by The Gun Club. 'I had an impression of what Creedence were supposed to be about, partly because I'd already gotten into The Gun Club and heard 'Run Through The Jungle' from their second album [1982's *Miami*]. It triggered off some echoes of what I'd heard of Creedence. So I made this demo, 'Swamp', trying to capture the same vibe. It didn't have the tremolo figure on it, but it had the slide part in regular concert tuning. It was quite a pretty figure, but only hinting at what it became. It was still quite passive, nowhere near as intense as it got.'

Marr had already given a copy of 'Swamp' to Morrissey when supplying him with demos for all three tracks that would appear on the 'William, It Was Really Nothing' single. After completing the first two A and B sides by the Friday evening, the following afternoon Marr began jamming his 'Swamp' riff with Rourke and Joyce. 'I remember us playing it for a while and me really hoping we could make it sound like a Smiths track, because the chances were it might not have. So I had me fingers crossed that it was gonna be like us, already liking it myself and having given it to Morrissey.'[58]

While the track slowly came together, its mysterious, trippy atmosphere proved irresistible for the three musicians and producer John Porter, all of whom were known to indulge in a recreational spliff when the mood suited. By the evening, they'd even made amendments to the studio fixtures and fittings to match their mellow disposition. 'We just took all the lights out in the studio,' confesses Joyce, 'and put red bulbs in and got, well, stoned. Off our tits. That was it really.'

'We were always stoned,' laughs Porter. 'Vast quantities of hashish were consumed, and weed and whatever else we could lay our hands on. At first, I told them to play it for as long as they needed, a good four of five minutes. We did it and I got two good takes. Then I got both takes and cut out the bits which weren't good and chopped them together. That's why it ended up as long as it did.'

'We kicked it around until it *did* feel like us,' continues Marr, 'but I could hear that it had something lacking. So I saw my opportunity to throw the tremolo part down that I'd been looking to use for quite a while.'

At least three different records can lay claim to the inspiration for this, the track's celebrated quivering guitar texture. Marr would have been just 11 years old when he heard the first, Hamilton Bohannon's 1975 UK Top 10 hit 'Disco Stomp'. 'I was obsessed with that track. I remember hearing it in the back of the car with my parents, driving back from Wales on a hot day. The sound of it just really turned my head.' Equally important was 'I Want More', a rare UK hit for Can in 1976, though Marr wouldn't discover its influential shuddering rhythm until much later amongst the inherited record collection

58 This version of the making of 'How Soon Is Now?' contradicts that printed in the first edition of this book published in 2002, which Marr dismisses as incorrect. 'The idea that it was an experimental jam and that Morrissey just came in and heard it and sang over it first time, as capable as he was, it doesn't make sense. He was working to my rough portastudio demo. But I'm not trying to take away anyone's credit or input into the song at all, because it's magical enough as it is.'

of his friend, Pete Hunt. Last but not least was Bo Diddley, another of Marr's musical obsessions during the summer of 1984, who'd pioneered a distinctive, oscillating tremolo guitar style back in 1955 (one need only listen to Diddley's 'Mona' to spot a discernable antecedent for 'How Soon Is Now?'). 'So it was my boyhood love of 'Disco Stomp', Can's 'I Want More' and then tying the whole thing together with the Bo Diddley bow, as it were. That was the whole thing.'

The compelling effect in question was achieved without the aid of samplers or digital simulators, but manually on traditional analogue equipment. The first step involved taking the basic rhythm guitar part, which had been recorded as a 'dry' DI (Direct Input) take, without any effects.[59] This dry guitar pattern was next relayed to four Fender Twin Reverb amplifiers, each with its own vibrato tremolo switch. As Marr's plain rhythm was played back through the four speakers, Porter and Marr controlled the vibrato on one pair of amplifiers apiece to create the swampy, shuddering texture required. Whenever their tremolo slipped out of sync, the recording was stopped, the tape spun back and recommenced, sometimes recording in bursts of only ten seconds at a time.

Marr and Porter still had a couple more ingenious finishing touches up their sleeves overdubbed at the end of the session, including its mesmerising, punctuating guitar slide. 'Layering the slide part was what gave it the real tension,' Marr later verified. 'As soon as I played that bit on the second and third strings, John Porter put an AMS harmoniser[60] on it. Then we recorded each individual string with the harmoniser, then we tuned the B string down a half step and harmonised the whole thing.'

Finally, a separate guitar melody played in harmonics (a natural pinging tone achieved when a muted string is plucked) was dropped in as one of Marr's more obscure, and unlikely, homages; a secret nod to the man who first coined the phrase 'hip hop', New York rapper Lovebug Starski. 'The very first night we played New York,' explains Marr, 'after the Danceteria show, we were all a bit bugged out. He came over and was very nice and took care of me. I was really excited by that music. I'd heard his records in Manchester but he was still this pretty obscure hip-hop guy. So to suddenly be there in

59 Porter was already in the habit of taping a DI safety guitar track for every Smiths recording in case he needed to alter or manipulate the sound at a later point in the mixing process. The song's texture was further enhanced by Porter's employment of noise gates and the same dry guitar track fed through a quarter note delay signal. 'I had all these combinations which were pretty much all the same guitar but through various faders,' says Porter, 'each with slightly different sounds on. It was a combination of all these things.'

60 A harmoniser is an effects unit that allows recorded parts to change octave within the same key without losing time signature. It's used on many Smiths recordings, eg the slaughterhouse soundscape on 'Meat Is Murder' and the 'Ann Coates' chipmunk voice on 'Bigmouth Strikes Again'.

New York and meet him, at the time I was like "Whoa! There he is! Lovebug Starski!" So that bit in 'How Soon Is Now?' is a figure he'd used on one of his records, just a little motif that I thought was unusual and appropriate, so long as it worked. Which it did.'

Morrissey himself had remained at home in his Kensington flat the whole day, perhaps just as well since his admonitory attendance would have no doubt scuppered the opium den of stoned creativity executed in his absence. 'By then our sessions eventually got into a pattern,' says Porter. 'We would pretty much do the tracking and then everybody would just leave me and Johnny to it. Mozzer wouldn't even be there, unless it was a song they already knew. Most of the time we'd make these things up in the studio so it was pretty much done by the time he came in and put a vocal on top. I'd normally post a copy of what we'd been doing that day through his letter-box on the way home and then he'd come in the next morning with his notebook of lyrics and write something that seemed to fit.'

Though Porter posted a cassette of a rough mix through Morrissey's letter-box late that Saturday evening, Marr is keen to stress that the singer would have already spent some time drafting lyrics to his 'Swamp' demo.[61] Morrissey duly joined his fellow Smiths back at Jam the next day and laid down his vocal in just a couple of takes. When Porter first heard the song's opening line, he misinterpreted them as the ethereal metaphor 'I am the sun and the air.' 'Great,' he exclaimed to the others assembled around the mixing desk, 'he's singing about the elements!' The actual lyric itself was in fact adapted from George Elliot's *Middlemarch*; 'to be born the son of a Middlemarch manufacturer, and inevitable heir to nothing in particular.'

A sublime expression of disconsolate social inadequacy and raw human yearning, the power of 'How Soon Is Now?' lay in its universal scenario of unrequited desire. The ballad of a bad night out – the desperate, masochistic quest to find love in the essentially loveless environment of a nightclub – becomes the catalyst for a broader decree of aching existentialism, one that aggressively demands affection in the face of recurrent rejection. Writing for New York's *Village Voice Rock & Roll Quarterly* in 1989, Jon Savage took Morrissey's lyric as specifically evocative of Manchester's gay club scene during the late-Seventies and early-Eighties. 'How Soon Is Now?', according

61 A rogue theory that 'How Soon Is Now?' was originally called 'Father And Son' was later refuted during a 1985 *Melody Maker* interview in which Morrissey was cross-examined by a select panel of fanzine writers. Whatever 'Father And Son' may or may not have been, it never materialised despite Morrissey's forewarning 'it's about to emerge and I'm sure it will change your life.' Considering that in the same feature he joked that their next album would be called *Retreat!*, the very existence of 'Father And Son' ought to have been taken with a healthy shovel of salt. It's certainly doubtful – as some fans later intimated – that the song Morrissey referred to was a cover of the Cat Stevens track of the same name.

to Savage, 'captures that experience exactly – except the last line: home and sleep were not upsetting but a relief.'

The original unedited vocal track saw Morrissey yodel an alternate melody during its instrumental passages. Removed from the final master (though a barely audible trace can still be detected at 2.10), an earlier trial mix just clipping seven minutes which was later released – possibly by accident – as the B-side to the Italian edition of 'William, It Was Really Nothing' contains Morrissey's unabridged vocal track, complete with humming interludes and a spoken 'OK?' directed at Porter once his singing has finished. Comparing his delivery with that of the Troy Tate sessions 12 months earlier and the extent of Morrissey's transition from green novice to assured, vocal powerhouse is dazzlingly apparent. In interviews of the period he admitted to having had voice coaching, though made light of its merits. However, it's clear from the Jam sessions, 'How Soon Is Now?' in particular, that Morrissey's inherent talents as a singer were now in full bloom. His opulent poise, from submissive first entry to its soaring chorus clarion call ('I need to be loved') is magnified by an undaunted conviction, which sees him imperturbably break out into a merry whistle at 4.30. Throughout, the richness of his natural timbre amplifies the song's breast-beating humanity to the point where 'How Soon Is Now?' simply engulfs the listener.

The simplicity and directness of its lyrics was all the greater for Marr's iridescent yet spacious background score. Maintaining his beat to a mechanical constant (though in concert he'd excitedly integrate some sportive snare fills), Joyce's steady Diddley pulse was the solid vertebrae around which Marr's bayou tremolo shimmy, unearthly harmonic sparks and Rourke's converse, carefree funk wanderings bound themselves in a vibrating wall of supernatural sound. At over six-and-a-half minutes, sonically, technically, lyrically and aesthetically, 'How Soon Is Now?' was a heroic achievement.

'I was really pleased and really excited about it,' says Porter. 'I felt we were breaking new ground. I remember calling up Geoff on the Sunday night and saying "we've just done this great track, you've got to come down", so he did with Scott Piering. I could tell Geoff didn't like it very much. He just kept looking at me constantly and I could sense him thinking "what the fuck is this?" Scott dug it, I could see like me he thought it was cool. So I was very disappointed by Geoff. I got the vibe that he thought I was pushing them in a direction he didn't want them to go in.'

Despite pressure from the producer to save it for a separate A-side, it was finally issued as planned on the 12-inch B-side of 'William, It Was Really Nothing' that August. Night-time radio began to pick up on it almost immediately; by the autumn 'How Soon Is Now?' was the most frequently demanded Smiths track by listeners of John Peel, Janice Long (who had taken over from David Jensen's early evening slot) and Annie Nightingale's Sunday night request show. 'Obviously it came out as a single in its own right later,' defended Travis after the event. 'Maybe you could say we made a mistake not releasing that as the A-side [instead] of 'William... '.'

Its inclusion on November's *Hatful Of Hollow* compilation offered some solace yet only when the song provided The Smiths with their first number one – in John Peel's end of year Festive 50 poll – did Rough Trade begin to seriously recant on their initial decision not to publish 'How Soon Is Now?' as a single. Partly in response to the Festive 50 result, in late January the song was belatedly released in a radio-friendly three-and-a-half minute edit as The Smiths' sixth UK 45; a rare anomaly in which the previous single's B-side was now being promoted as their latest chart contender. Rough Trade justified the venture by claiming it was to spare British fans having to fork out "an extortionate price" for a Dutch 7-inch import released the previous autumn, which paired the shorter radio edit with 'Please Please Please Let Me Get What I Want'.

Alas, the label's dilly-dallying backfired. 'How Soon Is Now?' failed to follow its three predecessors inside the Top 20 and confused their fan base who, despite the obligatory draw of new B-sides, were less than enthusiastic about parting money for old rope. Furthermore, the release of 'How Soon Is Now?' thwarted plans to precede the imminent *Meat Is Murder* album with a foregoing single ('Barbarism Begins At Home' had been the strongest candidate, itself issued as a promotional DJ 12-inch that same month). Although Morrissey and Marr approved its release, 'How Soon Is Now?' stalled the momentum of The Smiths' discography, which had previously always thrilled with the shock of the new. 'They threw it away,' mourns Porter. 'By the time everyone got hip to it everybody had already bought it, twice. So they shot themselves in the foot.'

Yet across the Atlantic, in the words of Nick Kent it alerted 'a young Anglophile audience to a group whose every US press clipping initially seemed to view them as some wacky gay-rock crusade until ['How Soon Is Now?'], bolstered by an unsolicited video for MTV rotation, did the trick.' The aforementioned unauthorised promo film aside, although it paid dividends by alerting left-field America to The Smiths, Morrissey was deeply depressed by its US single release in an 'abhorrent sleeve' and Sire's further butchering of *Meat Is Murder* where it was unceremoniously tacked on.

The fact that today it remains without doubt their most popular recording is a sweet if mildly ironic consolation for both their own and their label's failure to highlight its brilliance with an adequate single release first time round (when reissued by WEA in September 1992 it fared marginally better, reaching number 16 in the UK singles chart). More than any other Smiths track, 'How Soon Is Now?' has crossed over into the fabric of mainstream pop culture. It was famously sampled on 'Hippy Chick', a UK Top 10 hit by Soho in 1991 (for which Morrissey and Marr claimed a quarter of all royalties), used as the soundtrack to an international advertising campaign by Pepe Jeans, since covered by both rock and dance artists and licensed to all manner of 'classic rock' compilation albums. As performed by The Psychedelic Furs' offshoot band Love Split Love, it's been adopted as the TV theme tune to the cult US lipstick 'n' witchcraft series *Charmed*. Even chart-topping faux lesbian Russian pop sensation TATU famously covered the song in 2003. For those who hate The Smiths, 'How Soon Is Now?' is their populist saving grace; the exception to the rule.

'This sounds incredibly egotistical,' Marr once recalled, 'but [with 'How Soon Is Now?'] I wanted an intro that was almost as potent as 'Layla'. When that song plays in a club or a pub, everyone knows what it is instantly.' With the ageless opening shimmer of 'How Soon Is Now?', time has declared Marr's mission accomplished. If nothing else, The Smiths will always be remembered for this unparalleled and outlandish modern masterpiece.

In Concert

Live, 'How Soon Is Now?' posed a major problem for The Smiths. Conceived as a technically adventurous studio piece, its distinctive guitar effect was near impossible to recreate in concert as Andy Rourke confirms: 'It was the bane of our live career, we never got it right. Johnny used to try layering it up but compared to the record it just ended up sounding dead wimpy. It always used to go pear shaped.'

Accordingly, 'How Soon Is Now?' was tackled from various approaches. Debuted at Gloucester Leisure Centre (24/9/84), at first Marr tried to play the whole riff alone, based around the basic Bo Diddley shuffle. As the result sounded inevitably thin, by the *Meat Is Murder* tour, he attempted to expand its dimensions by adding a pre-recorded slide overdub, which he would trigger with a foot pedal when required. Marr also toyed with a tremolo pedal on his accompanying rhythm part with mixed results; some nights he'd get the tempo right, other times the vibrato shudders would go horribly out of sync with Joyce's beat. It remained in this shaky state of flux until the autumn Scottish tour, after which it was dropped.

With the addition of Craig Gannon in the summer of 1986, The Smiths had another crack at 'How Soon Is Now?', re-introducing it for their epic Canadian/North American expedition (twice as set opener) and the final UK tour that October. Yet even with two guitarists, it was still hit and miss with Marr deciding to rock out during the climax with some needless improvised soloing. This, its final imperfect translation, was last performed at their penultimate concert at Manchester Free Trade Hall (30/10/86).

Television

Their first *Top of the Pops* visit of 1985, The Smiths' appearance on the programme to promote 'How Soon Is Now?' on 14 February (Valentine's Day) saw Morrissey's infamous machine-gun mime, spraying the audience with imaginary bullets much like Tom Courtenay's similar fantasies in *Billy Liar.*[62]

To the band's disgust, as previously mentioned, their American label, Sire, concocted an unauthorised promotional video for the single's US release. Accredited to Paula Grief and Richard Levine, it comprised of lo-fi camcorder footage shot by tour soundman Grant Showbiz (including a priceless clip of Marr teaching Morrissey some guitar chords) and a blonde-haired girl sullenly posing in chiaroscuro intercut with library stock of industrial chimneys. 'It had absolutely nothing to do with The Smiths,' Morrissey bitterly protested to US rock magazine *Creem* later that year, 'but quite naturally we were swamped with letters from very distressed American friends saying "why on earth did you make this foul video?" And of course it must be understood that Sire made that video, and we saw the video and we said to them "you can't possibly release this... this degrading video." And they said, "well, maybe you shouldn't really be on our label". It was quite disastrous, and it need hardly be mentioned that they also listed the video under the title 'How Soon Is Soon?' which... where does one begin, really?'

Radio

After the July Jam session, Porter recorded The Smiths for their third John Peel engagement on 1 August at BBC Maida Vale Studio 5. The booking was primarily a means of plugging the imminent 'William, It Was Really Nothing' single and its intended follow-up 'Nowhere Fast', with the other two tracks selected from their respective B-sides. Knowing that 'How Soon Is Now?' wouldn't be possible to recreate within the time constraints of a one-day BBC radio session, Porter brought with him the Jam studio master, sampling its infamous juddering guitar to save time, as Marr freely confirms: 'It was done from the studio tapes, obviously. We just rejigged it 'cos we would have been there doing it all day doing otherwise.'

Two live versions were also aired by the BBC; the first, recorded at the Oxford Apollo (18/3/85) was broadcast on Janice Long's *Evening Show* in

62 The same *Top of the Pops* clip was briefly shown the following week on the BBC's lunchtime magazine show *Pebble Mill At One* during an interview with Morrissey (21/2/85).

May. The second, taped at Kilburn National Ballroom (23/10/86) featuring Craig Gannon on rhythm guitar, was included on April 1987's *In Concert* programme. Although this gig later became the basis for 1988's posthumous live album *Rank*, 'How Soon Is Now?' was omitted from Morrissey's final running order.

28

'Fast One'

Recorded **July 1984, Jam Studios, London**

Produced by **John Porter**

Studio out-take

Originally, the July Jam sessions had been intended to stockpile enough material for a couple of singles to release at regular intervals throughout the autumn (hence Rourke's boast to *Record Mirror* in September that 'we recorded the next three singles in two days flat, we work fast'). The first, 'William, It Was Really Nothing', was issued as planned, though its intended follow up, 'Nowhere Fast', (which probably would have been backed with versions of 'This Night Has Opened My Eyes' and 'Rusholme Ruffians' also recorded at Jam that month) was scrapped.

Other than the six completed songs, Marr also used the time to rehearse musical sketches with Rourke and Joyce for future reference. Among them was an unnamed instrumental given the working title 'Fast One'; a wonderfully punchy number just under three minutes, propelled by a strident bass line from Rourke. Echoing the kind of vivacious tempo and euphoric melody Marr later perfected with 'I Want The One I Can't Have', this is the same instrumental Mike Joyce later referred to in a 1993 *Q* feature, hazarding a guess that it had been recorded at the same time as 'Girl Afraid'.[63]

In October 1984, The Smiths were scheduled to embark upon their first major tour of the US, yet after three mainland UK gigs in late September intended as a warm-up, these American dates were cancelled at the eleventh hour. With band and crew waiting to board the plane at Heathrow Airport,

63 Another untitled instrumental also survives from this period. Referred to in the first edition of this book as 'Untitled Instrumental (Jam '84)' it may actually have been recorded a few weeks earlier during a curtailed session at Matrix Studios in early June (this would tally with John Porter's recollection of being called away from a Smiths session at Matrix to attend the birth of his daughter, born June 1984). The track in question is recognisably 'Smiths-like' and vaguely similar in pattern to 'Well I Wonder', but nothing more than an indistinct working draft of a half-formed melody.

Morrissey suddenly decided they weren't going. 'It wasn't unusual,' remembers Rourke. 'It happened a few times. Once we were supposed to be doing some gigs in Europe and Morrissey hadn't shown at the airport. Me and Johnny ended up going round his flat and knocking on his door. We knew he was in, but he just wouldn't answer. That was just his way of dealing with that situation, I don't think he was capable of telling us any other way, which is a statement in itself really.'

Morrissey also had concerns about their forthcoming single. Although 'Nowhere Fast' was still being named as the next Smiths 45 by *Melody Maker* in November (and prematurely heralded as such in the introduction to the first sheet music collection of The Smiths published that autumn), the record was shelved and with it John Porter's future as in-house producer.

With an unexpected gap in their calendar after the cancellation of the US tour, Morrissey and Marr seized the opportunity to devote themselves to making a second album. It now seemed obvious given Morrissey's instinctively insular temperament and Marr's grounding in the mechanics of mixing and recording from Porter, that they would produce it themselves. 'The whole idea with *Meat Is Murder*,' Morrissey later divulged, 'was to control it totally and without a producer things were better. We saw things clearer.'

Meantime, Stephen Street had followed The Smiths' career with great interest blighted only by moderate envy. Despite taking his phone number during the 'Heaven Knows I'm Miserable Now' sessions back in February, it looked as if Morrissey and Marr had no intention of contacting him for future work. The release of 'William, It Was Really Nothing', made without his involvement, confirmed Street's fears that theirs had been an empty promise, until in early October he received a phone call from Geoff Travis. Though Morrissey and Marr had decided to produce the next album, they still needed an engineer they could trust. So began Street's fruitful relationship as The Smiths' newly adopted recording whiz-kid, one which saw his steady graduation to co-producer come their final studio album two and a half years later.

'We were really lucky to have Stephen Street,' stresses Marr. 'He was exactly the right person for us at that time because he was so talented and, crucially, round about the same age as us. He was also fledgling, if you like, and not too experienced so his trajectory was similar to us. He had his own agendas that he wanted to bring in that were really in synch with ours so he was a very sympathetic guy to be around. So much has been made of my relationship with John Porter that it might give the impression that the band's relationship with Stephen wasn't as intense. But it was, in a different sort of way. He was absolutely crucial and really we couldn't have made the album we did without Stephen. I can't praise him highly enough for the work he did on *Meat Is Murder*, and all the other records we made.'

Having settled on their recording personnel, the band resisted London in favour of the North. Nick Kent would later reiterate that 'both Morrissey and Marr [stressed] how essential it was that sessions for their second LP took place in Liverpool's Amazon studios amidst earthy Northern badinage as opposed to studios in London where they were made to feel like nuisances and timewasters in the proximity of lavish multi-track equipment.'

Amazon itself was anything but hi-tech, as Street remembers: 'The studio was in Kirby, on this godforsaken industrial estate outside Liverpool. It wasn't what you'd call the most salubrious place in the world, put it that way. When we turned up, I found that the speakers were all wired out of phase – a technical term – but it was a bit of a dump. To make things worse we had this terrible white Mercedes car, which we used to travel back and forth between Liverpool and Manchester every day. We just used to pile into it first thing in the morning, work till late at night at the studio, then pile back in and be chauffeured home to Manchester every night. But it was a great session.'

Unlike its predecessor, what became *Meat Is Murder* was only half-written when The Smiths first set foot in Amazon. Marr later joked that they needed to return to the North to get rained on as it improved their creativity. Be that the case, it must have been pissing down in Liverpool, as the album The Smiths fashioned in Amazon that October[64] represented a gargantuan leap forward in every direction. Marr was acutely aware of their audience's expectations and relished the prospect of trouncing such anticipations and testing the mettle of The Smiths as a versatile musical unit capable of cruising down whatever tangent he wished to veer. 'I don't want the second album to sound like a logical or credible step forward,' he enthused to *Sounds* earlier that year, 'I want it to be unexpected Smiths.'

29

'The Headmaster Ritual'

Recorded **October-November 1984, Amazon Studios, Liverpool/Ridge Farm Studios, Surrey**

Produced by **The Smiths**

Album track from ***Meat Is Murder*, February 1985**

Johnny Marr had been working on the raw musical material of 'The Headmaster Ritual' since the summer of 1983. 'The first time I came up with the chords was sitting around when we were working with Troy Tate. I

64 Though technically the bulk of *Meat Is Murder* was recorded at Amazon, a separate overdub session took place at Ridge Farm Studios in Surrey in early November.

had it for that long but it was always looking for a home. I thought if you could play those chords on acoustic then I could see shades of Joni Mitchell in them.[65] But what use would sounding like Joni Mitchell have been to me at that time? So like a lot of the things that we did, it went through the weird labyrinth of influences.'

It was only after Marr moved to London in early 1984 that the guitarist began some serious remodelling of the tune, blending the chorus and bridge from another, separate work-in-progress until it resembled its final, intricate character. 'As my life got more and more intense, so did the song' he later reflected. Adopting an open 'drop D' tuning (with a capo at the 2nd fret to bring it up to E), Marr's riff also possessed a strong trace of Beatles, specifically 'I Feel Fine', which played with a similar melody based around a major chord shape. He'd later admit that the riff was indeed consciously influenced by George Harrison, and actually played on a classic Rickenbacker model once owned by The Byrds' Roger McGuinn (acquired by John Porter via Roxy Music's Phil Manzanera). 'People always think I love that tune for what I'm doing on the verses,' adds Marr, 'but for me it's the chords I'm playing in the intro and outro.'

Rourke and Joyce had never rehearsed the song until arriving at Amazon, where it was swiftly jammed into shape. Upon hearing Marr's opening, staccato chords, Joyce instinctively followed suit; thus creating the compelling rat-a-tat intro that would lead to the track's eventual placing as the album's suitably forceful opener. Rourke's muscular bass cleverly weaved between the gaps of Marr's Harrison homage, surging above the surface during the choruses to assert his instrument's indispensability within The Smiths' unique sound. Marr himself multi-tracked something close to a dozen guitars, all in open tuning save the jingling climax featuring an Epiphone Coronet in 'Nashville tuning' (a standard guitar strung with the high-octave doubles from a 12-string set) for that 'really zingy' effect.

Morrissey honoured the detail and vision of Marr's groundwork with a fittingly grand lyric that transposed the domestic savagery of 'Barbarism Begins At Home' into the school classroom. Its potent tableau of senseless canings and locker-room bullying was especially suggestive of Ken Loach's magnificent *Kes*, not least Brian Glover's darkly comic portrayal of a merciless PE teacher who rules his pupils with the back of his hand.[66] For once

65 Speaking about 'The Headmaster Ritual' to *Guitar Player* magazine in 1990, Marr commented: 'I fancied the idea of a strange Joni Mitchell tuning, and the actual progression is like what she would have done had she been an MC5 fan or a punk rocker.'

66 The actual 'grabs and devours' phrase used to describe the games teacher is taken from Elizabeth Smart's *By Grand Central Station I Sat Down and Wept*, one of Morrissey's main resources when composing the lyrics for the *Meat Is Murder* album **[see also 30, 31 and 39]**. Smart's book, 'a masterpiece of poetic prose', relays the emotional chaos at the heart of her tempestuous real-life love affair with the poet George Barker.

though, Morrissey didn't have to rely on second-hand experiences inherited from Sixties kitchen-sink dramas, as he was only too eager to share with the press. 'The Headmaster Ritual' was, he explained, openly autobiographical of his time at Stretford's St Mary's secondary modern during the mid-Seventies; 'If you dropped a pencil you'd be beaten to death. It was very aggressive. It seemed that the only activity of the teachers was whipping the pupils – which they managed expertly.' The strength of his antipathy towards his alma mater was illustrated in a moving if somewhat self-mythologising feature for BBC2's *Oxford Road Show* screened on 29 February 1985, in which he took the cameras on a tour of his pre-Smiths past. Stood outside the gates of St Mary's, he appeared genuinely distressed; 'Five years of education here proved to have no effect on me whatsoever, and I'm sure no effect on anybody else except in a very adverse sense. Not to be recommended.'[67]

'The Headmaster Ritual' is a compelling emotional release of such adolescent hangovers. For the first time, Morrissey sullies his language with coarse vernacular, labelling his former tutors 'spineless bastards', before venting his wrath in an unearthly, double-tracked yodel of random gibberish; a final, cathartic primal scream to purge the frustrations of his past. In its condemnation of comprehensive schooling and institutionalised misery, the song still packs some clout, though corporal punishment itself has since been abolished in the British education system. To that end, it was shrewd of Morrissey, a decade later, to write a reverse thesis of 'The Headmaster Ritual' – the self-explanatory 'The Teachers Are Afraid Of The Pupils' – on his 1995 solo album *Southpaw Grammar*.

Throwing down the gauntlet of *Meat Is Murder*'s implicit catalogue of violence, Morrissey's opening gambit – 'Belligerent ghouls run Manchester schools' – remains the greatest opening line of any Smiths album, showcasing an incisive vocabulary and poetic pith that made its entry into the UK album charts at number one in February 1985 an even sweeter victory. The Manchester Education Committee wasn't nearly so impressed, and tried – in vain – to prevent The Smiths from playing within their jurisdiction. The controversy resulted in an amusing confrontation between Morrissey and Tony Wilson during a Granada TV news report coinciding with the album's release, in which the singer not only defended his 'right' to attack his former

67 Morrissey painted an equally grim picture of life at St Mary's in an earlier TV interview on Channel 4's *Earsay* (broadcast 7/6/84): 'I went to a school which ultimately got global attention for being the most brutal school in the country for capital punishment ... It was really quite an absurd school, working class, and the only thing you could possibly do was woodwork. Obviously when you left school you would go to a factory or something, there was no question of being articulate or reading books. I remember one instance when all the pupils were asked to write about their favourite book and I wrote about the dictionary. I remember I was virtually expelled for being so obstreperous and perverse. It was *that* kind of school!'

school governors but impertinently suggested Wilson should try his hand at being a pop star himself.

Relations between these two opposing leviathans of the Mancunian music scene curdled considerably thereafter. When Wilson called Morrissey 'a woman trapped in a man's body', the latter replied that the Factory Records' boss was a 'pig trapped in a man's body' and that 'the day somebody shoves Wilson in the boot of a car and drives his body to Saddleworth Moor, that is the day Manchester music will be revived.' Asked to defend the severity of these comments by *The Observer* in 1992, Morrissey digressed; 'Actually I was misquoted on that one. What I actually said was that he is a man trapped in a pig's body.'

In Concert

Considered by many critics as the high point of the second album, surprisingly, 'The Headmaster Ritual' had a relatively short lifespan in the ruthless climate of the Smiths' ever-changing set-lists. Introduced on the first night of the *Meat Is Murder* tour at Chippenham Golddiggers (27/2/85), it was played for the duration of 1985 only to be dropped following the final date that year at Inverness Eden Court Theatre (1/10/85).

Despite being sound-checked at Liverpool Royal Court in February 1986, 'The Headmaster Ritual' was never actually performed again, although Marr was prone to tinkling a slowed-down arrangement of its infectious opening riff in between songs as a crowd teaser, segueing it into the intro of 'Meat Is Murder' on their final UK tour in late '86.

Television

The second of two mimed songs on BBC2's *Oxford Road Show* on 22 February 1985, 'The Headmaster Ritual' saw Morrissey frenetically gesticulating its brutal imagery (acting out the 'elbow in the face') culminating in a welcome reappearance of his machine gun dance first featured on the previous week's *Top of the Pops* 'How Soon Is Now?' performance **[see 27]**.

Radio

A live version of 'The Headmaster Ritual' recorded at the Oxford Apollo (18/3/85) was broadcast by BBC Radio 1 on Janice Long's *Evening Show* on 9 May 1985.

30

'What She Said'

Recorded October-November 1984, Amazon Studios, Liverpool/Ridge Farm Studios, Surrey
Produced by The Smiths
Album track from *Meat Is Murder*, February 1985
Subsequently released as B-side to 'Shakespeare's Sister', March 1985

A return to the harder-edged sound not heard in their set since the likes of 'Handsome Devil', 'What She Said' saw the intensity of Marr's sneering, multi-tracked lead and Joyce's thunderous backbeat push the group, unbelievably, into quasi-heavy metal territory; a bemused if approving diagnosis shared by the majority of critics such as the *NME*'s Paul Du Noyer who deemed it 'a storming guitar attack your average metal guitarist would rip off his chest wig to emulate.'

Another Morrissey/Marr composition written together 'eyeball-to-eyeball', the band utilised group sound-checks on the Gloucester, Cardiff and Swansea dates in September 1984 to busk a rough design into shape. Shortly before entering Amazon, a more polished arrangement, then stretching to five minutes and featuring a drum-solo breakdown, was rehearsed alongside 'Well I Wonder'. Both songs would contain explicit references to Elizabeth Smart's 1945 novella *By Grand Central Station I Sat Down and Wept*, which Morrissey would repeatedly plagiarise. In this instance, Smart's jaded admission, 'I have learned to smoke because I need something to hold on to' and the equally dejected resignation 'I wonder why no one has noticed I am dead and taken the trouble to bury me' would both be knitted into 'What She Said' with little alteration.

Over Marr, Rourke and Joyce's combined metallic clamour, Morrissey revisits the dictum of 'Handsome Devil' – that there's more to life than books – in a half-mocking portrait of a traumatised intellectual with romantic visions of suicide who receives a rude awakening courtesy of a 'tattooed boy from Birkenhead'. Following the fairground violence of 'Rusholme Ruffians' and ongoing battle between mind and body expressed in 'I Want The One I Can't Have', 'What She Said' was perfectly placed as the penultimate track of *Meat Is Murder*'s first act. Another trump card in The Smiths' curriculum vitae of genre-hopping malleability, it was an ideal choice of flipside for the non-album follow-up single 'Shakespeare's Sister', which also drew inspiration from Smart's profound paean to feminine suicidal tendencies.

In Concert

Previewed on 1984's winter tour of Ireland (beginning at the Waterford

Savoy 11/11/84), 'What She Said' would become a hard-rocking perennial of Smiths gigs henceforth, staying in the set for all of 1985 and right through to the summer of 1986.

Played at their first concert with Craig Gannon – Glasgow Barrowlands (16/7/86) – it disappeared from the next two shows at Newcastle and Manchester's G-Mex Festival, only to return at Salford University (20/7/86) having been restructured as a medley with 'Rubber Ring' **[see 44]**. This new version, book-ended by the latter's funky intro and wailing erratic finale (as heard on *Rank*) would be a staple fixture for the majority of dates on the final tours of Canada, America and the UK, last played at Manchester Free Trade Hall (30/10/86).

Radio

A live version of 'What She Said' – recorded during their Oxford Apollo show (18/3/85) – was broadcast by BBC Radio 1 on Janice Long's *Evening Show* in May 1985; later that month it was also made available on a free 7-inch EP given away with the *NME*.

The 'Rubber Ring'/'What She Said' medley, as performed at Kilburn National Ballroom (23/10/86) was also broadcast on Radio 1's *In Concert* in April 1987. The same recording would eventually be included on 1988's posthumous live album *Rank*.

31

'Well I Wonder'

Recorded **October-November 1984, Amazon Studios, Liverpool/Ridge Farm Studios, Surrey**

Produced by **The Smiths**

B-side to **'How Soon Is Now?', February 1985**

Subsequently featured on the album ***Meat Is Murder*, February 1985**

Composed by Johnny Marr at his Earls Court flat during the late summer of 1984 ('I wrote it in from scratch and made a demo with Andy on acoustic in one afternoon'), the demurely melancholic chords for 'Well I Wonder' had been nesting up the guitarist's sleeve for some time. Apart from a distantly related instrumental taped during the summer Jam sessions with John Porter, a rare home recording from late 1983 discovered in the tape archives of Mike Joyce reveals Marr experimenting with a similar, arpeggio chord structure (more surprising still, the guitarist can be heard singing a random vocal melody over the top) before progressing to a jerkier, flamenco arrangement. 'It wasn't that I was looking for a home for those chords,' says Marr, 'I had a theme knocking around subconsciously that just worked with acoustic. They're very typical of the chords that I play so it doesn't surprise me that they were in the air at that time.'

Recorded after 'What She Said', the contrastingly glum 'Well I Wonder' also shared a debt to Elizabeth Smart's *By Grand Central Station I Sat Down and Wept*, borrowing a clutch of stanzas; 'the fierce last stand of all I have', 'lies gasping, but still living' and the novella's closing line 'do you hear me where you sleep?'. Morrissey's crushing soliloquy shared the sentiment of Klaus Nomi's 'Death'; a distressing interpretation of a Henry Purcell aria from 1982's *Simple Man* LP, which he named in an interview of the period as the 'most Biblical record' in his collection,[68] even quoting its lyric 'remember me, but forget my fate' (a possible antecedent of 'please keep me in mind'). Arguably Morrissey's finest performance on the entire album, 'Well I Wonder' climaxes in a chilling, twittering falsetto worthy of Nomi himself.

The addition of Marr's muted Buddy Holly-style bridge vamp and the overdub of drizzling rain from a sound effects LP – an accidental homage to the miserable showers featured on The Ronettes' classic Phil Spector production 'Walking in the Rain' – distended the morose ambience. 'That was Morrissey's idea,' says Marr. 'He was always good at adding these little bits of atmosphere.'

'Well I Wonder' boasted a beautifully understated arrangement (note the way Rourke's bass hesitates at the beginning of the first verse before plunging in on the B-minor with breathtaking precision) that Marr was justly proud of. In the circumstances then, that it was never performed in public makes it the most surprising omission from The Smiths' concert career and the only track from their first three studio albums never to be played live. A fortnight prior to its release on *Meat Is Murder*, 'Well I Wonder' was actually first issued as the B-side to 'How Soon Is Now?'

32

'Nowhere Fast'

Recorded **October-November 1984, Amazon Studios, Liverpool/Ridge Farm Studios, Surrey**

Produced by **The Smiths**

Album track from ***Meat Is Murder*****, February 1985**

Another title seemingly plucked from the vocabulary of Shelagh Delaney (Nell quotes the phrase in Act I of *The Lion in Love*), the eloquent

68 Klaus Nomi's 'Death' would later be selected by Morrissey for inclusion on his 2003 compilation album of favourite artists, *Under The Influence* (DMC).

'Nowhere Fast' presaged the sensationalist monarchy-bashing Morrissey would famously return to in 'The Queen Is Dead' **[see 54]**.

By the end of 1984, his media persona, as prodded and probed by interviewers fascinated with pop's premiere celebrity celibate, had shifted from 'ailing Victorian romantic with a permanent health problem' to opinionated bigmouth whose cutting asides on The Smiths' *Top of the Pops* peers, Princess Diana, Thatcher and the IRA bombing of the October Tory party conference in Brighton ('I feel relatively happy about it') made excellent copy. With 'Nowhere Fast', in which he fantasises about dropping his trousers Brian Rix-style to bare his bottom to Her Majesty, the inflammatory beliefs he'd expressed in such interviews were now seeping further into his lyrics.

Never one to avoid a decent drubbing of the House of Windsor, Morrissey went so far as to tell one journalist that the Queen was a 'fascist', in doing so evoking the seditious bile of The Sex Pistols' monumental 'God Save The Queen' seven years earlier; 'To me there's something dramatically ugly about a person who can wear a dress for £6,000 when at the same time there are people who can't afford to eat. When she puts on that dress for £6,000 the statement she is making to the nation is: "I am the fantastically gifted royalty, and you are the snivelling peasants." The very idea that people would be interested in the facts about this dress is massively insulting to the human race.' Within the context of 'Nowhere Fast', the monarchy's existence merely adds to its author's overwhelming sense of disparagement. Yet again, the small town frustrations of 'William, It Was Really Nothing' (written at roughly the same time) resurface, though here Morrissey's locale is worse than 'humdrum': a graveyard where passing trains mock with the promise of escape and 'each household appliance is like a new science'.

When interviewed by Tony Wilson for a local *Granada Reports* TV feature upon the album's release, Marr played its trim, twanging intro as direct evidence of the 'Sam Phillips influence'[69] on his writing; its sliding lower string hammer-ons being a blatant homage to the nimble fretwork of Scotty Moore, guitarist on Elvis' early Sun sides recorded for Phillips between 1954-55. The final album version was a vast improvement on the fine, if slightly flat, interpretation cut with John Porter at Jam back in July that had originally been flagged as the follow-up single to 'William... '. Its stark, rockabilly ambience is enhanced by Marr's subtle whammy-bar shivers and Joyce's drums, cleverly utilised during the instrumental middle eight in a remarkable piece of onomatopoeic production; recreating the ephemeral

69 A giant within the history of rock, producer Sam Phillips was the man behind Jackie Brenston's 1951 R&B hit 'Rocket 88' (commonly regarded as the first bona fide rock 'n' roll record) and later founded the Sun Records label in Memphis, which would launch the careers of, among others, Elvis Presley, Jerry Lee Lewis and Johnny Cash.

clatter of a passing train while panning from speaker to speaker in a steam of vaporous reverb.

Yet if there's one instrument that powers 'Nowhere Fast', paramount to all others, it's Rourke's bass. On *Meat Is Murder*, The Smiths' rhythm section was finally freed from Porter's well-meaning constraints, with Rourke in particular taking a more prominent position in the mix. His *pièce de résistance* 'Barbarism Begins At Home' notwithstanding, the majority of tracks on The Smiths' second album apportion their tuneful propensity to the assertive bass melodies Rourke conjures up as a compliment to Marr's overall design. 'Nowhere Fast' is a case in point; Marr provides the delicate, treble frills, but during the verses it's Rourke's athletic bass scales that commandingly bind the disparate elements together.

A fierce opener for *Meat Is Murder*'s second half, oddly it seemed that Marr himself was never fully satisfied with the finished record. '*Meat Is Murder* I still rate very highly,' he divulged to *Melody Maker* towards the end of 1985, 'but again stuff like 'Nowhere Fast' could have been done better.'

In Concert

'Nowhere Fast' was debuted as the opening number at the GLC 'Jobs for a Change' Festival in London (10/6/84). It remained at the beginning of the set for their remaining UK dates that month, including their Glastonbury Festival appearance (23/6/84) becoming a permanent fixture of Smiths concerts from thereon; played for the rest of 1984, all of '85 and up until early '86. It was last performed at Belfast Queens University (12/2/86), the final gig prior to the arrival of Craig Gannon.

Television

As part of a special report on BBC2's *Whistle Test* (12/2/85), The Smiths were interviewed while putting the finishing touches to *Meat Is Murder*. The feature itself was a contrivance for the benefit of the cameras, filmed while mixing down at Island Records' 'Fallout Shelter' studio in London, not Amazon in Liverpool where the album was actually recorded. Excerpts from several album tracks were included, ending in 'Nowhere Fast' in its entirety featuring Morrissey and a noticeably Keith Richards-esque Johnny Marr (complete with precariously placed cigarette dangling from his bottom lip) miming to the track with headphones on while Joyce, Rourke and engineer Stephen Street watched from the control booth.

Radio

Along with 'William, It Was Really Nothing', 'Rusholme Ruffians' and the dubious BBC mix of 'How Soon Is Now?', 'Nowhere Fast' was recorded for

The Smiths' third John Peel session produced by John Porter at Maida Vale Studio 5 on 1 August 1984. An earnest rendition, though lacking the stylised flair of the definitive *Meat Is Murder* master, it was eventually released as the 12-inch extra track of the final Rough Trade single, 'Last Night I Dreamt That Somebody Loved Me', in December 1987.

A live version recorded at the Oxford Apollo (18/3/85) was also broadcast by BBC Radio 1 on Janice Long's *Evening Show* on 9 May 1985 and later issued as a 12-inch extra on the 'That Joke Isn't Funny Anymore' single.

33

'Rusholme Ruffians'

Recorded **October-November 1984, Amazon Studios, Liverpool/Ridge Farm Studios, Surrey**

Produced by **The Smiths**

Album track from ***Meat Is Murder*, February 1985**

Created at the Jam Studios sessions in July, 'Rusholme Ruffians' (Rusholme, like Whalley Range in 'Miserable Lie', being another specific reference to a Manchester locale) began as a freeform improvisation based around '(Marie's The Name) His Latest Flame', Elvis Presley's 1961 hit written by Doc Pomus and Mort Shuman and heavily influenced by the rhythms of Bo Diddley. 'That was blatantly done,' says Marr. 'Morrissey said to me "let's do a song about the fair" and for some reason my association with the fair was to pull out that Elvis riff. We tried, but we couldn't get away from it.'

Originally a seven-minute jam, Joyce bashed out a double-timed, metronomic thump over which Marr cruised between the D/B minor change, experimenting with all manner of melodic variations, creating a much less explicit echo of its Presley source matter than the final studio master. Once again, Rourke's bass would prove the vital component, finding a separate, secular riff within Marr's looser skiffle-style chord cycle. Morrissey was enthusiastic enough to apply an outstanding preliminary vocal that lasted the full seven minutes, in doing so splitting up the verses so as to leave four instrumental bars between each couplet, ad-libbing furiously ('the pulses being beat are mine!') and launching into a tremendous falsetto finale. Trimmed and tidied into a four minute rockabilly takeoff, the eventual 'Rusholme Ruffians' marked a shift in The Smiths' oeuvre; the first of many 'organic' works, brewed up in the studio as a working band rather than the calculated Brill building principle Morrissey and Marr had first clung to.

As first uncovered by Johnny Rogan in his biography *Morrissey & Marr: The Severed Alliance*, the lyrics of 'Rusholme Ruffians' were shamelessly derived from 'Fourteen Again', a bitter-sweet nostalgic homage to fairground romances by comedienne Victoria Wood. The citations are manifold: Wood writes of 'the last night of the fair', 'behind the generators', 'when I was funny, I was famous' and of lights 'reflected in the Brylcreem in his hair'. Yet 'Fourteen Again' is only half the story. Another Wood song from the same period, the George Formby-esque 'Funny How Things Turn Out' contains the key line 'my faith in myself is still devout', which Morrissey adapted for his song's final pronouncement of his resolute belief in love.

Sharing its theme of a cheap engagement ring with 'William, It Was Really Nothing' and regurgitating the solitary walk home of 'How Soon Is Now?' (which here becomes a march of blind faith rather than a suicidal slink of pessimistic resignation), 'Rusholme Ruffians' was also Morrissey's first flirtation with thuggish low-life, a topic he'd return to in later Smiths compositions and throughout his ensuing solo career. At least here, the violence in the song appeared to be first hand, a cathartic address of his own unpleasant experiences at fun fairs while growing up in Manchester. 'In the Sixties [Manchester] was a very violent place,' he told *The Observer* in 1992. 'I remember being at a fair at Stretford Road; it was very early, about 5.00 pm, and I was just standing by the speedway. And somebody just came over to me and head-butted me. He was much older than me, and much bigger. I was dazed for at least five minutes. What I find remarkable is the way you just accepted it. That was just the kind of thing that happened. I don't think it was even that I looked different in those days. There never needed to be a reason.'

When recorded for posterity at Amazon for *Meat Is Murder*, The Smiths and engineer Stephen Street imbued 'Rusholme Ruffians' with added colour; attaching a whirling intro of fairground noises (from one of Morrissey's many BBC sound effects LPs) and loosening Joyce's beat to a rattling shuffle – in perfect tandem with Marr's shaking acoustic – far more evocative of its theme than his original lumpen pacesetter. The end result is a vivid frieze of cheap, and dangerous, working class thrills, where the adrenalin rush of fast rides quickly escalates into a taut atmosphere of potential stabbings and suicides; a waltzer ride of emotions providing its own spinning rock 'n' roll soundtrack. Like Albert Finney's fatal fairground liaison with Rachel Roberts in Karel Reisz's 1960 kitchen-sink classic *Saturday Night and Sunday Morning* condensed into the language of pop, with 'Rusholme Ruffians' The Smiths' music, lyrics and new-found production sensibilities gelled superbly.

In Concert

First previewed at Gloucester Leisure Centre (24/9/84), 'Rusholme Ruffians' was played at the majority of that year's remaining concerts, usually segueing into 'This Charming Man' as their first medley.

A permanent fixture of the 1985 *Meat Is Murder* tour and subsequent European and American shows, the track underwent a slight makeover prior to that autumn's Scottish sojourn. Beginning with Marr and Rourke's intro in D-major, the song followed its original chord descent from A to G before sliding abruptly into F# for the first two verses of '(Marie's The Name) His Latest Flame' – the 1961 Pomus/Shuman penned Elvis hit that had been Marr's initial musical foundation for the song – then reverting back to 'Rusholme Ruffians' (as heard on *Rank*). Morrissey would also often perch on the monitor amps at the front of the stage, theatrically hurling himself backwards as he sang of leaping from 'the top of the parachute'.

Introduced at Irvine Magnum Leisure Centre (22/9/85), this latter medley would be revived the following year with Craig Gannon as an encore for their July 1986 UK dates, only to be dropped for most North American shows (save only a handful towards the end). On the final UK tour, it was reinstated yet again, last played at Manchester Free Trade Hall (30/10/86).

Television

A short clip of the band with engineer Stephen Street listening to playback of 'Rusholme Ruffians' in the studio was broadcast as part of BBC2's *Whistle Test* report on the making of *Meat Is Murder* on 12 February 1985 [see 32].

Radio

A basic version (with Joyce's simplified beat) produced by John Porter at BBC Maida Vale Studio 5 on 1 August 1984 for their third Peel session was later issued as the 7-inch B-side to the final single, 'Last Night I Dreamt That Somebody Loved Me', in December 1987.

The live medley of Elvis Presley's '(Marie's The Name) His Latest Flame' with 'Rusholme Ruffians' was also broadcast on BBC Radio 1's *In Concert* on 18 April 1987. Recorded at Kilburn National Ballroom the previous year (23/10/86), an edited account of the gig later became 1988's posthumous live album *Rank*, upon which this same medley appears. The inclusion of 'His Latest Flame' was one of the album's major draws, even though their rendition was an undemanding and purely cursory nod towards Marr's musical foundations for 'Rusholme Ruffians' itself and, more to the point, lasted all of 40 seconds.

34

'Barbarism Begins At Home'

Recorded October-November 1984, Amazon Studios, Liverpool/Ridge Farm Studios, Surrey

Produced by The Smiths

Album track from *Meat Is Murder*, February 1985

The oldest song on *Meat Is Murder* (and, at 6.57, the longest track they ever committed to vinyl), 'Barbarism Begins At Home' was written at the band's Crazy Face rehearsal room in the summer of 1983. 'I came up with the riff the day that Troy Tate came up to Manchester to meet us,' reveals Marr. 'It was almost because our first proper producer was about to arrive that I thought we needed a new song, maybe, and it was a sunny afternoon. We played it in the daytime, which was unusual because there were machinists working downstairs on the floor below, and we wouldn't want to be working stuff out at high volume. There was no drums there, it was just me and Andy jamming like we used to when we were 14 or 15.'

As debuted at London's Electric Ballroom in Camden (19/12/83), the tune was always intended as a six-minute-plus epic, though its earliest incarnation – as bootlegged at that same Camden show – was a meandering, half-baked quagmire of blind improvisation. Missing Marr's solid, overture riff and with Rourke's bass line only a sketchy framework whose dots had yet to be connected, it was a bold addition to their repertoire, if still underdone. Even Morrissey's lyrics took the shape of a freeform, spontaneous bluster; 'a crack in the groin is what you get, because you never asked me' he hollered, 'a crack on the head, a warp of your mind, I've always been such a decent lad!' These, and other impulsive digressions – 'I don't know what came over me today!', 'I am the man to keep you in place' – would be discarded by the time it re-emerged a month later in its finished state during their spring UK tour to promote *The Smiths*.

For Marr and Rourke, 'Barbarism Begins At Home' was essentially a nostalgic throwback to their pre-Smiths days rehearsing with drummer Simon Wolstencroft as the instrumental funk ensemble Freak Party. Consequently, the vibe Marr was aiming for – heavily influenced by the stylised chopping guitar of Chic's Nile Rodgers – was second nature to Rourke, whose resultant bass line has since been nominated as both his greatest contribution to The Smiths' legacy and, moreover, one of the greatest bass lines of all time. If ever there was a case to challenge the Morrissey/Marr composer credit, Rourke's input to 'Barbarism Begins At Home' is surely such a nominee. 'I know a lot of fuss has been made and Andy is, quite rightly, proud of the bass line,' says Marr, 'but, personally, harmonically I don't think that bass line comes anywhere near Andy's other stuff. 'Nowhere Fast', 'That Joke Isn't Funny Anymore', 'The Headmaster Ritual', all tower above it.'

For all Marr's qualms, 'Barbarism Begins At Home' is a staggering achievement. One of The Smiths' most radical departures from their beaten track of white guitar pop into potentially uncharacteristic dance-floor territory, it reveals them to be adaptable chameleons, effortlessly acclimatising to its funk parameters. As a direct commentary on corporal punishment, Morrissey's dour remarks on parental discipline (taking the form of a repetitive, hypnotic nursery rhyme) helped enforce the album's unifying themes of institutionalised brutality and mankind's predilection for violence of one form or another (ditto the sadism of 'The Headmaster Ritual', the stabbing in 'Rusholme Ruffians', the murder of a policeman in 'I Want The One I Can't Have' and the final bloodletting of 'Meat Is Murder' itself). Speaking to the *NME* after the album's release, Morrissey admitted there was a degree of role play within 'Barbarism Begins At Home'; '[It's] not from my experience really. It was simply another recognition that the only channel of communication open to a lot of parents is violence.' His lyrics also contained another likely (and by this stage, increasingly predictable) connection with Shelagh Delaney's *A Taste of Honey*, in which Geoff exclaims to Jo 'you want taking in hand' (Act II:1).

With its potentially controversial subject, emphasised by the resonant smacks overdubbed during its yodelling choruses, it was mildly surprising that 'Barbarism Begins At Home' was very nearly The Smiths' sixth UK single instead of 'How Soon Is Now?' Its vicious lyrics notwithstanding, the song's contagious rhythm, alluring bass and Morrissey's unusual, high-pitched screams would have probably set it in good stead had it actually been released commercially (as opposed to the promotional 12-inch issued in February 1985 for radio only).

Ironically, the song's biggest critic is the Smiths guitarist himself. 'To me it was one of those things where it was a good idea at the time,' confesses Marr, 'but later, as we played it, I didn't think it really represented the band. The overall thing, all of it, was a little bit corny.'

In Concert

As described above, a primitive version of 'Barbarism Begins At Home' was introduced at London's Electric Ballroom (19/12/83) before being smartened up prior to the spring 1984 UK tour to promote *The Smiths*. The song remained in the set for the rest of the year, despite its continued absence on record. When finally released, 'Barbarism Begins At Home' became a regular encore of the 1985 *Meat Is Murder* tour itself.

Left out of the set for their only Italian concert in Rome that summer, it was momentarily reinstated for their two Spanish gigs in Barcelona and Madrid before being cut from the first week of their ensuing American dates. By popular demand, it returned as a final encore halfway through the same US tour, often spun out into an epic ad-libbed funk jam in excess of ten minutes. Its last ever performance at the Laguna Hills Irving Meadows Amphitheater (29/6/85) stretched to an incredible 15-minute curtain-closing marathon.

Perhaps its strangest live rendition was that performed at London's Royal Albert Hall a few months earlier (6/4/85), where Morrissey was joined on stage by Pete Burns to sing 'Barbarism Begins At Home' as a duet. At the time, Burns was basking in the success of his band Dead Or Alive's recent UK number one 'You Spin Me Round (Like A Record)', a stylised hunk of programmed populist disco-fodder produced by Stock, Aitken and Waterman, which Morrissey subsequently declared 'a hallmark of British music, it will never date' (even though he would later slur the same production team as 'Stock, Face-ache and Waterbed').

Indeed Morrissey had been singing Burns' praises in the press for several months prior to their Albert Hall duet. After the event, the Smiths frontman would hint that he and Burns might perhaps record together, since 'making a record with Pete would be great fun because it's always hysterically funny to be around him.' Yet as with many of his high-profile celebrity friendships, Morrissey's dalliance with Burns soured in the wake of a *Smash Hits* cover feature in October 1985, in which they were interviewed together as part of a tongue-in-cheek stitch-up. 'They made us look like a couple of dippy queens,' he later complained.[70]

Television

Nearly a year before its release on *Meat Is Murder*, 'Barbarism Begins At Home' was played live in the studio of Channel 4's *The Tube* on 16 March 1984. Still being broken in on the debut album tour, without so much as an accompanying on-screen caption this funky new six-minute epic would have been unfamiliar to fans watching at home.

The last of three numbers (following 'Hand In Glove' and 'Still Ill'), Andy Rourke was on top form, his vigorous fretwork visibly propelling the song's rhythm. Sliding across the stage with his jumper tied around his waist, Marr's fluid jangling gathered to a manic plectrum-grinding crescendo, culminating in both he and Morrissey dancing around one another in air-punching, arm-flailing harmony. This divine, ritualistic fandango of

70 Burns has since claimed he and Morrissey fell out because 'I bought a fur coat and he blew up.'

wordsmith and composer twisting together in pure poetic motion was already a familiar sight in concert, with Marr often putting down his guitar altogether so he was free to gyrate as he pleased (as seen on the version from their Paris El Dorado concert in May 1984, filmed for French TV's *Les Enfants Du Rock*).

Mike Joyce, however, would remember this *Tube* performance for less constructive reasons, noticeably fluffing a drum fill near the song's finish. 'Even my mum, who was in her sixties at the time, recognised that I'd cocked up,' laughs Joyce, 'so I knew if she sussed I had then everybody else watching must have.' A year later, this same *Tube* clip was repeated during an interview with Morrissey to promote *Meat Is Murder* on ITV's *Studio One* in May 1985 [see 37].

Radio

A live version of 'Barbarism Begins At Home' recorded at the Oxford Apollo (18/3/85) was broadcast by BBC Radio 1 on Janice Long's *Evening Show*, 9 May 1985.

35

'That Joke Isn't Funny Anymore'

Recorded **October-November 1984, Amazon Studios, Liverpool/Ridge Farm Studios, Surrey**
Produced by **The Smiths**
Album track from ***Meat Is Murder*, February 1985**
Subsequently issued as a **Single A-side, July 1985 (Highest UK Chart Placing #49)**

Often cited by Johnny Marr as one of his favourite Smiths tracks and the focal point of *Meat Is Murder* for many critics, like 'What She Said' the august 'That Joke Isn't Funny Anymore' had come together during the sound-checks of their Gloucester, Cardiff and Swansea gigs the previous month when Marr, Rourke and Joyce had busked a rough arrangement of its main verse structure. By the time they arrived at Amazon, Marr had honed this sophistically minimal semi-waltz foundation into a monolithic ballad of tender yet imposing grace; a score of unreserved, raw beauty that Morrissey dutifully complemented with one of his frankest lyrics to date.

In a revealing character-study of The Smiths' frontman for *Uncut* in 1998, Dave Simpson inferred that the song was inspired by an 'intimate friendship with a journalist around 1984-5' who nowadays 'steadfastedly refuses to talk about Morrissey.' It was certainly true that a select group of journalists, such as *i-D*'s Jim Shelley (who was personally thanked in the sleeve notes of their debut album), were closer to The Smiths' camp than others. Even at the time of its release, the singer divulged to *Melody Maker* that it was, indeed, a direct response to journalistic cynicism and The Smiths backlash that had been gathering pace throughout 1984 ('this contest of wit, trying to drag me down and prove that I was a complete fake'). Conversely, the sketchy details of a sexual liaison in a parked car on 'cold leather seats' read like a sober sequel to the whimsical flirtation begun in 'This Charming Man'. Additionally, its final disclosure adapted from a similar line in the 1935 Katharine Hepburn movie *Alice Adams.*[71] ('I've watched this happen in other people's lives and now it's [happening in mine]') surely ranks as one of the most heart-rending vocal passages Morrissey has ever recorded.

Technically, its climactic deluge of cooing guitar streams soaked in reverse-reverb, cardiac drum rumbles (Joyce's best performance on a Smiths track up to that point) and compound vocal howls was a remarkable feat of production for their first turn behind the mixing console. The false fade-out at 3.50, a playful homage to the ending of Elvis Presley's 'Suspicious Minds', was another inspired twist suggested by engineer Stephen Street. 'We loved the fade on it,' he explains, 'as it felt like it had to disappear at a certain point. But I said to Johnny "it would be really nice if it could come back in again because it's just really majestic." So we did, but to get it that length we had to fade it out, spin back the tapes and then fade it back up because the original take wasn't quite long enough.'

As an album track, 'That Joke Isn't Funny Anymore' was *Meat Is Murder*'s pivotal emotional set piece. Consequently, the decision to belatedly release it as the album's sole spin-off single in the summer of 1985 was a dubious move, on a par with their previous fidgety reissuing of 'How Soon Is Now?' as an A-side that January. For the second time that year, The Smiths' discography had gone askew. Their failure to act upon the album's contents at the time cost them dearly; Morrissey had moaned prior to the release of 'Shakespeare's Sister' that 'I feel quite edgy because something from the LP should be released because I think they're too good to be buried.' Danny Kelly's optimistic forecast in the *NME* that it was the most likely track off *Meat Is Murder* to be played on daytime Radio 1 proved very much mistaken. The single bombed, barely scraping the Top 50, hampered by the absence of

71 Directed by George Stevens, *Alice Adams* is a light, Depression-era romantic drama set in small-town America about a poor girl who attempts to impress the rich socialite she's fallen in love with. The film has dated extremely badly in its detrimental racial stereotyping and is rarely screened on terrestrial UK television. The line comes at the very end of the film. Fred Stone (Hepburn's on-screen father) remarks 'I've seen this happen in other people's lives and now it's happening in ours.'

new B-sides (save some interesting but unessential live tracks), a severe lack of promotional activity and the 7-inch being chopped to lose its cherished false-fade (as included on 1987's *The World Won't Listen* compilation). Undoubtedly one of Morrissey and Marr's finest songs, as a pop single, 'That Joke Isn't Funny Anymore' was a lost cause.

In Concert

First performed at Chippenham Golddiggers (27/2/85) on the opening night of the *Meat Is Murder* tour, 'That Joke Isn't Funny Anymore' remained an integral part of The Smiths' live set for all of 1985 and the majority of 1986. Audibly lean with just one guitar, it improved with the addition of Craig Gannon, freeing Marr to reproduce the record's haunting slide coda. On the October UK *The Queen Is Dead* tour itself, the song was played on the first night at Carlisle Sands Centre (13/10/86), but dropped from thereon until Manchester Free Trade Hall two weeks later (30/10/86), their homecoming finale, where it was last performed.

Television

A short clip of Andy Rourke miming his bass part in the studio was also included on BBC2's *Whistle Test* report on the making of the *Meat Is Murder* album screened on 12 February 1985 **[see 32]**.

To coincide with its release as the summer single, The Smiths were due to perform the song on BBC1's *Wogan* on Friday 19 July 1985. The thrice-weekly prime-time chat show would have been tremendous exposure that 'That Joke Isn't Funny Anymore' desperately needed, having charted the previous week at a lowly number 49. While Marr, Joyce and Rourke obediently turned up for rehearsal at BBC's Shepherds Bush theatre that afternoon, Morrissey was a no-show having decided at the eleventh hour that *Wogan* was a mainstream compromise they didn't need. Without their singer, the band made their apologies and cancelled their scheduled appearance. The following week, the single dropped to number 70.

Radio

Recorded at the Oxford Apollo (18/3/85), a live take of 'That Joke Isn't Funny Anymore' was broadcast by BBC Radio 1 on Janice Long's *Evening Show* on 9 May 1985.

36

'I Want The One I Can't Have'

Recorded **October-November 1984, Amazon Studios, Liverpool/Ridge Farm Studios, Surrey**
Produced by **The Smiths**
Album track from ***Meat Is Murder*, February 1985**

Surprisingly for such an accomplished track, 'I Want The One I Can't Have' came together during the *Meat Is Murder* sessions as the result of an extemporaneous jam (though admittedly it bore some of the melodic tics Marr had been grappling with in their earlier 'Fast One' instrumental demo **[see 28]**).

Returning to the theme of the brain versus the body first eulogised within 'Still Ill', Morrissey's verses leap from a cynical itinerary of working class material expectations ('a double bed and a stalwart lover') to perverse awe of a teenage murderer, concluding with a flashback to another early song, 'These Things Take Time', with the invitation of sexual shenanigans in the shadow of a rail yard. The mythical 'tough kid who sometimes swallows nails' would become a recurring motif in later works such as 'The Queen Is Dead' (with its 'nine-year-old tough') and 'Sweet And Tender Hooligan'. Its original take also saw Morrissey's juvenile rogue commit matricide instead of slaying a policeman ('He killed his mother when he was thirteen').

'The riches of the poor' was a phrase probably appropriated from Edith Sitwell's *English Eccentrics*, which Morrissey had already used in a previous interview with *The Face* about his days subsisting on the DHSS **[see 17]**.[72] Later, he clarified the lyric to the *NME*, shortly before the album's release: 'That came from a sense I had that, trite as it may sound, when people get married and are getting their flat – not even their house, note – the most important thing was getting the double bed. It was like the prized exhibit; the cooker, the fire, everything else came later. In the lives of many working class people the only time they feel they're the centre of attention is on their wedding day. Getting married, regrettably is still the one big event in their lives. It's the one day when they're quite special.'

Marr's crisp, multiple overdubs were among his most flamboyant on the whole album, while Joyce's beat – an ebullient, up-tempo strike – instilled a blithe velocity worthy of an A-side. Indeed, Morrissey took it upon himself

72 Found within Sitwell's chapter on 'Quacks and Alchemists', the quote is actually attributed to an 'illustrious Spanish doctor' called Don Lupus: 'O Health, Health, the blessing of the Rich, the Riches of the poor.' Cecil Beaton's portrait of Sitwell featured on the Seventies Penguin paperback edition of *English Eccentrics* was later used by Morrissey as a stage backdrop on his 1991 *Kill Uncle* tour.

to announce it on their tour of Ireland that winter (their first live dates after recording *Meat Is Murder*) as 'our next single'. Of all the candidates rumoured to be in the running for their sixth 45 (the others being 'Nowhere Fast' and 'Barbarism Begins At Home'), 'I Want The One I Can't Have' was easily the strongest. Controversial enough to antagonise the pop establishment without being banned, its spirited melody and bristling rhythm would have made it a bankable Top 20 contender. That it lost out to the reissued 'How Soon Is Now?' was, in retrospect, a grave error – doubly so as five months after the album's release it was again foolishly passed over as an A-side in favour of 'That Joke Isn't Funny Anymore'. Their missed opportunity was bitterly highlighted in the summer of 1986 when Hull band The Housemartins enjoyed a UK top three hit with 'Happy Hour', a tune Marr criticised as a lazy 'I Want The One I Can't Have' rip-off.

In Concert

Introduced along with 'What She Said' at the Waterford Savoy (11/11/84), 'I Want The One I Can't Have' became one of the most prevalent standards of their concert career, rarely absent from Smiths gigs henceforth. Usually slotted early on in the set, it was last played at the London Palladium (26/10/86).

Television

A brief segment featuring Mike Joyce pretending to record a bongo part for 'I Want The One I Can't Have' was broadcast on BBC2's *Whistle Test* report on the making of *Meat Is Murder* screened 12 February 1985 **[see 32]**.

37

'Meat Is Murder'

Recorded **October-November 1984, Amazon Studios, Liverpool/Ridge Farm Studios, Surrey**

Produced by **The Smiths**

Album track from ***Meat Is Murder*****, February 1985**

Closing the second album, its sepulchral title track saw The Smiths venture away from their established catalogue of lovelorn existential angst and Delaney-esque sketches of working-class dilemmas into socio-political, dogmatic mission statements. Although its sensationalist sloganeering would set a precedent for later works ('The Queen Is Dead', 'Shoplifters Of The World Unite'), 'Meat Is Murder' remains unlike anything else within The Smiths' repertoire; not so much a song as a manifesto.

Those unsympathetic to the cause of vegetarianism – carnivorous Smiths fans included – have dismissed it as histrionic melodrama; its unsubtle employment of mooing cows and fabricated abattoir machinery over-egging the pudding to the point of comical overkill. Such borderline kitsch production theatrics, however extreme, were merely in keeping with the album as a whole, rife with symbolic musical metaphors and random sound effects (eg the till at the end of 'Rusholme Ruffians', the helicopter-blade fade in on 'I Want The One I Can't Have'). 'Meat Is Murder' actually benefits from these vivid decorations, turning a gloomy-bordering-on-dreary protest song into an electrifying, sonic experiment that tested the limits of their collective invention.

Stephen Street savoured the challenge to make the grazing cows, sourced from one of Morrissey's BBC sound effects LPs, sound as if they were in a slaughterhouse. After much trial and error, he gathered random mechanical noises – from revving engines to closing doors – and filtered them through a harmoniser, before drenching them in reverb until they sounded suitably abattoir-like. The animals' impending horror was amplified by Marr's sporadic piano tremors, which Street transformed using one of his favourite tricks of the trade, the reverse echo. This effect, used in many of Street's Smiths recordings, was achieved by turning the master tape reels over and adding reverb to the necessary instruments as the music ran backwards. When the tape was then flipped back over the right way round, the echo would precede the affected note, or beat, to create a slow fade in with an abrupt climax. 'Meat Is Murder' utilises this technique with tremendous cunning, its distressing piano groans acting as the ideal precursor to its plodding, minor-key dirge. 'That was a riff I'd been playing around with for a few days before,' says Marr. 'Really nasty, in open D. I didn't know the lyrics but I knew the song was gonna be called 'Meat Is Murder' so it just all came together in the take.'

As a fan of Melanie, it's not beyond reason to ponder whether Morrissey drew some scrap of influence from her quirky 1970 protest song 'I Don't Eat Animals' ('I don't eat animals 'cos I love 'em you see, I don't eat animals, I want nuthin' dead in me'). However, where Melanie is derisively whimsical, Morrissey is far graver in articulating his vegetarian beliefs, exploiting every available lyrical device: aggressive propagandising ('do you know how animals die?'), emotional blackmail ('this beautiful creature must die'), sharp alliteration ('fancifully fry') and impassioned metaphors ('screaming knife'). His intention, to convey a direct statement about meat being directly connected to the slaughter of animals as opposed to a benign food product that simply appears on the dinner plate with no moral liability, is wholly realised. Morrissey's chorus vocal is made all the more disquieting thanks to Street's subtle application of the harmoniser once more; though barely audible, this comical 'chipmunk' effect would be given more prominence on 'Bigmouth Strikes Again' recorded the following autumn **[see 46]**.

At the end of the album sessions, The Smiths' mandatory group meal provoked an amicable debate about the vegetarian issue. As a direct result – of both the song's lyrics and Morrissey's persuasive line of reasoning at that meal – Mike Joyce became a vegetarian though, like Marr, drew the line at fish for the time being (tuna sandwiches were the staple of the guitarist's rider even though pre-gig nerves meant they were more often than not vomited back up before taking the stage). Rourke also feigned allegiance to the veggie cause, though admits that after 18 months he was at breaking point, eventually sneaking out for surreptitious steaks with members of their road crew exasperated by Morrissey's strict catering regime of bland boiled potatoes and broccoli; apart from abstaining from meat and fish, Morrissey was also notoriously hostile to garlic, onions and any form of spice or flavouring.

Understandably, the subject dominated the majority of interviews given circa the album's release in February 1985. By far one of the most amusing was their first *Smash Hits* cover story of the new year, in which Morrissey grappled with the mordant wit of the brilliantly eccentric Tom Hibbert. Having admitted to a 'bacon fetish' in his carnivorous past, Morrissey also gave his support to extremist animal welfare groups such as the Animal Liberation Front, currently in the news for a hoax Mars bar scare in which they claimed to have injected an unknown percentage of the confectionery with mercury. Combined with his anti-royalist statements and implicit support for the IRA's Brighton bombing, his hearty championing of the ALF was yet another fearless feather in Morrissey's cap of controversy.

In Concert

Debuted on the first night of the *Meat Is Murder* tour at Chippenham Golddiggers (27/2/85), the anthemic title track was usually reserved for the second or third last song of the evening, with its disturbing slaughterhouse sound effects recreated using backing tapes. Marr would climactically grind his guitar in surround-sound delay, while it was usually left to Mike Joyce to bring the song to a stand still with a galley-slave tom-smacking finish.

Morrissey would often make a point of highlighting the song's message by reminding carnivores in the audience of their folly: 'Every time you bite into a fat juicy sausage, remember it's somebody's mother!' Ironic, then, that during this same tour he was once infamously struck in the face with a string of sausages – each one inscribed with the album title – by a severely misguided fan. 'They hurled it so accurately,' he told the *NME*, 'that I actually bit into it in the action of singing the word "murder". I thought at first that it was something else, something extreme.'

Played for the duration of 1985, it became an unlikely set opener for the latter half of their American sojourn in June and again at Inverness Eden Court Theatre (1/10/85), the closing night of their Scottish mini tour. By the summer of 1986, 'Meat Is Murder' was conspicuously absent from their July UK and Canadian dates before returning to the set after the first week of the North American leg (Washington Smith Center 8/8/86 onwards), where it remained until their penultimate concert at Manchester Free Trade Hall (30/10/86).

Television

A specially made video for 'Meat Is Murder', featuring stock news footage juxtaposing grazing cattle with graphic scenes of butchered carcasses inside an abattoir, was screened on ITV's *Studio One* on 24 May 1985 during a lengthy interview with Morrissey to promote the album.[73] Speaking to host Muriel Gray about vegetarianism, The Smiths' image and his own acidic tongue, Morrissey was also treated to a zodiacal prediction about his destiny as a 'flag-bearer for future values' by the show's resident astrologer.

A brief excerpt of 'Meat Is Murder' live on stage at Glasgow Barrowlands (25/9/85) was also included as part of a special report on The Smiths' Scottish tour broadcast on Channel 4's *The Tube* on 25 October 1985.

Radio

A typically intense live rendition from the Oxford Apollo (18/3/85) was aired by BBC Radio 1 on Janice Long's *Evening Show* in May 1985. Originally, The Smiths planned to issue a live 12-inch EP sourced from this broadcast with 'Meat Is Murder' as the lead track, backed with 'William, It Was Really Nothing', 'Nowhere Fast', 'Stretch Out And Wait' and 'Miserable Lie'. Though white labels were pressed, the proposed *Meat Is Murder* EP was shelved. Instead, four tracks from the BBC Oxford Apollo gig were issued in Europe on the reverse of a Dutch 12-inch of 'The Headmaster Ritual'. In July 1985 the same format was repeated in the UK substituting 'That Joke Isn't Funny Anymore' as the A-side. The Oxford Apollo recording of 'Meat Is Murder' was featured on both 7- and 12-inch formats of the latter.

73 The same clip was also incorporated into ITV's posthumous *South Bank Show* documentary in October 1987.

38

'I Misses You'

Recorded **December 1984, 'Fallout Shelter' (Island Studios), London**

Studio out-take

With the bulk of *Meat Is Murder* laid down at Amazon, in early November The Smiths moved to Ridge Farm studios in Surrey to add further overdubs prior to a short tour of Ireland. In the meantime, Rough Trade released *Hatful Of Hollow* – the magnificent, budget-priced interim compilation of BBC sessions, B-sides and non-album singles that gave them a second UK Top 10 album that winter.

After their last show of the year in Paris on 1 December (not for the first time further European dates were brusquely cancelled), they returned to London to fine-tune *Meat Is Murder*'s final mix with Stephen Street at Island Studios' subterranean 'Fallout Shelter' (it was here that The Smiths were filmed by BBC's *Whistle Test* pretending to record the album for the benefit of the cameras **[see 32]**).

As ever, the economically conscious Marr found time to rehearse a couple of instrumental ideas with Rourke and Joyce for future reference. The first was a long, lumbering dry run of the 'Never Had No One Ever' riff **[see 48]**. The second is much more intriguing, not least because, according to the studio master reels, it was given a working title – 'I Misses You' – which would suggest that Morrissey may have had a lyric in mind. 'I remember the title,' says Marr, 'but it would've bitten the dust if I didn't follow it up.'

Vaguely reminiscent of the bright, jangling flightiness of 'The Boy With The Thorn In His Side', the tune also contained passing chord changes and motifs similar to those later employed on 'Unloveable'. What's most interesting, though, about these recordings is that they illustrate Marr's admirable prescience. Before *Meat Is Murder* is even released, here he is in December 1984 already developing the body of work that will form the next Smiths album, *The Queen Is Dead*.

Part 3

'... *Take me anywhere, drop me anywhere...*'

Recordings 1985

By the time *Meat Is Murder* was released in February 1985, The Smiths had decamped from their various London residences and returned to their native Manchester. First to flit back North was Morrissey, who bought a house in what the *NME* later lampooned as 'the Cheshire stockbroker belt'. Marr, Rourke and Joyce were only too happy to find an excuse to travel back home and soon followed suit.

Meat Is Murder itself was a phenomenal achievement, annulling its predecessor's shortcomings with transcendent poise. The Smiths' only number one studio album (displacing Bruce Springsteen's *Born in the USA*), it's easily their most vivacious; bursting with bright ideas, frisky experimentation and a discernable sense of author satisfaction. 'It just wasn't what people expected,' asserts Stephen Street. 'Good as the first album was, it was pretty traditional, whereas on *Meat Is Murder* Johnny and Morrissey were free to be more creative, bringing in elements of studio trickery. There's a real joy of the whole band working together on that album, which definitely comes through.'

Critically lauded, it was even hyperbolically hailed by one reviewer as The Smiths' equivalent of The Beatles' *Sgt Pepper* – an exceptional feat for a second LP. The album where they finally walked it like they talked it, there are enough flickers of genius in its nine tracks to validate a convincing argument that *Meat Is Murder* is not only The Smiths' most musically diverse long player – a metamorphic kaleidoscope of pop, rockabilly, funk, folk and metal – but their most accomplished.

Unfortunately, 1985 turned out to be a far more difficult year for The Smiths than they had imagined, as they struggled to maintain their UK singles profile in the face of renewed contractual quarrels and lack of proper management. Still, if only for the time being, the considerable chaos without The Smiths did little to encumber the art within.

39

'Shakespeare's Sister'

Recorded **January 1985, Ridge Farm, Surrey**
Produced by **The Smiths**
Single A-side, March 1985 (Highest UK Chart Placing #26)

After spending Christmas of 1984 in Manchester, The Smiths returned to the studio in the first week of January with Stephen Street. The very morning they were due to travel south, back to Ridge Farm in Surrey, Morrissey called round Marr's house. 'We were getting ready to leave,' says Marr, 'when I said to him "check this out" and played this thing, this guitar figure that I was flipping over at the time.' Morrissey was equally taken with the tune, inspired by a classic R&B riff from The Rolling Stones' '19th Nervous Breakdown' ('It's also in Bo Diddley's 'Diddley Daddy' and Chuck Berry's 'You Can't Catch Me',' says Marr, 'I was obsessed with it'). By the time they arrived at the studio several hours later, Marr's sketch had fully blossomed into the finished 'Shakespeare's Sister'.

'I also saw it as my chance to get some of the ghost of Johnny Cash into one of our tunes,' adds Marr. 'I loved it. To me it had everything, those Stones echoes, exactly the feeling of 'Have You Seen Your Mother Baby?'. Quite audacious and a little bit satanic. There was some weird stuff in there.' Driven by a boogie-woogie piano vamp and unusually short of the three-minute norm, as Marr acknowledges 'Shakespeare's Sister' is very much The Smiths' equivalent of The Rolling Stones' 1966 single 'Have You Seen Your Mother Baby, Standing In The Shadow?' It was also no accident that its composition coincided with Marr's gradual image transformation – in dress, haircut and even stage poses – all clearly indebted to mid-Sixties Keith Richards.

Lyrically, it represented something of an overspill from Morrissey's *Meat Is Murder* cycle, with yet more citations from Elizabeth Smart's *By Grand Central Station I Sat Down and Wept.*[74] Indeed the song's scenario – a theatrical deliberation on suicide – seemed directly inspired by the predicament outlined in Smart's novella. However, the title was actually an extremely clever lateral reference to Virginia Woolf's 1928 feminist thesis *A Room of One's Own,* in which she argues that if Shakespeare had had a sister who was every bit his creative equal, her sex would have denied her the privilege of his education. As a woman, presupposes Woolf, she would also never have been allowed to enter the theatre, but instead would end up abused,

74 Namely: 'the rocks below could promise certain death', 'our bones groaned', 'I am going to meet my lover'.

exploited and ridiculed for sharing her brother's ambition. To that end, Shakespeare's sister would have been driven to end her misery by committing suicide.

Morrissey had told Ireland's *Hot Press* the previous year that he himself had felt close to taking his own life on a number of occasions: 'People who have never been close to it cannot hope to understand it, and the idea that it was illegal until recent years is of course laughable. But I think to me it's quite honourable in a way, because it's a person taking total control over their lives and their bodies.' A recurring theme in his lyrical tenet, Morrissey would treat suicide both with solemn reverence ('Asleep', 'There Is A Light That Never Goes Out') or – as in the case of 'Shakespeare's Sister' and the casual 'Death At One's Elbow' – inflated comedy.

Another likely muse is an obscure 1962 Billy Fury B-side, 'Don't Jump'. 'I was standing at the edge of a cliff top high above and I was looking right down below' sings Fury, stricken with depression having just been jilted. Ethereal voices summon him to hurl himself where 'the sea rushes in around the rugged rocks', though ultimately he manages to repel his fatal urges. Morrissey's predicament in 'Shakespeare's Sister' is one and the same. Like Fury's morbid 'death disc', as he sings of the rocks below beckoning 'throw your skinny body down, son' one senses Morrissey's tongue very much planted in the side of his cheek. Its final verse, in which he muses on his failed attempt as a protest singer ('I can laugh about it now but at the time it was terrible') seems to dismiss these same suicidal howls as a mere passing teenage whim.

Originally, the song opened with a startling guitar prologue – hazily reminiscent of Buddy Holly's 'That'll Be The Day' intro – which, had it not been edited out, would have ranked as a nimble feat of plectrum perfection to rival Marr's equally stunning foreword to 'Girl Afraid'. The section was later cut, opening instead with a highlighted slide-guitar quiver. As on 'Oscillate Wildly', cut at the same session **[see 40]**, Rourke was encouraged to add a cello part (though its middle eight, which originally featured a much more prominent cello line, was barely audible on the finished record). Joyce was also audibly revitalised after the *Meat Is Murder* sessions, delivering a furious rhythm that added further grist to the track's rockabilly mill. Marr later enthused that it possessed 'one of the best rhythm patterns and grooves I have ever heard.' Speaking about the record to *Melody Maker*, in the same breath he also made a point of praising their rhythm section's contribution; 'If Elvis Presley had had Mike Joyce and Andy Rourke in his band he would have been an even bigger name. I'm sure of it.'

Stephen Street wasn't nearly so convinced. 'I remember it coming out and I remember cringing thinking "god, I really could have mixed this one better". It just didn't sound right and I wasn't surprised when radio didn't take to it.' Journalist Nick Kent, who attended the song's mixdown at Utopia studios, was one of many who blamed its production, describing the finished record as 'an abomination of the song's potential' According to Kent, 'it was a sobering example of the hopeless impracticalities of 'group democracy'. Each member had his finger on the level adjustment dial pertaining to his particular instrument.'

During his time shadowing the band for *The Face,* Kent became privy to some shocking revelations about their private lives. Although both Morrissey and Marr would scold Kent's article when published in May 1985 (a revealing investigation of The Smiths' roots that unearthed a couple of skeletons Morrissey in particular would have preferred to have kept in his closet), he was honourable enough to reserve the most damaging information – his discovery that Andy Rourke had a heroin problem – until another article for the same magazine two years later (by which time, Rourke's plight had since become public knowledge). According to Kent, while completing 'Shakespeare's Sister', Marr had confided in him that 'things are bloody horrendous at the minute. Morrissey's just found out about Andy and he's going frantic demanding he leave the group. And I'm in the middle trying to hold everything together.'

'Nick Kent was right what he said about that,' confesses Marr, 'he came down to interview us and saw a lot of what was going on. He was sort of perched on our shoulders the whole time, like something out of Edgar Allen Poe.' Kent was also witness to the stresses of being manager-less, as 'Rough Trade employees kept collaring members in order to get their signatures on numerous documents – bills, dockets, and pieces of paper with the odd five zero figure on them.' By the end of the year, the pressure that Kent glimpsed during just one mixing session would snowball out of control and threaten to crack The Smiths completely.

Released in March, 'Shakespeare's Sister' was sadly shunned by radio (Morrissey was convinced this was on account of a derogatory remark about the BPI awards that resulted in an unofficial blacklisting) and only just scraped into the Top 30. For the first time since 'This Charming Man', the band were denied the opportunity to promote their new single on *Top of the Pops*. Its failure would be a major turning point in their relationship with their label. '[They] released the record with a monstrous amount of defeatism,' Morrissey would fume to the *NME* 'They had no faith in it whatsoever. They liked it but they allowed it to dribble, to stall. They didn't service it or market it in any way.'

'It was the beginning of the end with Rough Trade as far as Morrissey was concerned,' confirms Street. 'He felt that every record of theirs deserved to be in the Top 10. He wasn't amused that radio didn't go for it.' Admittedly, Rough Trade's promotional machine left a lot to be desired. One need only scour the pages of the music weeklies during The Smiths' first 18-month ascension for evidence to uphold Morrissey's claim that, compared to their less prominent, less prolific peers, full-page press ads for Smiths product were virtually non-existent. 'The subject of flyposting wasn't broached till The Smiths' ninth single,' he mourned to Kent five years later, long after the group had split. 'Nothing was utilised and Rough Trade are largely to blame.'

Its chart disappointment and the apathy of Geoff Travis aside, its authors were justly satisfied with the finished record. 'Regardless of what many people feel,' said Morrissey, '['Shakespeare's Sister'] was the song of my life. I put everything into that song and I wanted it more than anything else to be a huge success and – as it happens – it wasn't.' Even so, a Top 30 single in a month dominated by Phil Collins, Madonna and the archaic West End warbles of Elaine Paige and Barbara Dickson that romanticised teenage suicide to a fittingly torrid two-minute rockabilly fanfare was a triumph of pop audacity that, in March 1985, only they alone could have gotten away with. Unfairly tarred by rock historians as the runt of The Smiths' single litter, 'Shakespeare's Sister' is their unsung masterwork.

In Concert

Debuted at Chippenham Golddiggers on the first night of the *Meat Is Murder* tour (27/2/85), 'Shakespeare's Sister' would be performed at every concert in 1985, providing the set opener for both the autumn Scottish tour (except Inverness 1/10/85) and their first few dates of 1986.

Still in the set of that summer's UK and Canadian dates, 'Shakespeare's Sister' was played only twice during the North American leg and dropped altogether from the first half of the final UK tour of October '86. Reinstated at Kilburn National Ballroom (23/10/86), it stayed for the following night at Brixton Academy before its last outing at the London Palladium (26/10/86). Even with two guitars, without its driving piano boogie the live translation of 'Shakespeare's Sister' never lived up to the record, even if its energetic torrent allowed Joyce adequate space to drum up a storm.

Television

A month before its release as a single (with even its predecessor 'How Soon Is Now?' still climbing the charts) The Smiths insisted on giving 'Shakespeare's Sister' a premature debut on BBC2's *Oxford Road Show* on 22 February 1985. The first of two mimed performances (alongside 'The Headmaster Ritual' **[see 29]**), Morrissey seemed to have finally shed the flower-waving foppishness of the previous year by appearing in a plain black blazer and white open shirt. Marr, once again, looked a model Keith Richards clone in the same denims worn the week before on their *Top of the Pops* 'How Soon Is Now?' performance (14/2/85). It was a brilliant demonstration of hammy gesticulation on Morrissey's part; dropping to his knees, pleading to heaven during the 'mama let me go' choruses and rocking on his haunches in melodramatic suicidal pretence.

A sound-check of 'Shakespeare's Sister' at Glasgow Barrowlands (25/9/85) interrupted mid-song by Margi Clarke was also shown as part of *The Tube*'s report on The Smiths' Scottish tour broadcast in October 1985.

Radio

Introduced by Morrissey as a song 'about the greatest woman that ever lived', a live take of 'Shakespeare's Sister' recorded at the Oxford Apollo (18/3/85) was first broadcast by BBC Radio 1 on Janice Long's *Evening Show* in May 1985, before being officially released by Rough Trade on the 12-inch B-side of 'That Joke Isn't Funny Anymore' that July.

40

'Oscillate Wildly'

Recorded January 1985, Ridge Farm, Surrey

Produced by The Smiths

B-side to 'How Soon Is Now?' (12-inch format only), February 1985

Alongside 'Shakespeare's Sister', the Ridge Farm session would also result in their first 'proper' instrumental, based upon a piano riff Marr had worked out on 'a crappy old upright' he'd recently inherited when moving into his new home. 'We did it really quickly in just one evening,' says Marr, 'but it came together so beautifully.' Christened 'Oscillate Wildly' by Morrissey (an impish pun on his literary hero Oscar Wilde), the track was subsequently mixed down back in London prior to its imminent release on their next 12-inch.

Apparently, Geoff Travis requested that Morrissey try and write an accompanying lyric, only to be informed by the singer that it was strong enough to stand up on its own. Morrissey told the *NME* after their split that all along, the concept was his idea; 'I suggested that 'Oscillate Wildly' should be an instrumental; up until that point Johnny had very little interest in non-vocal tracks. There was never any political heave-hoing about should we/shouldn't we have an instrumental and it was never a battle of powers between Johnny and myself. The very assumption that a Smiths instrumental track left

Morrissey upstairs in his bedroom stamping his feet and kicking the furniture was untrue! I totally approved but, obviously, I didn't physically contribute.'

'That's absolutely right,' verifies Marr. 'There was never any plan for it to have lyrics. It was always going to be an instrumental and Morrissey encouraged me all the way.' Like 'Shakespeare's Sister', 'Oscillate Wildly' saw Rourke try his hand at cello after Morrissey expressed a desire to introduce strings of some kind or another (their first use of the instrument since 'Pretty Girls Make Graves' with Audrey Riley **[see 5]**). Budget restrictions aside, the orchestral grandeur that Marr's haunting melody required posed something of a problem in the studio. 'Morrissey was very, very reluctant to use synthesizers or anything electronic,' explains Street. 'The only way Johnny and I could get around that was by trapping guitar notes into these extended infinite reverbs that would hold for a long, long time then use the fader to bring it in at the right moment. It sounds like a string-type effect but really it's just guitar notes. That's the way 'Oscillate Wildly' was built up. Johnny was still working with guitars but we were trying to stretch the possibilities and sounds of what we could do with it.'

Their first track to use piano as the lead instrument, its sonic texture of guitar, cello, faux-string surges and synthetic woodwind (their one concession to electronic invention, concocted on an Emulator keyboard) would be another turning point for Marr, one which he'd hone to perfection during the *The Queen Is Dead* sessions later that year (notably 'There Is A Light That Never Goes Out').

In Concert

Their only instrumental not to be performed live (though it would make it as far as being sound-checked on their 1986 US tour), 'Oscillate Wildly' would instead be included on their pre-gig interval tapes during 1985.

41

'Stretch Out And Wait'

Recorded January 1985, Utopia Studios, London

Produced by The Smiths

B-side to 'Shakespeare's Sister' (12-inch format only), March 1985

Alternate version later released on *The World Won't Listen* compilation, March 1987

Having chosen 'Shakespeare's Sister' as the next single, in late January The Smiths reconvened at Utopia Studios in Primrose Hill to finalise the mix and cut a new B-side: the tender yet sanguine 'Stretch Out And Wait'. With its fluttering acoustic chords and the gentle patter of Joyce's snare brushes, the song would boast one of Marr's most superbly understated arrangements, disturbed only by the sporadic shake of a tambourine (or in the case of the alternate version featured on 1987's *The World Won't Listen*, some soft Phil Spector-ish thunderclaps).[75]

Against such unimposing accompaniment, Morrissey delivers an atypical celebration of the sexual act; a sharp and unexpected aesthetic U-turn on the impotent sentiments of 'Pretty Girls Make Graves'. Explaining his singular viewpoint on gender politics to *Melody Maker* in 1986, Morrissey made a direct reference to its lyrics: 'In the song 'Stretch Out And Wait', there is a line "God, how sex implores you". To make choices, to change and to be different, to do something and make a stand. I always found that very, very encroaching on any feelings that I felt that I just wanted to be me, which was somewhere between this world and the next world, somewhere between this sex and the next sex.'

The song's closing concern as to the end of the world occurring in the day or at night was inspired by an identical exchange between James Dean and Sal Mineo during the climactic planetarium scene of Nicholas Ray's 1955 *Rebel Without a Cause*. Further stimulation came from *Men's Liberation*, a 'new definition of masculinity' by American gay activist Jack Nichols. Back in June 1983, Morrissey had told *Sounds*' Dave McCullough: 'the quote that best sums up The Smiths is from Jack Nichols' book *Men's Liberation*: "We are here and it is now".' What Morrissey conveniently failed to mention was that Nichols himself was actually quoting from Charlton Heston in the 1968 film *Planet of the Apes*. Regardless of its incongruous sci-fi origins, 18 months later, 'Stretch Out And Wait' presented Morrissey with the opportunity to employ the same phrase.[76]

As with many of their B-sides, it said much for The Smiths that they could consign a song of such grace and sensitivity to a 12-inch extra track. An overpoweringly beautiful work.

In Concert

Tested live on the second and third nights of 1985's *Meat Is Murder* tour (Guilford 28/2/85 and Brixton 1/3/85 respectively) 'Stretch Out And Wait' was temporarily dropped for a week until Ipswich Gaumont Theatre (11/3/85), becoming a set regular from then on.

75 Other than the subtle storm sound effects, the alternate mix recovered for 1987's *The World Won't Listen* compilation is distinguishable by its echoing guitar postscript and a completely different opening lyrical couplet.

76 Journalist Nick Kent, present during the track's mixdown, would also refer to *Men's Liberation* as 'shaping what has since become a key concept in [Morrissey's] own lyrical observations.' Nichols quotes Heston during his chapter on male 'Instincts'.

Absent from the first three Canadian concerts of 1986's North American tour, it was reinstated at Montreal University (3/8/86) and remained for the duration of that summer's US leg until St Petersburg, Florida (10/9/86); their final American concert and the song's last public performance.

Radio

A live version of 'Stretch Out And Wait' recorded at the Oxford Apollo (18/3/85) was first broadcast by BBC Radio 1 on Janice Long's *Evening Show* in May 1985 before being officially released by Rough Trade on the 12-inch reverse of 'That Joke Isn't Funny Anymore'.

42

'Untitled Instrumental' (Hanley)

Recorded **Hanley Victoria Hall, March 1985**

Engineered by **Grant Showbiz**

Informal sound-check rehearsal

With an extensive touring schedule in place for the first half of 1985, it would be another six months after the 'Shakespeare's Sister' single sessions at Ridge Farm and Utopia before The Smiths properly set foot in another studio. Meantime, as Mike Joyce substantiates, organised group rehearsals were practically non-existent. 'I remember asking Johnny once about practising,' the drummer recalls, 'and he said to me "what do you think sound-checks are for?"'.

Indeed, Marr was extraordinarily proactive in his approach to sound-checks, turning a technical obligation into a chance to sketch rough ideas with Joyce and Rourke, often capturing the results on tape through the mixing desk of sound engineer Grant Showbiz for future reference. The spring UK *Meat Is Murder* tour was no exception, with working instrumental versions of 'Bigmouth Strikes Again', a loose 'Rubber Ring' and 'The Boy With The Thorn In His Side' all coming together at various sound-checks in March 1985.

That same month Marr outlined another tune, which unfortunately went no further than an instrumental jam. A taut R&B adrenalin rush, it featured a typically stupefying high-octave lead riff from Marr (a distant cousin of 'Some Girls Are Bigger Than Others' but more abrasive) over an express bass riff taking its cue from the opening scale of Ray Charles' 'What'd I Say'. Repeating the same chord cycle ad infinitum, the tune becomes a vehicle to hone the band's twangy, rock 'n' roll spirit previously unleashed on

'Nowhere Fast' and 'Shakespeare's Sister', echoing Marr's comments to *Melody Maker* soon after the *Meat Is Murder* tour that the next album would be 'very much in the R&B groove' The best surviving tape of the track this author has uncovered is a sound-check from their Hanley Victoria Hall concert (16/3/85).[77]

43

'The Boy With The Thorn In His Side'

Recorded **August 1985, Drone Studios, Manchester/RAK Studios, London**

Produced by **The Smiths**

Single A-side, September 1985 (Highest UK Chart Placing #23)

Subsequently remixed for inclusion on ***The Queen Is Dead*, June 1986**

After four months promoting *Meat Is Murder* with tours in the UK, Europe and their first haul across America (during which Marr married his long-term girlfriend, Angie, in San Francisco), in the summer of 1985 The Smiths returned to Drone Studios in Chorlton. Though originally intended as a demo, a relatively simple 8-track take of 'The Boy With The Thorn In His Side' captured at Drone was subsequently tidied up at RAK Studios back in London and deemed good enough to be released as the next single.

One of several new tracks rehearsed at sound-checks during the latter stages of the *Meat Is Murder* tour, Marr employed a classic Stratocaster guitar model for the first time on a Smiths record, hoping to achieve a 'twangy Hank Marvin sound'. In the event, 'The Boy With The Thorn In His Side' owed more to the scratching funk rhythm technique of Chic's Nile Rodgers and the bright, optimistic guitar patterns of the 'highlife' genre.[78] 'I never called it highlife,' refutes Marr. 'I mean the Nile Rodgers thing with the rhythm, absolutely, but I didn't know I was playing highlife until John Porter said it. There was no other way of playing that tune. I just wanted that melody out of it and we did a really good job. It was just a chord change that I was kicking around at home and I was imagining a tune on top of it. It wasn't until we got the bass and drums behind it that I could play the topline. It just made me feel good.'

Interviewed by actress Margi Clarke for Channel 4's *The Tube* shortly after its release, Morrissey revealed that the song was a metaphorical expression of The Smiths' status within both the press and the music industry at that

77 The tune follows the following four-bar chord loop: F#m/ Bm, C#m/ Bm, C#m/ D, E.

78 'Highlife' is a particular style of West African guitar music, notably upbeat in melody and tempo.

time. In the wake of *Meat Is Murder*, Morrissey had been subject to a succession of interviewers who he regarded as hostile cynics. 'I think the mission of most journalists is to expose me,' he'd previously warned *Jamming!* magazine, 'because they have this notion that I'm totally fake – as though I'm secretly some mad sex monster. People are ready, in wait, for the cloak to drop and to see me photographed in the Playboy Club. They're trying to unravel me.' As he also told Margi Clarke, 'the thorn is the music industry and all these people who would just never believe anything I said, tried to get rid of me, wouldn't play the records. So I think we've reached the stage where we feel "if they don't believe me now, will they ever believe me?" What more can a boy do?'

Arguably the most melodically gratifying single of their career, 'The Boy With The Thorn In His Side' somehow lacked the bite of the bulk of its predecessors. Of greater concern at the time, its moderate chart placing just outside the Top 20 would also further Rough Trade's unease over the group's commercial future. Nine months after its single release, the song reappeared in slightly more polished form on *The Queen Is Dead*.[79]

In Concert

Introduced at Irvine Magnum Leisure Centre (22/9/85), as the current single (or as Morrissey termed it 'our monthly complaint') 'The Boy With The Thorn In His Side' was played throughout the 1985 Scottish tour, remaining a perennial live favourite for the rest of their career with the exception of one date during the summer American tour (Houston 5/9/86) and the notorious aborted 1986 Preston Guildhall show (27/10/86).

Featured within the final concert at Brixton Academy (12/12/86), since the recorded version faded out, live renditions of 'The Boy With The Thorn In His Side' closed on a reprise of its four bar intro (as heard on *Rank*).

Television

'The Smiths will never make a video because our music speaks for itself. I think that by now people have accepted the fact that they are never going to see us in a video – ever.' So protested Andy Rourke to the press in September 1984, just two months before Morrissey informed *Melody Maker* that they would 'never make a video as long as we live!' with equal self-assurance.

79 The album version of 'The Boy With The Thorn In His Side' differs from the single version. Completed during the final album sessions at Jacobs Studios in November, it features extra guitar overdubs as well as an additional string arrangement, played by Marr on an Emulator. The two versions are easily distinguishable at 0.07; a symphonic surge pre-empts Morrissey's opening line on *The Queen Is Dead* version, whereas the original single mix bears only the plain marimba three-note scale up.

Having adopted such a fierce stance against pop promos, it was actually surprising how lightly they'd be let off by the press when finally The Smiths surrendered to the pressure to make their first video for 'The Boy With The Thorn In His Side'.

Admittedly, their past couple of singles hadn't exactly smashed into the Top 10 (or Top 20 for that matter), but at least by sticking to their no video doctrine what they lost in sales they gained in integrity. 'The Boy With The Thorn In His Side' was a regrettable compromise which, says Marr, was purely to silence Rough Trade who blamed the disappointing chart success of their previous singles on their refusal to make such promos. 'We said, "Okay, if you want to film us you'll have to come to the studio 'cos we're not leaving. And bring lots of red wine." It was horrible, so we just got drunk.' Filmed at RAK, where the band were involved in preliminary recordings for *The Queen Is Dead*, this understandably stagy, mimed performance was directed by Ken O'Neil, whose track record included The Kinks' celebrated 'Come Dancing' promo.

When the single charted the band still opted to make a studio appearance on the 10 October edition of *Top of the Pops* rather than substitute the video. Fresh from their triumphant tour of Scotland, Morrissey writhed in a pelvic trance with the word 'BAD' scrawled on the side of his neck. Presenter Steve Wright – their arch nemesis who would later inspire 'Panic' **[see 58]** – was also seen tediously mimicking Morrissey's dancing as the cameras pulled back.

A short clip of the song being played in concert at Glasgow Barrowlands (25/9/85) was also screened on *The Tube* in October 1985 as part of a lengthy feature on The Smiths' recent tour of Scotland.

Radio

A live version of 'The Boy With The Thorn In His Side' recorded at Kilburn National Ballroom (23/10/86) was first broadcast on BBC Radio 1's *In Concert* series in April 1987 and later included on 1988's posthumous live album *Rank* adapted from the same show.

44

'Rubber Ring'

Recorded **August 1985, RAK Studios, London**

Produced by **Morrissey and Marr**

B-side to **'The Boy With The Thorn In His Side' (12-inch format only), September 1985**

Among the many riffs jammed during sound-checks on the spring *Meat Is Murder* tour was a steady 4/4 minor-key garage rock vamp, which shared its rolling blues tempo with Booker T & The MGs' soul chestnut 'Green Onions'. By the time The Smiths upped sticks to London's RAK Studios in St John's Wood that August, Marr had adapted this rough sketch into what would become 'Rubber Ring'; shifting key and introducing a more disjointed rhythm in keeping with the Chic-inspired funk of 'The Boy With The Thorn In His Side'. Another superb bass line from Rourke emphasised this mystical funk ambience, lacquered with some wraithlike strings (created, once again, synthetically on an Emulator) and a surging backbeat from the ever-impressive Joyce.

The 'Rubber Ring' of the title is an incisive metaphor for The Smiths' repertoire, as perceived by their most ardent admirers, emotionally dependent on Morrissey's every word. 'I understand that form of expression, that form of drama,' he later sympathised when describing the wealth of hysterical letters he regularly received, many from distraught adolescents threatening suicide. 'I think it primarily stems from feeling quite isolated and believing that the people who make the records you buy are your personal friends, they understand you, and the more records that you buy and pictures you collect the closer you get to these people. And if you are quite isolated and you hear this voice that you identify with, it's really quite immensely important.'

The genius of 'Rubber Ring', in celebrating the consoling passions of 'the songs that saved your life', is its cynical sting in its tail. Morrissey seems bluntly resigned to the fact that with 'the passing of time' (another maxim culled from Elizabeth Smart), these same melodramatic back bedroom casualties are more than likely to grow out of this music – his music – as they enter the stability of adulthood. As he wickedly pictures them years later 'finally living', his ruthless rebuke 'hear my voice in your head and think of me kindly' assumes an unsettlingly spectral timbre; a haunting reprimand from the other side.

Morrissey's own voice from the dead is echoed in the unnerving sample culled from an obscure EP originally distributed with Dr Konstantin Raudive's 1971 book *Breakthrough: An Amazing Experiment in Electronic Communication with the Dead*. Often referred to as EVP – Electronic Voice Phenomenon – these 'Raudive Voices' were allegedly recordings of the deceased collected by the Latvian psychologist on special laboratory equipment. The woman's voice heard on 'Rubber Ring' is that of Nadia Fowler, Raudive's English translator, interpreting one such message from his former collaborator, the Swedish parapsychologist Professor Gebhard Frei who had recently died. Frei's message to Raudive is a mixture of Swedish and German; 'Du sovas, willst nicht glaube!'/ 'you are sleeping, you do not want to believe'. 'It was always exciting when Morrissey brought in these little ideas,' comments Street. 'He'd just bring in these records and say "I want this on" and we'd experiment with it, cue it up and drop it in when it sounded right. I think Johnny in particular really appreciated these little soundscape ideas that set them apart from other bands.'

An extra spoken word sample was provided by a 1969 EMI Music for Pleasure audio recording of Oscar Wilde's *The Importance of Being Earnest.*[80] Two excerpts of dialogue from John Gielgud as Jack in Act I were spliced together; 'is that clever?' and 'everybody's clever nowadays'. The latter quip, if only by coincidence, also served as a deferential homage to the 1979 Buzzcocks single 'Everybody's Happy Nowadays'.

After completing a provisional mix at RAK, Morrissey and Marr were later called back by Rough Trade to add some last minute overdubs. 'There was some matter of urgency that we had to finish the record because it was incomplete,' recalls Marr. 'So when we were mixing 'Rubber Ring', there's that lyric "hear my voice in your head and think of me kindly." Morrissey said "we need a sound effect of this noise". I said "what noise?" He said "like a lift shaft". So he checked his pockets and for once he never had any sound effects records on him. But he was specific about this sound that it needed. I said to him "well what's the sound you're after?" and he said "kind of like a lift shaft?". I said "well how's a lift shaft sound?" and he said like this "whoooooosh!". I said "well, just do that!" So that's what we did. He went in to the recording both, cupped his hand over the microphone, I put a load of reverb on it and he made this whooshing sound. It was fantastic.'[81]

A B-side of devastating originality and emotional potency, 'Rubber Ring' easily elbows its way into The Smiths' shortlist of all-time bests. Sadly, its appearance on all subsequent compilations called for an abrupt edit of the Raudive voice coda. The original 12-inch of 'The Boy With The Thorn In His Side' blended its two separate B-sides together into one continuous eight-minute piece of music; as 'Rubber Ring' ends, 'you are sleeping, you do not want to believe' repeats into a gradual fade, simultaneously merging with the howling wind ushering in 'Asleep'. Together they make a spectacular combination. To that end, this author strongly recommends seeking out the Rough Trade 12-inch of 'The Boy With The Thorn In His Side' to hear both 'Rubber Ring' and 'Asleep' concurrently as The Smiths first intended. 'Absolutely,' agrees Marr, 'that whole piece of music is really well executed.'

80 This snippet has been frequently misquoted as stemming from Anthony Asquith's 1952 film version, despite the fact that Gielgud does not appear (the role of Jack ably played by Michael Redgrave) nor the dialogue itself, which Asquith edited from his screenplay interpretation.

81 Morrissey's 'lift-shaft' can be heard buried in the final mix at 2.18.

In Concert

'Rubber Ring' itself was never played live as a song in its own right. Marr would however construct a teasing medley that began with its slick, funky guitar intro, then ricocheted into 'What She Said' before eventually reverting back to the yodelling, frenetic outro of 'Rubber Ring' again. This segue-way was first debuted at Salford University (20/7/86) and included on the ensuing Canadian/North American tour and their final UK dates that autumn, last played at Manchester Free Trade Hall (30/10/86).

Radio

The 'Rubber Ring'/'What She Said' live medley from the Kilburn National Ballroom (23/10/86) was broadcast on BBC Radio 1's *In Concert* in April 1987 and later included on 1988's live album *Rank*. Both the production notes of that BBC broadcast, and *Rank* itself, refer to the track as 'What She Said' only.

45

'Asleep'

Recorded **August 1985, RAK Studios, London**

Produced by **Morrissey and Marr**

B-side to **'The Boy With The Thorn In His Side', September 1985**

Having spent a whole day in early August laying down 'Rubber Ring', at around eight o'clock in the evening, Johnny Marr announced to Stephen Street that he had 'a little piano thing I want to put down with Morrissey'.

The roots of Marr's 'little piano thing' stemmed from the very origins of The Smiths in the summer of 1982; specifically the discarded coda of 'Suffer Little Children' **[see 19]**, which had featured a similarly morose piano melody. Three years later, 'Asleep' offered a more mature arrangement loosely based upon this same blueprint; though in different keys, the opening 'sing me to sleep' descent is patently derived from the first bar of that abandoned 'Suffer Little Children' epilogue. 'Undoubtedly it is similar,' confirms Marr, 'because that's how I play piano, I can't play it any other way. That was another one worked out on the upright I inherited when I moved into the house in Bowden, the same piano I wrote 'Oscillate Wildly' on. It had a pleasingly eerie quality about it. You could only play certain things on it. Weird, doomy music, which suited us fine.'

'The piano went down first,' recalls Street, 'after which Morrissey handed me one of his BBC sound effects records and told me he wanted this wind noise on. It was only so long so I had to keep playing it backwards and forwards to make it stretch the whole song.' Another effect, of a music box playing Burns' traditional New Year's toast 'Auld Lang Syne', was also incorporated, varying its speed to synchronise with the song's key. 'The whole thing – the piano, the vocal take, the sound effects – just came together beautifully,' Street concludes. 'It only took about two hours.'

Of all Morrissey's many lyrics concerning suicide, 'Asleep' is by far the bleakest. More than eloquently articulating an unshakeable world-weariness simply for poetic effect, 'Asleep' actively eulogises it. The sleep of the dead Morrissey desires is exactly the same as that fantasised by Hamlet in Shakespeare's celebrated 'To be or not to be?' soliloquy:

> *'... To die: to sleep;*
> *No more; and by a sleep to say we end*
> *The heart-ache and the thousand natural shocks*
> *That flesh is heir to, 'tis a consummation*
> *Devoutly to be wish'd. To die, to sleep;*
> *To sleep: perchance to dream ... '*
>
> (Shakespeare, *Hamlet* III:1)

Taking one's life becomes the entry into 'another world', 'a better world' (Hamlet's 'undiscovered country'). Yet unlike the flippant melodrama of 'Shakespeare's Sister', as a blustering 'goodbye cruel world' farewell, 'Asleep' is terrifyingly sincere. The cause of the protagonist's death-wish is his fatigue over constantly waking up alone (a scenario soon to be repeated in 'I Know It's Over' and the later 'Last Night I Dreamt That Somebody Loved Me' **[see 51 and 78]**), though as he slips from this life to the next, his final macabre wish is to be serenaded. Groaning his dying breath, the closing exhortation of 'Auld Lang Syne' suggests that the suicidal act is now complete; a new year, free of old acquaintances, has begun in the afterlife.

The whistling, Brontë-esque wind was another adroit tactic, evoking the stormy 'death discs' of the Sixties (eg, John Leyton's 1961 hit 'Johnny Remember Me' with its 'singing in the sighing of the wind'), while making it the perfect companion piece to the equally morose 'Rubber Ring' on the original 'The Boy With The Thorn In His Side' 12-inch B-side's uninterrupted segue-way **[see 44]**. That 'Asleep' was, and still is, perhaps the most achingly desperate advocate of suicide ever constructed within the medium of popular music, was another cross Morrissey would have to bear when accused of promoting a 'suicide-chic'; exacerbated by the fact that the relatives of at least half a dozen 'alarmingly dedicated' fans who had taken their own lives had contacted the group for consolation. As the *NME*'s Ian Pye pointed out to the singer, there were a handful of Smiths songs that could be easily categorised as 'aesthetic Exit manuals'.

Illustrating The Smiths – minus Rourke and Joyce that is – at their darkest emotional ebb, 'Asleep' is as beautiful as it is ghastly; a song of assiduous despair that befits the predominantly undeserved 'miserablist' stigma that hounded them. Stained with what Elizabeth Smart herself metaphorically termed 'the cold semen of grief', 'Asleep' is the harsh and authentic clamour of the human soul at its most nihilistic.

In Concert

'Asleep' was played live just once on the final date of the 1985 Scottish tour at Inverness Eden Court Theatre (1/10/85). The catalyst for its sole public performance was the discovery of a piano at the side of the stage during the sound-check. Unable to move the instrument, come the gig itself later that evening, Marr had to disappear into the wings to play it, thereby secreted from the view of his audience. Rourke and Joyce stayed to improvise a sparse accompanying rhythm section that was only moderately successful, while, to the bemusement of the rowdy Highland audience, Morrissey ended the song by curling into a foetal ball in the centre of the stage. 'That was a really brilliant gig,' adds Marr, 'partly because we knew we were gonna do 'Asleep' so we had this strange kind of "is it gonna work?" thing hanging over us.'

46

'Bigmouth Strikes Again'

Recorded **September-November 1985, RAK Studios, London/Jacobs Studios, Farnham**

Produced by **Morrissey and Marr**

Single A-side, May 1986 (Highest UK Chart Placing #26)

Subsequently featured on the album ***The Queen Is Dead*, June 1986**

Following 'The Boy With The Thorn In His Side' and 'Rubber Ring', 'Bigmouth Strikes Again' would be the third and final instalment in Morrissey's highly personal triptych, written consecutively in the summer of 1985, which scrutinised his art and the industry that sustains it. The first ('The Boy With The Thorn In His Side') admitted a hopeless vulnerability to the slings and arrows of music biz and media cynicism being hurled in his direction. The second ('Rubber Ring') addressed his audience, questioning their loyalty and the validity of his work with it. The third – 'Bigmouth Strikes Again' – was the cycle's vaudevillian conclusion, addressing the same issues of 'The Boy With The Thorn In His Side' but inverting the accusations of his detractors to set himself up as a pop martyr.

All three songs originated from riffs that Marr had introduced at sound-checks during the March *Meat Is Murder* tour. He would later famously confess that with 'Bigmouth Strikes Again' he set out to write his equivalent of The Rolling Stones' 'Jumpin' Jack Flash': 'I wanted something that was a rush all the way through, without a distinct middle eight as such. I thought the guitar breaks should be percussive, not too pretty or chordal.'

Recorded at the preliminary *Queen Is Dead* session at RAK,[82] Marr's dark, downcast score was perfectly complemented by Joyce's gnashing snare rolls and Rourke's twisting bass, amplifying the scornful homily of Morrissey's lyrics. Originally it had been their intention to feature a cameo from Kirsty MacColl on backing vocals. 'That's the first time we met her,' explains Marr. 'She came down to the studio and put on these *really* weird harmonies.' Though impressed enough with MacColl's performance to invite her back to sing on the following year's 'Ask' **[see 60]**, Morrissey and Marr decided to erase her from the finished mix. As a quick-fix replacement, Morrissey instead substituted a semi-comic helium vocal (achieved by filtering his normal speed take through a harmoniser), which, upon Marr's suggestion, would be humorously credited to fictitious guest vocalist 'Ann Coates' (a pun on the Ancoats district of Manchester). In the shortlist for pseudonyms, Joyce had suggested the equally corny 'Sally Ford' ('as in Salford'). Press officer Pat Bellis would also draw inspiration from its lyrics for her own photographic alter-ego 'Jo Novark' ('Joan of Arc').

Naturally, the eponymous Bigmouth is Morrissey himself. When questioned by the *NME* in June that year if there was anything he'd regretted saying, he retorted 'I can't think of one sentence!', later admitting that 'we're still at the stage where if I rescued a kitten from drowning they'd say, "Morrissey Mauls Kitten's Body." So what can you do?' Thus 'Bigmouth Strikes Again' is an ingenious double-edged sword of chromic self-effacement and sarcastic critical deflection. Its first, and only, verse presaged the domestic violence of 'Girlfriend In A Coma' with its troubling juxtaposition of 'Sweetness' beside retracted threats of teeth smashing and bludgeoning. For his troublesome tongue, Morrissey is then prepared to be burned alive like Joan of Arc; another throwback to Patti Smith's 'Kimberly' ('the sea rushes up my knees like flame, and I feel just like some misplaced Joan of Arc') also recalling Sandie Shaw's earlier description of 'Hand In Glove' as 'real Joan of Arc stuff' **[see 21]**.

82 Final overdubs were added at Jacobs Studios in November, including the dramatic baying guitar slides (doubled on a harmonised Les Paul and Rickenbacker) and Morrissey's wailing background vocals.

Urban myth has it that the melting Walkman scenario was inspired by a sketch on *The Kenny Everett Television Show* in which the comedian obliviously listens to a personal stereo while being burned at the stake. By the end of the second chorus, though, the song's autobiographical undercurrent surfaces beyond all reasonable doubt, when it becomes a hearing aid now being engulfed by the flames. Questioning his right to 'take my place with the human race', it soon transpires that all this graphic self-deprecation is merely an elaborate joke to infuriate his tormentors. Laughing maniacally into the fade out, it's clear that Bigmouth has no intention of disappearing without a struggle. He will – and he did – strike again.

Less amusing were the behind-the-scenes struggles in seeing the record released. The interminable delays imposed by Rough Trade shortly after the completion of *The Queen Is Dead* resulted in a gap of almost nine months (the longest of their career) between 'Bigmouth Strikes Again' and its predecessor, 'The Boy With The Thorn In His Side'. Once the dispute between artist and label was settled, Geoff Travis was adamant that 'There Is A Light That Never Goes Out' **[see 47]** should be their 'comeback' record. Luckily, Marr stubbornly insisted that his original choice, 'Bigmouth Strikes Again', be selected instead, though Travis's regret was sustained by its alarming failure to return The Smiths to the Top 20. This commercial shortfall aside, the record more than reassured fans who'd feared for the band in their prolonged absence, while whetting the appetite for the imminent third album. If not necessarily their best single overall, the song's violent comedy and rhythmic ferocity ('Jumpin' Jack Flash' meets *Saint Joan* with added GBH) certainly ranks 'Bigmouth Strikes Again' among their most intrepid pop creations.

In Concert

Along with 'Frankly, Mr Shankly' and 'The Boy With The Thorn In His Side', 'Bigmouth Strikes Again' was the first of the new *The Queen Is Dead* material to be previewed live; introduced shortly after its recording (but eight months before its release) on the 1985 Scottish mini-tour, beginning at Irvine Magnum Leisure Centre (22/9/85).

By the summer of '86, as the new single it provided the set opener for the first three UK dates that July (Glasgow, Newcastle and Manchester's G-Mex 'Festival of the Tenth Summer') before being moved to the encore from thereon. Closing the majority of their Canadian and US summer shows, it stayed as the last bow of their October 1986 UK tour up to and including Manchester Free Trade Hall (30/10/86) before being moved to the second number for their final gig at Brixton Academy (12/12/86). In concert 'Bigmouth Strikes Again' was longer than the recorded version, utilising its brief middle eight a second time towards the climax before repeating the chorus ad infinitum (since the studio version faded out, Marr conceived a powerful coda of [A /B/G#-minor/C#-minor] as captured on *Rank*).

James Maker also made a brief appearance on stage during the encore of 'Bigmouth... ' at Cornwall's St Austell Coliseum (17/10/86). 'The Smiths had invited my group, Raymonde, to tour support them in 1986,' Maker explains. 'I was backstage that night when I heard the chords of 'Bigmouth Strikes Again' strike up. Spontaneity, instinct, and Remy Martin drove me out onto the stage – just briefly – to join them. It seemed fitting and ironic. Johnny was beaming. Afterwards, Morrissey dispatched me an Agatha Christie book titled, *Murder Is Easy*. To which I sent him the Sandie Shaw single, 'Message Understood'.'

Television

After a seven-month absence from British TV screens, The Smiths unleashed 'Bigmouth Strikes Again' live on BBC2's *Whistle Test* on 20 May 1986; their first TV appearance with Craig Gannon on rhythm guitar. They were introduced by Radio 1's Andy Kershaw, who related how he'd spent the previous evening trying to make a list of 'the truly great British bands of the 1980s, bands whose recordings and influence would endure'. 'After nearly an hour,' said Kershaw, 'I was staring at a sheet of paper with only one name on it: The Smiths!'

With that, the new five-man ensemble launched into a mighty rendition of their latest single. Morrissey, still wearing a mock hearing aid and dressed like some wayward school teacher in blazer and tie, cut a menacing figure; poking his fingers into the camera as if to blind the viewer at home before cackling demonically as the track reached its thunderous finale. Marr kept a lower profile, while Rourke – making his first appearance since being fired and rehired a few months earlier – now sported a luminous bleach-blond quiff. Most conspicuous of all, however, was new boy Craig Gannon, sheepishly strumming his Rickenbacker in the background, head permanently bowed.

The overall sound was a coarse cacophony, with Marr's arpeggio instrumental break fighting for breath in the imbalanced mix. But visually, this was The Smiths' most awe-inspiring broadcast yet and, along with 'Vicar In A Tutu' from that same programme **[see 55]**, perhaps even the greatest TV performance of their career.

Radio

As the final encore at Kilburn National Ballroom (23/10/86), a guttural live take of 'Bigmouth Strikes Again' was first broadcast on BBC Radio 1's *In Concert* series in April 1987, later included on 1988's posthumous live album *Rank*.

The sweet and tender hooligans. Outside Salford Lads Club during the *Queen Is Dead* photo shoot, December 1985. Left to right: Johnny Marr, Morrissey, Andy Rourke, Mike Joyce.
(photo by Stephen Wright)

Above:
Marr, Rourke and Joyce prepare to storm Versailles. Backstage in Paris, December 1984.
(photo by Paul Slattery)

Left:
'A boy in the bush'.
(photo by Howard Tyler)

Above:
A flower-like life. The Smiths at Manchester's derelict Central Station in the summer of 1983.
(photo by Paul Slattery)

Right:
Shoplifters of the world unite! Marr keeps a watchful eye for security at Manchester's Arndale Centre, December 1985.
(photo by Stephen Wright)

Miserable now? Serious times for The Smiths, spring 1987.
(photo by Lawrence Watson)

Morrissey celebrates his victory over 'The Headmaster Ritual' at BBC Manchester's *Oxford Road Show*, February 1985.
(photo by Stephen Wright)

This page: Rare promotional posters from Rough Trade.

Right: 'How Soon Is Now?' featuring Sean Barrett as Frankie in the Ealing Studios drama *Dunkirk* (1958).

Far right: 'The greatest woman that ever lived' – *Coronation Street*'s Pat Phoenix becomes 'Shakespeare's Sister'.

THE SMITHS
7" (RT 176) B/W WELL I WONDER
12" (RTT 176) WITH EXTRA TRACK OSCILLATE WILDLY

Right: From Vietnam to vegetarianism. An unknown soldier from Emile de Antonio's *In The Year Of The Pig* announces The Smiths' war on carnivores.

Far right: 'The King of Rock 'n' Roll' becomes an unlikely advocate for petty theft. Elvis graces the cover of 'Shoplifters Of The World Unite'.

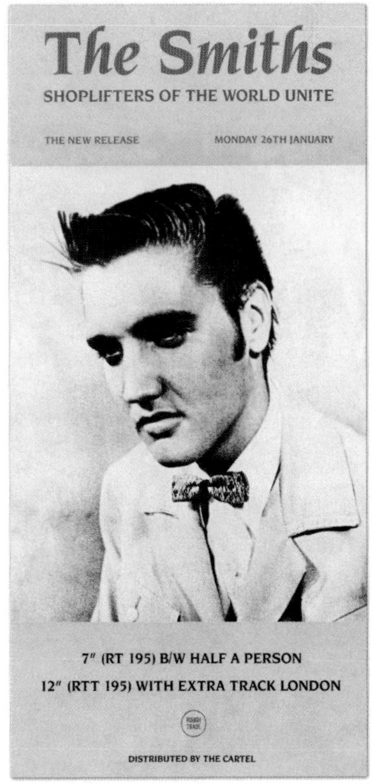

This spread:
Morrissey's celluloid influences.

Opposite above:
'Them was rotten days.' Shirley Anne Field and Albert Finney in *Saturday Night and Sunday Morning* (1960).

Opposite below:
'The dream is gone but the baby is real.' Murray Melvin and Rita Tushingham in *A Taste of Honey* (1961).

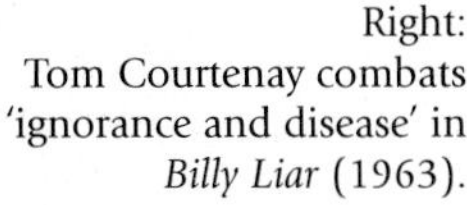

Right:
Tom Courtenay combats 'ignorance and disease' in *Billy Liar* (1963).

Below:
Terence Stamp tries to 'pin and mount' Samantha Eggar in *The Collector* (1965).

'Murder at the Wool Hall'. The making of *Strangeways, Here We Come* is interrupted for the final group photo call, March 1987.
(photo by André Csillag)

'Compulsive non-viewing'. Actress Justine Kerrigan coaxes Morrissey's post-Smiths 'acting debut' in the 1988 *Brookside* spin-off, *South*.

47

'There Is A Light That Never Goes Out'

Recorded **September-November 1985, RAK Studios, London/Jacobs Studios, Farnham**

Produced by **Morrissey and Marr**

Album track from ***The Queen Is Dead,*** **June 1986**

One late summer's evening in 1985, Morrissey paid a visit to Marr's house in Bowden for a routine writing session. It was to prove an especially lucrative night's work, resulting in the basis of 'Frankly, Mr Shankly' and 'I Know It's Over'. But it was the genesis of a third song that would mark the evening out as one of the most significant in the duo's creative relationship. 'Morrissey was sat on a coffee table, perched on the edge,' recalls Marr. 'I was sat with my guitar on a chair directly in front of him. He had a Sony Walkman recording, waiting to hear what I was gonna pull out. So I said "well, I've got this one" and I started playing these chords. He just looked at me as I was playing. It was as if he daren't speak, in case the spell was broke.' Dumbstruck and spellbound, Morrissey listened to 'There Is A Light That Never Goes Out' for the very first time.

If 'How Soon Is Now?' is the populist Smiths favourite, among scholarly fans of the group opinion is almost unanimous that this, *The Queen Is Dead*'s penultimate track, is the quintessential Morrissey/Marr classic. Attaching Morrissey's emotional intensity of the beautiful-yet-doomed 'Hand In Glove' relationship and the suicidal extremes of 'Asleep' to the multi-layered melodic texture of Marr's earlier 'Oscillate Wildly', the song encapsulates The Smiths at their most morbidly romantic; a love song that celebrates the existential transience of human mortality by fantasising about being cut down in the prime of happiness. Preserving bliss, but only through death.

The song's lengthy recording process began during the autumn RAK sessions. A first raw rehearsal in an ill-fitting higher key was taped on 2 September prior to a lower, more comfortable, monitor mix completed four days later. Though commonly attributed to The Velvet Underground's 'There She Goes Again' from 1967's *The Velvet Underground & Nico*, the song's signature stammering bridge was actually an intentional steal from The Rolling Stones' cover of Marvin Gaye's 'Hitch Hike'.[83] As Marr later told *Select* magazine, this was a conscious embezzlement to gauge the wisdom of their critics: 'There's a little in-joke in there just to illustrate how intellectual I was getting. At the time everyone was into The Velvet Underground, and they

83 'Hitch Hike' first featured on The Rolling Stones' third album, 1965's *Out Of Our Heads*, which Marr nominated as his joint favourite LP in the *Meat Is Murder* tour programme earlier that year alongside The Four Tops' *Greatest Hits*.

stole the intro to 'There She Goes Again' – da da da-da, da da-da-da, Dah Dah! – from The Rolling Stones' version of 'Hitch Hike', the Marvin Gaye song. I just wanted to put that in to see whether the press would say, "oh, it's The Velvet Underground!" 'Cos I knew that I was smarter than that. I was listening to what The Velvet Underground were listening to.'

Marr utilised an Emulator to concoct a breathtaking artificial string arrangement credited on the finished album as the fictitious 'Hated Salford Ensemble'. 'We'd lightened the rules a bit,' opines Stephen Street, 'we were starting to use the Emulator more to create other orchestral sounds. Once Johnny knew that he had the freedom to use the Emulator as well as guitars he really got encouraged to push the boat out.' The Rough Trade budget, which would have immediately ruled out the possibility of recording with a real string section, no doubt helped Morrissey overcome his cautious cynicism towards synthetic strings. 'There was also that thing of letting outsiders in,' confirms Joyce, 'I just don't think it would have worked in the studio if we'd have brought in a load of classical musicians. The Smiths were a closed shop.'

The track was completed later that winter during their residency at Jacobs Studios in Surrey, where Marr attached its integral, lingering flute melody (originally conceived as a guitar part and, again, played on an Emulator), while Morrissey redid his vocal twice more. It's intriguing to note how on his initial vocal takes, the literal meaning of the song's title was clarified in the final refrain 'there is a light in your eye and it never goes out'. Oddly, this explanatory revelation was omitted from the finished record, which procured greater ambiguity as a result.[84]

As their most 'treasured' song, the effusive, soul-penetrating lyrics of 'There Is A Light That Never Goes Out' are among the most commonly and contentiously discussed, many taking the idealistic romantic view that its words amount to a wholly autobiographical confession of Morrissey's feelings towards his songwriting partner. However, its presiding narrative is also vaguely similar to the plight of Jim (James Dean) and Judy (Natalie Wood) in *Rebel Without a Cause*; escaping a hostile parental home in the passenger seat of an unconsummated love interest's car. There's even a gentle allusion to Karel Reisz's 1960 film version of Alan Sillitoe's *Saturday Night and Sunday Morning*, where Shirley Anne Field protests to Albert Finney: 'why don't you take me where it's lively and there's plenty of people?'

Thrilled at the outset of a carefree nocturnal drive on the open road, Morrissey soon becomes wracked with the fresh anxiety of whether or not to

84 This original lyric may have been a throwback to another of Morrissey's favourite girl groups, The Shirelles, specifically their 1961 Gerry Goffin/Carole King penned classic 'Will You Love Me Tomorrow?' and the line: 'Tonight the light of love is in your eyes'.

realise his desire towards the vehicle's owner 'in the darkened underpass.' The singer would refer to this passage as 'lines that I can never bear to listen to because I find them so close ... I can't listen to those lines willy-nilly. I have to sit down. It's like somebody hitting me with a hammer.' In the event, he fearfully resists, returning to the song's dominant fantasy that at any moment the car should collide with an articulated lorry or double-decker bus; a perverse prayer that the passion they cannot realise in life will be gratified in death, binding passenger and driver together for all eternity in a serendipitous suicide pact (such a grisly scenario was the stuff of your typical 1960s 'death disc', notably The Shangri-Las' hysterical 1965 single 'Give Us Your Blessings', in which an eloping teenage couple are killed in an automobile accident).

Although Geoff Travis was anxious to release the track as the belated follow-up single to 'The Boy With The Thorn In His Side' instead of 'Bigmouth Strikes Again', it seems unlikely that such an explicit glamorisation of suicide would have endeared 'There Is A Light That Never Goes Out' to daytime radio schedulers. At any rate, it provided The Smiths with their second number one in John Peel's 1986 Festive 50 poll and was subsequently included on the following spring's *The World Won't Listen* compilation by way of a celebratory lap of honour. In December 1992, the song was finally issued as a posthumous A-side in its own right by WEA in support of the *Best 2* compilation. Ironically, it only reached number 26 in the charts – the same position as 'Bigmouth Strikes Again' some six years earlier.

In a straw poll among Smiths fans today, 'There Is A Light That Never Goes Out' would more than likely still come out victorious; the perfect balance between the genius of Marr as a composer – unquestionably one of his most elegant arrangements – and Morrissey as a lyricist touching raw nerves of adolescent angst and unrequited ardour with a poetic dexterity that was without equal in the British pop environ of the mid-Eighties. 'I didn't realise that [it] was going to be an anthem,' Marr later admitted, 'but when we first played it I thought it was the best song I'd ever heard.' As it happens, audio evidence of his initial awe has survived. Following the song's first rehearsal at RAK on 2 September 1985, the tapes were left rolling long enough for the microphones to pick up Marr's excited adulation of his co-writer. 'Aw, your singing on the end of that,' he glows towards Morrissey, 'was *brilliant*.'

In Concert

Although it was rehearsed during sound-checks on the autumn '85 Scottish tour (having been laid down at RAK the previous month), 'There Is A Light That Never Goes Out' wasn't introduced until the 'From Manchester With

Love' show at Liverpool Royal Court (8/2/86), which The Smiths shared with The Fall and New Order. The gig was a political benefit for the city's Labour council who faced crippling legal fees after its militant leaders refused to bow to Thatcherite government policy, which would have cost them 5000 jobs. Morrissey personally sent deputy council leader Derek Hatton copies of their three LPs to date, along with a letter pledging his support. Sadly, their affinity soured come the night of the show when, much to Marr's aggravation, Hatton tried unsuccessfully to force Morrissey on stage during The Fall's set.

With the exception of Dundalk (11/2/86) and the aborted Preston Guildhall show (27/10/86), 'There Is A Light That Never Goes Out' would be played at every Smiths gig thereafter, the final show at Brixton Academy included (12/12/86). Considering its esteemed reputation within their repertoire, The Smiths always played it mid-set resisting the temptation to save it for an encore. Curiously, in concert Morrissey always refrained from singing the song's title at the finish as he does on the record. Instead, following the last chorus, after four instrumental bars of the verse it closed with another 'Hitch Hike' bridge.

Television

With Channel 4's *The Tube* off air during the summer of 1986, a one-off themed European special dubbed *Eurotube* was staged on 5 July. Their second TV appearance with Craig Gannon, the new five-man Smiths played two songs live in the studio in front of an Alain Delon *The Queen Is Dead* backdrop, the first being a rousing take of 'There Is A Light That Never Goes Out'.

The song would also form the middle segment of Derek Jarman's *The Queen Is Dead* film **[see 54]**. The least memorable of the three tracks featured, Jarman's video for 'There Is A Light... ', consisted of barely distinguishable flaming cars mixed with prolonged close-ups of a sleeping figure bathed in pale blue light and slow-motion pools of rippling water. Amateur home video footage of the song performed during the final Brixton Academy concert (12/12/86) was briefly included on ITV's *South Bank Show* documentary screened in October 1987. Following the break up of The Smiths, the video for Morrissey's debut solo single 'Suedehead' in February 1988 also contained a hidden reference to his past; a bathmat, filmed in plain view, embroidered with the words 'There Is A Light That Never Goes Out'.

Radio

Although a live version recorded at Kilburn National Ballroom (23/10/86) was broadcast on BBC Radio 1's *In Concert* series in April 1987, in spite of its overwhelming popularity with critics and fans alike, 'There Is A Light That Never Goes Out' never made it onto 1988's *Rank*, the posthumous live album edited from the BBC Kilburn tapes by Morrissey himself.

48

'Never Had No One Ever'

Recorded **September-November 1985, RAK Studios, London/Jacobs Studios, Farnham**

Produced by **Morrissey and Marr**

Album track from ***The Queen Is Dead*, June 1986**

The least immediate track on *The Queen Is Dead*, 'Never Had No One Ever' was also the oldest, dating back to an instrumental jam taped at the *Meat Is Murder* mixdown session at Island's 'Fallout Shelter' in December 1984 **[see 38]**. Along with 'Bigmouth Strikes Again' and 'There Is A Light That Will Never Go Out', a more advanced template was completed during the RAK session in early September. Annotated by Joyce as the 'blind buskin' Moz' mix, this first proper attempt at the song would be the only occasion when Morrissey would lay down an indecipherably sketchy vocal before his lyrics were finalised (dimly murmuring 'I'm waiting outside your house' ad infinitum during the verses). Clocking in at over five minutes, this first take featured some extraordinary high-pitched yelps from the singer during its ceaseless end section. Morrissey's canine whines and gurgles were reminiscent of, and perhaps inspired by, his friend Linder Sterling, whose own work with Ludus often featured similarly outlandish primal screams. Though it would never make the finished master take, both Morrissey and Marr later admitted to one another that in erasing this same vocal track they'd made a mistake. 'It was a really great two part harmony he sang on the fade,' agrees Marr. 'It wasn't any words, just a sort of lilt thing. Years later he finally agreed with me that we should have kept it on.'

During the next album session at Jacobs beginning in October, Morrissey had now completed its two curt verses, also overdubbing some deranged laughter towards the finale. This second stab at 'Never Had No One Ever' (slightly shorter at 4.38) would be one of two alternate 'Trumpet Versions' that never made it onto *The Queen Is Dead*. During its plodding, repetitive climax, Morrissey's bizarre vocal shrieks are complimented by jazzy trumpet wails, raising its mournful sentiment to that of a New Orleans funeral procession. The addition of a trumpet – which couldn't be successfully mimicked on an Emulator like strings or woodwind – appears to have been Morrissey's idea, as Mike Joyce elaborates: 'We got in this BBC orchestra guy, he was about 50. He was very polite, he seemed very straight and he just asked "what do you want me to do?" But the thing was he was quite eccentric himself. So when he started playing this wild jazz it sounded ridiculous. I remember us all trying not to laugh. I think the moment Morrissey heard it he just creased up.'

Like the ditched trumpet take of 'Frankly, Mr Shankly' **[see 56]**, this experimental jazz version of 'Never Had No One Ever' would surely have radically altered the tone of *The Queen Is Dead.* 'It was just experimentation really,' says Marr, 'I don't remember much about it, other than it being hilarious.' Pared down to three-and-a-half minutes, the final master was instead swamped in ethereal guitar, while a lone whistle now replaced Morrissey's primitive burbling. Joyce enhanced his performance on the previous takes with some excellent, intense snare fills as Marr imbedded a simple yet inspirational Duane Eddy twang deep into the heart of the hymnal backwash. As the track fades, Morrissey's original laughter track – heavily distorted with reverb to assume a frosty sobbing quality – can still be clearly defined.

Lyrically, 'Never Had No One Ever' is self-explanatory. Morrissey would later refer to its opening verse as being about 'the frustration that I felt at the age of 20 when I still didn't feel easy walking around the streets on which I'd been born, where all my family had lived. They're originally from Ireland but had been here since the Fifties. It was a constant confusion to me why I never really felt "this is my patch, this is my home, I know these people. I can do what I like, because this is mine." It never was. I could never walk easily.' Marr was even more frank about the song and its muse during the notoriously pressured recording of *The Queen Is Dead*: 'We had no manager, so me and Morrissey were trying to run the whole band, plus we were still on an independent label, but out of all that adversity we still managed to make this great album. A song like 'Never Had No One Ever' could only have come out of that mindset – fucked-up.'

When placed after 'I Know It's Over' on the album's first side, 'Never Had No One Ever' becomes *The Queen Is Dead*'s depressing nadir, crushing the listener in a double blow of poetic disheartenment. 'I remember at the time thinking that those two tracks together weren't right,' agrees Street. 'It was just a bit too down. Looking back, as good as I know that album is, we just weren't playing to our strengths with that running order. But if that was what Morrissey wanted, that was what Morrissey got.'

In Concert

First played at Glasgow Barrowlands (16/7/86), 'Never Had No One Ever' remained in the set for the rest of the year with the exception of that summer's G-Mex festival appearance, their first two Canadian shows and the last two British concerts. Like 'I Know It's Over', The Smiths never performed this track without Craig Gannon, its final outing being at the London Palladium (26/10/86).

49

'What's The World?' *(Glennie/Gilbertson/Whelan/Booth)*

Recorded **25 September 1985, Barrowlands, Glasgow**

Produced by **Grant Showbiz**

B-side to **'I Started Something I Couldn't Finish' (cassette format only), October 1987**

In response to criticisms from fans north of the border that the March *Meat Is Murder* tour had neglected their Scottish audience, in late September, after wrapping up the preliminary sessions for *The Queen Is Dead* at RAK, The Smiths embarked upon a short seven-date tour of the country to coincide with the release of their new single, 'The Boy With The Thorn In His Side'.

As an exclusive treat for these few Scottish dates, each night they performed a cover of 'What's The World?', the debut single from Manchester's James,[85] released on the Factory label the previous year. Inspired by James's performance as support on that earlier *Meat Is Murder* tour, Morrissey's decision to promote the repertoire of a new, up-and-coming band would set a precedent that he'd return to in his solo career (championing Bradford's 'Skin Storm' and Suede's 'My Insatiable One' with similar gusto).

As a cover, The Smiths' interpretation of the track was unremarkable if maintaining the spirited thrust of James' admittedly superior original. It is unlikely that such a live recording was ever planned for general release since its eventual issue as a cassette single extra track on 1987's 'I Started Something I Couldn't Finish' was instigated purely out of desperation for new B-sides in the wake of the split. Consequently the agreeable if dispensable 'What's The World?' is of trivial significance within The Smiths' history, as Marr confirms. 'Morrissey had his reasons for wanting us to play that but I was never really mad about it, it never really felt like us. It added another slightly different dynamic to the live set, that's all.'

85 James would later become one of Britain's most popular alternative guitar bands of the Nineties, their turbulent beginnings salvaged by the 'Madchester' movement which provided them with a number 2 UK hit in 1991, 'Sit Down'. The following year, James also substituted for Morrissey at the last minute when he pulled out of his scheduled Glastonbury Festival performance (26/6/92). By way of a barbed homage, they opened their set with a cover of his recent solo single 'We Hate It When Our Friends Become Successful'.

In Concert

Introduced at Irvine Magnum Leisure Centre (22/9/85), 'What's The World?' was played throughout the 1985 Scottish tour up to and including Inverness Eden Court (1/10/85).

50

'Unloveable'

Recorded **October-November 1985, Jacobs Studios, Farnham**

Produced by **Morrissey and Marr**

B-side to **'Bigmouth Strikes Again' (12-inch format only), May 1986**

Marr was 'playing his guitar and watching TV with the volume down' one evening at home in Manchester when he first happened upon the simplistic, pleasant major chord loop of 'Unloveable'. He was sufficiently impressed with the tune to commit it to tape and drive it round to Morrissey's house the same night.

Against this innocuous harmonic template, Morrissey played to type with an apologetic lyric lamenting his own romantic incapability, which, by this stage in their career, cruised dangerously close to self-parody. Within his rueful confession of material poverty and inborn strangeness he'd cunningly paraphrase the chorus of Sandie Shaw's 'Message Understood', also weaving in an apparent homage to the original 'Man In Black', Johnny Cash.

First taped during the September RAK sessions prior to their short tour of Scotland,[86] 'Unloveable' was properly recorded during their later residency at Jacobs Studios that winter. Early mid-production album mixes indicate that the song had actually been earmarked for inclusion on *The Queen Is Dead* (one such trial track listing, retained by Mike Joyce, places it as the penultimate number on side two) though in the event the late arrival of 'Vicar In A Tutu' **[see 55]** pushed it out of the running. Released instead as the 12-inch extra track to 'Bigmouth Strikes Again', 'Unloveable' was a satisfactory B-side but nevertheless ranks among Morrissey and Marr's lesser achievements.

In Concert

The Smiths never performed 'Unloveable' in front of a live audience. A full sound-check version, with vocal, recorded at Inverness Eden Court Theatre (1/10/85) exists on bootleg, suggesting they at least toyed with the idea of

86 At this point The Smiths had either recorded or demoed over half of *The Queen Is Dead*: 'The Boy With The Thorn In His Side'; 'Bigmouth Strikes Again'; 'There Is A Light That Never Goes Out'; 'Frankly, Mr Shankly'; 'Never Had No One Ever'; and the backing music for 'I Know It's Over'.

bringing the song into the main set at that stage. Ultimately, even after its release, 'Unloveable' was never considered strong enough to feature in their final tours of 1986.

51

'I Know It's Over'

Recorded **October-November 1985, Jacobs Studios, Farnham**
Produced by **Morrissey and Marr**
Album track from ***The Queen Is Dead*, June 1986**

Beside 'There Is A Light That Never Goes Out' and 'Frankly, Mr Shankly', 'I Know It's Over' was among three songs Marr first played to Morrissey one evening at the guitarist's house during the summer of 1985.[87] The tune was subsequently demoed as a then-unnamed instrumental during the September RAK sessions; its first rehearsal notable for Rourke's original staccato bass pulse, which, if only by coincidence, bore a strong similarity with Rita Pavone's 1966 UK hit 'Heart' (an English translation of her Italian original 'Cuore'), which Morrissey had previously cited as one of his favourite records in the *NME* two years earlier.

Having already written half of *The Queen Is Dead*, 'I Know It's Over' was the first new set of lyrics Morrissey completed during the album's main Jacobs residency in October. By this stage in their career, though they would still rehearse some tracks as a full band with vocal, for the majority of their latter recordings Morrissey had developed a working method similar to that of Roxy Music's Bryan Ferry, whereby he would wait for the backing track to be completed, taking notes and listening to instrumental run-throughs on tape, before adding his part at the very end. Just as the other members of Roxy Music were unaware of Ferry's plans, so Marr, Rourke and Joyce were often in the dark about the song title, lyrics and vocal melody until they heard Morrissey sing it for the first time over their finished score. 'Sometimes it was slightly frustrating,' says Rourke, 'because we'd have all the music done and Morrissey would come in and put a vocal on the top and in hindsight you'd think "well if I knew that's what he was going to do I would've played that differently." But maybe that's what made it so special.'

87 Marr may well have been referring to 'I Know It's Over' when interviewed by *Melody Maker* around the same period, telling the paper that the previous evening he'd written 'a real beaut ... along the lines of 'The Hand That Rocks The Cradle' or 'Reel Around The Fountain', so I'm feeling pretty chuffed about that.'

Such was the case with 'I Know It's Over'. Marr would later describe watching Morrissey come in and deliver his vocal as 'one of the highlights of my life', telling Johnny Rogan that 'every line he was hinting at where he was going to go I was thinking, "Is he going to go there? Yes, he is!" It was just brilliant.' The first take itself contained a few minor alterations (for example, Morrissey's bed is 'icy' as opposed to 'empty') but was still a turbulently passionate recital fully deserving of Marr's extraordinarily high praise.

Often regarded somewhat understandably as among Morrissey's 'bleakest' works, it might be fairer instead to categorise 'I Know It's Over' as his most isolationist. Admittedly, the unsettling suicidal narrative established in 'Asleep' and 'There Is A Light That Never Goes Out' is carried over with the blatant anxiety that 'the knife wants to slit me', yet the main thrust of the song is the frank realisation of the protagonist's exclusion from the loving relationships the rest of us take for granted. The death being graphically described – buried alive while crying for his mother – is more metaphorical than literal, as the lyrics amount to a determined letter of resignation from the human race. Even as he prohibits himself from ever finding reciprocal love, Morrissey pauses to advise those more fortunate than himself to count their blessings ('handsome groom, give her room').

The crux of the song's power and one of Morrissey's most ingenious feats as a lyricist occurs after the first chorus where, having gained our confidence through his own self-deprecation, he cleverly switches into an imagined first person conversation to reflect this same resolute self-disgust back out at the listener. Each of the rhetorical questions that Morrissey purports to have borne from his own unrequited love – 'if you're so funny, then why are you on your own tonight?' – we also must address. It's an incredible passage that transforms 'I Know It's Over' into a test of its audience's character; an interactive experience commanding the listener to acknowledge their own base insecurities.

Arguably the closing track on *The Queen Is Dead* that should have been, like 'There Is A Light That Never Goes Out' it would swiftly assume a unique place within The Smiths fans' creed. In its musical execution (the subtlety of Marr's acoustic chimes and emulated strings contrasting with the raw fury of Joyce's drum rolls), emotional weight and sheer scope, 'I Know It's Over' was, in every sense, an epic.

In Concert

Introduced at Glasgow Barrowlands (16/7/86), 'I Know It's Over' was a dramatic focal point of The Smiths final shows, habitually played as the last number before the encore. Morrissey would often symbolically retreat into the womb during the song's finale, stretching his T-shirt over his head akin to a child having trouble getting undressed.

Never performed without Craig Gannon, it remained in the set for the remainder of 1986 with the exception of the Canadian dates of that summer's North American tour and the final Brixton concert. 'I Know It's Over' was last played at Manchester Free Trade Hall (30/10/86).

Radio

A stunning seven-minute, live version of 'I Know It's Over' recorded at Kilburn National Ballroom (23/10/86) was first broadcast on BBC Radio 1's *In Concert* series in April 1987 and later included on 1988's posthumous live album *Rank* adapted from the same Kilburn performance.

52

'Some Girls Are Bigger Than Others'

Recorded **October-November 1985, Jacobs Studios, Farnham**

Produced by **Morrissey and Marr**

Album track from ***The Queen Is Dead*, June 1986**

'Some things just drop out of the heavens,' says Marr, 'and 'Some Girls... ' was one of them. It's a beautiful piece of music.' Possessing one of his most alluring guitar melodies (a return to the folk inspired arpeggios of earlier Smiths material, delivered with lucid dexterity) if Marr's tune was heaven-sent, then it seemed very nearly blasphemous of Morrissey to christen it 'Some Girls Are Bigger Than Others' and bestow it with its notoriously frivolous lyric. 'I do want to write about women,' the singer explained. 'The whole idea of womanhood is something that to me is largely unexplored. I'm realising things about women that I never realised before and 'Some Girls... ' is just taking it down to the basic absurdity of recognising the contours to one's body. The fact that I've scuttled through 26 years of life without ever noticing that the contours of the body are different is an outrageous farce!'

Sure enough, its words offered scant enlightenment beyond its titular observation, save the muted political bite in referring to 'the dole age' (the national unemployment figures still at crisis point during the Thatcher government of the mid-Eighties) and Morrissey's mysterious closing paraphrase of Johnny Tillotson's 1962 rock 'n' roll ballad 'Send Me The Pillow You Dream On'. Though commonly attributed to 1964's *Carry On Cleo*, the notoriously camp Antony and Cleopatra scenario detailed in the second verse was merely an extension of Morrissey's own whimsical sense of the absurd, echoed in the album's other vaudevillian interludes 'Vicar In A

Tutu' and 'Frankly, Mr Shankly' and, contrary to longstanding myth, bears no relation to the comedy itself.[88] Even so, it was maybe no coincidence that around the time of the album's release, Morrissey should choose to extol his love of the *Carry On* series to the *NME*. 'There were 27 films made in all and at least six of them are high art. They finished artistically in '68 but it went on, I think, to '76 or '78. When you think of Charles Hawtrey, Kenneth Williams, Hattie Jacques, Barbara Windsor, Joan Sims, Sid James... the wealth of talent!'

Completed midway through the Jacobs sessions, though it seemed an unlikely album closer, as the final track on *The Queen Is Dead*, 'Some Girls Are Bigger Than Others' worked as a flippant palate cleanser after its more emotionally intense peaks. Engineer Stephen Street would also add his own stamp on the record with a twist on the false fade out he'd previously suggested for 'That Joke Isn't Funny Anymore' **[see 35]**. 'The song, as it was, just faded in, so I thought we had to do something a bit more interesting. Basically I put all the reverb on the drums up so it sounded like it was coming in from some large hall, then faded it down really quickly. Then I took all the reverb back off and faded it up again. The effect was supposed to be like the music's in a hall somewhere, it goes away, then it comes back and it's nice and clean and dry. A bit like opening a door, closing it, then opening it again and walking in.'

In Concert

Though briefly tested at sound-checks on their 1986 US tour, 'Some Girls Are Bigger Than Others' wouldn't be introduced into The Smiths' live set until their final concert at London's Brixton Academy (12/12/86) with the band back to the original four-piece line up after Craig Gannon's departure.

Luckily, its belated live debut was taped for posterity and later released by Rough Trade as an extra track on both the 12-inch and cassette single of 'I Started Something I Couldn't Finish' in October 1987. The recording itself is a fairly crude mixing desk effort, low on ambience with the audience response noticeably weak in the mix. As a snapshot of the Smiths' last stand, however, it reveals Marr as a guitarist who, stripped of studio trickery and the support of Gannon he'd come to rely on in concert, could still dazzle with some extraordinarily delicate and adept picking. If Gannon had given him

88 At no point during *Carry On Cleo* does actor Sid James, as Mark Antony, turn to Amanda Barrie, as Cleopatra, exclaiming 'oh I say' whilst opening a crate of beer. Even *Severed Alliance* author Johnny Rogan has claimed, erroneously, that James is seen cracking open a bottle of ale during the film despite the fact that, as it is set in Roman times, he is only ever seen drinking from pitchers and goblets of wine. Ironically, *Carry On Cleo* does actually contain an unrelated Smiths reference, albeit tenuous: during the meal onboard the Roman galley, Charles Hawtrey mutters 'stop me if you've heard this before' **[see 75]**.

space to breathe, space to show off even, here was concrete proof that Marr had lost none of his ability to fill the gaps on his own with characteristic flair.

The live version of 'Some Girls Are Bigger Than Others' is also something of a rarity in containing an extra third verse not featured on *The Queen Is Dead*. Driving the song's title home just that bit further, Morrissey informs us of a 'Girlie' calendar that is 'as obvious as snow, as if we didn't know.'

53

'Cemetry Gates'

Recorded **October-November 1985, Jacobs Studios, Farnham**
Produced by **Morrissey and Marr**
Album track from ***The Queen Is Dead,*** **June 1986**
Subsequently issued as the B-side to **'Ask', October 1986**

Even before the critical veneration of *The Queen Is Dead*, Morrissey and Marr were being hailed, in the words of the latter, as 'The Great New Songwriters'. 'I was on the train,' Marr later reflected, 'thinking, "right, if you're so great, first thing in the morning, sit down and write a great song." I started with [the] 'Cemetry Gates' B-minor to G change in open G.'

Though this simple yet effective contiguity of major and minor chords was all the inspiration Marr needed, he certainly wasn't the first to exploit their united melodic temper. Twenty-two years earlier, Paul McCartney's reverse drop from G to B-minor while composing 'I Want To Hold Your Hand' dumbfounded John Lennon who, as legend has it, enthused, 'That's it! Do that again!' History was to repeat itself when Morrissey heard Marr strum the same chords while allegedly tuning up in his kitchen and keenly interrupted 'that's the song!'.

In spite of its foundation Beatles pattern, Marr would quote The Kinks as his original influence; its breezy, acoustic air possibly endeavouring to capture the harmonious agility of Ray Davies' maturing catalogue circa 1968's *The Kinks are the Village Green Preservation Society*. The resulting genial melody – underscored by a fittingly relaxed rhythm section, sequined with added Nashville-style electric sparkles and the comforting major-key drones of a harmonium – provided the album with some much needed levity (especially at the close of side one after the relentless sequence of 'I Know It's Over' and 'Never Had No One Ever').

Typically, Morrissey would subvert its inherent beauty by using the tune to eulogise the eldritch pastime of visiting graveyards. Though feasibly one of several references on the album that could be linked to the film *Billy Liar* (namely Tom Courtenay's courtship of Helen Fraser in the local cemetery), Morrissey told the press he was already a regular grave-watcher himself, sometimes accompanied by former Magazine singer Howard Devoto ('it's a most gripping pastime I can assure you'). In fact, Morrissey had been rambling between tombstones for pleasure since the late-Seventies, his original haunt being Manchester's Southern Cemetery in the company of Linder Sterling. The song's morbid premise and misspelled title notwithstanding (the latter appears to have been a genuine syntax error on its author's part), 'Cemetry Gates' would improbably become one of Morrissey's more optimistic portrayals of romantic human relationships. The song's central couple share genuine happiness speculating on the lives of the departed, while playfully attempting to outwit one another in tit-for-tat intellectual charades.

It was also a coy confessional of Morrissey's own literary plagiarism. A firm believer in 'talent borrows, genius steals' (a maxim commonly attributed to Oscar Wilde and later etched into the run-out groove on the B-side of 'Bigmouth Strikes Again' **[see Appendix II]**), the singer had all too often been rumbled by critics who happily exposed his sources from films such as *Sleuth* ('This Charming Man') and *A Taste of Honey* ('Reel Around The Fountain' et al). In 'Cemetry Gates', he impishly preaches the virtues of originality while arguing the merits of Keats, Yeats and Wilde before he and his partner's literary jockeying escalates into a nonsensical lexicon of cod Shakespearean gobbledygook; specifically the bastardised translation of 'the early village-cock hath twice done salutation to the morn' from *Richard III*, V:3.

Within this scheme it wasn't so much cynical as knowingly ironic of Morrissey to integrate another chunk of appropriated dialogue from a hitherto untapped cinematic resource. The 1942 Hollywood adaptation of Hart & Kaufman's play *The Man Who Came To Dinner* already had great personal resonance, as during his pre-Smiths ventures into freelance rock journalism Morrissey had written under the pseudonym of 'Sheridan Whiteside'; the film's eponymous scoundrel played by Monty Woolley. A precocious 'critic, lecturer, wit, radio orator, intimate friend of the great and near great', Whiteside is a pompous irritant, who, after slipping on an ice cube on the steps of a wealthy Ohio family's home one Christmas, feigns invalidity and proceeds to take over their entire household while threatening to sue. Whiteside's unbearable self-importance is best summed up in his nurse's complaint that 'if Florence Nightingale had ever nursed you, Mr Whiteside, she would have married Jack the Ripper instead of founding the Red Cross.' What attracted Morrissey to usurp the *nom de plume* of this blustering charlatan in the first place, one can only guess. It's doubly curious that following The Smiths' split, their final two Rough Trade singles – 'I Started Something I Couldn't Finish' and 'Last Night I Dreamt That Somebody Loved Me' – would both feature hidden matrix messages naming fictitious X-certificate movies 'starring Sheridan Whiteside' **[see Appendix II]**.

'Cemetry Gates' contains a lengthy citation from *The Man Who Came To Dinner*, though not from Whiteside himself. Instead it is the character of Lorraine Sheldon, played by Ann Sheridan, who towards the end of the movie reminisces about a visit to Pompeii. 'All those people – all those lives. Where are they now?' she mourns before describing one particular mummified victim: 'Here was a woman – like myself – a woman who once lived and loved, full of the same passions, fears, jealousies, hates. And what remains of it now? … I want to cry.'

One of the last songs to be completed for the album, engineer Stephen Street remembers 'Cemetry Gates' vividly as a track 'where everything we tended to try just worked like a dream.'

In Concert

One of a handful of *The Queen Is Dead* tracks previewed at the Liverpool Royal Court 'From Manchester With Love' benefit (8/2/86), 'Cemetry Gates' would stay in their live repertoire for the rest of the year up to and including the final concert at Brixton Academy (12/12/86).

Radio

'Cemetry Gates' recorded live at Kilburn National Ballroom (23/10/86) was first broadcast on BBC Radio 1's *In Concert* series in April 1987 and later included on 1988's posthumous live album *Rank* adapted from the same Kilburn performance.

54

'The Queen Is Dead'

Recorded **October-November 1985, Jacobs Studios, Farnham**

Produced by **Morrissey and Marr**

Album track from ***The Queen Is Dead*, June 1986**

The Smiths' greatest singular recording, it fits that 'The Queen Is Dead' was the perfect hybrid of Morrissey and Marr's carefully considered song-writing masterplan with the band's unpredictable flair for studio spontaneity. According to Marr, the musical concept had been fermenting in his mind for several months prior to its recording.[89] His intention had been to merge the raw garage fire of early-Seventies Detroit punk pioneers the MC5 with the cooler sophistication of The Velvet Underground. The latter's 'I Can't Stand It', a 1969 out-take that had only just been posthumously issued on 1985's *VU* compilation, was to be Marr's main foundation stone; borrowing its loose rock 'n' roll template and even appropriating Lou Reed's same scratching guitar rhythm during its lengthy instrumental finale. From this basic agenda Marr, began to jam his ideas with Joyce and Rourke, whose resultant bass riff ('a killer' in the words of Stephen Street) would earn the guitarist's accolade of 'one that [other] bass players still haven't matched.'

Its first instrumental take stretched to over eight minutes of furious cyclical repetition through Marr's untethered wah-wah crests, Joyce's equally impulsive snare drum ricochets and Rourke's vibrant bass scales. The gilt on the frame, however, would be Marr's ghostly, controlled-feedback whistle, winding through the entire track. The effect in question was discovered purely by chance. 'I'd done the rhythm track and left the guitar on the stand,' Marr later explained, 'the wah-wah pedal just happened to be half open, and putting the guitar down made it suddenly hit off this harmonic. We were back at the desk playing back the rhythm track and I could still hear this harmonic wailing away, so we put the tape back on to record while I crept back into the booth and started opening up the wah-wah, thinking "don't die, don't die!"'. As Stephen Street confirms, 'Johnny did it pretty much live in one take. It was just one of those inspired performances. He just got this great harmonic feedback from his Les Paul and as he changed the angle on the pedal, it changed the note.'

Even before the lyrics had been added, Morrissey had already embellished the studio master with its sampled frontispiece of 'Take Me Back To Dear Old Blighty', culled from Bryan Forbes' 1962 film adaptation of Lynne Reid Banks' kitchen-sink drama *The L-Shaped Room*. Originally, the film's 90-second sequence – in which the elderly lesbian played by Cicely Courtneidge sings this relic of WWI music hall jingoism for the amusement of her fellow lodgers in a Notting Hill boarding house – was tacked on in its entirety, before being later abbreviated to its final chorus alone. The song's faltering stop, which sounds like a clumsy edit, is actually on account of the pregnant lead character played by Leslie Caron whose sudden collapse forces Courtneidge to trail off (as she sings 'I should like to see my best girl').

89 Marr had already been forewarned by Morrissey of the designated title 'The Queen Is Dead'. The alternative of 'Margaret On The Guillotine' had briefly been considered but was abandoned because, in the singer's own words, its lyrics 'didn't fit any music that was presented at the time.' The latter title would of course be salvaged for Morrissey's 1988 solo debut *Viva Hate*.

The final piece of the jigsaw was Joyce's tribal drum intro, which was added after the main backing track had been put down. 'We had this very antiquated sampler called a Window,' Street clarifies, 'you could only record for so long but you could loop it. So we got Mike to play this rumbling rhythm and then sampled a small section of it. That's what you hear at the beginning of 'The Queen Is Dead', not live drums but a repeated sample. It's actually quite complicated so all credit to Mike that he learnt how to replicate that sample going into the main song when they played it in concert.'

The elaborate and spellbinding intensity of its score deserved nothing less than Morrissey at his lyrical zenith. Marr wasn't to be disappointed, later citing its words as his favourite that his partner had ever written. The title itself was lifted from an especially disturbing chapter from Hubert Selby Jr's controversial novel *Last Exit to Brooklyn* (the subject of several obscenity trials in the UK and the US upon its original publication in 1964). In its new milieu, the phrase became the perfect inflammatory umbrella under which Morrissey could fan his monarchy-bashing ire, previously only hinted at in 'Nowhere Fast' **[see 32]**. As an attack on the House of Windsor expressed through the medium of popular music, 'The Queen Is Dead' very nearly surpasses The Sex Pistols' 'God Save The Queen', which famously provoked the outrage of a nation blinded by the rose-tinted, flag-waving nostalgia of 1977's Silver Jubilee celebrations. But where John Lydon's brilliance was one of grand sarcasm, the insolent sneer of punk's two-fingered salute born of mid-Seventies frustration, Morrissey's greatest weapon in his storming of the palace is wit, which had been sharpened to the deadliest of razor-fine tips.

The effrontery of Morrissey's prose is as perceptive as it is profound. His blunt dismissal of the monarchy as outmoded, uncaring and parasitical is also a rejection of England itself. This arch invective takes the form of a farewell address to his native soil in harsh and acerbic contrast to Courtneidge's yearning for 'dear Old Blighty'. Morrissey begins by venting his own aggravation at England's 'cheerless marshes' as the land Courtneidge yearns for is revealed to be a desecrated carcass of its former Imperial stature, offering its subjects little solace beyond drink, the money-grabbing clergy and hard drugs (sold by prepubescent tearaways). While speculating on the mortality of Elizabeth II, the actual dead Queen Morrissey cries of is far more metaphysical.

Between this sobering decree, the listener is also witness to a hilarious turn of vaudeville humbug beginning with treasonous fantasies of 'her very Lowness' in the gallows. Her eldest son, Prince Charles, is next to be targeted with the provocative suggestion of closet transvestism, while the far-right editorial of *The Daily Mail* is also cocked a snook in the same breath. The extent of Morrissey's gall is evident when later he pictures himself as an intruder breaking into Buckingham Palace. The scenario was already far too close to comfort for the Queen who, on 7 July 1982, had been woken in her bed by a real-life trespasser, Michael Fagin, whose surmounting of Buckingham Palace's shoddy security caused a national scandal. Morrissey puts himself in Fagin's shoes, armed with a rusty spanner and sponge, presumably to bludgeon Her Majesty before mopping up the mess. The imagined dialogue between sovereign and singer is at once self-effacing and brazen. Like some brusque Northern stand-up comic spinning an improbable yarn for the sake of a fittingly absurd punch line (the mischievous rhyming of 'spanner' with 'piano'), Morrissey's vision is a one man *Carry On Up The Monarchy*.

Outside of this ribald Royal farce and Morrissey's acrid obituary for Old Blighty, there lies a third and far more ambiguous subtext. From the frightful sketch of Prince Charles' cross-dressing urges, the narrator then describes his shame at discovering 'some old queen' in his own family tree. Later, in a scene provoked by the 1963 film version of *Billy Liar* in which Tom Courtenay hopes to get his wicked way with Helen Fraser by suggesting 'let's go for a walk, where it's quiet', Morrissey finds himself frustrated both at his inability to discuss castration with his companion and the weather's adverse effect on his hairdo. Most curious of all is the unprinted lyric, heavily disguised in reverb, where he also mourns 'lies about make up and long hair'. Collectively, these details hint at a more esoteric interpretation, thematically in keeping with Selby Jnr's original chapter about 'a hip queer' named Georgette: 'Queen' in the effeminate homosexual sense.

Regardless of any such alternate readings, perhaps understandably the press focussed wholly on the song's portrayal of the Royals as flawed mortals. Finally released in 1986, five years after the wedding of Charles and Diana and only a year before Prince Andrew and Sarah Ferguson's nuptials, the British monarchy was then very much a sacred institution, whose fallibility in the eyes of the public wouldn't be exposed until the early-Nineties with the divorce of both marriages and the death of Diana in 1997. Though the reaction wasn't to be anything as dramatic as that previously created by The Sex Pistols' equation of the monarchy with a 'fascist regime', at the time 'The Queen Is Dead' was still an incredibly brave assault on the nation's most sacred cow. As always, Morrissey's justification of their actions made superb copy. 'When one looks at all the individuals within the Royal Family,' he told the *NME*, 'they're so magnificently, unaccountably and unpardonably boring! I mean Diana herself has never in her lifetime uttered one statement that has been of any use to any member of the human race.'

Having finally completed the track at Jacobs, prior to the assembly of the finished album a debate ensued as to whether 'The Queen Is Dead' was too long in its master cut of just over seven and a half minutes. 'I remember telling Johnny that I thought it was a bit long and that we should bring it down,' says Street, 'but he said no at first. Then after we'd mixed it we all finally agreed that it was just slightly too much, so I did a manual edit from the half-inch tape master.' Street made four cuts in total to reduce it to a snappier 6.23.[90] In retrospect, the shortening of 'The Queen Is Dead' showed fantastic judgement and quality control. The famed unedited 'director's cut', as it were, actually takes its instrumental finale into unnecessarily repetitious territory, even if as a self-indulgent wallow in the sound of Marr, Rourke and Joyce firing on all cylinders it's as sensational as one might imagine.

With 'The Queen Is Dead', the band finally shed their skin as a mere sharp, consummate pop group, revealing themselves to be fundamental rock 'n' roll agitators of peerless courage, intellect and musical forethought. Its execution was a separate triumph for each and every band member however one wishes to read it; be it Morrissey's caustic Magna Carta, the decisive poise of Rourke's bass line, Joyce's idiomatic drumming upon the palace gates or Marr's uninhibited freak out in his infinite wah-wah vortex. The ultimate expression of Marr's 'rock from a housing estate' manifesto and as close to perfection as The Smiths ever achieved, 'The Queen Is Dead' is their unequivocal masterpiece.

In Concert

Perhaps their most awesome live set piece, 'The Queen Is Dead' was introduced shortly after its vinyl release at Glasgow Barrowlands (16/7/86), the first gig by the five-strong Smiths enhanced by Craig Gannon on second guitar. Initially featured towards the end of the set during their summer UK shows and Canadian/American tour, from their last few US dates onwards it was switched to become their apocalyptic set opener, remaining the first song of the night for their final British tour in October (except for Manchester Free Trade Hall 30/10/86 where it was preceded by 'Ask').

During performance, Morrissey would proudly raise a mounted placard inscribed with the song's title (as the tour progressed, the message changed to the more curious 'Two light ales please' instead). Marr also had his own gimmick, one that was to backfire drastically one fateful night at their third-to-last concert at Preston Guildhall (27/10/86). As Mike Joyce began his drum intro, Marr would stand by Joyce's kit, tapping the crash cymbals with a separate drumstick. When the first verse finally kicked in, Marr would routinely shimmy to the front of the stage, banging his guitar strings with

90 The version of 'The Queen Is Dead' that was officially released has three separate 14 second/four bar sections removed at 4.55, 5.09 and 5.51, while a final 28 seconds/eight bars have been cut away at 6.04.

the same drumstick before tossing it into the crowd with reckless abandon. Alas, on this occasion, a member of the audience hurled it back on stage where it struck Morrissey on the head.[91]

Exactly one week after a show at Newport Leisure Centre had to be aborted when Morrissey fell off stage **[see 59]**, the Preston gig started and finished with 'The Queen Is Dead', making it the shortest engagement of The Smiths' career. With Morrissey ferried to casualty (he waited for an hour in Preston Royal Infirmary, after which he gave up and went back to Manchester without seeking medical assistance), the remaining Smiths escaped to the jeers of an understandably pissed-off lynch mob of paying punters congregating outside.

Joyce recalls the atmosphere surrounding the venue as they arrived earlier that day as one of ominous hostility. 'It was pandemonium, there were gangs of skinheads giving it the 'Seig Heil!' salute so we were really frightened. It was supposed to be a homecoming gig of sorts because it was Preston, the North, not that far from Manchester, so we couldn't understand what had gone wrong. It might have been Johnny's drumstick that got thrown, but at the time I remember being told it was a coin that had struck Morrissey's head. Everybody was so hyped up and with us playing such a short set the place went mad. I remember talking to one of the roadies afterwards and he said "if I told you what we found on that stage you'd never go out and play live again".' As Andy Rourke also notes, such episodes did little to quell Morrissey's own nerves; 'After about the fifth missile incident I think he started getting paranoid about being shot.' Marr would later blame the Preston fiasco on the press for encouraging a hooligan element to attend Smiths concerts. The following night's scheduled concert at Llandudno Astra (28/10/86) was cancelled as a result.

For the final gig at Brixton Academy (12/12/86), 'The Queen Is Dead' was saved as an encore played third from the end; the first and only time it was performed without Craig Gannon.

Television

First screened on BBC2's short-lived annual music all-nighter *Rock Around the Clock* on 20 September 1986, *The Queen Is Dead* was a short film by Derek Jarman (co-directed with John Maybury and Richard Heslop).[92]

91 Rough Trade were adamant the missile was a coin, not Marr's drumstick, even though crowd testimonials printed in the following week's *Melody Maker* hinted otherwise: 'Many fans who were at the front saw him get hit with a piece of wood. It's absolute rubbish to say it was a sharpened coin or any other sort of coin.'

92 Jarman's *The Queen Is Dead* triptych was also released theatrically in the autumn of 1986 as a support feature to Alex Cox's *Sid and Nancy* at selected UK cinemas.

Comprised of three separate abstract film montages for the album tracks 'The Queen Is Dead', 'There Is A Light That Never Goes Out' and the single 'Panic', anybody familiar with Jarman's more notorious feature-length works like *Jubilee* or *Sebastian* (both screened on Channel 4 at the time, much to the displeasure of Mary Whitehouse, President of the doggedly conservative National Viewers and Listeners Association) would have found the film typical of his art-school, handheld-camera technique.

The main 'The Queen Is Dead' segment begins with an androgynous young woman in shorts and braces spraying the song's title onto a concrete wall in a derelict wasteland followed by a cornucopia of superimposed motifs; from roses, crowns and guitars to goldfish, burning records and Buckingham Palace. Unusual, if very repetitious, Jarman's Smiths shorts would have made ideal back projections for live shows, but weren't totally successful as individual films in their own right. Morrissey, however, would refer to their unpopularity with the public as a marker of Jarman's talent.

Radio

A spirited live version of 'The Queen Is Dead' recorded as the opening number at Kilburn National Ballroom (23/10/86) was first broadcast on BBC Radio 1's *In Concert* series in April 1987 and later included on 1988's posthumous live album *Rank* adapted from the same Kilburn performance.

55

'Vicar In A Tutu'

Recorded **October-November 1985, Jacobs Studios, Farnham**

Produced by **Morrissey and Marr**

Album track from ***The Queen Is Dead,*** **June 1986**

Subsequently issued as the B-side to **'Panic', August 1986**

The last piece of music to be written for *The Queen Is Dead,* 'Vicar In A Tutu' arose from a spur-of-the-moment studio jam in the final week of recording at Jacobs. That it lacks Marr's usual premeditation is glaringly obvious. Not only is it based upon a repeated twelve-bar cycle with no bridges, middle eights or other such deviations, it also reprocesses the same chord pool already employed in 'Bigmouth Strikes Again', 'There Is A Light That Never Goes Out', 'Frankly, Mr Shankly' and 'Some Girls Are Bigger Than Others'.[93] It's also the only section on *The Queen Is Dead* to lapse into musical pastiche,

93 'Vicar In A Tutu' is rooted in E, but with a chorus that yet again sees Marr juggling the ubiquitous C# minor with A and B majors.

a transparent mimicry of Sun rockabilly and the sub-country picking style of Elvis's original lead guitar player Scotty Moore (one need only compare Marr's predominant riff with Moore's mercurial solo on 1955's 'Mystery Train' to note the song's unmistakable muse).

To a large degree, 'Vicar In A Tutu' may have been contrived, but what it lacks in invention it accounts for in naturalism. Apart from Marr's own polished restraint (resisting the temptation to switch into fifth gear as on past rockabilly dalliances such as 'Shakespeare's Sister' or 'Rusholme Ruffians'), Joyce's breathless brush work also lends the track a tactile radiance unique within the album's track listing, even if the drummer himself freely confesses to the irregularity of the song's rhythm. 'It's all over the place,' comments Joyce, 'you try putting a click track on top of it and it's just impossible.'

Morrissey plays the joker card yet again by applauding the eccentricity of the song's eponymous clergyman, who chooses to preach the gospel half dressed as a ballerina. It's a softer dig at religious convention than the straight accusations of corruption mentioned within 'The Queen Is Dead', but potentially no less disdainful of the church hierarchy. His one-off situation comedy is brilliantly realised with a vivid cast of supporting players; Rose with her collection plate, the 'monkish Monsignor' and Morrissey himself as a petty criminal stealing lead from the spires of Manchester's Holy Name Church. The lyrics also feature another of the album's many references to the 1963 film *Billy Liar*, in which Tom Courtenay daydreams about the state funeral of his grandmother who 'struggled valiantly to combat ignorance and disease'. As a last addition to *The Queen Is Dead*, 'Vicar In A Tutu' successfully nudged the inferior 'Unloveable' out of the running order even if, on its own merits, the song was ostensibly an amusing but lightweight filler.

In Concert

Introduced at Liverpool Royal Court (8/2/86), 'Vicar In A Tutu' stayed in the set during the spring Irish tour, their summer UK dates introducing Craig Gannon and the four Canadian concerts in late July, but was dropped from the following month's North American itinerary altogether. A routine fixture of the final UK tour, it was last played at Manchester Free Trade Hall (30/10/86). Unlike the album version's sudden start, in concert 'Vicar In A Tutu' opened with an instrumental chorus prologue.

Television

On 20 May 1986, 'Vicar In A Tutu' was given its national broadcast premiere on BBC2's *Whistle Test*. The second of two tracks played that evening **[see also 46]**, Andy Kershaw offered a teasing first glimpse of the cover art of *The*

Queen Is Dead by way of introduction before the band let rip, attacking 'Vicar In A Tutu' with such ferocity that the final album version released a month later would seem almost lame by comparison.

Joyce kept the rhythm to a taut express-train pace, while the dual guitars of Marr and new-boy Craig Gannon exploded in an angelic treble fusion of sliding rockabilly licks. For the song's wailing climax of 'I am a living sign', Morrissey crouched on his knees in mock religious fervour bringing a truly inspirational performance to its end.

Radio

A live version of 'Vicar In A Tutu' recorded at Kilburn National Ballroom (23/10/86) was first broadcast on BBC Radio 1's *In Concert* series in April 1987 and later included on 1988's posthumous live album *Rank* adapted from the same show.[94]

56

'Frankly, Mr Shankly'

Recorded **December 1985, Wessex Studios, London**

Produced by **Morrissey and Marr**

Album track from ***The Queen Is Dead,*** **June 1986**

The pinnacle of Morrissey's recurring thesis on the monotony of regular employment, 'Frankly, Mr Shankly' also presented The Smiths at their most vaudevillian extreme. The manifest music-hall wit of its lyrics transpose even to Marr's complementary, tongue-in-cheek score, given a final slapstick shove from Joyce's Salvation Army stomp and Rourke's quirky Tyrolean bass. Marr took the inspiration for its jaunty, oompah rhythm from 'Yesterday Man', a 1965 top three hit for Sandie Shaw songwriter Chris Andrews. 'That was the idea,' says Marr, 'but it didn't *quite* work out that way.'

Repelling the futility of the nine-to-five grind, Morrissey's rhetoric is almost Marxist; dismissing what Marx himself would call 'acquisitive activity' as a corrosive and inhuman hindrance to his artistic bent. Though the name of Shankly seemed a plausible nod to the late legendary Liverpool football manager Bill Shankly, as a cocksure fantasy resignation speech the song was more in keeping with *Billy Liar* and Tom Courtenay's tribulations in the

94 The version of 'Vicar In A Tutu' on *Rank* sees Morrissey actually sing 'head of a child' as annotated on *The Queen Is Dead*'s printed lyrics. Strangely, on the album itself he sings 'head of a goose'.

employment of his undertaker boss Mr Shadrach (Leonard Rossiter). Its periodically hysterical verses were as close to the comedy repertoire of Morrissey's heroes George Formby (whose 'Why Don't Women Like Me?' was played as interval music during The Smiths' latter concerts) and Victoria Wood as he'd ever ventured. There's even a possible nod to Wood herself, when speculating on making Christmas cards with psychiatric patients. In Wood's 'Funny How Things Turn Out' **[see 33]**, she too has a similar desire to 'sing Lerner and Lowe to the mentally ill'.

Considering how successfully the lyrics work as a universal anthem for disaffected employees of whatever vocation, it was surprising to learn that Morrissey's objectives were far more personal with the butt of his joke being his own boss-of-sorts, Geoff Travis. As Rourke and Joyce both confirm, the 'bloody awful poetry' referred to an incident in which Travis had composed what he regarded as a humorous ode in an attempt to impress Morrissey. 'Geoff kind of saw himself on the same level as him intellectually,' verifies Joyce, 'but I don't think Morrissey saw it that way at all.' In the event the song uncannily foretold the dispute between the band and the label that was to besiege the release of *The Queen Is Dead*, and which culminated in their eventual defection to EMI the following year.

Its actual composition dated back to the summer of 1985 during one of Morrissey and Marr's infrequent 'eyeball-to-eyeball' song-writing sessions at the guitarist's house in Bowden (the same night Marr would also give Morrissey the music to 'I Know It's Over' and 'There Is A Light That Never Goes Out'). Demoed at RAK Studios in September prior to their Scottish mini-tour, an alleged technical mishap during the main Jacobs sessions would ensure that 'Frankly, Mr Shankly' had to be re-recorded after *The Queen Is Dead* had been provisionally completed, thus becoming the last master take to appear within its eventual running order. The accepted story, according to Stephen Street, is that the studio's new digital desk malfunctioned to create a second of dropout (total silence) halfway through the original.

Though there's no reason to doubt this established anecdote, what it fails to explain is the radical difference between the first 'Frankly, Mr Shankly' – which has survived, curiously devoid of any such dropout – and that which appeared on the finished album. Like its sibling draft of 'Never Had No One Ever' **[see 48]**, the song initially featured a cameo from the same BBC orchestra trumpet player. This inappropriate brass part is introduced during its premature middle eight, before offering a peculiar four-note bugle response call to 'Mis-ter Shank-ly!' during the next verse. The tone was very much that of early David Bowie (during his late-Sixties 'Anthony Newley period'), in particular his 1966 Deram single 'Rubber Band'.

Whatever the intended effect, the trumpet take of 'Frankly, Mr Shankly' was shelved, making its re-recording a necessity, dropout or not. Out of time at Jacobs, a last gasp renovation session was swiftly scheduled back in London at Wessex Studios in Highbury. With Marr now mentally and physically exhausted, he called upon the emergency services of John Porter, who hadn't worked with the group in over a year, to engineer a new version of the track. 'Johnny was a bit burned out on the whole thing,' says Porter, 'he'd reached a point when he just had enough.'

The ensuing delay fortuitously allowed Morrissey time to hone his lyrics, making a few subtle but important improvements. Originally, he'd complained of being 'a tremulous wreck' (an adjective which he may have felt he'd already exhausted on 'Rusholme Ruffians') who wished to 'do something' as opposed to the much more uproarious 'catch something' to bring him shame. The vital pay-off groan of 'give us yer money!' was also absent from its earlier take.

Miniature in stature perhaps, 'Frankly, Mr Shankly' was still a minor gem in The Smiths' crown that worked both as pure comedy and as a wonderfully comforting catharsis for long-suffering workers the world over.

In Concert

Alongside their current single 'The Boy With The Thorn In His Side', 'Frankly, Mr Shankly' and 'Bigmouth Strikes Again' were the first songs from *The Queen Is Dead* to be introduced live during the mini tour of Scotland in September 1985, debuting at Irvine Magnum Leisure Centre (22/9/85). Last played as a four piece at Liverpool Royal Court (8/2/86), it was absent from their turbulent February Irish dates but returned with Craig Gannon added to the ranks at Glasgow Barrowlands (16/7/86) to remain in the set for the duration of their Canadian/US tour bar the last four American shows.

A popular crowd favourite on the final UK tour in October, it was last played at Manchester Free Trade Hall (30/10/86), their penultimate gig and Gannon's final appearance with The Smiths.

Radio

A live version recorded at Kilburn National Ballroom (23/10/86) was first broadcast on BBC Radio 1's *In Concert* series in April 1987. Although the posthumous live album *Rank* was adapted from the same Kilburn performance, 'Frankly, Mr Shankly' was not selected within Morrissey's final running order.

57

'Money Changes Everything'

Recorded **December 1985, Wessex Studios, London**
Produced by **John Porter**
B-side to **'Bigmouth Strikes Again', May 1986**

Having engineered 'Frankly, Mr Shankly' after being excluded from The Smiths' recording career for the best part of 17 months, John Porter's readmission into the fold was secured when he stayed on at Wessex to produce 'Money Changes Everything', their second instrumental B-side.

Marr later explained that he discovered its bluesy, octave-leaping riff by accident on his home 4-track portastudio, when he heard a different guitar part running back to front coming through on the reverse of the cassette he was working with. He was impressed enough to 'learn it backwards then play it backwards'. Together, Marr and Porter constructed the track alone using a heavily synthetic Linn drum guide (later overridden by Joyce's static beat). Originally much sparser and less twangy, Marr was especially proud of its rounded intro of feathery chord surges created by precision twiddling with his guitar's volume control.

Morrissey had no involvement with the track whatsoever (bar its portentous title), though claimed a joint composer credit. As Stephen Street speculates, his estrangement may well have been a reflection on the return of Porter himself. 'I think Johnny formed a stronger relationship with John Porter than he did with me,' admits Street. 'They definitely had a great understanding and a real bond. Morrissey was probably envious of that. If Johnny had had his way, I think he'd have wanted John to do the albums as well as just the odd single here and there, whereas Morrissey didn't.' As it transpired, John Porter remained on board to produce the majority of their sessions over the next 12 months, until Morrissey persuasively barred him from the band's insular clique once and for all.

'Money Changes Everything' was later to assume a new lease of life as Bryan Ferry's 'The Right Stuff'; a single from the Roxy Music singer's 1987 solo LP *Bête Noir*, which amounted to a slick cover version of the same Smiths instrumental with an accompanying Ferry lyric ('it's mountain high, river deep – the right stuff'). Ferry had first contacted the group through Warners in America before introducing himself during a visit to Livingston Studios in May 1986, while The Smiths were recording the 'Panic' single **[see 58]**. 'He came down to meet the band because we were all big fans,' explains Marr. 'So it was news to me when I found out years later that another person was unhappy about me doing this. It wouldn't have been a problem for me to say "of course you can cover it Bryan but I don't have to be there". If I thought it was upsetting the band then I wouldn't have done it.'

Nevertheless, Marr's involvement in 'The Right Stuff' would upset not only Morrissey, but the majority of The Smiths' audience; principally because the single was released in October 1987 amid the fall-out of the group's shock split. Despite the fact that 'The Right Stuff' had been recorded months previously, its unfortunate scheduling gave the misleading impression that Marr had deserted Morrissey and hopped straight into the studio with Ferry – a heretical betrayal in the eyes of The Smiths' obsessively loyal fan base. 'The Right Stuff' was to finally stall in the UK singles charts at 37.

Though not included on the original *The World Won't Listen* LP, the solid if inconsequential 'Money Changes Everything' did appear as an extra track upon the compilation's first 1987 cassette and CD release.

In Concert

The first instrumental The Smiths ever played live, 'Money Changes Everything' was introduced at Salford University (20/7/86) prior to that summer's lengthy tour of Canada and North America, where it was routinely slotted in as the first encore. The Salford gig was a particularly riotous evening, largely considered to be among the best of their career. 'We'd played to a massive crowd at G-Mex the night before,' remembers Joyce, 'but Salford University was a thousand times better. We were rocking, the whole place was rocking. The roadies had to climb up on top of the PA stack to stop it falling over. You could see it bowing in. The place went nuts, it was like the building was gonna collapse. They even had to evacuate people downstairs.'

With Craig Gannon added to the ranks, Marr could finally bring his instrumentals to life as part of The Smiths' stage show. 'Money Changes Everything' was an opportunity for the band to indulge in an exhibition match of their united musicianship without the distraction of a vocalist, also granting Morrissey respite to change his shirt and take a pre-encore breather. Its success encouraged Marr to repeat the experiment with 'The Draize Train' on the final autumn UK tour. Consequently the Salford show was the only time 'Money Changes Everything' was performed in the UK.

Part 4

'... *Liverpool, Leeds or Birmingham, but I don't care!*'

Recordings 1986-1987

As Christmas 1985 approached, *The Queen Is Dead* was ready to release. Yet what The Smiths hadn't anticipated was the sheer gravity of their behind-the-scenes contractual row with Rough Trade, which had been a constant psychological burden during its recording. With the label refusing to release any Smiths product until a legal compromise was settled, the band were thus plunged into crisis, with Marr even making an unsuccessful bid to steal back the album's master tapes as a bartering tool.[95]

'I thought that was so fucking noble,' smiles Marr. 'The concept only occurred to me and [guitar technician] Phil Powell at about midnight. So we took off from Manchester in an absolute blizzard, this full-on snow storm, and drove down to Jacobs in Surrey. It took about seven hours! By the time we got there it was breakfast. One of the owners woke up and said "Oh? Hi Johnny, what are you doing here?". So I was dead straight with him and said "I've come for the tapes. It's okay I'm just taking them home." But he couldn't release them without Rough Trade knowing. Really they just wanted the money for them. Had I handed over a cheque it would have been a different matter.'

In the interim, Morrissey's return South after acquiring a second home in Chelsea's Cadogan Square represented another change in their equilibrium. Their release schedule still frozen, as 1986 began The Smiths had only a short tour of Ireland in February to look forward to, preceded by appearances at two separate political benefits in Newcastle and Liverpool.

The first of these, an impromptu cameo on the Labour Party affiliated Red Wedge tour on 31 January, is among Marr's proudest memories. 'The Red Wedge gig at Newcastle City Hall was one of the best things we ever did. Andy and I had done a couple of gigs already with Billy Bragg in Manchester and Birmingham the week before. It was fun hanging out with Billy and we enjoyed playing with him, but the atmosphere around the other bands on that tour was really shitty. They treated me and Andy pretty scrappily.

95 Such an exercise had previously worked for Dexys Midnight Runners, who in similar circumstances outwitted their EMI superiors by repossessing the studio masters of their 1980 debut *Searching for the Young Soul Rebels*, thus gaining the upper hand in a dispute over their contract.

Anyway, I was telling Morrissey about it and he was fairly up for just doing an impromptu show. So we drove up to Newcastle, without telling anyone. I walked into the sound-check, having already been a bit of a feature the week before, but this time with *the gang*. We had no instruments, so we borrowed The Style Council's equipment and just tore the roof of the place. The other bands were a little bit perplexed as to what we were doing there. In the middle of the set we just walked on to this announcement and the place went bananas. I was so proud of the band. It was like *my* mates showed up and shut everybody up. It was great.'

Sadly, the euphoria of the Newcastle Red Wedge show evaporated come the Irish dates less than a fortnight later. Though Andy Rourke's drug dependency was never evident in the studio, on the road and away from his regular dealer, the cracks were finally beginning to show – both on and off stage. When Marr invited Rourke into The Smiths back in 1982, he had full knowledge of the bassist's problems. Yet for their first full year together, he'd successfully managed to shield Morrissey, known for his naivety on the matter of recreational narcotics, from the grim reality that the band had a regular heroin user in their midst. 'In certain situations you could say I protected Morrissey,' Marr later reflected. 'Andy had been my friend from the age of 14, so I knew all his problems but I always thought, "It's going to be over soon, it's just going to stop."'

Exasperated with the situation, Morrissey decided Rourke's fate for him, choosing a characteristically peculiar non-confrontational method of communication; a note left upon his car windscreen outside his house in Manchester.

'At first I thought it was a note that a fan had left because you used to get fans hanging around the house,' Rourke remembers. 'It just said 'Andy' on it. It was almost like a parking ticket. But it was unmistakably Morrissey's handwriting. It said "Andy, you have left The Smiths. Goodbye and good luck" and that was it. I was in bits, inconsolable for a few days. I think I phoned Johnny up, blubbing. He took me round his house and said "Morrissey's decided enough's enough." It was a good kick up the arse really.'

That their detractors never sussed the full details of the Rourke scenario at the time was a godsend. Nick Kent had tentatively insinuated his history with drugs, coyly referring to a 'barb problem' in Rourke's teens in his infamous March 1985 *Face* article. All the same, Morrissey's later proclamations – 'I despise drugs' – effectively set The Smiths up as narcotic abstainers in an age dominated by government funded anti-heroin adverts, the doctrine of anarchist-rockers New Model Army that 'Only Stupid Bastards Use Heroin' and that year's *Grange Hill* campaign to 'Just Say No'. It's therefore understandable that when alerted to the hypocrisy of having a 'smackhead' bassist, Morrissey coldly discharged Rourke to save face and avoid scandal.

'They'd stuck by me, but there came a point when I needed a short, sharp shock,' says Rourke. 'They fired me for a couple of weeks. I didn't know it was gonna be a couple of weeks, I don't even know if they did. I cleared my act up because that's all I had at that time, that's all I wanted to do. I think they thought if they left me in the lurch I'd go even more downhill.' As it happened, initially Rourke did slide further into the mire. Within a fortnight of being sacked, he was arrested in a drugs raid at a dealer's house. That the London music press never picked up on the bust was quite miraculous, though the swoop was reported in a local Manchester paper where a slipshod picture researcher had accidentally printed a mugshot of Mike Joyce instead of Rourke. The drummer naturally demanded an apology, while Morrissey, strangely amused at the mix-up, sent Joyce a biscuit through the post with a handwritten letter instructing him it was to provide him with sustenance for his imminent trial.

It was no laughing matter for Rourke, however, who stood to face a lengthy custodial punishment. Fortunately, he was reprieved with a fine and a suspended sentence, before being immediately welcomed back into The Smiths. The bassist's firing and re-hiring was so fleeting that the media barely had a chance to make an issue of the subject (by the time the music weeklies reported his departure during the third week of April, Rourke was already back in the group). As Morrissey later asserted 'his leaving seemed more wrong than his staying in.' Marr echoed this sentiment: 'I guess something positive has come out of it, particularly in relation to that "Morrissey, Marr and the session guys" shit. We found we really missed [Andy] and he discovered just how important he is.'

Yet even before reinstating Rourke, Marr had already begun meddling with The Smiths' tried and tested group dynamic by tentatively introducing a new member. Salford-born Craig Gannon was only 19, but already an experienced guitarist, having played with Aztec Camera, The Bluebells and latterly Terry Hall's The Colourfield alongside former Freak Party drummer Simon Wolstencroft **[see 1]**. 'Me and Simon became friends,' says Gannon. 'He was still in with The Smiths so one day he said "Johnny Marr wants to get in touch with you". I didn't have a clue what it was about so I just gave him my number. Eventually Johnny Marr rang us and said "do you want to get together?" Before that I didn't even realise that they were looking for another guitarist. They probably weren't.'

Since his entry into the fold coincided with Rourke's brief exit, it's always been assumed that Gannon was hired by Marr as a replacement bassist. 'To be honest that's a myth,' refutes Gannon. 'What happened was, I went up to Johnny's house and we had a big meeting there for a couple of hours. Mike was there as well. Johnny was saying that they wanted to get rid of Andy because he was a junkie and "we'd love you to be in the band as a guitar player, but if you fancy playing the bass, you can join now." So the original offer wasn't to do with playing bass. I'm not a bass player, especially on the lines of what Andy Rourke could play. I couldn't imagine anyone filling his shoes easily. So that was the only time it was ever mentioned about playing the bass and I never once picked up a bass with The Smiths.'

Following that first meeting in Manchester, it was decided that Marr and Joyce should take Craig down to London the following week to meet Morrissey. 'I got on really well with him so everything was fine' says Gannon. It was only when he arranged to attend a rehearsal in the basement of Joyce's house a few days later that Gannon received an unexpected surprise. 'Andy was there. They'd obviously decided to keep him in. It was the first time I'd met him so I didn't ask too many questions. I was happy to play with Andy anyway, but nobody really explained what was happening.'

Marr, however, still insists that Gannon was taken on board as a potential replacement for Rourke: 'Craig was *always* brought in to play bass. I mean the very short, honest, truthful version of it is that he came in to play bass, which was quite an exciting prospect for him as you can imagine. And then because Andy, quite rightly, came back and we got his hopes up, it just felt really cruel to fire Craig before he'd even had a chance to be in the band, so we let him stay. We just saw it as a way to turn that to our advantage. It wasn't that I was trying to turn the group into a big rock sound. He'd had a few weeks of getting excited about the idea of being the new Smith and I just didn't have the heart to take it away from him.'

Whatever his original job description, the opportunity to become the official 'Fifth Smith' on 'Second Guitar' was too good to pass up. 'Straight away I thought it sounded fantastic,' says Gannon, 'right from that first rehearsal. I'd never felt that before, maybe a little bit in Aztec Camera, but nothing like The Smiths. It was real chemistry, you could just feel it in the room.' Morrissey trusted Marr's judgement, commenting on the group's unintentional metamorphosis into a quintet with self-satisfied pragmatism: 'Now Craig Gannon has also joined we sound more formidable as you'll hear on the next single, so perhaps Andy's brief departure was a benefit.'

This 'formidable' regeneration process occurred just as the Rough Trade dispute reached its conclusion and, at long last, *The Queen Is Dead* was finally given a release date for 16 June. Even so, the experience of the last six months would certainly quicken their determination to find an alternate label before the year was out.

Since hailed as their undisputed masterpiece, *The Queen Is Dead* was undoubtedly their only studio album that truly seemed to typify its age;

capturing the imagination of an ever-widening audience (as the hysteria of their final UK tours would testify) and consolidating their critical standing as the benchmark against which all other contemporary English groups ought to be evaluated. After the kaleidoscopic genre hopping displayed on *Meat Is Murder*, *The Queen Is Dead* captured the band in their maturity, featuring many of their pioneering, personal bests ('There Is A Light That Never Goes Out', 'Bigmouth Strikes Again' and not least the title track). And while at times exhausting in its aching sadness ('I Know It's Over'), few could now dispute the counterbalance of Morrissey's humour, which shone through like never before, from the opening palace break in to the deadpan saucy postcard conclusion that 'Some Girls Are Bigger Than Others'.

Visually, the prostrate Alain Delon in a deep bottle green tint was also their most graphically striking LP cover yet. Just as iconic was Steve Wright's inner gatefold band photo posed outside the Salford Lads Club.[96] The venue itself inevitably became a Mecca for Smiths pilgrims, who defaced its brickwork with so much graffiti that eventually the club was forced to erect railings to prevent its constant vandalising. The committee had also attempted to sue Wright for photographing the premises without their permission, further complaining to Rough Trade that none of the band were ever affiliates of the club and that the album's contents may be mistakenly viewed as those shared by its members.

The consensus regarding its prominence above their other studio albums remains unchallenged to this day – in 1999, *Melody Maker* even voted it the greatest album of the millennium. Only The Smiths themselves have contested this opinion, the last word on the subject perhaps best given to Morrissey himself. '*The Queen Is Dead* is not our masterpiece,' said the singer in 1995. 'I should know. I was there. I supplied the sandwiches.'

96 Wright was a post-grad student in Manchester supplementing his income as a freelance music photographer. After sending some live Smiths shots to Rough Trade (including the famous 'Bum and flowers' image, which Morrissey particularly liked), Wright was officially commissioned to take the Salford Lads Club pictures in December 1985. 'Basically Morrissey gave the opportunity to take a picture to a fan who was learning to become a photographer, that's the bottom line,' says Wright. 'I had a fairly crude set up. I processed those photos in a darkroom converted from a bedroom which I slept in using chemicals which I kept in a Corona bottle. It was a really grimy, dark day when we took them. In an ideal world you would've said "sod this it's too dark."' In response to Morrissey's later comment that during the shoot 'while we were setting up a gang of ten-year olds came and terrorised us, everyone in the street had a club foot and a vicious dog', Wright's memories are much less hysterical. 'Kids were coming up on their bikes who should've been in school. But it was just that kind of Salford locale, what you'd expect.' Morrissey loved Wright's photos so much that he sent him a thank you card, written on Boxing Day 1985; 'A sweeter set of pictures were never taken. I smiled for a full minute (phone Roy Castle that's a record). I quite fancy Southport's wet sands next, or the tropical shores of Belle Vue. It must be done. Fatal regret: I should have worn my mud-coloured cardigan, Oh well, we shall meet when Venus is under Capricorn, so keep your lenses dry and thank you. Morrissey'.

58

'Panic'

Recorded **May 1986, Livingston Studios, London**

Produced by **John Porter**

Single A-side, August 1986 (Highest UK Chart Placing #11)

Having been out of the studio for nearly six months while they battled over their contract with Rough Trade, it was with great relief that in May 1986 The Smiths finally resumed their recording career at Livingston Studios, situated in Wood Green, North London.[97] The session would also prove an acid test for both Rourke and Gannon; the former having to validate his band mates' trust in allowing him back, the latter equally obliged to prove himself worthy enough a musician to contribute to their already established group dynamic. In the event, both would pass their respective tests with flying colours. On 'Panic', Gannon was more than competent as Marr's second fiddle, while Rourke's virtuosity was as impressive as ever.

The well-worn fable over the song's genesis has it that on 26 April, just over a week before entering the studio, Morrissey was paying a visit to Marr's home where the pair were listening to BBC Radio 1 in the kitchen. After a news report detailing the shocking nuclear disaster at the Chernobyl plant in the former USSR, DJ Steve Wright recommenced his programme by playing Wham's current single, 'I'm Your Man'. 'I remember actually saying, "What the fuck has this got to do with peoples' lives?"', said Marr. 'We hear about Chernobyl, then, seconds later, we're expected to be jumping around to 'I'm Your Man'.' Though the guitarist has since referred to this story as being slightly inflated, he still admits to this episode being a likely influence on the lyrics Morrissey presented nine days later as 'Panic'; borrowing the title of a rare 1968 Reparata & The Delrons B-side, later to become a hit on the Northern Soul circuit.

Prior to Chernobyl, the lyrical concept and chosen title had already cropped up in conversation three months earlier during an incident on the band's tour bus in Belfast. As they drove through the city, the band were impressed to see an overabundance of fly posters advertising that evening's

97 Marr and producer John Porter were already acquainted with Livingston, having worked there the month before on Billy Bragg's third album, *Talking With the Taxman About Poetry*. Marr made a cameo on the tracks 'Greetings To The New Brunette' and 'The Passion', as well as recording a beautiful acoustic rendition of 'Walk Away Renée' (originally by The Left Banke, later a hit for The Four Tops in 1967) issued as the B-side to Bragg's 'Levi Stubbs' Tears' in June 1986. On the latter disc, Marr was credited under the pseudonym 'Duane Tremelo'.

concert at Queens University. Morrissey invited Marr to speculate on what would happen if the entire British isles were fly-posted in this manner, before comically holding up a pre-prepared postcard upon which he'd written the word 'PANIC!'. It followed that the song itself, which Nick Kent later described as a mandate for 'rock terrorism', should begin with a nationwide tour of Britain in chaos; from Dundee down to Carlisle, through to London and across the Irish Sea to Dublin. The root of this 'Panic', we soon discover, is the state of pop itself, which, in Morrissey's words, 'says nothing to me about my life'. The solution is nothing less than a violent pop revolution – to 'burn down the disco'[98] and 'hang the DJ!' (the latter creed repeated ad infinitum and underscored by the amusing juxtaposition of a school assembly-style chorus echoing Morrissey's bloodthirsty command with juvenile glee).

For once, there was little ambiguity about Morrissey's intent. 'Panic' was squarely aimed at daytime radio and its roster of DJs such as Steve Wright (the band even commissioned a 'Hang The DJ!' T-shirt bearing Wright's portrait). 'I thought the song was extremely funny, I really did,' Morrissey later divulged. 'To hear it on national daytime radio on the few occasions it was actually played in the mish-mash of monstrous morbidity. I think it was quite amusing, a tiny revolution in its own sweet way.' But not everyone was laughing, especially those critics who misconstrued the song's ferocious rejection of 'the disco' and 'the DJ' as an ambiguous attack on black music. The racism charge, which would harangue Morrissey beyond The Smiths and throughout his solo career, had already been fuelled by such inflammatory quips as his notorious diagnosis that 'reggae is vile'.[99] It was only when, two months after the single's release, an unforgettably candid interview with *Melody Maker*'s Frank Owen in September 1986 saw Morrissey sounding off about a 'black pop conspiracy' that aspersions were cast as to the song's ulterior motive.

Morrissey's comments, as isolated by Owen, were admittedly absurd and alarmist ('to get on *Top of the Pops* these days one has to be, by law, black'). However, the singer's remarks against Diana Ross and Stevie Wonder were purely a musical concern (why else would Morrissey name fellow Motown artiste Martha Reeves & The Vandellas' 'Third Finger, Left Hand' as one of his favourite records of all time in the same breath?). Marr was especially incensed by the accusations, threatening that if The Smiths ever crossed Owen's path again, they would 'kick the shit out of him'. 'To those who took offence at the 'burn down the disco' line, I'd say please show me the black

98 A vague allusion to The Trammps' 1977 'Disco Inferno' with its 'burn baby burn' slogan inspired by the 1965 LA 'Watts riots'.

99 Morrissey made this notorious throwaway comment when asked by the *NME* to list his favourite 'Reggae Act' of 1984.

members of New Order,' argued Marr. 'For me, personally, New Order make great disco music, but there's no black people in the group. The point I'm making is that you can't just interchange the words 'black' and 'disco', or the phrases 'black music' and 'disco music'. It makes no earthly sense.'

The tune itself was only slightly less controversial, being Marr's wholesale mimicry of T.Rex's 1972 number one hit 'Metal Guru'; based around a carbon copy glam rotation between G and E-minor complete with a heavy Bolan-esque slide overdub. 'Johnny rang up and said "we need to do another single," remembers John Porter, 'so I said "what'll we do?" and he said "let's make a T.Rex record." So that was the kind of brief, but it was symptomatic of the kind of latitude we were on back then.' Marr himself remains rightly unapologetic: 'The thing about 'Panic' is that yeah, *of course* it was deliberate, but it doesn't sound like T.Rex. It still sounds like us. It still sounds like The Smiths.'[100]

As his first major Smiths recording in almost two years, Porter's enthusiasm at being back in the producer's chair was obvious. Buried within the final mix is a veritable spider's web of guitar tracks; Marr and Gannon's separate arpeggio jangling, banks of delayed twang, a wall of slide crescendos and even the harsh peel of high-range bells. Joyce's meaty, beaty brontosaurus stomp would also be emphasised with a single overdubbed thump at the end of each bar as a final glamtastic trimming. Porter's only concern was the song's brevity. A first take on 5 May was copied and re-spliced by the producer, repeating the first verse at the song's finish to stretch to a more acceptable three minutes. Unimpressed with this arrangement, the group were content to leave 'Panic' as it was. Since the unedited master cut drew to a spontaneous halt after just two minutes and twenty seconds, the final edit faded out just two seconds short of this bumbling climax.

Porter was also instrumental in the novel addition of the children's chorus during the 'Hang The DJ!' coda, assembling pupils from a local school. 'I think that was probably Mozzer's idea,' says Porter. 'We were in Wood Green, so I suppose I must have gone round to the nearest school with a bag of lollipops.' The last time such a device had been used effectively in pop had been Pink Floyd's 1979 single 'Another Brick In The Wall Part 2'. However, it's more likely that Morrissey's muse in tacking a kiddies' choir onto a Smiths record – other than the obvious arch subversion – was Keith West's 1967 psychedelic oddity 'Excerpt from a Teenage Opera' with its severely catchy 'Grocer Jack' refrain.[101]

100 Significantly, T.Rex's 1971 single 'Jeepster' was the first record Marr ever bought.

101 A twee ballad about a small town thrown into chaos by the death of its only fruit and veg vendor, Keith West's 'Excerpt from a Teenage Opera' wasn't so far from Morrissey's own provincial dramas.

Capitalising on their critical and commercial rejuvenation after the overdue release of *The Queen Is Dead* a month previous, 'Panic' was perfectly timed to return The Smiths enticingly close to the Top 10 in the late summer of '86. Between the inane Stock, Aitken and Waterman fodder of Sinitta's 'So Macho' and Chris De Burgh's nauseating 'The Lady In Red', Morrissey's DJ-lynching call to arms seemed a very rational argument indeed. As provocative agitprop or mere glam racket, 'Panic' was indisputably one of the strongest 45s of their career, voted not only 'Single of the Year' in the following spring's *NME* readers' poll, but – somewhat incongruously for such a famously anti-disco diatribe – the sixth 'Best Dance Record' to boot.

In Concert

'Panic' joined The Smiths' live repertoire at Gannon's inaugural Smiths gig, Glasgow Barrowlands (16/7/86), and was played at virtually every concert henceforth, the majority of those as the second song of the night. It was briefly employed as the opening number at Salford University (20/7/86) and the first two Canadian dates of the summer US tour, while at their final Brixton Academy concert (12/12/86) it was moved towards the end of the set list (the only time it was ever performed without Gannon).

For the rousing chorus of 'Hang the DJ!', Morrissey would normally utilise the macabre stage prop of a hangman's noose, twirling it around his head centre stage. Bizarrely, Radio 1's Steve Wright – the man supposedly vilified in the song – asked to appear on stage at their London Palladium show (26/10/86) to join in the chorus as an ironic publicity stunt. The Smiths, of course, were only too delighted to refuse.

Television

'Panic' was premiered prior to both its vinyl release and inclusion in concert live on Channel 4's *Eurotube* summer special on 5 July 1986. Joyce led the way with a pounding, floor tom intro before its deliriously catchy might was proudly unleashed. Halfway through the song, a young boy (later rumoured to be Johnny Marr's nephew, but in truth a child actor of no relation) came bouncing on stage strumming air guitar in school uniform with a hearing aid and Morrissey-patented bush clipping sprouting from the rear of his shorts. Marr beckoned him towards a pre-prepared low mic-stand, where he nervously joined Morrissey in the relentless chant of 'Hang the DJ!'. Recognising the lad's shyness, Marr grinned over at him encouragingly while even Morrissey proffered a fatherly pat on the head at the end of the performance. Partly due to the bizarre novelty of their juvenile guest, this broadcast was as dynamic a proclamation of the new single as could have been wished for.

By the time 'Panic' was finally released, The Smiths were already into their gruelling North American tour. As a result, all further TV promotion relied on the Derek Jarman film included as part of his *The Queen Is Dead* feature **[see 54]**. The original, finally screened on BBC2's *Rock Around the Clock* that September, was both the most inventive segment of Jarman's three-song presentation and the simplest, based around a camera's eye view of an outstretched hand leading the viewer down an alleyway in jerky monochrome. Morrissey later commented that of all the Smiths' promotional films, it was the only one he actually liked.

Sadly, Jarman's footage was later doctored by Rough Trade by superimposing shots of The Smiths miming to the song at a recent sound-check in Canada (Ottawa Capitol Congress Centre, 2/8/86). Like 'The Boy With The Thorn In His Side' video, the bastardised 'Panic' promo seemed an unnecessary compromise on The Smiths' behalf, one they would repeat with the similar sabotage of Jarman's 'Ask' video **[see 60]**.

Radio

A live version of 'Panic' recorded at Kilburn National Ballroom (23/10/86) was first broadcast on BBC Radio 1's *In Concert* series in April 1987, and later included on 1988's posthumous live album *Rank* adapted from the same Kilburn performance.

59

'The Draize Train' (Marr)

Recorded **May 1986, Livingston Studios, London**

Produced by **John Porter**

B-side to **'Panic' (12-inch format only), July 1986**

In keeping with their track record for exclusive B-sides, The Smiths hoped to use the remainder of the Livingston session to complete enough supplementary new material to accompany 'Panic'. The first of these, an early version of 'Sweet And Tender Hooligan' complete with vocal, was ultimately rejected **[see 67]**. The second, cannily confined to the single's 12-inch, would eventually emerge as 'The Draize Train'; Marr's third and final Smiths instrumental, which, unlike its predecessors, would be credited to him alone. 'I was asked to write words for [it],' Morrissey later confessed, '[but] I thought it was the weakest thing Johnny had ever done. Geoff Travis came to see me one day with the tape of it and said, "It's the best thing Johnny's written and it's a number one single if you put words to it." But I said, "No,

Geoff, it's not right."' For once, Morrissey found an unlikely ally in John Porter: 'I never thought it quite worked. We were trying to create that groove that people were starting to get into at the Hacienda, that's what Johnny was after. I think I could have made it work as a song, but Mozzer didn't want to sing on it. In the end I thought it was a bit of a throwaway.'

Its title honoured Morrissey's firm anti-vivisection rhetoric (the 'Draize test' – created in the Forties by American scientist John Draize – is a rightly reviled practice in which commercial chemicals are administered into the eyeballs of animals, usually rabbits, to assess their irritancy level), though it also seemed Marr's admission of the tune's similarity to The Doobie Brothers' 'Long Train Running'. 'It honestly wasn't,' disputes Marr, 'but I can see how people could make that comparison because of that little guitar figure. But for me, that funky riff was secondary to the chord change. To me the music was so romantic.'

As with their work on the previous instrumental 'Money Changes Everything' **[see 57]**, Marr and Porter built the track up from an overtly artificial Linn drum foundation. A more progressive studio monitor mix also featured a pre-acid house stuttering synth pulse, uncannily evocative of Marr's later work with New Order's Bernard Sumner in Electronic. That in its final state 'The Draize Train' developed into one of Marr's more ostentatious displays of fret-wizardry, with the majority of its electro outlines rubbed out, bears all the hallmarks of his silent partner's influence. Morrissey even made a point of bragging to the press a few months later that their rivals had made the mistake of 'going through their heavily electronic period', a trap that The Smiths were definitely not about to fall into as far as he could see, as Rourke verifies: 'The electronic thing was something me and Johnny wanted to get into but it was sort of beaten out of us by Morrissey. The only keys we were allowed to use were acoustic piano and emulated real sounds like strings. It's strange because I'd have liked to have pushed us more in that direction. Certain tunes Morrissey would say I really like that but I don't think I should sing on it. Whether that meant he couldn't write anything for it I don't know.'

Regardless of any compromise on Marr's part, it still managed to reflect its author's innate love of music-making. As well as his trusty Nashville-tuned Epiphone Coronet, he particularly relished the opportunity to noodle on a couple of Rickenbackers owned by The Who's Pete Townshend (after telling his guitar technician that he wanted 'a Townshend sound'). Presumably, the return of his 'love of booze' (as he proudly informed *Record Mirror* journalist Eleanor Levy, who interviewed him midway through the session) also played its part in heightening Marr's creative spirits.

As an exhibition of The Smiths as a taut instrumental unit, 'The Draize Train' was a creditable success, not least Marr's note-bending solo extravagances and Rourke's characteristically animated bass line. Nevertheless, as the only Smiths recording to bear a singular composer credit, it would be the first to throw light upon the hitherto unthinkable possibility of a fracture within Morrissey and Marr's musical partnership.

In Concert

Having successfully interpreted 'Money Changes Everything' live on the US tour of 1986, Marr decided to replace it in the set of what would be the final UK excursion that October with 'The Draize Train'. Introduced at Carlisle Sands Centre (13/10/86), with Craig Gannon's slick rhythm adding to Joyce and Rourke's solid backbeat, it provided Marr with a solo show piece that he clearly adored playing (routinely slotted as the first encore before Morrissey returned to the stage).

The only time it ever closed a set was at their semi-disastrous Newport Leisure Centre show (19/10/86), when after just nine songs, Morrissey was pulled off stage by the eager Welsh throng, only to crack his head open upon landing. While doctors attended to the dazed singer backstage, the rest of the band brought 'The Draize Train' forward as the last number, to compensate for the brevity of an aborted gig. Soundman Grant Showbiz was struck by a bottle as he then made the announcement on stage that the concert was over, after which a minor riot ensued in which six people were arrested.

Five days later, at their penultimate visit to Brixton Academy (24/10/86), 'The Draize Train' was given added vivacity thanks to honorary guest Fred Hood from The Impossible Dreamers, who shadowed Joyce's beat on a separate second drum kit.[102] The track was last performed at Manchester Free Trade Hall (30/10/86).

Radio

An excellent live version (far superior to the studio original) recorded at Kilburn National Ballroom (23/10/86) was first broadcast on BBC Radio 1's *In Concert* series in April 1987 and later included on the posthumous live album *Rank*. Compiled by Morrissey himself from the full 90-minute BBC concert tapes, upon its release in September 1988 his decision to include 'The Draize Train' was interpreted by many as a peace offering towards Marr – who would recoup greater royalties as a result – at a time when rumours of post-split acrimony abounded in the music press.

102 Hood was an associate of soundman Grant Showbiz. Johnny Marr had also produced The Impossible Dreamers' 'August Avenue' single (RCA, 1985). After The Smiths, Hood would briefly join Marr again in a new line-up of The Pretenders.

60

'Ask'

Recorded June 1986, Jam Studios, London
Produced by John Porter, Mixed by Steve Lillywhite
Single A-side, October 1986 (Highest UK Chart Placing #14)

Barely a month after the Livingston 'Panic' session, The Smiths returned to the studio with John Porter to stockpile more material prior to their imminent seven-week tour of Canada and the US. Once again, the objective was a three-track single though, like the Livingston version of 'Sweet And Tender Hooligan', a solid rendition of 'Is It Really So Strange?' **[see 66]** taped at Jam that June was never released. Instead, only two tracks were fully completed; an expendable cover of Twinkle's 'Golden Lights' **[see 61]** and 'Ask', both of which would be interfered with in post-production much to Porter's dismay.

It's no secret that Morrissey was extremely circumspect when it came to Marr's working relationships with people other than himself, an unhealthy state of protective paranoia that was to worsen throughout The Smiths' career. John Porter was one of many unfortunate enough to get too close to Marr for Morrissey's comfort. Threatened by their studio camaraderie, Morrissey used the eventual release of 'Ask' as a way of expressing his dissatisfaction with, and ultimate power over, Porter's presence. Having invited singer Kirsty MacColl to provide backing vocals at the end of the session, Morrissey would later commission her husband, producer Steve Lillywhite, to remix 'Ask' once Porter had finished with it.[103]

'I was disappointed about that,' says Porter. 'Originally 'Ask' was a bit of a *tour de force* and it was pretty complicated. We'd done all these little guitar parts, all this intricate kind of highlife playing. I had a graph which was a plan of how all these things would interlock, it was pretty fantastic. Then there was this bit in the middle where they wanted the sound of a waterfall crashing, all with guitars. It was fucking amazing, we even had seagull sounds. So there was a lot of stuff on tape but it didn't make any sense unless you knew this map of how and where we were gonna pick out these little bits. It was a jigsaw puzzle. You needed six hands to mix it properly and we didn't have automation at Jam studios, so I knew I was going to have to mix it somewhere else at a later date.'[104]

103 Significantly, Lillywhite would go on to produce three of Morrissey's solo albums in the mid-Nineties (*Vauxhall & I*, *Southpaw Grammar* and *Maladjusted*), while MacColl would also guest on his 1989 single 'Interesting Drug'.

104 Automation, now standard in all modern recording studios, is where each individual track (eg vocals or a guitar part) can be pre-programmed by computer to fade in or out at the appropriate point without having to adjust any levels by hand.

'So then they went off to tour America straight after that. I went out to see them in LA, which was great. We just chilled out and smoked a lot of dope. I remember saying to Mozzer "when you get back to England we'll get round to mixing 'Ask'". He said nothing but then I eventually heard from somebody else "Lillywhite's done it because Mozzer didn't like your mix". I was so pissed off. I said "well I haven't even mixed the bloody thing." So, it came out and it did okay and it was alright but the thing is there was a plan to that record and what came out just didn't have the plan. It should have been the best single they did. I really think it could have been.'

'It wasn't dramatically different,' states Marr, 'but yeah, it felt kind of a little bit muted when it came out. Less spirited, absolutely. At the time I couldn't understand why it was being tampered with because it all came together very simply and with a definite sense of purpose.' In sharp contrast to its predecessor (Morrissey even referred to it as a 'slight antidote to 'Panic'') 'Ask' was unadulterated pop whimsy, at times bordering on anodyne. Marr's jovial chord cycle (G, A-minor, C and D, which he would use again on 'I Won't Share You' **[see 79]**) was certainly catchy but perhaps his least imaginative arrangement since 'Unloveable'. Significantly, Craig Gannon would controversially claim that the chord structure was actually *his* doing. 'When we were at Livingston doing 'Panic', we played around with a basic chord progression,' explains Gannon. 'But then at the next session at Jam we started doing 'Ask' and I thought, "hang on, I came up with that!". It's no big deal and it didn't really bother me too much. It's bothered me a lot more since.'

Short on melodic originality maybe, the lyrics were an equally lightweight paean to adolescent bashfulness, partly inspired by Morrissey's youth as a manic letter-writer. 'I spent every solitary penny on postage stamps,' he confessed, 'I had this wonderful arrangement with the entire universe without actually meeting anybody, just through the wonderful postal service. The crisis of my teenage life was when postage stamps went up from 12p to 13p. I was outraged.' A superficial plea to liberate one's inhibitions, the crux of 'Ask' appears to be its protagonist's own fizzling sexual repression, amplified in Morrissey's exaggerated use of uppercase in its printed lyrics and his vivid metaphor of sexual desire as a unifying explosive.

A dynamic first take on 9 June augured well for the end product with Marr and Gannon attacking its basic chord run with all the rhythmic gusto of The Ramones (regrettably diluted in the final mix). The original middle eight also saw Joyce erupt in an abandoned tom-hammering frenzy not unlike the tribal surf rhythm of The Surfaris' classic instrumental, 'Wipe Out'. Porter's aforementioned complex infrastructure of individual guitar parts was assembled from a twin acoustic foundation and various overdubs using both a Rickenbacker 12-string and a classic Stratocaster model. Marr also added a simple harmonica vamp, purposely overdriven through a Seventies 'Boom Box' stereo, to great effect.

Though Porter would publicly slate Lillywhite's remix for failing to exploit these various ingredients to the full, and by no means one of The Smiths' best, upon its release in the last week of October 1986, 'Ask' was still an accomplished pop 45. Bristling with tuneful optimism, its entreaty that 'nature is a language, can't you read?' was another welcome fly in the ointment of daytime radio and the antithesis of Berlin's risible 'Take My Breath Away', then at the top of the British charts. Yet as a Smiths single, 'Ask' was definitely more froth than fire.

In Concert

Months before its release as a single, 'Ask' was introduced into the set at Glasgow Barrowlands (16/7/86), the first performance from the new five-man Smiths with Craig Gannon on second guitar. Though played at their first two concerts in Canada, it was excluded from the rest of their North American dates in August and September though, as their new single upon returning home, was a necessary staple of their October UK tour. At their final two shows – Manchester Free Trade Hall (30/10/86) and London Brixton Academy (12/12/86) – 'Ask' was The Smiths' last ever set opener.

Television

Following his *The Queen Is Dead* triptych, from which the 'Panic' promo was taken, Derek Jarman was commissioned to make another video to accompany 'Ask'. Sticking to the same stylised, handheld, super-8 approach of its predecessor, 'Ask' offered a colourful and more literal interpretation of the song's lyrics. Shot on waste ground near the banks of the Thames, it starred a caricature Morrissey substitute trying to overcome a hammy Chaplin-esque shyness, whilst presenting a girl with a bouquet of flowers. The couple are joined by mock Fifties dancers in leather jackets, playing pass the parcel with a cartoon black, spherical bomb. Britannia is also seen dancing back and forth, a favourite motif of Jarman's – referring to his earlier 1978 punk/art-house feature *Jubilee*.

Having initially resisted the very notion of pop promos, with Jarman The Smiths were courageously trying to do something visually that stood apart from the mainstream. 'Ask' very nearly succeeded, though, as with 'Panic', they were forced to make a ridiculous compromise in the name of prime-time television. Despite being shown untampered on ITV's *The Chart Show*, it was still far too avant-garde for *Top of the Pops*, who insisted on a crude superimposition of Morrissey singing.

Radio

A live version recorded at Kilburn National Ballroom (23/10/86) was first broadcast on BBC Radio 1's *In Concert* series in April 1987 and later included on 1988's posthumous live album *Rank*.

61

'Golden Lights' (Ripley)

Recorded **June 1986, Jam Studios, London**
Produced by **John Porter**, Remixed by **Stephen Street**
B-side to **'Ask' (12-inch format only), October 1986**

The worst record ever accredited to The Smiths, 'Golden Lights' should have been a routine cover version of a minor Sixties hit, but ended in a sabotaged atrocity for reasons best known to Morrissey alone. The tragedy of this, their first studio cover version, was twofold, in that the 1965 original by Twinkle, a sullen 16-year-old aristocratic mod (born Lynn Ripley), was a UK girl group classic that should never have been tampered with in the first place. Written by Twinkle herself (an almost unheard of feat in Britain's chauvinistic mid-Sixties pop scene), 'Golden Lights' was a remarkably astute ballad about fame's fatal effect on a teenage romance, inspired by her own relationship with the Bachelors' singer Dec Clusky. Its central themes of lost love and the perils of stardom were a perfect vehicle for Morrissey, as was its alluring, if somewhat kitsch, major-key melody.

It was certainly no fault of John Porter that 'Golden Lights' ended up so terrible a recording. His finished mix, though hardly groundbreaking, was a competent adaptation with some beguiling acoustic guitar and mandolin runs from Marr and Gannon lending it a South American bossa nova feel (almost radical when placed beside Twinkle's original). Most importantly, Morrissey delivered a confident, orthodox vocal, devoid of the ghastly flange effect added in its later remix. All the same, neither Andy Rourke nor Mike Joyce contributed to the track, unable to muster up the requisite enthusiasm (John Porter provided bass, while the beat was maintained using a minimal Linn track). 'I was never really into that song either,' agrees Gannon. 'We listened to the original a couple of times in the studio to learn, but there was so little on it guitar-playing wise. It was all getting a bit weaker.'

The Smiths' 'Golden Lights' would have been, at best, a mere dispensable footnote had Morrissey not stepped in at the eleventh hour, instigating its metamorphosis into the discography blemish that was to finally appear four months later. As with its respective A-side, 'Ask', Porter's handiwork was remixed, this time by a reluctant Stephen Street. The resultant hatchet job simply defies logic; drowning the subtleties of Marr and Gannon's guitars, burying its forceful, staccato intro (which honoured the Twinkle arrangement), needlessly over-stressing the hitherto understated background harmonies of Kirsty MacColl and imbuing Morrissey's voice with a horrendous delay effect equivalent to him singing while trying to drink a glass of water simultaneously.

'Mozzer didn't have much of a musical clue,' says Porter. 'I remember him saying when we recorded it "can we not start with everything out of tune? Do we have to tune the instruments?" So either me or Johnny had to point out to him that it wouldn't work, that music had to be played in a set key. Like 'Ask', I remember thinking 'Golden Lights' could have been great. We did a brilliant monitor mix of it and it was starting to sound really lovely. But I could see Mozzer stood there, not liking it at all. He just wanted it to be weirded out, which it was in the end. It was fucked up deliberately and I didn't understand why.' What Morrissey aimed to achieve by spoiling Porter's efforts we can only presume. Then, as now, the shameful 'Golden Lights' has no place within The Smiths' legacy.

By July 1986, even though Rourke was 'cleaned up' and back in the band, his part in a Manchester drug bust earlier in the year now jeopardised his chances of acquiring a visa to join The Smiths on their upcoming tour of Canada and North America. Rather than abort the trip, Marr reasoned they should continue with the tour as promised, using a session player if need be. Accordingly, during rehearsals at Stanbridges near Brighton in mid-July, bassist Guy Pratt was employed as an emergency stand-in. Against the odds, Rourke's visa came through at the eleventh hour – something of a disappointment for Pratt who had shorn his hair in preparation at Morrissey's behest: 'I'm not going on stage with anyone with a ponytail!'[105]

Beginning in late July and scheduled to finish in the middle of September, their second and final US tour was the most daunting concert itinerary of their career, a challenge which they'd rise to with heroic resolve. 'I've never seen a band rip up 10,000 people like they did on those Stateside gigs,' recollects tour soundman Grant Showbiz. 'The ripples of madness going through the crowd was incredible, night after night. It was like when you saw old clips on TV of what The Beatles or The Stones did, and realising *this* was it! This was that same feeling. Seeing The Smiths live was like a holy communion. The band had that faith in the audience and vice versa,

105 Pratt would later work with Marr on the Kirsty MacColl albums *Kite* (1989), *Electric Landlady* (1991) and Electronic's *Raise The Pressure* (1996) and *Twisted Tenderness* (1999).

there was this unique empathy between them. That's what it was. Pure faith.'

Mike Joyce singles out a show at LA's Universal Amphitheater as indicative of their communicative energy. 'It was about 15,000 capacity, a lovely open-air, seated amphitheatre but there were about 30 of the local jocks from the American football team acting as security. These college guys were all six feet wide, all wearing headphones and earplugs so they couldn't hear the music. They were in this line across the front of the stage and as the fans tried to get close they were literally battering people. So Morrissey stopped and said something like "stop hurting the people" at these bouncers.[106] Then he looked out into the audience and said "remember there's only 30 of them, there's 15,000 of you." The crowd just went oomph! This great big wall of people suddenly stood up out of their seats. You could see in the faces of the security, these jocks were scared. That's the kind of relationship we had with the fans, we were in this together.'

Off stage however, things weren't nearly so harmonious. To begin with, there was the increasing tension between Marr and recent recruit Craig Gannon. 'It was nothing musical,' says Gannon, 'it was just a personality difference. I started feeling like maybe we didn't like each other. The vibe started to change. We all began splitting off into separate camps.'

There was also the running farce that was The Smiths' vegetarian catering needs. Joyce explains: 'We just weren't eating properly, it was hilarious looking back. I remember once in Dallas this woman was dishing out beans for us all and there was this big knuckle, this big pig's trotter in there. And I said "what the hell's that?" and she said "it's OK, you don't eat that it's just to give it flavour". And I was like, "well no, *you* don't understand!" God knows what would have happened if Morrissey had seen it. Over there most of the Americans thought that as vegetarians we were part of some strange religious cult.'

'It's true that we were on some weird fucking diet that no one's yet put a name to,' adds Marr. 'We'd be eating yoghurt and crisps, and that was on a good day.' The band's own dietary trauma was only half the story. According to Rourke, the meatless regime practically instigated a mutiny amongst their undernourished roadies. 'Morrissey wouldn't allow any meat or any money to be spent on meat. So imagine an American crew into T-bone steaks and they'd get nut roast every night with a floret of broccoli. They'd be like, "What's this fuckin' shit!". A few threatened to walk out if they didn't get any

106 Though true, Joyce is actually paraphrasing here. The concert at LA's Universal Amphitheatre (26/8/86) is available on bootleg. During 'I Know It's Over' Morrissey can be heard uncharacteristically losing the plot, screaming 'Jesus Christ! Don't be so stupid!' in a dramatic tirade against the venue security.

meat because the stupid thing was they didn't find out till after they were hired that they couldn't eat it. Nobody had warned them. So they turned up thinking it was normal crew work and on top of everything else they learn they've got to eat shit food for six weeks. In the end I used to sneak out for steaks with the crew myself. I was going mad.'

'I ate meat at the time too,' comments Gannon. 'Sometimes we'd sneak off to diners, me and Mike or with Jim, Morrissey's minder. I was never told not to eat meat but the crew were told you couldn't spend your earnings on meat. A couple of times the band used to fly between gigs. I was petrified of flying so if it was the choice of a two-hour journey on a plane or a twelve-hour drive with the crew, I'd sometimes take the crew bus. When we used to stop to get something to eat the crew would be a bit nervous, looking at me thinking "if we buy meat will he grass us up?" In the end I just said "look, it's totally up to you what you spend your money on."'

Their malnourished tour fatigue was exacerbated by well-documented post-gig blitzes of booze and cocaine ('It could get a bit rock 'n' roll,' says Gannon, 'but we were just a group of lads in a big band'). 'People were beginning to crack, not just the band but the road crew as well,' concurs Showbiz. 'I mean, if you stay up partying till 4 o'clock every morning and get up the next day but don't eat any food and then you do the same thing over and over gain, you're going to feel shit sooner or later. Morrissey was only eating – I don't know – custard perhaps, so it got to that point where he was bound to fall over. Some of those gigs were like 100 degrees, it was unfathomably hot. People were sick with dehydration. Even Morrissey was wearing shorts by the end of it.'

'The thing about The Smiths was we were a DIY band,' says Marr, 'we had no real connection with the record company because we had no tour manager, we did it ourselves. But that didn't really quite work when we were playing seven weeks in America expecting to get up in front of 15,000 people in the sweltering heat. The knock-on effect of that DIY mentality was we weren't eating, we were travelling around in some really weird way because we had to sort it ourselves, which in turn causes massive financial problems on tour which is then dropped on a 22-year-old sicky boy who's trying to just keep his partner happy, keep himself happy and write songs at the same time. And it just couldn't be done. But the point was, we did it together, whatever the dynamic of the band.'

As if a vitamin deficient life on the road with no proper management in a boiling hot foreign country wasn't stressful enough, behind the scenes Marr was also having to brace the legal fallout from The Smiths' furtive negotiations to sign with EMI Records. Events came to a head at LA's Universal Amphitheater, when a senior executive at Warners, the band's US licensees, confronted the guitarist backstage. 'This guy was someone I really liked and had a lot of respect for,' recalls Marr, 'a gentle, lovely man who got close to violence with me in a dressing room because we'd signed to EMI and somebody hadn't told him. He was so upset he put his fist through a plasterboard wall. This is someone who epitomised Californian calm. His tan turned chalk white. That situation really set alarm bells ringing.' A few nights later in Phoenix, Andy Rourke remembers being called to Marr's hotel room by his wife Angie, finding the guitarist 'in bits on the bed' and fearing that he was witnessing his friend in the midst of an actual nervous breakdown. Marr numbed the pain with alcohol, later admitting to downing a bottle of Remy Martin a night. All things considered, that the tour ended a week prematurely through sheer lack of steam came as no surprise.

At least in the interim their prominence back home had grown during their absence with 'Panic', which rewarded them with their highest UK singles chart position in two years. Nonetheless, a fortnight after their return, The Smiths were to face fresh criticism when their departure from Rough Trade to EMI was officially announced. This move, from indie to major, was regarded as nothing short of 'defection' in the eyes of an audience for whom EMI represented a corporate beast destined to sap The Smiths' maverick autonomy. As a facet of the arms-funding Thorn-EMI conglomerate, it also appeared depressingly hypocritical of the group's allegiance to the Campaign for Nuclear Disarmament (a charge Morrissey would struggle to deflect with audible unease in a radio interview with Dave Fanning of Ireland's RTE the following spring).

With the specifics of their remaining contractual obligations to Rough Trade still in doubt, The Smiths attempted to carry on regardless. From the outside looking in at least, it was business as usual. Marr, however, was already considering the worst. 'When you sort of decide that something might be over you start to notice the cracks. Once the decision's been made, to change things and change your fate, that's when you start to tick things off...'

62

'You Just Haven't Earned It Yet, Baby'

Recorded **October 1986, Mayfair Studios, London**

Produced by **John Porter**

Album track from the compilation ***The World Won't Listen*, March 1987**

Their first recording session after returning from America would also be Craig Gannon's last. After his initially prosperous bedding-in period,

Morrissey would later refer to their arduous US tour as the acid test of Gannon's compatibility as a full-time Smith: 'When we toured America, which was a very long time, you get to know people very well and it all came forth as it were. Craig wasn't terribly interested, in a nutshell. We had to force him to come to the studio, we had to force him to come to rehearsals and so on.'[107]

Five days were spent at Mayfair Studios in Primrose Hill, North London; the first with John Porter at the helm, the remainder with Stephen Street. 'It couldn't have been more obvious at that point,' says Porter of the increasingly tetchy group politics. 'It was almost like Johnny's way of saying "I want Porter" and then Mozzer saying "then I want Street the next day." So that's what happened. I suppose it was their idea of a compromise.'

On 2 October, recording commenced with Porter taping a run-through of the proposed lead track, 'You Just Haven't Earned It Yet, Baby'. Boasting a luxurious Marr melody harking back to the archetypal Smiths designs of two years previous, its simplistic verses allowed the guitarist to indulge in some characteristically glittering arpeggios (doubly so during its late middle eight breakdown) fractured by a spine-tingling chorus propelled by Joyce's stomping, staccato beat. Its title was allegedly inspired by an offhand comment by Geoff Travis, which Morrissey would recycle again on 'Paint A Vulgar Picture'. 'Obviously Geoff was staunchly against it,' said Morrissey, 'because he thought it was a personal letter addressed to him.' However, as a universal anthem to frustrated ambition it tapped directly into the same nerve as 'Frankly, Mr Shankly', offering the listener an emotional double blow of empathetic wisdom and converse torment.

That such a memorable tune, and lyric, was never actually issued as a single (or indeed played live) was, in retrospect an opportunity wasted, even if the decision to replace it with 'Shoplifters Of The World Unite' was a justifiable switch. Although Morrissey expressed his dissatisfaction with Porter's mix – a dazzling wall of multi-tracked guitars jangling to infinity – some have opined that his increasing distrust of the producer also played a part in vetoing 'You Just Haven't Earned It Yet, Baby' as the next single ('I can never remember Morrissey and John Porter actually speaking to each other' states Gannon).

Instead, it was to become the only new composition exclusive to the budget compilation album *The World Won't Listen*, issued in the spring of 1987. An ostensible *Hatful of Hollow* 2, *The World Won't Listen* mopped up their past few non-album singles and B-sides. Prior to the compilation's release, an alleged

107 In his defence, Gannon personally blames the brewing tension he felt between himself and Marr. 'After America the hostility was even worse so, yeah, I was spending a lot of time out of the studio.'

'pressing mix up' resulted in 'You Just Haven't Earned It Yet, Baby' appearing on a limited number of 12-inch versions of the 'Shoplifters Of The World Unite' single in January 1987 (now a rare collectors item).

An alternate mix of 'You Just Haven't Earned It Yet, Baby' was subsequently included on the Sire compilation *Louder Than Bombs* (a title culled, again, from one of Morrissey's oldest sources, Elizabeth Smart's *By Grand Central Station I Sat Down and Wept*). Slightly weaker overall, this version can be distinguished by a more gradual build-up of guitar overdubs during the instrumental third verse and a marginally shorter fade out. After The Smiths, Marr would also perform on Kirsty MacColl's cover of the song in 1989.

63

'Half A Person'

Recorded **October 1986, Mayfair Studios, London**

Produced by **Morrissey and Marr**

B-side to **'Shoplifters Of The World Unite', January 1987**

After completing 'You Just Haven't Earned It Yet, Baby' with John Porter, another four days were spent at Mayfair working on its projected B-sides with Stephen Street. Marr already had the chord changes in place for what would become 'Half A Person', though it wasn't until he and Morrissey sat alone together on the studio staircase that the song came into being; 'We officially wrote it on the stairs at Mayfair. Morrissey got his part of it together overnight, and it was amazing. That was probably the best writing moment I think me and him ever had because we were so close, practically touching, and I could see him kind of willing me on, waiting to see what I was going to play. Then I could see him thinking "that's exactly where I was hoping you'd go!" It was a fantastic, shared moment.'

Stephen Street also singles out this track as one of his personal favourite Smiths recordings. 'I remember Johnny and Craig were both playing acoustic guitars, which we set up separated with one in the left and one in the right speaker. That was put down together, very simply, with just a few overdubs on top. I was really chuffed with it, I thought it was a beautiful song.'

Indeed, 'Half A Person' was an awe-inspiring addition to the Morrissey/Marr songbook; a triumph of confessional tenderness and melodic sobriety. Its romantic lamentation of a clumsy, teenage runaway bound South was a theme Morrissey had already examined with more humour on 'Is It Really So Strange?' (written several months earlier), and with more cynicism on its accompanying B-side 'London'. As he later told Nick Kent in

The Face, the obsessive relationship/six-year stalking detailed in the lyrics was apparently 'all absolutely true'.

Taking its name from a passage in John Fowles' original novel of *The Collector,*[108] Morrissey's wordplay throughout 'Half A Person' is truly magisterial. Expressing that his life could be surmised in five seconds flat was a quip of self-deprecatory genius, as was the ambiguity in his hesitant phrasing when revealing that he sought lodgings at the YWCA (Young Women's Christian Association). The latter seemed a purposely camp inversion of Elvis Presley's 1968 'Guitar Man' in which the King thumbs it to Memphis and finds board 'at the YMCA'. However, it's more likely that the lyric is a nod to Terence Stamp. In the 1962 drama *Term of Trial,* Stamp plays Mitchell, a teenage hooligan who during a school trip to London harasses teacher Laurence Olivier by teasing 'let's all go to the YWCA.'[109] The song's closing refrain was also a probable bow towards The Velvet Underground's 'That's The Story of My Life' from their eponymous third album of 1969.

Because of its absorbing acoustic texture and the mesmerising quality of Morrissey's compassionate narrative, 'Half A Person' has long been one of their most popular works. Sadly, The Smiths would never perform it in concert.

Radio

A subtly brighter version of 'Half A Person' was re-recorded after Craig Gannon's departure for their final John Peel session at BBC Maida Vale Studio 4 on 2 December, 1986. Produced by John Porter, it features perhaps one of Morrissey's best vocals on a BBC session recording.

64

'London'

Recorded **October 1986, Mayfair Studios, London**

Produced by **Morrissey and Marr**

B-side to **'Shoplifters Of The World Unite' (12-inch format only), January 1987**

The aggressive twin sibling of 'Half A Person', 'London' was a fervid fireball of a song which saw Morrissey offer an alternate perspective on

108 Miranda, the imprisoned art student, decides to nickname her captor 'Caliban' after Shakespeare's *The Tempest,* writing in her journal that 'Caliban is only half a person at the best of times'.

109 Morrissey was familiar enough with *Term of Trial* to suggest a still from the film depicting Stamp being caned by Olivier as a possible sleeve for the 1985 Dutch single of 'The Headmaster Ritual'. Since Olivier failed to give his consent in time, a replacement sleeve was eventually sought instead.

North to South migration. Its scenario drew obvious parallels with the climax of the film *Billy Liar* in which Tom Courtenay is about to board a midnight train to the capital but is crippled with nervous disinclination. Leaving friends, family and lover behind, the flight from the humdrum provinces brings guilt and pessimism instead of the expected relief of escape. That 'London' is also the title of a 1968 Sandie Shaw B-side is perhaps coincidence, though Morrissey's explicit citation from Elizabeth Smart's *By Grand Central Station I Sat Down and Wept* – 'because you notice the jealousy of those that stay at home' – is quite deliberate.

The protagonist's dilemma as the train hurtles South is amplified by the high-speed momentum of Joyce's rip-roaring beat and Marr's stammering, discordant Morse-code feedback. Street also left his mark upon its quasi-punk fresco: 'I remember saying to Johnny that I could hear these little descending guitar lines. We tried it with him playing it down the bottom of his guitar neck, but it wasn't low enough. In the end he did it on the bottom E string, playing it open but turning the tuning head each time so it scaled down.'[110]

After 90 seconds, 'London' is almost done, bar a ballistic minor-key instrumental finale in which Marr slips into more familiar lightning picking mode and Joyce pounds his heart out to an impressively mental climax. Interestingly, London itself is never mentioned in the song by name, only Euston station, where the majority of trains from Manchester arrive. Contrary to the clichéd northern fear and hatred of the city expressed in its lyric, Morrissey freely confessed in interviews of the period that since living in the capital he had actually grown 'attached to London' and its 'cosmetic fake glamour'.

For Craig Gannon, 'London' marked the end of his recording career with The Smiths, surviving in the group for one more month to see out their final UK tour before being abruptly dismissed. Yet even as the Mayfair session was wrapping, Stephen Street was to learn that Gannon was already being primed for the chop: 'I'd never worked with him before so as we finished I remember saying to Johnny that I thought it went pretty well with Craig. He took me aside and said "I don't think he's going to be around much longer." I didn't say anything, but it was obvious, before the tour had started, that Craig's days were numbered.'

In Concert

A spirited live favourite, 'London' was introduced at Carlisle Sands Centre (13/10/86) and played throughout their final tour. Crowd reaction to the song was routinely ecstatic, despite the fact that it had yet to be released (by

110 The twanging plunge Street refers to are those heard at 0.21, 0.47 and 1.14.

the time it was, The Smiths would sadly never play live again). For the last ever concert at Brixton Academy without Craig Gannon (12/12/86), Marr constructed an ingenious medley, segueing the outro of 'London' into the second half of 'Miserable Lie'.

Radio

By far the best version of 'London' was that recorded at BBC Maida Vale Studio 4 on 2 December 1986 for their final John Peel session. Produced by John Porter, its foremost improvement was Marr's brilliant use of controlled feedback, bending high-pitched screeches with a whammy bar which soared spectacularly behind Joyce's vigorous rhythm.

'London' as recorded live at Kilburn National Ballroom (23/10/86) was also broadcast on BBC Radio 1's *In Concert* series in April 1987 and later included on the posthumous live album *Rank* adapted from the same show. This version was also issued as a free flexi-disc with *The Catalogue* in September 1988, the reverse of which featured Morrissey's entertainingly camp 'Poppycocteau' poem, in which he surrenders his trousers to two merchant seamen outside a Liverpool nightclub ('well you've got to make the most of life, haven't you?').

65

'Shoplifters Of The World Unite'

Recorded November 1986, Trident Studios, London

Produced by Johnny Marr

Single A-side, January 1987 (Highest UK Chart Placing #12)

Craig Gannon's brief career in The Smiths ended at Manchester Free Trade Hall on 30 October 1986, with the last night of their autumn UK tour. 'By that point, myself and Johnny were just trying to avoid each other,' says Gannon. 'It was maybe two weeks after the Free Trade Hall gig. Johnny had rung up and left a message. I'd try to ring him back and left messages, we kept missing each other. Then a few weeks after that a mate of mine, Gary Farrell, the drummer in [fellow Rough Trade signings] Easterhouse, rang me up and said "Er, I don't think you're in The Smiths anymore. I think you'd best ring up somebody to find out". I think Geoff Travis had probably let it slip to him. It was a horrible way to find out but really, by then, I didn't even want to be in the band anymore.'

Initially, Gannon saved face by informing the press he'd taken the decision to leave because he wanted to form his own group. He also expressed the opinion that his drinking on the final tour may have also served to distance him from the other Smiths ('They all do it, but I just do it more'). Rough Trade immediately contested this, stating that the band had chosen to fire Gannon for his indifferent attitude to rehearsals as well as fresh accusations that he'd forced them to cancel a *Top of the Pops* appearance by failing to show up.[111] Marr would later go as far as to call Gannon 'a lazy bastard', while Morrissey also pulled no punches in publicly chastising him for his alleged lack of enthusiasm and commitment.

A fortnight after the Free Trade Hall show, a scheduled Anti-Apartheid benefit gig at London's Royal Albert Hall on 14 November was cancelled at the last minute with the worrying news that Marr had been involved in a near-fatal car accident two days before. Luckily, his injuries were not serious, though the incident left him understandably shaken and suffering with what press officer Pat Bellis described as 'on-off bouts of extreme physical weakness'. Marr later admitted that he'd been driving under the influence of alcohol after a night out with Mike Joyce and his girlfriend and had careered into a wall only a few yards from his house.

With the Anti-Apartheid show rescheduled to Brixton Academy a month later, ten days after his crash Marr was sufficiently fit enough to return to the studio to both record and take sole production responsibilities over a replacement A-side for the designated 'You Just Haven't Earned It Yet, Baby' single, pencilled in for the new year. His recovery was doubtlessly aided by the choice of studio. Trident, just off London's Wardour Street in Soho, was famous as the location where The Beatles cut 'Hey Jude'. Morrissey would have been similarly encouraged knowing that David Bowie's *Hunky Dory*, *The Rise and Fall of Ziggy Stardust and the Spiders from Mars* and Lou Reed's *Transformer* were also made there.

During the four-day session spent on 'Shoplifters Of The World Unite', the recuperating Marr had to contend with playing and producing, while wearing a fitted neck brace. As the patron saint of self-styled 'disability chic', Morrissey was particularly taken with his writing partner's medical accessory, to the point where he expressed something approaching envy that he couldn't have one himself. 'He thought it was my best fashion statement,' laughs Marr, 'It was "At last! He's got it together!"'

Andy Rourke's opinion that on 'Shoplifters… ' they were 'trying too hard to recreate the same vibe as 'How Soon Is Now?'' certainly merits consideration.

111 On reflection, this slur seems highly dubious. Of the two singles Gannon appeared on, 'Panic' was released when they were overseas and therefore physically unable to appear on the programme, while 'Ask' didn't chart until the week after the tour had finished, when his future in the group had already been decided. More critically, taking on board Morrissey's track record for similar last-minute cancellations (eg, his famous *Wogan* no show in July 1985) the allegation seems a little surprising. Gannon himself told this author that the allegations were 'complete lies.'

The textural combination of Marr's swampy guitar scratches and Rourke's thickset bass (catapulting between low and high E) were admittedly reminiscent of their earlier John Porter-produced epic. Nevertheless, on 'Shoplifters... ' Marr, Rourke and Joyce achieved a rare rhythmic synchronicity, finding its mysterious groove together over a series of extraordinarily powerful live instrumental takes prior to the addition of Morrissey's vocal.

Marr was also to indulge himself with his first 'authentic' guitar solo on a Smiths record, one which caused an outcry among purist Smiths militants fearing their worst suspicions about his closet rock-god ambitions were coming true. 'It was played on Radio 1's *Round Table*,' recalls Marr, 'and [The Cult's] Billy Duffy, being one of my oldest friends, in his own inimitable way decided to say it sounded like Brian May. That sort of stuck then.' In his defence, Marr explained that his 18-second burst of layered harmonising played through an open wah-wah pedal had been influenced by Nils Lofgren as well as the patron saint of squealing harmonics, blues legend Roy Buchanan.

The title slogan itself, though paraphrased from Karl Marx's celebrated instruction to workers of all countries in *The Communist Manifesto*, was actually another nod to the mid-Sixties pop of Morrissey's youth; specifically David & Jonathan's 1967 Top 10 hit 'Lovers Of The World Unite'. Beneath its inciting chorus, 'Shoplifters... ' was a much more ambiguous lyric than the title may have suggested, clouded in wordplay (Morrissey's 'list of crimes' becoming 'a listed crime' in the second verse) and jagged with existential digressions (resisting 'the real world' as boring, while demanding to be loved for all eternity). The shoplifters revolution is actually one of resigned nihilism in a world where a scaremongering Channel 4 documentary detailing the imminent apocalypse[112] or a criminal reprimand bringing a six-month sentence are met with desensitised apathy. Any clues as to its governing hypothesis was further clouded by Morrissey's own explanation that the song was about shoplifting in the 'spiritual' sense.

Representing a fairly radical change from their past 45s – musically less immediate but sonically more adventurous (even *with* that guitar solo) – 'Shoplifters Of The World Unite' peaked at number 12 in early February after whipping up a right royal media brouhaha. The Smiths' parliamentary

112 Morrissey's lyric in this instance bears the influence of Joni Mitchell. The title track of her 1977 album *Don Juan's Reckless Daughter* contains the couplet 'Last night the ghost of my old ideals/Reran on channel five'. When given the opportunity to interview Mitchell in the mid-Nineties, Morrissey divulged, 'Everything about that record completely mesmerises me. When I first saw the lyric sheet and the vastness of these words I actually had to close the record. I thought "I have to leave this for another day, this is just – a monster!"' Incidentally, the same album's closing track, 'The Silky Veils of Ardor', would also provide a lyrical template for Morrissey's 'Seasick, Yet Still Docked' featured on his 1992 solo LP *Your Arsenal*.

nemesis Geoffrey Dickens once again raised his head to denounce the band in the tabloids, expressing his moral outrage that such a brazen glorification of petty theft be even allowed to exist. *Smash Hits* magazine also landed themselves in hot water when they mischievously reprinted the song's lyrics using a background graphic incorporating a Tesco's shopping bag (the incensed supermarket chain threatened to sue). Meanwhile, Rough Trade were shrewd enough to milk its provocative potential by distributing their own limited edition 'Shoplifter' carrier bags to participating record shops during its first week of release. All of which Morrissey found hilarious: 'I heard [the song] once on the radio. A chart rundown, it was a new entry. They had to play it. They had no choice. And I laughed hysterically as I listened to it.'

'I still think it's a great record,' says Marr. 'Really direct as well. I really liked the words on that. "Alabaster crashes down" – I thought that was brilliant.' As his first solo production credit, Marr was justly proud of 'Shoplifters Of The World Unite'. Ironic, then, that his enjoyment in completing the record single-handedly would inadvertently reinforce a growing sense of isolation from his fellow band members; a feeling that he couldn't, and wouldn't, ignore as events progressively deteriorated over the next six months.

In Concert

A month before its release as the next single, 'Shoplifters Of The World Unite' was premiered at London's Brixton Academy (12/12/86). As this unwittingly became their final gig, 'Shoplifters… ' was the last new song ever to be introduced into The Smiths' concert repertoire. They would play it live only once more in public on Channel 4's *The Tube* the following April (see below).

Television

'Shoplifters… ' was first featured on *The Tube* on 23 January 1987, when Morrissey took part in a two-way interview with Liverpudlian teenage playwright Shaun Duggan (whose drama *William*, inspired by 'William, It Was Really Nothing', was currently being staged at the Royal Court in London).[113]

113 Duggan was something of a minor celebrity amongst Smiths fans. Significantly, at one point Morrissey asks him about the Channel 4 Liverpool soap *Brookside*. 'I adore *Brookside*' enthuses Duggan, 'I could easily write for it.' Sure enough, within a decade he was one of the show's main scriptwriters. After Morrissey confessed to the press that he too was 'hopelessly addicted' to the soap, it was rumoured he was to make a *Brookside* cameo as a prospective buyer for the bungalow owned by the curmudgeonly Harry Cross. Morrissey finally did make his acting debut in March 1988, not in *Brookside*, but in its two-part spin-off series *South*, playing himself in the reception of London's Capital Radio offices: 'I know who you are' says Tracy Corkhill (actress Justine Kerrigan). 'So do I' mutters Morrissey. 'You're Morrissey!' she gasps. 'I know' he retorts. It was, as he told the *NME*, 'compulsive non-viewing'.

Asked about The Smiths' recent activities, Morrissey named the new single, in doing so confessing that he'd never actually shoplifted but that the record was about using things to one's own advantage. The song was then given a brief airing over old footage from *The Tube*'s 1985 Margi Clarke interview with Morrissey in Edinburgh.

With the single firmly lodged in the UK Top 20, on 5 February The Smiths gave an especially enigmatic mimed performance on *Top of the Pops*, their first since 'The Boy With The Thorn In His Side' 15 months earlier. In a denim two-piece and Elvis Presley T-shirt, Morrissey curled in a series of slow, deliberate pelvic grinds, playing to the camera like a skilled master of the pop charade and underlining every lyric with flawless theatricality (thrusting an outstretched palm into the lens whilst demanding 'hand it over'). Marr cut an especially fine model of rock 'n' roll chic with a restored quiff and denim turn-ups. Even the routinely deadpan Andy Rourke managed a smirk or two, proof if any that The Smiths were, for now, still an impenetrably happy family.

In bitter contrast, their final live TV appearance on *The Tube* on 10 April felt like the beginning of the end. The last edition to feature Jools Holland as presenter (his job security perishing the moment he innocently murmured 'groovy fuckers' live on air during a previous programme), The Smiths closed the show with their new single, 'Sheila Take A Bow', followed by 'Shoplifters Of The World Unite'. Though musically both songs sounded fine, visually it was a depressing spectacle; particularly when two typically self-conscious young males leapt on stage only for Marr to be seen mouthing 'get them off' to roadie Phil Powell who obligingly shooed them back into the audience.

'I remember that,' explains Marr, 'but what's important to understand is that quite often when people would jump on stage, leads would come out, amps would go over and it was a real damp squib. So when those two guys jumped on stage and we're on live television, I don't want the plug to be literally pulled. That's why those two guys had to go. I never had anything against fans who crashed the stage. There's photos of me at Glastonbury in 1984 physically pulling people out of the audience to come up and go mad with us. There were just a few times where the stage invasions killed the gig off and I felt quite badly for the other 75 per cent of the audience. But it was only because we were live on Channel 4 that I asked for those fans to be taken down.'

66

'Is It Really So Strange?'

Recorded **December 1986, BBC Maida Vale Studio 4, London**

Produced by **John Porter**

B-side to **'Sheila Take A Bow', April 1987**

The Smiths' formative BBC radio sessions for John Peel and David Jensen had played a vital role in their media ascent during their first year together. As a magnanimous gesture honouring their debt to the programme, their decision to record a new Peel session at the end of 1986 marked a surprising but welcome return to their grass roots. Of the four songs recorded, two would eventually be licensed out as B-sides to the 'Sheila Take A Bow' single in April 1987 – 'Is It Really So Strange?' and 'Sweet And Tender Hooligan'.

Both songs were among the first tunes Marr had written in the aftermath of *The Queen Is Dead*, assembling a basic drum machine demo of each in early 1986. First attempted at the 'Ask' session at Jam studios that June, John Porter helped modify Marr's draft by suggesting he approach the tune in a similar style to guitarist Scotty Moore's rockabilly picking on 'That's All Right', an old Arthur 'Big Boy' Crudup blues that Elvis Presley had refashioned as his debut Sun single in 1954; the very roots of rock 'n' roll.[114] Accordingly, Marr eagerly applied stylised Fifties' rock 'n' roll motifs, resulting in a familiar 12-bar framework laced with twanging blues scales and added seventh hammer-ons. This tongue-in-cheek Fifties feel was given even greater prominence on its first few takes, thanks to Marr's Link Wray-style elastic tremolo contractions.

The rock 'n' roll vibe was continued within Morrissey's lyrics; a classic hitch-hiking travelogue that may well have based its title and chorus upon an obscure Elvis Presley 1957 EP track – Faron Young's 'Is It So Strange?'. Just as the King smoulders 'is it so strange to be in love with you?', Morrissey opens his heart with 'cause I love you – and is it really so strange?'. As the

114 Though their respective sessions were nearly two years apart, since both 'How Soon Is Now?' and 'Is It Really So Strange?' were recorded at Jam Studios, John Porter has since attributed the 'That's All Right' story to influencing the former song; an error reiterated in the earlier edition of this book where this author suggested Porter had helped Marr sculpt 'How Soon Is Now?' via this same Elvis influence. Johnny Marr is adamant that this isn't the case. 'I remember John suggesting the figure for 'That's All Right', and why I'm so clear about it is because I was playing my Gretsch. Now I didn't play my Gretsch on 'How Soon Is Now?' but I did on 'Is It Really So Strange?' I remember John literally breathing down me neck with his arm around me and showing me the riff. So that's where he's getting confused. If you compare the demo of 'Is It Really So Strange?' with the record then you can hear the Sun riff and tell the difference because there's sevenths all over it.'

first in Morrissey's triptych of songs about southbound journeys (carried on with 'Half A Person' and 'London' **[see 63 and 64]**), 'Is It Really So Strange?' was also the quirkiest. Chasing the disinterested object of his desire from North to South and back again, in his lovelorn confusion Morrissey confesses to murdering first a horse, then a nun. The unrequited amour corrupting his every move is, he claims, invincible enough to even withstand physical violence from his averse love-interest. Alas, this black comedy ends with the grim realisation that, with the blood of a Bride of Christ on his hands, just like Gene Pitney in Bacharach and David's '24 Hours From Tulsa', he can 'never, never go back home again' (ditto The Shangri-Las' 1965 classic 'I Can Never Go Home Anymore').

Speaking to *No 1* magazine that summer, Morrissey said he found 'that mood of a Northern person going to London and then returning home very poignant. You can't describe how you feel when you go from South to North, stopping at the service stations. It hits a deafening note'. This might explain his specific namedropping of Newport Pagnell, a popular service stop on the M1 just outside Milton Keynes where the song's narrator loses his bag. John Peel shares a telling anecdote on the subject: 'One time I met Morrissey at one of those motorway services just south of Newcastle. I was coming down from Edinburgh and I was feeling tired. So I went in there and saw him and I was like "Oh! Hello!". And Morrissey said "This is my favourite motorway service station". And I thought "How extraordinary!" that *anybody*, particularly Morrissey, could have a favourite motorway service station!'

The Smiths were sufficiently dissatisfied with the Jam studio recording of 'Is It Really So Strange?' not to release it. Six months later, their fourth Peel session provided them with a golden opportunity to tackle this whimsical rocker a second time with the end result deemed good enough for commercial release; first as a B-side and later as a tantalising opener for Sire's *Louder Than Bombs* compilation. A live version of 'Is It Really So Strange?' recorded by the BBC at Kilburn National Ballroom (though never broadcast) was later included on 1988's *Rank*.

In Concert

First played nearly eight months before its vinyl release at Glasgow Barrowlands (16/7/86), 'Is It Really So Strange?' would remain a set regular from thereon up to and including the last ever gig at Brixton Academy (12/12/86), the only time it was performed live without Craig Gannon.

67

'Sweet And Tender Hooligan'

Recorded **December 1986, BBC Maida Vale Studio 4, London**

Produced by **John Porter**

B-side to **'Sheila Take A Bow' (12-inch format only), April 1987**

Among Morrissey and Marr's first songs of 1986, 'Sweet And Tender Hooligan' was written that spring at the same time as 'Is It Really So Strange?', originating as one of Marr's four-track home drum machine demos and using a chord loop similar to the rebounding minor-key drop and return of 'Some Girls Are Bigger Than Others'. It took Rourke and Joyce to fully exploit the tune's inherent menace when it was first recorded at the start of the Livingston 'Panic' session in early May as a potential B-side **[see 58]**. Yet despite several strong takes (with vocal) to choose from, 'Sweet And Tender Hooligan' was never completed.

Deciding against introducing it in concert, the song would gather dust for seven months until their December Peel session, where they attacked it with renewed fervour. The sped up 'Sweet And Tender Hooligan' was a refreshing return to the savage unruliness of 'Handsome Devil'; a fittingly rumbustious charge of spitting guitars and fuming drums (Joyce's off-beat tom fills between the second and third snare-hits quaking like a bovver-boy stampede). John Porter also made the most of Marr's intro, frenetically panning it from left to right to create a fittingly vicious prologue.

Morrissey's vivid portrait of a baby-faced geriatric murderer appealing for judicial clemency with his 'mother-me eyes' was an inevitable development of his earlier references to juvenile crime in 'I Want The One I Can't Have' and 'The Queen Is Dead'. This controversial theme was one he would return to with increasing frequency during his solo career. Although in these later works, such as 1989's Kray homage 'The Last Of The Famous International Playboys', he would be repeatedly accused of glamorising the subject (even confessing in 1988's 'Sister I'm A Poet' – 'how I love the romance of crime!'), 'Sweet And Tender Hooligan' is more sardonic than sympathetic to its eponymous thug. His derisive counsel that 'he'll never, never do it again – at least not until the next time' expressed a lack of faith in the British penal system that was strangely conservative, especially when contrasted with the graphic horror of the young lad's misdeeds.[115]

115 Originally it had been 'a three *ring* fire' that caused the pensioner's accident and a 'poor old girl' who'd been strangled.

As Rourke's pummelling bass and Marr's punkish tumult build to a gory climax, Morrissey recites from the standard church burial service as famously subverted by American wit Ethel Watts Mumford that 'in the midst of life we are in *debt*', eventually so consumed by the horror and futility of the situation that his words crumble into trance-like gibbers. Culled from their December Peel session along with 'Is It Really So Strange?' as B-sides to 'Sheila Take A Bow', the tremendous 'Sweet And Tender Hooligan' would later be issued as a posthumous European single in its own right.

In Concert

'Sweet And Tender Hooligan' was never performed live by The Smiths but was played as the final encore at Morrissey's live solo debut at Wolverhampton Civic Hall on 22 December 1988 **[see Epilogue]**. Though significantly inferior to The Smiths' original (and desperately missing Marr) the Wolverhampton 'Sweet And Tender Hooligan' was later issued as the 12-inch/CD extra track to Morrissey's fourth solo single 'Interesting Drug' released on EMI's HMV imprint in April 1989. Excerpts from the gig, including the scenes of pandemonium outside the venue, were filmed by Tim Broad and included on Morrissey's *Hulmerist* video collection in 1990.

68

'Sheila Take A Bow'

Recorded **January 1987, Good Earth Studios, London**

Produced by **Johnny Marr, Morrissey and Stephen Street**

Single A-side, April 1987 (Highest UK Chart Placing #10)

On Friday 12 December 1986, The Smiths played their rescheduled Anti-Apartheid concert at London's Brixton Academy. Back to a four piece again after Craig Gannon's severance, neither the band nor their audience would have suspected that it was to be their last. The euphoria of the gig itself offered no ill omens, while the group's own determination to soldier on into 1987 was evident in their booking of another recording session commencing the very next day.

Tired and a little worse for wear, Marr, Rourke and Joyce rolled up as planned at Paul Weller's Solid Bond studios in Marble Arch that weekend, where John Porter was waiting. Unfortunately, Morrissey failed to show, much to the chagrin of Sandie Shaw who had also been invited along to add backing vocals on the proposed new song, 'Sheila Take A Bow'. 'There was no sign of Morrissey for a couple of hours,' remembers Joyce. 'Sandie was getting a bit frantic. In the end she phoned up Morrissey and managed to get hold of him. She was saying "just hum me the tune down the phone that you want me to do!". I think she took it all personally.' According to Shaw's 1991 autobiography, *The World at my Feet,* Morrissey explained he was 'desperately unwell'. The Solid Bond session was cancelled.

After Christmas, the group reconvened with Porter and Shaw at Matrix studios, where they'd originally recorded her version of 'Hand In Glove' nearly three years earlier. Sadly, Sandie's vocal failed to fit 'Sheila Take A Bow' as planned, a disappointment which she genially put down to incompatible musical mathematics: 'Morrissey had written the melody around the fifth harmony of Johnny's tune, and because of the key and my range all I could sing was the third below. This put Morrissey and me in a two-part harmony reminiscent of the Sinatras' duet 'Something Stupid'. It was squirmy.' The original take also differed in its introduction featuring a sitar-like Indian melody (played by Porter on an Emulator), which recurred throughout the rest of the song in its post-chorus bridges. By the time the master mix was finished, Sandie had already been dropped out of the arrangement though, in any case, this version would never be released.

Instead, in late January the band shifted camp to Good Earth, the West End studios owned by venerated glam producer Tony Visconti, to record the song from scratch with Stephen Street. The ignominy of having his trial run rejected notwithstanding, Porter was further disheartened to discover a guitar part that he'd recorded had been sampled onto the remake without his permission. Street explains: 'There was this certain guitar sound on John's version which they really liked[116] but we only had so much time to do it in. So in the end Johnny just said "sod this, let's just take it off the other recording" which we did. I heard John Porter was upset about it, but the way Johnny saw it was that it was his guitar figure anyway, so why shouldn't he just lift it? It was purely to save time at the end of the day.'

'Well I wouldn't have minded if anybody had said anything to me but they didn't,' comments Porter, who would never work with The Smiths again. 'Looking back I would say that I was disappointed more than anything. I felt that I never really got to make a proper album with them because that first one was so rushed. They were getting better all the time, but I don't think we'd got it as good as we could. It all felt like a rehearsal for the great album we never made. That's my only regret. But all the bullshit I understood. I mean it's the music industry – shit happens! As soon as a band becomes successful, well, money changes everything as somebody once said.'

116 Namely, its background chord surges in E and D during the chorus.

Admittedly, their second stab at 'Sheila Take A Bow' was manifestly burlier than Porter's draft, harking back to the retro-glam of 'Panic' Their early-Seventies pop muse was fed by the studio surroundings, when they fortuitously stumbled upon some of Visconti's original T.Rex reels which they mischievously played around with; listening to the individual tracks of the actual Bolan masters between takes. The result was a rollicking glam attack, goaded by Joyce's quaking floor-tom rumbles and Marr's dirty sweet Bolan vamps, which profited from past sound-checks jamming T.Rex's 'Get It On' and Gary Glitter's 'Rock And Roll Part 2'. Porter's Indian intro was also swapped for a Salvation Amy brass band sampled from David Lean's 1954 northern comedy *Hobson's Choice*, which was sped up to synchronise with Marr's fuzzy singular ringing B chord.

It fitted that Morrissey's words imbued the Seventies glam tableau, echoing David Bowie's 'Kooks' off his 1971 album *Hunky Dory*, in which he promises 'if the homework brings you down, then we'll throw it on the fire' That the lyrics were an obvious homage to Salford-born playwright Shelagh Delaney (though he decided against using the Gaelic spelling of her Christian name), suggested Morrissey was indeed treading water. No matter, his inspirational cry to go forth and 'boot the grime of this world in the crutch' made for a stimulating pop record, as did its titillating gender-swapping finale. The latter subtext of sexual identity was exhibited in the single's sleeve depicting Warhol transsexual 'Superstar' Candy Darling **[see Appendix II]**. 'To be able to inflict Candy Darling on the record buying public', bragged Morrissey, 'was a perfect example of my very dangerous sense of humour.' The insurrection of its transvestite cover was all the greater since, along with 'Heaven Knows I'm Miserable Now', 'Sheila Take A Bow' became the only Smiths single to make the UK Top 10 and, discounting WEA's 1992 reissue of 'This Charming Man', their joint biggest hit ever.

Television

On 10 April 1987, 'Sheila Take A Bow' was performed on Channel 4's *The Tube* as part of their last live TV appearance **[see also 64]**. Translating well to a basic four-piece arrangement (beginning with its *Hobson's Choice* intro played on a backing tape), this, its only public performance, was a fair indication of how it might have sounded in concert. A fortnight later it would also instigate their last TV engagement of their career when they mimed to 'Sheila Take Bow' on the 23 April edition of *Top of the Pops*.

Their return to the Top 10 for the first time in three years was marked with a masterful display of pop prowess. Morrissey was as charismatic as ever, a disposition shared by the triumphant, Lennon-cap wearing Marr, shaking his rump with arms outstretched in time with the thudding oompah rhythm. The inter-group chemistry was still a fluorescent, almost visible harmony of intense comradeship. Far from a band on the brink of implosion (unbelievably, in six months they would be no more), here The Smiths looked invincible.

69

'Girlfriend In A Coma'

Recorded **January-April 1987, Good Earth Studios, London/Wool Hall Studios, Bath**

Produced by **Johnny Marr, Morrissey and Stephen Street**

Single A-side, August 1987 (Highest UK Chart Placing #13)

Subsequently featured on the album ***Strangeways, Here We Come*, September 1987**

Between the re-recording of 'Sheila Take A Bow', The Smiths made economical use of the Good Earth session. Marr, Rourke and Joyce found time to cut two instrumental demos annotated as 'Jam 1' and 'Jam 2' The first hinted at the rudimentary glam groove of 'I Started Something I Couldn't Finish' **[see 74]** while the second possessed feint traces of another future *Strangeways, Here We Come* track, 'Stop Me If You Think You've Heard This One Before' **[see 75]**. More importantly, the 'Sheila' session allowed them time to lay down the basic foundations of another new song, complete with vocal, also destined for their fourth album.

'Girlfriend In A Coma' was a further stylistic departure for the group, particularly during its first two takes which accentuated Marr's jerky Jamaican upstrokes to lend the song an unusual rocksteady feel. 'That song came out of mine and Morrissey's love of Bob & Marcia's 'Young, Gifted And Black',' reveals Marr.[117] 'We both absolutely adored it. So 'Girlfriend In A Coma' was trying to capture the spirit of that. If you listen to the string parts on both you can maybe see it.'[118]

Of all Morrissey's pop *coups d'état*, the ability to craft a hit single with the dour and distasteful title 'Girlfriend In A Coma' was among his most remarkable. The lyrics were an ingenious twist on the classic Sixties' 'death disc' scenario, lamenting a hospital-ridden lover after a ghastly accident (as in Ricky Valance's 1960 number one 'Tell Laura I Love Her'). In this instance, the anxiety that his injured sweetheart will survive is multiplied by the

117 In later interviews Morrissey would confirm his love of Bob & Marcia's 'Young, Gifted and Black' (a UK number 5 in early 1970), also compiling the song on his live intermission tapes during his solo tour of 1997.

118 Once again it was the trusty Emulator that allowed Marr to weave in this resplendent string part during the final *Strangeways* album mixdown at The Wool Hall later that spring.

guilty memories of their bitterest arguments. The first draft had Morrissey divulge 'there were times when I could have *cheerfully* strangled her', then retracting his initial refusal to see his beloved's critical condition by begging 'with tears in my eyes, I ask you!' All too soon, the drama is steered towards its grimmest possible conclusion, with a morbid recitation of Reparata & The Delrons' 1965 girl group oldie 'Bye Bye Baby' (later a 1975 UK number one for The Bay City Rollers). Chillingly juxtaposed against Marr's jovial major-key backcloth, the curtain falls with Morrissey preparing himself for the dreaded 'last goodbye'. In what was to be their shortest (and most macabre) single ever, the emotional gauntlet of life, hope, guilt, regret and death rattles past the listener in just two minutes and two seconds flat.

Wretchedly, 'Girlfriend In A Coma' was released in the aftermath of press reports confirming Marr's acrimonious exit from The Smiths. The single was even previewed on Janice Long's Radio 1 show in early August the very evening his 'resignation' was announced. Although The Smiths had yet to officially call it a day (and the record peaked at a respectable number 13)[119], its deathly subject matter seemed to symbolically scrawl their looming termination on the wall for all to read: 'I know – IT'S SERIOUS.'

In Concert

One of the great tragedies of The Smiths' disordered break-up was that they were never to perform 'Girlfriend In A Coma', nor any of *Strangeways, Here We Come* in concert. In one of his last interviews shortly after completing the album, Marr vowed that on their next tour 'all [we] want to play is the new material and some of the old material that we feel we'd still like to play – some bits off *The Queen Is Dead*, 'Shakespeare's Sister', 'Panic', 'Ask'.' Alas, Morrissey was much less enthusiastic, informing *Q* magazine that for him, the thrill of live performance was 'totally, totally gone'. Fate decreed that the sights, sounds and setlists of the *Strangeways* tour that never was would remain the fodder of idle fan fantasy alone.

Television

Unable to perform the song on *Top of the Pops* due to Marr's sudden departure, a substitute video for 'Girlfriend In A Coma' was hastily completed in 24 hours by Tim Broad, featuring Morrissey miming over superimposed footage from the 1963 Rita Tushingham kitchen-sink/biker drama *The Leather Boys*, (his 'favourite film' at the time).

119 Many associates of the band verify that Morrissey was obsessed with chart positions. In a letter to Stephen Street the following week, he would express great unhappiness that 'Girlfriend In A Coma' missed the Top 10, grumbling that 'it was number 7 midweek'.

70

'Heavy Track'

Recorded **March 1987, Wool Hall Studios, Bath**

Studio out-take

After rerecording 'Sheila Take A Bow', The Smiths spent February 1987 promoting the current single, 'Shoplifters Of The World Unite', with a media tour of Eire and Europe, even joining indigenous peers such as Spandau Ballet, Pet Shop Boys and The Style Council at Italy's San Remo Pop Festival (a mimed performance for foreign TV, sometimes inaccurately referred to as their last gig). Upon returning home, spirits were buoyed by their conquering of the music press' annual readers' polls, topping the *NME*'s 'Best Band', 'Best Album' and 'Best Single' categories, while Morrissey had the privilege of also being declared 'Best Singer' and 'Most Wonderful Human Being'.

Consequently, when The Smiths commenced their month's residency at The Wool Hall studio near Bath that March, the mood of the troops was justly victorious. It was ironic then that *Strangeways, Here We Come*, the album they produced there with Stephen Street, was to be their last. 'I didn't want it to be our last record,' reflects Marr. 'I would have been really happy for it not to be our last record. But if the business and management pressures were gonna carry on being on my shoulders then I'd made the decision that spiritually, emotionally and physically I wasn't gonna collapse under the weight of it. But it was a really liberating feeling making that album. We all had a great time, maybe because *I* was having such a good time.'

'Everybody thinks as it was the last album that we were falling apart but we weren't,' Rourke concurs. 'The four of us really came together and it was probably the best time we ever had as a group.' With all mod cons and an endless supply of beer and wine, the band had no excuse not to make themselves at home. Joyce elaborates: 'We used to party every night. Because it was a residential studio, there was no kind of getting a cab back so we had to stay. It didn't matter what time you played to either as we were out in the middle of nowhere. It couldn't have been a better place really.'

The evening bacchanalia routinely dissolved into a record-playing session, relaxing to Prince's *Sign O' The Times* or – in Street's case – drunkenly dancing to Sister Sledge. Marr further amused himself with his new state-of-the-art camcorder, documenting hours of studio tomfoolery between recording. The band were also, as Street puts it, 'going through a Spinal Tap phase'. In tribute to Rob Reiner's 1984 *This Is Spinal Tap* mockumentary, cigarette packets were arranged into mini replicas of Stonehenge, while after-hours jams saw Marr, Rourke and Joyce boisterously bash their way through the Tap songbook – 'Big Bottom' included. 'It's true that our night times were spent in revelry,' says Marr, 'but only after ten or twelve hours of making some really great music, not as a substitute. I just wasn't going to be choked or suffocated by the situation so it gave me a sense of liberation.'

Conspicuous by his absence in such laddish shenanigans was, of course, Morrissey. 'We were having really good fun listening to funk music, pissing about with the Spinal Tap thing,' says Street, 'but obviously when Morrissey wasn't around. It wasn't really his bag. He'd usually go to bed about 10.30 or 11.00 every night, which was fair enough. But the rest of us would carry on working for another hour doing overdubs and then the records would start going on and we were off, partying till all hours.'

Strangeways kicked off with Marr, Rourke, Joyce and Street arriving at The Wool Hall the day before Morrissey and taking the opportunity to lay down the hedonistic ground rules that evening. Street recalls their flagrant first jam and their excessive alcohol consumption, in which the inebriated Marr fell off his piano stool during an early run through of 'A Rush And A Push And The Land Is Ours' before taunting the producer with an altogether different hard-rock work out: 'Johnny was a bit plastered. It was strange because Morrissey wasn't there, so they were just rocking out and doing their own thing and I remember Johnny shouting up through the intercom[120] "'ere Streety. You don't like it when we do this, you like us to be all jingly-jangly don't you?". And I didn't know how to take it, I didn't know if he was having a go at me or if he was just pissed.'

Marr had long since tired of The Smiths restrictive 'indie' pigeon-holing and was now clearly determined to stretch their remit as far as he could, eager to shatter all audience preconceptions in the process. The extent of his sonically harder ambition was evident in one of their fist jams at The Wool Hall – an instrumental transcribed on the master reels as the self-explanatory 'Heavy Track'. At least two takes of this fierce rocker survive, taking its cue from the abrasiveness of 'What She Said' and 'London', but with stronger hues of early-Seventies metal. The best comparison would perhaps be The Who circa 1970's *Live at Leeds* in so far as Joyce's drumming is a bombastic exhibition of Moonish lunacy, while Rourke's dynamic bass noodling likewise tips its cap towards John Entwistle. The riff itself employed a favourite Marr chord grouping, holding in E-minor for four bars before

120 Unlike traditional studios The Wool Hall's recording room and control booth were on separate levels with both parties only able to communicate through a CCTV intercom system.

rising to C then D for a bar apiece (its second take ran to early five minutes, rotating in key between E and A minors). Marr's charging high-gain assault left plenty of room for a vocal melody, while the guitarist himself was clearly besotted with the tune as the studio tapes pick up: 'Cool!' he beams, 'I really, really like that!'

Alas, Morrissey didn't, and the otherwise nameless 'Heavy Track' was taken no further. Had it been, it would have heightened the drama and diversity of *Strangeways* just that bit more, while the inclusion of weaker fare like 'Death At One's Elbow' made its loss all that more pertinent.

71

'Death Of A Disco Dancer'

Recorded March-April 987, Wool Hall Studios, Bath

Produced by Johnny Marr, Morrissey and Stephen Street

Album track from *Strangeways, Here We Come*, September 1987

After rocking out with 'Heavy Track', the first proper song taped for *Strangeways* was possibly its best, and ranks alongside even 'The Queen Is Dead' as one of the most extraordinary pieces of music The Smiths ever created in the studio.

From its first full band rehearsal, 'Death Of A Disco Dancer' tapped into the exclusive improvisational chemistry between Morrissey, Marr, Rourke and Joyce, wringing their individual tacit musical instincts for all they were worth. This simplest of melodies jammed around Marr's twist on The Beatles' 'Dear Prudence' from 1968's *White Album* became the catalyst for a mesmerising atonal freak out.[121] While never losing sight of its principal chord pattern, it's as if all four musicians simultaneously disrobe their inhibitions just short of the three-minute mark. As Rourke momentarily raises his bass scale an octave, the backdrop explodes: Marr slashes at his strings in a Velvet Underground 'Sister Ray' frenzy, Joyce flays his kit in a cold voodoo sweat, while Morrissey encourages the hallucinogenic chaos in an epilepsy of tumultuous, avant-garde piano.

'We just jammed it,' confirms Joyce. 'The first time we did it Johnny was looking at me over the kit going, "Carry on, more, more, more!" We just let ourselves go.' Its first raw run-through hammered on for nearly seven minutes, in which Morrissey improvised a whistled solo and wailing

121 'It's true,' admits Marr, 'that 'Death Of A Disco Dancer' was trying to capture everything about the atmosphere of *The White Album*.'

falsetto harmonies, showing his keenness by exclaiming 'Great! Let's listen, listen, listen!' the moment the band had ground to a halt. Snipped to a tidier five and a half minutes, 'Death Of A Disco Dancer' was still an epic composition. 'There was a great aura of energy coming from Mike on that track,' Street enthuses over Joyce's opportunity to shine during its instrumental climax. 'The recording area wasn't actually that big so we couldn't get a huge drum sound. Instead, we just whacked up the room mics to make it as powerful as we could. I thought Mike's playing on that was really inspiring.'

Morrissey's infamous debut as a pianist was merely a spur-of-the-moment whim during the song's overdubbing process. 'I just fell onto a piano and began to bang away' he later joked when describing his disjointed, Bartok-style tinkling, similar to the radical jazz piano interlude on the title track of Bowie's 1973 *Aladdin Sane.* According to Street it wasn't quite so comically casual. 'Morrissey suggested it. He just went down and said, "can I try this piano thing" and did it. I don't even know if he was sure what notes he was hitting, but it seemed to work really well.' The singer duly made merry hell on the ivories (much of which was later cut out or concealed) earning his way to his only instrumentation credit on a Smiths record. Completing the tune's unsettling eeriness was a crooked background string drone played on an Emulator. 'That's one of the best things about it,' laughs Marr. 'For me, that Emulator thing, that drone, it really captures the band. It's almost like 'Goldfinger' on bad acid. Which is kind of The Smiths in a nutshell.'

After 'Panic', it wasn't any great surprise that Morrissey's concern over the death of a regular disco goer didn't stretch beyond *blasé* disinterest ('I'd rather not get involved'). Yet what is truly astounding about his lyrics – written in early 1987, a good year before the acid-house boom and the proliferation of smileys and ecstasy – was just how predictive they came to be. Even before 'the Second Summer of Love' had begun, Morrissey saw through the rave era's hedonistic promise of 'love, peace and harmony' (curiously swapped as 'peace, love and harmony' during his first vocal take) with a condescending 'very nice' and the sobering thought that such things may be possible, but only after death. The chipmunk tones of 'Ann Coates' **[see 46]** make an uncredited cameo to further mock the naivety of those unfortunate enough to be duped by this lifestyle. Aside from the high profile media stories of teenage E-casualties in the years that followed, the song's nonchalant remark that such deaths occur regularly 'round here' were an uncanny forecast of the drug-related gun crime that played a major part in the close of Manchester's Hacienda club in the early Nineties.

Today, the song remains one of their most consistently overlooked masterpieces; possibly on account of its unrepresentative simplicity and the challenge of its trippy, sonic pandemonium. When ruminating on The

Smiths' finest moments a decade later, Morrissey divulged that he occasionally sang it 'as I'm rolling out pastry', though for an authoritative validation of its worth, one need look no further than the very end of 'Death Of A Disco Dancer' as it appears on *Strangeways* itself. Just as the song finishes (about 5.23 on a CD counter), crank up the volume as high as you can for just a moment and you should be able to hear Marr begin a sentence with the words 'some bits... ' The track cuts off before he has a chance to finish, but what you are hearing is the start of Marr's ecstatic comment to the rest of the band picked up on the studio mic when they finished its original live take. 'Some bits of that were incredible.' Enough said.

72

'Paint A Vulgar Picture'

Recorded **March-April 1987, Wool Hall Studios, Bath**

Produced by **Johnny Marr, Morrissey and Stephen Street**

Album track from ***Strangeways, Here We Come*, September 1987**

One of the earliest songs laid down for *Strangeways* was Morrissey's masterful indictment of the music business and is mercenary attitude towards rock 'n' roll martyrs, 'Paint A Vulgar Picture'.

The title stemmed from the song's original lyrics in which Morrissey actually sang 'so they paint a vulgar picture of the way they say that you were'.[122] Early drafts were also more accusatory with a reworded line pinched from Twinkle's 1964 'death disc' 'Terry': 'it's too late to tell him how great he really was' (subsequently adjusted to 'it took his death for you to see how great in life he was', before being binned altogether). Morrissey would even plagiarise his own past as a struggling rock hack. In his 1981 book *The New York Dolls*, he writes of a fan throwing themselves at singer David Johansen after a show at LA's Whiskey-A-Go-Go. 'A very young girl clutched David's arm and pleaded "Take me with you pl-eeaasse, wherever you're going... "'

Marr's lengthy guitar solo, his first since 'Shoplifters Of The World Unite', was actually instigated by the removal of a whole verse, which left an instrumental gap of over 30 seconds that needed filling. The extracted lyrics graphically detailed the death of the song's tragic celebrity, strongly hinting at suicide: 'Anecdotes and stories/"Oh yes we were so close you know!"/So

122 Since this passage was omitted in the final draft, many would mistakenly assume 'Paint A Vulgar Picture' to be a steal from Oscar Wilde. Though Wildean in tone and explicitly suggestive of *The Picture of Dorian Gray*, it's neither a direct quote from that novel nor any other of his works.

why did the body lie for seven days/Before someone passed his way?'

Not surprisingly, when released after their split, 'Paint A Vulgar Picture' was zealously diagnosed as being Morrissey's personal premonition over his own mortality and the fate of The Smiths' back catalogue at the hands of their record company. 'It wasn't about Rough Trade at all,' Morrissey coyly deflected. 'I was a bit confused when Geoff Travis despised it and stamped on it. It was about the music industry in general, about practically anybody who's died and left behind that frenetic fanatical legacy which sends people scrambling, [like] Billy Fury, Marc Bolan.' It was a hollow defence, especially considering The Smiths' recent acrimonious contractual disputes with Rough Trade and their imminent move to EMI. His derisive remarks to the media in the past about the BPI, MTV and the BBC also contributed to a more autobiographical evaluation of its lyrics, as did the inclusion of a previous Smiths title – 'You Just Haven't Earned It Yet, Baby' – notoriously ascribed as coming from the mouth of Travis himself **[see 62]**.

'I know Geoff took umbrage with those lyrics,' admits Street, 'he felt quite hurt that the song was pointed at him. I think it's a shame really, because lyrically it's very clever, but in retrospect, Morrissey's the last one to talk about wanting to fleece people. I think it shows him up as a hypocrite. There he is having a go at record companies wanting to repackage things and then later on in life he does exactly the same thing himself. That's tainted it a little bit in that respect. Personally, I thought the song went on a bit too long anyway.'

The shrewd, unscrupulous marketing of extra tracks and 'tacky badges' aside, the song's most damaging blows were aimed at those on the extreme right of fandom's diverse political spectrum, the kind of character Morrissey knew only too well, as he told the press: 'There are some people who take train journeys to London to try and find me. They ring up the record company and appear at the doorstep and say "I am here and I am going to lie on the doorstep until Morrissey arrives." There are people like that. I don't disapprove of that situation. They're getting fresh air!' In 'Paint A Vulgar Picture' Morrissey runs the risk of finding humour just a little too close to home for these militant admirers to stomach, the track ending with his (quite purposely) audible vomiting.

It takes several rotations of Marr's knotty arrangement – repeatedly changing in key every other verse from D to B and back again – to grasp the essence of his melodic intent. Only after repeated listening can one start to appreciate the song's ambitious foundations and its confusing, unconventional off-bar chord changes. 'I was always intrigued by how Johnny came up with that,' says Street, 'because it was very clever, the way it bridged back and forth, but very odd as well.' Concern over the song's repetitive evenness resulted in the temporary addition of some emulated saxophone. The part in question never rested satisfactorily amid Marr's multi-tracked guitar rhythm score and was mostly erased.[123] After a dummy running order of *Strangeways'* final track listing was assembled in early April, the last effects to be tacked on were its backing handclaps and the fade-out's comical applause (all four Smiths giving themselves a standing ovation similar to that featured on their original 1982 Drone demo of 'What Difference Does It Make?' **[see 2]**).

Lyrically, 'Paint A Vulgar Picture' stood out as the album's most fascinating entry, a welcome diversion from the Morrissey/Marr songbook's presiding thesis on the impossibilities of love and human relationships. Yet as Street points out, taking into consideration the glut of posthumous compilations to have appeared after their back catalogue was sold to Warners in the early Nineties, with its infamous arraignment of 'Reissue! Repackage! Repackage!' The Smiths prophetically hexed themselves.

73

'Death At One's Elbow'

Recorded **March-April 1987, Wool Hall Studios, Bath**

Produced by **Johnny Marr, Morrissey and Stephen Street**

Album track from ***Strangeways, Here We Come*, September 1987**

The Achilles' heel of *Strangeways*, 'Death At One's Elbow' was among Morrissey and Marr's weakest offerings; so weak in fact that Marr has virtually no recollection of its recording. Its by now hackneyed Fifties shtick reeked of tokenism when placed beside its more convincing rockabilly predecessors – 'Shakespeare's Sister' or 'Vicar In A Tutu' – while Morrissey's lyrics were equally lacklustre.

Following a standard rock scale already exhausted on earlier Smiths melodies (e.g., 'What Difference Does It Make?' and 'How Soon Is Now?'), the track was originally driven by a different, distorted guitar vamp, which was later buried in a mock 'slapback' Sam Phillips pastiche. What the song lacked in ingenuity it at least compensated for in its meticulously layered production; making schizoid leaps from Marr's primary twang to rhythmic acoustic skiffle, panning tremolo bends and warped harmonica honks. A bizarre prologue also exposed Street's mechanical guide-track (which even Joyce struggled to enliven) meshed with the sound of a pneumatic road drill,

123 A trace of this synthesized sax can still be heard within the final album mix at 4.01 and 4.20.

sourced from one of Morrissey's sound effects LPs. 'I don't know why that went on there,' shrugs Street. 'I think we were struggling a bit with that track to be honest. We just went a little over the top on the comical side.'

The song's title was a quotation from the published diaries of Sixties playwright Joe Orton.[124] The entry in question, on Wednesday, 28 December 1966, referred to his return home the day before his mother's funeral. 'As the corpse is downstairs in the main living-room,' wrote Orton, 'it means going out or watching television with death at one's elbow.' Indeed Orton's fate, brutally hammered to death by his gay lover Kenneth Halliwell in August 1967, was vaguely reminiscent of the song's graphic threats of physical dismemberment with a hatchet.

Between its first draft in mid-March and its completion towards the end of the month, Morrissey made a mild adjustment to the song's narrative perspective. Originally, he'd specified a female subject ('how the frustration it renders her hopeless!'), which was altered to a first-person pledge of gory suicide retaining something of Orton's own darkly comic outlook. Yet, as his rare employment of coarse slang ('it's crap, I know') and obnoxious parting belch underlined, 'Death At One's Elbow' amounted to little more than throwaway ghoulish whimsy.

In Concert

'Death At One's Elbow' was never performed live by The Smiths, though along with 'Sweet And Tender Hooligan' and 'Stop Me If You Think You've Heard This One Before' it was to be one of three Smiths numbers integrated into Morrissey's solo debut concert at Wolverhampton Civic Hall on 22 December 1988 **[see Epilogue]**.

74

'I Started Something I Couldn't Finish'

Recorded **March-April 1987, Wool Hall Studios, Bath**

Produced by **Johnny Marr, Morrissey and Stephen Street**

Album track from ***Strangeways, Here We Come*, September 1987**

Subsequently issued as **Single A-side, October 1987 (Highest UK Chart Placing #23)**

Another transparent glam rock genuflexion, the brawny 'I Started Something I Couldn't Finish' originated from a leftover jam taped back

124 Interviewed by a Dutch magazine a few months earlier in November 1986, Morrissey mentioned that he'd just finished reading *The Joe Orton Diaries*.

in January while completing its parallel Bolan-ish predecessor, 'Sheila Take A Bow'. 'It was just a weird chord change that I had in my pocket for a while,' says Marr, 'and we needed a song so I pulled that out, just trying to get the key changes to work. I mean there was a lot of throwing stuff around with that album, a lot of jamming.' Marr had purposely opted for a heavier, electric sound on much of *Strangeways*, so that his guitar parts 'really counted' rather than becoming lost in the final mix as in the past. 'I Started Something… ' typified this harder agenda, where his focal rhythm track dominates the arrangement. An artificial saxophone line played on an Emulator provided a further retro-Seventies Roxy Music sheen, offset by Street's injection of an electronic snare for added tension. 'It wasn't that I wanted to replace Mike,' explains Street, 'I just wanted to add more sounds so that his drumming had more texture. Basically it was a glorified click track for Mike to play along with but I felt that it actually worked quite nicely as an extra element in itself.'

Morrissey would later dismiss the tune as indicative of their more 'bumptious' recordings he wasn't so keen on. Street remembers a specific incident during the song's mixing that highlighted both the singer's reticence over the track and the straining relationship between Morrissey and Marr. 'There was a little bit of a crack-up in the studio when we were doing some overdubs on 'I Started Something I Couldn't Finish'. I'd spent an afternoon working with Johnny, doing bits and bobs with guitars, and I took a cassette of it across to the cottage attached to the studio, where Morrissey was watching TV. I played it to him and he started complaining, "Oh no I don't like that bit" and "I don't like this bit". So I took the tape back to Johnny and said, "Mozzer doesn't like these things". And Johnny flipped. He snapped back, "Well fuck him! Let him think of something!" I think Johnny was getting exhausted always having to be the one to come up with musical ideas. I think we did fine tune a few things after that to please Morrissey, but Johnny really took it as, y'know, "Fuck him!"'

Rourke confirms this story as typical of the singer's unnecessary self-imposed exclusion from the day-to-day lay work: 'We were probably working on that for a couple of days. If he didn't like it, he should've been there with us listening to it at the time, not sat in another room watching telly waiting to say, "I don't like that". It's just wasting everyone's time isn't it?'

'It's true that we never argued,' says Marr, 'but at the time that was a bit much and whatever's been said about that incident since is right. Something else about 'I Started Something I Couldn't Finish' though, was that I'd been kicking it around for a while with Mike and Andy and it was the first time that I was aware of doing something that they didn't like. That really, really got to me. Big time. I'm not even sure they knew, but it made it more difficult trying to get that together when I could see we were on the scent of something really good. Morrissey was really into the song and he was sort of encouraging me, from on high as it were. But the thing with Mike and Andy on that track, it became another big tick in the box for me thinking about leaving.'

Despite such personal obstacles hampering its creation, 'I Started Something I Couldn't Finish' was an excellent late-period Smiths rocker, with an intriguing lyric about a platonic relationship ruined when the protagonist seemingly attempts to take this 'friendly venture' one step further using force. His actions are 'vile' enough to earn him '18 months hard labour' – a fate not so dissimilar from that of Oscar Wilde when convicted of sodomy in 1895 and sentenced to two years of soul-destroying prison graft, which effectively finished him. This pale comparison further develops the song's already hazy homoerotic overtones. Yet, as the track fades, the scenario is crudely annulled by the dippy inclusion of some technical *studio verité* with Morrissey's directive to Street in the control booth over the quality of his take ('Okay Stephen? Shall we do that again?').

It would later replace 'Stop Me If You Think You've Heard This One Before' as The Smiths' first post-split single in late October 1987. With B-sides comprised of demo and concert scrag-ends, 'I Started Something I Couldn't Finish' clawed to a disappointing number 23 in early November, an unjust suggestion of the song's lustrous pop potential had it been released in healthier circumstances.

Television

With The Smiths officially over by the time of its release as the penultimate single, 'I Started Something I Couldn't Finish' still called for an obligatory promotional video. Filmed by 'Girlfriend In A Coma' director Tim Broad, the intention was to catalogue a Smiths-centric tour of Manchester, focussing on key landmarks such as the *Strangeways* road sign, the Albert Finney shop facade and the steps of Salford Lads Club. A simple enough concept, yet by having Morrissey cycling the streets of his native city followed by 12 emaciated teenage lookalikes in hot pursuit, the end product sustained a detrimental comedy cliché of replica mini-Mozzers.

The dirty dozen clones were recruited by Rough Trade via the Bristol-based fanzine *Smiths Indeed*; the audition prerequisites being the ownership of NHS spectacles, a Smiths T-shirt, a bicycle and a quiff (the latter applied to both sexes). Shot one especially dreary Sunday in mid-October, Morrissey wore a T-shirt of the single's Avril Angers sleeve beneath a black jacket sporting a pertinent 'I am ill' badge. Stood outside the Salford Lads Club surrounded by his feckless entourage, Morrissey looked anything but a well man.

The Smiths' sightseeing tour of Manchester itself as mapped out in the video would later form an integral part of fan conventions in the years that followed. Pilgrims from across the country (and even abroad) would spend a weekend in a sleeping bag on the floor of a cold church hall for the privilege of being coach driven round similar landmarks. A comical, if depressing, account of one such convention was featured on the Channel 4 late night arts/music programme *Club X* in 1989 (the show's theme of the evening being fan worship). Those wishing to embark upon a similar excursion today should refer to Phill Gatenby's *Morrissey's Manchester* (Empire Publications, 2002).

75

'Stop Me If You Think You've Heard This One Before'

Recorded **March-April 1987, Wool Hall Studios, Bath**
Produced by **Johnny Marr, Morrissey and Stephen Street**
Album track from ***Strangeways, Here We Come*, September 1987**

Interviewed shortly after completing the album, Johnny Marr implied that this would be the first spin-off single from *Strangeways* ('Girlfriend In A Coma' would instead take its place). His pristine riff appears to have evolved from a tenuously related instrumental jam during the January Good Earth session **[see 69]**, which, though much simpler, featured a vaguely similar chord plunge and a comparably insistent rhythm.[125]

Marr, Rourke and Joyce put down most of the backing track at The Wool Hall during the second week of March along with the basics of 'Unhappy Birthday'. Its dramatic intro saw Joyce excel with a cannibalistic tom-tom assault, while Marr drew lightning from his Telecaster courtesy of kitchen cutlery. This, one of his favourite tricks, had first been used during 'This Charming Man', where a guitar tuned to an open chord is laid on top of a Fender Twin Reverb amplifier with its vibrato switched on and then exposed to a metal-handled knife dropped onto the strings to create a unique, echoing 'clang!' Marr was determined that the track should retain such random rough edges that their ever-improving musical skill may have unconsciously ironed out. '*Strangeways* sounds really accomplished,' says Rourke,

125 Though comparisons have been made between the song's introduction and that of Neil Young's 'I've Been Waiting For You' from his 1969 eponymous solo debut album, Marr denies it was ever an influence.

'but if you look at it another way, all the naivety's gone out of it. Playing-wise, it sort of loses its edge, but it makes up for it in other ways. It's not got that 'flying by the seat of your pants' vibe we perhaps had before.' Marr deliberately tried to counterbalance this dilemma by inserting some contrived inexperience in its closing guitar line 'I wanted it to sound like a punk player who couldn't play,' he admitted when describing how he extracted its melody with one finger on one string (inherent in many early Buzzcocks minimalist solos such as Pete Shelley's sublime break in 'What Do I Get?').

It was over a week before Morrissey came up with his ostentatious lyric, 'Stop Me If You Think You've Heard This One Before', which in title alone brilliantly disarmed criticisms over his repetitious subject matter. An exhausted articulation of a love that's 'only slightly less' intense than it first started, following on from 'Girlfriend In A Coma' Morrissey finds himself back in hospital. This time, however, it's he who is the casualty, after receiving a spleen-bruising kick-in from a third party as recompense for his alleged lies.

In its gratuitous detail and flippant self-pity, 'Stop Me… ' was Morrissey the peerless pop raconteur at his most entertaining. Unfortunately, his hilarious analogy that his near-fatal condition would make a passive Buddhist 'plan a mass-murder' would thwart initiatives to release the song as a posthumous single in October 1987. Two months earlier, on 19 August, lone gunman Michael Ryan went on a psychopathic killing spree in the Berkshire village of Hungerford, murdering 16 people before shooting himself. A girlfriend in a coma was one thing, but not even Morrissey would have gotten away with eulogising a bloodbath in UK pop that autumn. 'I desperately, desperately wanted that to be released,' he later reflected. 'Rough Trade sent white labels along to Radio 1, but they said they would never under any circumstances play it because of the line about mass murder. They said people would've instantly linked it with Hungerford and it would've caused thousands of shoppers to go out and buy machine guns and murder their grandparents.'

'I Started Something I Couldn't Finish' was finally substituted in its place. Morrissey remained unmoved: 'I think Rough Trade should've released 'Death Of A Disco Dancer' instead – just to be stroppy!'

In Concert

Never performed live by The Smiths, Morrissey would play 'Stop Me If You Think You've Heard This One Before' as the opening number of his solo debut concert at Wolverhampton Civic Hall on 22 December 1988 **[see Epilogue]**.

Television

The promotional video for 'I Started Something I Couldn't Finish' **[see 74]** was later re-dubbed with 'Stop Me If You Think You've Heard This One Before' to coincide with its inclusion on the *Best 1* compilation, and released on WEA's accompanying *The Complete Picture* video collection.

76

'Unhappy Birthday'

Recorded **March-April 1987, Wool Hall Studios, Bath**

Produced by **Johnny Marr, Morrissey and Stephen Street**

Album track from ***Strangeways, Here We Come***, **September 1987**

The melodically unobtrusive and acoustic-driven 'Unhappy Birthday' was another of Marr's personal favourites from the *Strangeways* sessions, stemming from a tune he'd been toying with on his 12-string acoustic for some time. An otherwise cheerful chord sequence was darkened by Marr's almost medieval fingering during its two drop out verses. Relatively effects-free, only in its disconcerting 'cat meow' slide did the guitarist resort to electronic gimmickry by using an extreme delay from the studio's Roland patch-board.

Marr's woolly design was spacious enough for Rourke to work in an imaginatively idiosyncratic bass line of his own. 'The music on 'Unhappy Birthday', what's going on between the bass and the guitar is one of the things that I still hold up as being unique and no one else has ever quite done,' Marr enthuses. 'There was *absolute* synchronicity between Andy and myself a lot of the time because we were best mates. And that took a less prominent place in the mythology and story of The Smiths but it was really the feet on the ground reality. The relationship between Morrissey and myself was obviously more creative in many ways, and more intriguing and more unusual and all the things that everybody knows about. But Andy and myself had that thing that friends have where you can actually sit around and not talk and it makes no difference. I took loads of video footage when we were making *Strangeways*. There's just tons of stuff of me and Andy just sitting round with guitars laughing. That, ultimately, is one of the sadder elements of things going down the way they did. Too many things weregetting in the way of me and him being able to take care of each other properly.'

The song's instrumental foundation was provisionally completed by Friday 20 March, stretching to over three and a half minutes in which Joyce eagerly picked up pace towards the fade with some added off-beat fills (these were sadly lost when the final master had to be shortened to 2.43). A very subtle harmonium riff would also be discreetly woven into the mix during the later stages.

Morrissey unveiled his vocal early the following week – a disappointingly one-dimensional lyric taking the form of a first-person poisoned birthday address from a jilted lover. The protagonist's spite is strangely devoid of his usual wit, other than the nonsensically surreal anecdotes about killing his dog and finally shooting himself, crowned by the equally sarcastic row of kisses included at the foot of the lyrics as they appeared printed on the inner of the finished album. Whether this was lazy role playing or a genuine expression of hate towards somebody in his own life, Morrissey's 'Unhappy Birthday' left a bitter aftertaste.

77

'A Rush And A Push And The Land Is Ours'

Recorded **March-April 1987, Wool Hall Studios, Bath**

Produced by **Johnny Marr, Morrissey and Stephen Street**

Album track from ***Strangeways, Here We Come*, September 1987**

Of all the musical departures *Strangeways* offered, 'A Rush And A Push And The Land Is Ours' was by far the most radical in its almost heretical absence of guitars (a first, bar 'Asleep'). 'I think Johnny really wanted to announce that this would be a new chapter in The Smiths' recording career,' comments Street. 'Until then, everyone was saying "great guitar player, blah, blah, blah" and I think he just wanted to prove he could write something without any guitars on it, which was quite brave.'

'That was me playing in the only key I could play in really,' explains Marr, 'but I was determined to have a track starting the album with no guitars on, I really had a bee in my bonnet. I was so adamant about getting away from this jingle-jangle thing. Musically, as a 23-year-old, I didn't want to be repeating myself. To somebody who'd lived and breathed music since the age of 11 to a freakish, insane degree, repeating myself was like death.'

Practiced during that first drunken evening at The Wool Hall, 'A Rush And A Push And The Land Is Ours' was properly recorded the following week. Marr's minor-key ivory vamp was not unlike that of Reparata's 'Shoes', a modest UK hit in 1975 and, significantly, among Morrissey's favourite singles. Its tempo was buoyed by Joyce's militaristic snare rolls, a more prominent feature on early mixes than on the final master, while the striding, guitar-less arrangement of mock piano, harmonium and marimba came courtesy of the 'Orchestrazia Ardwick'. As with *The Queen Is Dead*'s 'Hated Salford Ensemble', this fictitious Mancunian collective amounted to just Johnny Marr and an Emulator. 'We had this keyboard set-up which could practically do anything,' describes Rourke. 'A lot of the time we'd just click through sounds and mess about. With some string parts, Johnny would be playing one bit down one end and I'd be doing a little bit up the top, just because he ran out of fingers basically. Streety was really good on things like that too. That was sort of his speciality, making it sound authentic when we came to mix it.'

Though Wildean in title, 'A Rush And A Push And The Land Is Ours' actually took its cue not from Oscar but his mother, Lady Jane Francesca Wilde, who herself wrote radical Republican prose for Ireland's leading nationalist publication, *The Nation*, under the pseudonym 'Speranza'.[126] The song's abstruse lyrics commence with Morrissey welcoming the listener in a morbid trance as the spirit of 'Troubled Joe', hung 18 months earlier (a time-span shared in 'I Started Something… '), drifting in from the other side on Street's supernatural reverse echo. Awoken by his father, who chastises him over his caffeine intake and general indolence, the narrator blames his lethargy on his continued loneliness. Fearing the agony of romance, he is nevertheless bitterly envious of those 'uglier' and 'weaker' than himself who are considerably more successful in life and love. This desperate lack of understanding as to Cupid's mysterious ways was a fundamental stratum of The Smiths repertoire, dating back to their inception, though regurgitated here with Morrissey's poetic advantage of over four years perfecting his art.

Their guitar-less experiment was successful enough for The Smiths to confidently place 'A Rush And A Push And The Land Is Ours' at the front of *Strangeways* when the time came to select its running order. 'I think Johnny and Morrissey were at their peak as songwriters at that point,' adds Joyce, 'and it was such a brilliant move to take the guitars out and open with that track in particular.'

78

'Last Night I Dreamt That Somebody Loved Me'

Recorded **March-April 1987, Wool Hall Studios, Bath**

Produced by **Johnny Marr, Morrissey and Stephen Street**

Album track from ***Strangeways, Here We Come*, September 1987**

Subsequently issued as **Single A-side, December 1987 (Highest UK Chart Placing #30)**

The last of The Smiths' blockbusting tearjerkers, 'Last Night I Dreamt That Somebody Loved Me' was later cited by Morrissey as his favourite Smiths

126 The line itself was Lady Wilde's adaptation of a traditional Irish battle charge used to incite a potential uprising against the English garrison in the north of the province.

track (an opinion shared by David Bowie). *Strangeways*' emotionally raw, soul-baring centre reads like the final act in the tragedy of 'The Heir Of Nothing-In-Particular', now older, world-weary and rapidly losing the fight, staggering into the wings to an overpowering orchestral requiem, at once luxurious and moribund.

Though it was the penultimate song added to the album, its clever chord structure can be traced back to 14 October 1986, the day after The Smiths played Carlisle Sands Centre: 'Some writing moments you do remember really specifically and that was one,' elaborates Marr. 'We were coming down from Carlisle. I was sat on the tour bus, with my guitar, unplugged. I'd come up with this figure, I was absolutely ecstatic about it, but I couldn't work out how my fingers were playing it. So I was holding my breath in case I lost it.'

With the majority of the album already written and rough mixed by Friday 20 March, Marr spent most of the next week assembling the song's base with Rourke and Joyce. The crux of 'Last Night…' was duly completed by the following Thursday evening and, even without vocals, was already being earmarked as a potential album finale. Typifying the consummate musicianship illustrated throughout *Strangeways*, the individualistic performances were breathtaking. Joyce's beat was that of an exhausted heart shattering into a thousand tiny fragments, each eight-bar cycle ending with a sudden rhythmic cardiac arrest that altered shape every time. Rourke played a similar blinder with his spacious pauses suddenly corkscrewing off in between Marr's glacial, emulated symphony (a Royal Command Performance from his electronic 'Orchestrazia Ardwick'). Neither could Marr resist inserting a vivid guitar solo towards the finish. Although this impulsive frill would eventually be faded prematurely, the opening lick can still be heard entering at 4.32 before being buried under the swelling strings.

Essentially, the end product was two separate tracks sandwiched together. Marr had originally sketched its ambient two-minute piano prologue as a different song in its own right. However, the juxtaposition of this sedate tranquillity as a precursor to the histrionic dirge that followed turned out to be a genius move.

Like some precious Italian renaissance masterpiece, delicate finishing touches were added over the next fortnight before the tune achieved its full maturity. The same BBC sound effects LP Morrissey had used for the pneumatic drill intro of 'Death At One's Elbow' provided its disconcerting jeers of a violent crowd. Muted aquamarine flashes of whale song were also flecked onto its canvas. When, days prior to wrapping the album, The Smiths were called away to perform on Channel 4's *The Tube* (10

April),[127] Street was still fine-tuning its atmospheric preamble, dropping in some sub-bass notes as an adjoining flourish into the body of the song proper. The extreme swing sweep as the two halves crossover was also Street's doing. 'It was a very Eighties thing I know, those really dramatic orchestral 'whoomph' effects. Every Trevor Horn record had one at the time. Me and Johnny found it on the Emulator and ordinarily it wouldn't have suited a Smiths record I don't think, but dropped in just at that point it really increased the drama of the whole piece.'

Morrissey submitted his vocal at the end of the week. 'Another of those,' says Street, 'where he came in, did it and everybody watching just went "Whoa!". It's often said about Morrissey that he didn't do a lot of takes, which is true. If he could've gotten away with it I'm sure he would've liked to have done one take and just left it at that, but I'd always try and get him to do two or three. Morrissey would peak very quickly and I doubt if you'd get a better performance from him after the third time. But the reason he was that intense was because he used to really build himself up for it, almost like an actor. So with 'Last Night I Dreamt… ' and a few others, he just gave his all first time round, there was no need to have him do it over and over again until it lost all emotion.'

'Last Night I Dreamt That Somebody Loved Me' was as harrowing a realisation of loneliness as its title suggested. Not a dream but a nightmare, where love is forever unattainable and sleep is a torture of futile romantic fantasies. The lovelorn agony is magnified by the waking acquiescence of 'another false alarm' (a phrase borrowed from Joni Mitchell's 'Amelia' as featured on 1976's *Hejira*, one of Morrissey's favourite Mitchell albums) and the shatteringly hopeless resignation that this merciless solitude is the protagonist's life sentence. Morrissey's voice is all the more affecting for its lack of hysteria, baring his soul with an almost unbearable reconciled sincerity, breaking only during the last line with what the *NME* would describe as 'a [Bowie] 'Wild is the Wind' falsetto'. Though often belittled by those stony critics who cynically dismissed his graver, unloveable odes as a melodramatic image-conscious affectation, Morrissey's earnestness in this, The Smiths' most heartrending effusion of human desperation, is beyond dispute. Or as *Smash Hits* deemed it, 'the saddest, most woefully heart-sizzling Smiths song ever'.

Placed at the start of *Strangeways'* second half, it would also became their commercially unlikely, but symbolically poignant, Rough Trade swansong

127 Two weeks earlier, The Smiths decided to cancel a previous TV engagement so as not to disrupt their recording schedule. On Wednesday 25 March they had been due to play live in the studio of BBC2's *Whistle Test*, presumably to promote the current compilation, *The World Won't Listen*, and the forthcoming single, 'Sheila Take A Bow'

when released as a single in December (the 7-inch edit had to discard its protracted intro for radio purposes).

Since no promotional video was made and mimed performances were out of the question (Morrissey having by now declared himself a solo artist), 'Last Night I Dreamt That Somebody Loved Me' was never promoted on TV, sabotaging the chart hopes of an already disadvantaged single even further.

79

'I Won't Share You'

Recorded **April 1987, Wool Hall Studios, Bath**

Produced by **Johnny Marr, Morrissey and Stephen Street**

Album track from ***Strangeways, Here We Come*****, September 1987**

The last song to be added to *Strangeways* would become its much scrutinised denouement, 'I Won't Share You'. As the final track on their final album, this deeply affecting lullaby assumed a spookily profound poignancy in light of the group split and the breakdown between Morrissey and Marr.

By early April, the prevailing late-night party atmosphere the band brought to the Wool Hall had soured. The finger of blame points towards American manager Ken Friedman, who to his cost had accepted the poisoned chalice of the group's administration. Morrissey was visibly displeased. He wasn't alone.

'It created a lot of resentment,' says Rourke of Friedman's unwelcome studio visits to discuss business matters alone with Morrissey and Marr behind closed doors. 'It was like "Ken Friedman's here, let's drop everything!". Myself and Mike were never asked into the meetings so we'd just have to be sat watching telly for four hours killing time. It just made us feel separated from Johnny and Morrissey when a few hours earlier we'd all been having a great time together making music.' Joyce was equally nonplussed by Friedman: 'He just didn't feel the need to give me and Andy much time but I think the tension there boiled down to Morrissey feeling Ken wasn't right for the band. I never really liked him either if I've got to be honest.'

While Morrissey, Joyce and Rourke kept a suspicious distance, Marr had his own reasons for currying Friedman's favour as a matter of psychological survival. 'Johnny was sick and tired of managing their own affairs,' reasons Street, 'having to be the person to do all the hiring and firing of people. So

Ken seemed like the solution. But when he came down to the Wool Hall, it became quite obvious to me that Morrissey didn't want him to be the manager, didn't want to be involved with him and basically didn't like him. But Johnny felt that Ken was somebody who could come in and clear up all their business affairs and take a bit of pressure off him. He just wanted to get on with being a great musician and not deal with all that hassle. So I think Johnny felt Morrissey was really being unreasonable. That's when you could tell something was going wrong, because while we were recording and concentrating on the album it was fine, but once we started talking about the business with Ken, planning some video shoot or the next US tour – something outside of what we were actually doing in the studio – that's when the nightmares started.'

'One thing about Ken that's never been addressed is that I never brought him in,' stresses Marr. 'I didn't know who he was. But here was someone who started to get involved in important parts of our business and then was in complete confusion because phone calls weren't being returned, doors weren't being opened and he was really getting the cold shoulder.'

In early April, with the album almost completed, Friedman arranged a promotional video on location in London for 'Sheila Take A Bow', due for release at the end of the month. As Joyce describes it, Morrissey played 'his trump card' against their new manager by not showing up, forcing the video to be cancelled at great expense. According to Marr, the singer not only refused to offer an explanation but also refused to physically open his door to Friedman: 'It's not that I had any massive allegiance to Ken, but the way I saw it we'd upset somebody really bad so let's not talk to him through the fucking letterbox. That's not my way of doing things. I'm not gonna stand behind a door and not open it, it's not like he's a stranger. So even though I didn't bring him in in the first place, Ken comes running to me. Once again, it's dropped on my toes. Here was someone who is upset, who feels like he's being shat on, which I'd had to deal with before. People who wanted to take care of us who weren't quite capable who were having nervous breakdowns every five minutes because they thought they were the ones to be our saviours, they thought they could do the job and now they can't. I just couldn't do anymore at that point.'

As a soundtrack to his bubbling conflict with Marr over their managerial crisis, 'I Won't Share You' seemed like Morrissey's gesture of an explanatory olive branch. Stephen Street was moved to tears upon first hearing it, though points out its genesis was anything but contrived, instead blossoming from some eleventh-hour spontaneity. 'There was this auto-harp lying around in the studio,' Street explains. 'I remember it sitting in one of the windowsills as you went up the stairs, and one day Johnny dusted it down. It had been sitting around for ages so he tuned it up and started playing these chords. It sounded absolutely beautiful so we recorded it there and then. A few days later Morrissey came in and put his vocal on top. It was one of those tracks that sent a little chill down your spine.'

What Street failed to twig was that the chords Marr had first messed around with – G, A-minor, C and D – were those of an existing Smiths hit. Discounting their middle eights, 'I Won't Share You' is merely a slowed down, slovenly strummed version of 'Ask' Strangely, Marr was equally oblivious: 'I didn't realise it was the same chords as 'Ask' at the time and I'm glad I didn't because I might not have done it. I was just making a tune that sort of resonated with the day.'

Thankfully, any obvious familiarity was diverted by its exceptional ambience. Marr's zinging auto-harp quivers made for a dreamlike soundscape, drifting among his equally celestial guitar plucking and a faint but unmistakable lonesome harmonica fade out that symbolically returned The Smiths full circle to the melancholic mouth organ preface of 1983's 'Hand In Glove'. Rourke needed to add only the sparsest of bass lines to its heavenly minimalism. For sheer soul-stirring, heart-string-ripping emotional clout, 'I Won't Share You' did well to adhere to the 'less is more' maxim, even at the expense of Joyce's presence.

Nearly three years after he implored 'Pease Please Please Let Me Get What I Want', 'I Won't Share You' found Morrissey having achieved the ambitions hinted at in the former, but cagily unwilling to relinquish his newfound 'freedom and guile'. In closing, he'd also adapt a line which he'd first used on a rarely seen sleeve note for a retrospective of Linder Sterling's band Ludus, written in the winter of 1985: 'Oh Linder, Oh Linder. I will see you sometime, somewhere.' Given the song's specific gender stipulation ('the note I wrote as she read') it's not beyond reason to consider 'I Won't Share You' beside the early crop of 'Miserable Lie' and 'Wonderful Woman' as another of Morrissey's supposed 'Linder songs'.[128]

However, the more widely held presumption is that its sentiment was an open address to Johnny Marr. From Joe Moss through to Troy Tate, John Porter and now Friedman, those who in Morrissey's eyes threatened his exclusive relationship with Marr were habitually extradited from The Smiths' camp. For once, 'I Won't Share You' appeared to lay bare his honest feelings on the table. 'You know I wouldn't be surprised if the song was about Johnny,' says Street, 'but I wouldn't assume it's about him either.'

'I just heard a really lovely tune first off,' comments Marr. 'I was happy

128 Scheduled for release on the Belgian Crepuscule label, the Ludus compilation was eventually cancelled. Morrissey's accompanying sleeve note would remain unused.

that we had another unusual little 'star in our galaxy' or whatever. That's what it was like, this other little thing that just beamed down. The lyrics were brought to my attention by somebody, even before we got out of the studio. There were raised eyebrows and "whadya think of that then?". But it was all in a day's work for me really, still is. If I was bothered about it I'd say "well I ain't anyone's to fucking share, me" but that's really the truth. If, in fact, that sentiment was directed towards me then quite rightly I feel quite good about it. It's nice. It's okay. I'm not arsed about it.'

The Smiths' original objectives while writing and recording their fourth album were to be eclipsed by their break-up preceding its September release. The celebration that had routinely greeted its forerunners would become a wake, just as reviews would become post-mortems with fans and critics alike scouring its contents for clues as to why they'd split. In its multiple references to death and the elucidatory 'I Won't Share You', many thought they'd found some.

A reference to Manchester's famous Victorian prison, *Strangeways, Here We Come* was actually yet another paraphrase from the script of the 1963 film *Billy Liar.*[129] Morrissey would melodramatically expound to the press that the slogan echoed his current temperament where he 'wouldn't be surprised' if he himself wound up in *Strangeways* within the year: 'I don't have any particular crimes in mind but it's so easy to be a criminal nowadays that I wouldn't have to look very far.'

Revered at the time by the *NME* as superior to *The Queen Is Dead* ('in terms of poetic pop and emotional power'), it's only in the decade or more since its release that *Strangeways* has slipped into the background, rarely championed as their finest hour, despite Morrissey's own assessment that it 'said everything eloquently, perfectly at the right time and put the tin hat on it basically.' Though all four original band members now insist it's their best work, they appear to be in the critical minority. In many respects, *Strangeways* is in a state of suspended animation. Its ill-timed release as a posthumous last rite effectively strangled it before it could breathe. Nor did they have the chance to tour it, denying its contents the opportunity to be properly reciprocated by their audience in the live arena. Nevertheless, if one can clear the decks of all its emotional baggage and its debilitating reputation as a coded epitaph, *Strangeways* is their indisputable long-playing masterpiece. The proof is in the playing.

129 During the climax at the train station café, the character of Stamp, played by George Innes, drunkenly slurs 'Borstal, here we come!' The line only occurs in John Schlesinger's film adaptation, not Keith Waterhouse's original novel.

Even so, it's difficult not to torturously ponder on where The Smiths would have gone thereafter. 'When the dust has settled after *Strangeways* there will have to be some degree of rethinking,' Morrissey told the press that summer. 'We can't go on forever in our present form. Inevitably certain aspects of the band would become tarnished so a slight readjustment will have to be made – I think now is absolutely the right time to do it. When something becomes too easy and it's all laid out for you, one is robbed of the joy of achievement. When there's no need to fight any more, it'll be time to pull up the shutters on The Smiths.'

If only Morrissey had known that those shutters were hurtling towards the ground even as he spoke.

80a

'(Now And Then There's) A Fool Such As I' (Bill Trader)

80b

'Untitled Instrumental [Streatham #1]'

80c

'Untitled Instrumental [Streatham #2]'

Recorded **May 1987, Firehouse Studios, London**

Produced by **Grant Showbiz**

Studio out-takes

The strain between Morrissey and Marr rapidly accelerated in the weeks following the completion of *Strangeways* Outwardly, The Smiths were in their strongest commercial position at home that they'd ever enjoyed. The interim compilation *The World Won't Listen* had made number two in the album charts, while their April single, 'Sheila Take A Bow', returned them to the UK Top 10 for the first time in nearly three years.

Yet behind the scenes, the Ken Friedman situation had already reached breaking point. A press statement issued in the second week of May confirmed the manager's dismissal. Charges against Friedman included his alleged attempts to oust key personnel and the furtive promotion of two European festival appearances that summer without their consent.[130] Soon

130 An official press statement issued in April 1987 specifically warned fans 'not to be misled by newspaper advertisements' listing them on various European festival bills.

rumours of further dissension within their hitherto impenetrable circle began to filter through to the music press. In early May, the *NME* interviewed Craig Gannon's new band, The Cradle, also featuring Ivor Perry (formerly of Easterhouse), who would play his small part in the end of the affair a few months later. Careful to assert that The Smiths were still 'the only commercially viable, valid pop band in the world' in spite of Gannon's admittedly shoddy treatment, they nevertheless let slip that his former band were currently 'going through great personal turmoil.'

Sadly, for Marr, this turmoil offered only one solution: 'I'm a great believer in the idea that when something has to finish then events have a way of conspiring to make it happen. One of the things we do as humans is that we really absolutely don't want to look at the inevitability of something ending and when we know it's over, up until the bit when it actually finishes is where we put ourselves through the absolute torture and misery and where we avoid what our instincts, logic and reason are telling us is the right decision. That's the way I look at the end of The Smiths.'

With Friedman fired, the poisoned chalice of managerial responsibility inevitably boomeranged back on Marr yet again. Only this time, he wasn't prepared to carry it: 'We started off as a little band with one bass amp, one guitar amp, a drum kit and a microphone. We were homegrown, we were DIY, to the very end. We were still running it out of one's kitchen and it couldn't be done. We needed Joe [Moss] or someone to manage the changing dynamic between the band. Then on my own part, being 23, married and wanting to join the rest of the human race but at the same time I'm trying to keep my band together. It was *completely* emotionally fucked up. So the actual end was very intense, but it was very brief.'

In early May, the guitarist had an extremely emotional private summit with Morrissey at his Kensington flat where he laid his cards on the table. 'We sat down to sort things out,' Marr explains. 'We had some business things to sort out. Ken Friedman would have been one. We were also having problems with this lawyer who'd taken money from us through the move to EMI, which we had to recover in court. It was a highly pressured discussion about the business, but I didn't get together with Morrissey to say "I want to leave the band." He was so distressed by the pressures that he and I were under, in the spirit of real friendship and love, I said "well why don't we just go and get an annulment, and if we did I would see this huge misery and weight being lifted from your shoulders." To this day I don't think it was a selfish act. That wasn't me saying I wanted to leave, that was me trying to find a way out. I just thought we should sort our business affairs out and be separate agents. As it stood it had to change because it wasn't practical me being the manager and running the group.'

Following Marr's showdown with Morrissey, he summoned a cheerless group meal at Geales fish and chip restaurant in Notting Hill (as Rourke drolly puts it 'we actually split up in a chippy'). 'It was an emergency meeting, not a goodbye' states Marr. 'It seemed to me like the sensible way to deal with what was happening was to go and get some sunshine for 14 days and then, when I got back, just to think about where we were gonna go on the next record. When you put into context the intensity and the diversity that we put into that whole journey of recordings, it's impossible even now for me to imagine where it could have gone without coming up for air for a few months. It would have been a smart idea and by no means unusual for a band who'd been on the journey we had.'

'It was completely out of the blue,' recalls Joyce, 'we were just in shock. I think what Johnny really wanted was back up, but we couldn't give him any.' As far as his colleagues were concerned, Marr's suggestion of an immediate holiday and a rethink of The Smiths' musical direction sounded like a resignation rather than a resolution. 'We just couldn't comprehend it,' adds Joyce. 'That would've meant the band splitting up and that was the last thing we wanted.'

'So it was put to me by the band that if I didn't go into the studio immediately and do the B-sides for the next single, that wasn't yet to come out for ages, then I was letting the fans down and letting everybody down,' broods Marr. 'But we'd only just finished *Strangeways*, there was no need. That's why I said "well now's the time to rethink the group musically." Not, as people thought, big stadiums and becoming like U2. That was never going to happen. This idea that I wanted us to go on the road forever till we became like U2 and Morrissey didn't, just wasn't the case. Reason being I, to a fault, would put myself in a recording studio and not come out for ten years, whereas Morrissey's forte is when he's in front of his audience, that's when he comes alive. I wasn't meaning in the direction of Electronic either, that's something else people have misjudged. When we had that meeting, 'Last Night I Dreamt That Somebody Loved Me' was, to me, the best thing we'd done. It was my favourite track at that time and probably still is. So I was half in mind to consider that we become more orchestral because I was absolutely nuts about that track. Either that or what we'd done on 'Unhappy Birthday', which was getting away from electric and going more acoustic. But it had to change.'

Against his better judgement, Marr was persuaded not to take time out, reluctantly conceding to Morrissey's request of an obligatory B-sides session in preparation for the autumn release of 'Girlfriend In A Coma' The chosen location was Firehouse Studios in Streatham, South London; a converted barn run by tour soundman Grant Showbiz, who accepted production responsibilities for what was to become The Smiths' last stand. As Showbiz confirms, 'from day one, Johnny made it clear he didn't want to be there. That was very, *very* fucking obvious.'

Showbiz, who'd been a part of The Smiths' entourage since late 1983, was overjoyed that finally his chance had come to produce them. 'It was like – "At last!" – and in *my* studio as well. I was really looking forward to it because it was always a pleasure just being around them, but obviously that wasn't to be the case. It was a very spooky, very scary time. Everybody was disaffected, not just Johnny. The session went on for about a week but it seemed to last a bloody year. People were turning up at different times, it was totally disorganised. The problem seemed to be the level of communication, or lack of it. The atmosphere was so subtle, it was so 'cucumber sandwiches and tea' if you like, the knocking of the odd spoon off the saucer with the tea cup rather than outraged shouty confrontational stuff. But as I've said before, that was the only occasion where I was actually frightened, physically, of Morrissey.'

Accounts of the singer's behaviour at that final session are quite extraordinary. All first-hand testimonies concur that there were times where Morrissey was uncharacteristically aggressive, intimidating and, stranger still, seemed intoxicated. 'Morrissey's not a threatening, horrible person,' stresses Showbiz, 'but he got quite drunk one time. I remember him with a wine bottle in his hand and he was kind of reeling round the studio. He was slurring his words and crashing around, roaring "lezz go down and do it", meaning get on with recording. But Johnny was just looking at him in disbelief, kind of saying "go down and do *what?* What is it we're gonna do? Where are the songs?" Because there weren't any. There were just lots of little bits, half songs here and there, it just wasn't coming together.'

It was, in Marr's own words 'one of the low points of my life. I hated that session more than anything else. For a start I was sleeping in the control room, just to get it finished, and there was no need for that record to be finished. With Morrissey and how he was, I never felt intimidated by him. I just saw it as someone I cared about who was unhappy. I still, really hadn't decided to leave the band at that point. But throughout that week I was treated so badly. I felt as if everybody had lost the plot completely.'

Two tracks were eventually scraped together – the ill-omened Cilla Black cover 'Work Is A Four Letter Word' and the last Morrissey/Marr original, 'I Keep Mine Hidden'. A handful of unfinished demos were also committed to tape, including a cover of Elvis Presley's '(Now And Then There's) A Fool Such As I'. 'There was an Elvis song with a little bit of lyric' says Showbiz, 'half a song maybe, a very bad run through and a few other rough ideas. I had the tapes for a couple of years until I gave them back to Johnny for security. If he had any sense he probably burned them.'

Marr also confirms the existence of 'A Fool Such As I'; 'It's true that we did it, but I didn't like the song very much.' Elvis had recorded his version in 1958 as one of several stockpiled tracks to be released at regular intervals while he was serving in the US army. The song wasn't a hit until the following year, reaching number one in the UK on 15 May 1959, the week before Morrissey was born, and remaining there for another month. This historic detail almost certainly influenced Morrissey's decision to tackle 'A Fool Such As I', though it's just as likely he saw in its lyrics a chance to vocalise his most private feelings about Marr's potential departure, from its opening apology ('Pardon me if I'm sentimental when we say goodbye, don't be angry with me should I cry') to the more profound admission; 'You taught me how to love, and now you say that we are through/I'm a fool, but I'll love you dear until the day I die.'

Besides the aborted Elvis cover,[131] the Firehouse sessions also conjured up two accomplished instrumental backing tracks. Neither of these works-in-progress were ever given titles (though Showbiz has previously recollected seeing 'You Don't Know Anything' written down on paper as a suggested song name that week), though both could have made a more than acceptable flipside. After the heaviness of *Strangeways*, they found The Smiths in conventional trademark 'jingly-jangly' mode; a possible indication that Marr was glumly treading water perhaps, but fabulous tunes all the same.

The first was similar in tempo and yearning melodic sensitivity to 'You Just Haven't Earned It Yet, Baby' with a stunning chorus of off-beat cymbal crashes from Joyce, while Marr and Rourke unravel a beautifully simple chord loop.[132] The second was more lively, beating a harmonically similar path to 'Well I Wonder' (D, F#-minor, B-minor, G), but more urgent in tempo and driven by a more prominent twanging riff. Collectively, these recordings carry a profound sense of sadness in that they reveal a band who, though heading for the rocks, still cling to the mast united by a musical sixth sense. Every beat, every strum, still offers a grain of hope for their future. A future that was, nevertheless, ultimately hopeless.

131 According to Showbiz, 'A Fool Such As I' never saw the light of day because an engineer had accidentally wiped off the first verse.

132 The chords in question are: G/ D/ C/ D/ G/ D C/ D/ Em/ D/ C/ D/ Em/ D/ C/ D.

81

'Work Is A Four Letter Word' (Don Black/Guy Woolfenden)

Recorded **May 1987, Firehouse Studios, London**

Produced by **Grant Showbiz**, Remixed by **Stephen Street**

B-side to **'Girlfriend In A Coma', August 1987**

After they split, Marr would denounce this track, along with 'Golden Lights', as The Smiths' career low, and with good reason. For the first time ever, rather than tell Marr himself of his decision to cover a 1968 Cilla Black B-side, Morrissey first entrusted Joyce to break the news. 'That really pissed me off big time, that Mike was the one who told me we were gonna do that song, which I thought was just totally naff. It wasn't his role to tell me what song I was gonna produce and play on. To be fair, I think he was maybe trying to help by putting his hands on the wheel. I'm older now so I can see it was a desperate situation for everybody. But it was just *the end*.'

Rourke was equally discouraged: 'Morrissey played us the original because we had to weed out all the orchestration on it and learn the basic chords. But I could feel it was all getting less precious because we'd never have done that four years earlier.' As a desperate measure, Joyce was even roped into contributing some backing vocals which, as the drummer himself admits, 'shows how silly it was getting really!'.

Morrissey had first cited Cilla as one of his 'uncommon perversions' in *The Face* back in 1984. Her perky 1963 Lennon and McCartney penned debut single 'Love of the Loved' had been The Smiths' first walk-on theme during that year's spring tour. Given their collaboration with Cilla's leading contemporary, Sandie Shaw, perhaps it wasn't such a deplorable tangent for them to cruise down after all, particularly with the song's self-evident rejection of the work ethic in keeping with Morrissey's oeuvre. Rather, it was the stigma of Cilla herself who had since made the transition from Sixties chanteuse to prime-time TV light entertainment as the host of *Blind Date* and *Surprise, Surprise* (as well as being a keen Thatcher supporter) that rankled.

The title theme to Peter Hall's 1968 film comedy starring David Warner and Cilla herself, 'Work Is A Four Letter Word' was nowhere near as terrible as their butchering of Twinkle's 'Golden Lights'; at worst mediocre and at best, an admirable contemporary interpretation of an obscure Sixties pop curiosity. There was scarce indication if their hearts weren't in it, particularly during its active instrumental coda.[133] Morrissey was careful to discard its

133 The version of the song featured on the 7-inch of 'Girlfriend In A Coma' was an irrationally shortened edit fading out after two minutes and missing this end section completely.

opening stanza about 'girls who some men will slave for', perhaps as an exercise in kitsch-limitation, while his quip that 'people say that you were born lazy' seemed to echo 'Reel Around The Fountain' with its remark that 'people see no worth in you'. As with 'I Keep Mine Hidden', one could also speculate on its words being a subliminal expression of his feelings towards Marr at that critical moment before Johnny finally walked away from The Smiths: 'If you stay, I'll stay right beside you'.

When interviewed ten years later for a Channel 4 documentary on Cilla, Morrissey divulged that their cover was intended 'as a bit of a tease really – I wasn't really attempting to produce a great piece of Gothic art', before finally confessing with visible amusement that 'Cilla Black, unbeknownst to herself, actually broke up The Smiths!'

82

'I Keep Mine Hidden'

Recorded May 1987, Firehouse Studios, London

Produced by Grant Showbiz

B-side to 'Girlfriend In A Coma' (12-inch and cassette formats only), August 1987

The last word on Morrissey and Marr's extraordinary five-year creative partnership and its ultimate dissolution, 'I Keep Mine Hidden', their final collaboration, relays a crippling inability to express emotions. Partly blaming a stifled upbringing – 'where to be touched meant to be mental' – any chance of surmounting this psychological handicap is fogged by a 'yellow and green stumbling block'; a thinly veiled reference to the colour coding of temazepam capsules.[134]

In later years, Morrissey would openly confess to taking anti-depressants – 'I know little about Prozac. I've tried it of course' – as well as seeking professional therapeutic help from doctors and psychoanalysts. Grant Showbiz was particularly struck by 'I Keep Mine Hidden' and its lyrical candour: 'For me, that is the *key* song that sort of says everything. There are

134 Sometimes taking the form of green, or yellow and green gelatine capsules (often nicknamed 'greenies', 'green eggs' or 'yellow eggs'), temazepam is a short-acting benzodiazepine, commonly administered as a sleeping pill in severe cases of depression-related insomnia. Because of its potency (its strongest manufactured dose is a 20 milligram 'Temaze 20'), it is controlled by the Misuse of Drugs Act, while GPs are required to prescribe the pill for short periods only. As described by one UK medical journal, adverse side effects include confusion, euphoria and hyperactivity: 'behaviour may be exaggerated (often very talkative or over-excited, sometimes even hostile or aggressive) and judgement is impaired. Users may have a false sense of confidence, or even believe they are invincible or invisible.'

very few songs where Morrissey says "this is me", a lot of the time they're just these wonderful vignettes, but I think 'I Keep Mine Hidden' is a very personal song, a very direct song from Morrissey to Johnny.' Be that the case, then it reveals the crux of Morrissey's problem to be an envious incomprehension of his partner's ability to deal with his emotions more freely ('life is so easy for you because you let yours slide into public view'). Yet the sexual double-entendre inherent in its title and the tune's outwardly frolicsome disposition successfully throws the listener off the scent of such a revelatory reading. Resurrecting something of the thumping riposte of 'Sheila Take A Bow', Marr's arrangement has often been dismissed as 'music-hall', but is actually a standard Fifties rock 'n' roll pattern, very similar to that of Doc Pomus and Mort Shuman's 'A Teenager in Love'. Only in Morrissey's whistling milkman entrance does the track pass the point of no return into vaudevillian ham, though it was perhaps fortunate that a further 'whistling-solo' was later removed and replaced by Marr's uncomplicated monophonic guitar break. In the years immediately after the split, Morrissey would make a point of praising 'I Keep Mine Hidden' on several occasions as The Smiths song he always played first when reviewing their legacy; 'it's the one that makes me feel the happiest.' Marr is far less sentimental. ''I Keep Mine Hidden' was something that I knocked out on the first day of the session. I hated it, absolutely loathed it.'

There was no dramatic finale to The Smiths' last session, no final slamming of doors or smashing of crockery, no big bang, only a subdued whimper. 'Because nobody thought that *was* the end,' reflects Showbiz. 'Yes, there were bad vibes amongst the band, as there are amongst any band, but I always put that down to tiredness. They needed six months off, somebody to tell them to have time out, but the problem was that person wasn't there. I knew Johnny wasn't happy with what they'd recorded and I knew that I'd sort of blown my chance in a way. I had my opportunity to record The Smiths in my studio and it hadn't worked out. But never did I think that was it, *this* is the end. It was a weird time, yes, but even with all of that I didn't foresee the break up.'

Morrissey finished his vocals for 'I Keep Mine Hidden' on 19 May 1987, three days prior to his 28th birthday. It was the last occasion he and Marr would see each other for several years. Johnny stayed on at Firehouse with Rourke and Joyce for another few days, trying to make the most out of what he considered substandard Smiths fare, before flying to Los Angeles the following week. Yet what Marr had intended as a temporary break to clear his head after the stress of the past month, his fellow Smiths misconstrued as an abrupt and permanent exodus from the band.

'It was a really tragic week, that whole last session,' says Marr, 'but the idea that I was gonna go to Los Angeles and not come back to the band? That underestimated my loyalty so much that I just felt as though everybody had lost the plot, if that's what they thought. I felt that I'd taken care of everybody, I'd *always* have taken care of everybody and I loved everybody. I felt that I was a great friend and I just saw that friendship had fallen to pieces. Every rule in the book was broken during that week. That's kind of the crux of it, though. That I could be so underestimated. There was a vibe going out that I wasn't gonna return which really, *really* galled me.'

While over in LA, Marr obligingly took part in a promotional radio interview to promote the *Louder Than Bombs* compilation, which had just been released in the US on Sire. Marr sounded surprisingly optimistic. When asked about his feelings toward his partner, he forgivingly effused his love for Morrissey. 'He's brilliant, he's marvellous,' he gushed. 'I miss him, I haven't seen him for a week and I really miss him.'

It's plausible then that Marr may have had an iota of faith that their problems could be resolved. Unfortunately, outside forces were already deciding his fate for him. Returning to England, communication between the band hadn't improved. 'It was a total breakdown,' mourns Joyce. 'I know that Johnny has said in the past that nobody rang him for weeks, but it was all of us. He never rang me either. Morrissey was keeping quiet. Nobody knew what was going on.' In his defence, Marr stresses that he had made efforts to resume contact after all: 'I tried, and I know they say I never got in touch with them, but they were at home. I was the one who'd gone away.'

The stalemate ended with a controversial press statement on 30 July announcing that Marr had already left The Smiths. The origins of that statement have been furiously denied and debated ever since. 'That's the big question,' says Showbiz, 'if you could get to the bottom of who wrote that and who wanted that to be put in the press. That would be very interesting to know. At the time, I think the consensus was that it was Morrissey, because I knew he wasn't happy about Johnny. He'd told me himself that he wasn't happy about him going off to do this and that with Bryan Ferry and Talking Heads and whoever. But I think it might not be as simple as that. I was pretty damn certain that it never came from Johnny anyway. Will we ever know?'

If the objective behind the press statement had been to provoke a denial from Marr then it backfired. Rather than refute the allegations, the guitarist saw this as the final straw in the embittered psychological mind games surrounding the band. In the first week of August, without prior consultation with the other three members, Marr contacted the *NME* to confirm that he had quit. The Smiths were over.

Epilogue

'Only a flesh wound'

1987 and beyond

Marr was fully aware that by 'leaving' The Smiths, he was effectively disbanding them in the same breath. Although he was keen to impress upon the media that there was no acrimony between himself and the other three ('I've known them all a long time and I love 'em'), he was nonetheless horrified to learn his replacement was already being considered.

As Rough Trade issued that first contentious press statement confirming Marr's exit, so Morrissey began vetting potential substitutes. Among the first to be contacted was Kevin Armstrong, best known for his work with Thomas Dolby. 'I got a call out of the blue from somebody at Rough Trade,' says Armstrong. 'They said Morrissey wanted to meet me because he was considering a replacement for Johnny Marr. Now, The Smiths were one of my favourite bands so to step into Johnny Marr's shoes would have been amazing, but at the same time I thought he was mad.'

'When I met him at Rough Trade I was quite nervous but quite outspoken. He said he wanted to carry on The Smiths and I said "I don't think you should carry on because you and Johnny are a once-in-a-lifetime creative thing, you're not gonna repeat that straight away, he's not replaceable. But if you're thinking of going solo or something else then in that case it'd be great." He said "No, I'm going to carry on The Smiths. It doesn't need Johnny". And I said to him "look, you remind me of that knight in *Monty Python and the Holy Grail,* who has his arms and legs chopped off, sitting with blood pissing out, wriggling around shouting "come back, it's only a flesh wound!". Maybe he appreciated my candour, I don't know, but I thought it was a mental idea.'[135]

The Smiths minus Marr was indeed inconceivable, not that it prevented Morrissey from defending his resolve to soldier on with the famously hollow threat 'whoever says The Smiths have split shall be severely spanked by me with a wet plimsoll.' In private, though, the singer was all too aware

135 Armstrong would later work with Morrissey in 1989, co-writing the songs 'Piccadilly Palare', 'He Knows I'd Love To See Him' and the as yet unreleased 'Oh, Phoney'.

of the insurmountable legal machinery that would have prevented such a venture. 'When Johnny left I wanted to continue with the name,' he confessed to *Record Mirror* two years later, 'but contractually it would have to have been agreed by both of us, and he did not agree.'

With the legality of the name in doubt, it was still as 'The Smiths' that Morrissey, Rourke and Joyce entered London's Powerhouse Studios in early August, having found a prospective surrogate in Ivor Perry. Formerly guitarist with fellow Rough Trade signings Easterhouse (who toured Scotland with The Smiths in 1985), at the time of accepting the post Perry was still involved in Craig Gannon's new band, The Cradle. Hailing from Morrissey's native Stretford, Perry's indigenous Mancunian roots gave him a considerable advantage over rank outsiders like Armstrong. Unfortunately, the session was to prove a dreadful mistake, chiefly due to the eeriness of Marr's absence and Perry's unnecessary belligerence towards producer Stephen Street.

'I thought it was a strange idea,' Street reminisces. 'Ivor's gone on record saying he thought that *I* was bad for them. I think *he* was bad for them. He was never going to replace Johnny Marr and no, I didn't like him. Every other word was "fuck", the guy just couldn't talk properly. I thought he was completely the wrong person to go for as far as working with Morrissey was concerned.'

'It wasn't a *bad* atmosphere,' ponders Joyce, 'it was just a very *confusing* atmosphere because it wasn't The Smiths. If we had realised how confusing it was going to be I think we might've been able to cope with it a bit better. I've used this analogy before but the way I saw it, when a quarter of something you love has been taken away, then why discard the three quarters you already have? Why not keep hold of it? It took me a while to realise that four quarters make a whole, so to speak. So with Ivor, it sounded, well "okay". But we were listening back to some stuff at one point and somebody came through the door and I just automatically thought it was Johnny. Just for a split second. It was weird.' Street corroborates Joyce's confusion: 'I remember Mike sitting there and saying to me, "I keep turning to the door and thinking any minute Johnny's going to come in." It was kind of sad, it just really felt like it was a nightmare and any minute Johnny was going to come back and everything was going to be all right.'

Within this desperately unsettling climate, two new tracks were attempted. The first was a lolloping instrumental jammed between Perry, Rourke and Joyce, similar in tempo to 'I Know It's Over' with a more upbeat if mediocre melody (the session was aborted before Morrissey added lyrics or a title). On the second track, 'Bengali In Platforms', Perry's love of The Clash and his preference for an abrasive Joe Strummer-style guitar rhythm came to the fore. The main riff cut a figure very similar to Perry's earlier Easterhouse single 'Whistling in the Dark' (which was itself indebted to The Clash's 'London Calling'). Joyce instilled some verve with a steady tom-tom intro, though Rourke's input betrayed a noticeable lack of enthusiasm. Centred around a repeated chorus of 'Misguided Bengali! Misguided Bengali!', its lyrics were a clumsy portrait of an Indian immigrant's desires to ingratiate himself into Western culture ('and not to depress you – shelve your Western plans, Goodbye!'). Considering the notorious allegations of racism that would dog Morrissey in later years, it's fortunate that this condescending ballad of a 'misguided' Asian never saw the light of day (though a milder rewrite would later surface on *Viva Hate*).

Given the sour atmosphere and the friction gathering force between Perry and Street, it was miraculous that Morrissey got as far as putting a vocal down in the first place. The irreplaceable gap left by Marr was more than musical. Joyce, in particular, felt the strain of filling the guitarist's shoes as Morrissey's right-hand man, whose duty it was to relay the singer's peculiar demands to the rest of the crew: 'I felt as though I'd taken Johnny's mantle as being the interpreter of what Morrissey wanted. Because he didn't have Johnny to sound off or grieve to, he decided to go for me. I only had it for a few days but I just couldn't cope with it.'

After only two days recording, Joyce was cajoled by Morrissey into giving Perry his marching orders: 'He took me aside and said, "It's not working with Ivor. I don't want him to carry on with us." I said that was fair enough but then he said, "Can you tell him?" Now the weird thing was that I didn't even get Ivor in because he'd known Mozzer for years in Stretford, he even went to his school. I said to Morrissey, "I can't do that." He said, "I can't either." So I said, "Look, he's your mate, you got him in." And he actually said, "I *can't* tell him."'

Joyce eventually agreed to inform Perry that Morrissey wanted to have words. 'I went back to the hotel where me and Ivor were staying and rang his room to say, "Morrissey wants a word with you tomorrow about playing." Ivor sussed immediately. He was getting really defensive and began shouting, "Why can't he tell me himself? If he doesn't want me to play with him anymore why can't he tell me?" I said, "Look that's the way it is, you know what he's like." Then Ivor lost it, he was threatening to go round to Morrissey's flat in Chelsea. He was screaming, "I'm going to kick his fucking head in!". I had to calm him down.' The following morning Street was just about to leave for the studio when his phone rang: 'It was someone on behalf of Morrissey saying, "It's not going to happen, don't bother going in." And that was it.'

'I knew it was going on,' says Marr of the doomed Smiths Mk II. 'I was just glad to be out of it. But the name of the group was the name of the group that I'd started so no, I wasn't gonna let them be 'The Smiths'. There was no question of them ever going out under that name. Never.'

Though within the year Morrissey would profitably reinvent himself as a solo artist, it was an option he initially feared and resisted. 'Morrissey needed the band more than anybody,' explains Joyce, 'I don't think he was prepared to go solo at all. Absolutely not.' Rourke also noted the singer's distress. 'It was his life. The rest of us, we all had private lives whereas Morrissey really didn't. He was devastated, really devastated. Mind you, we all were.'

In a last-ditch bid to salvage whatever concept of 'The Smiths' remained after the Perry fiasco, Street sent Morrissey a cassette of some demos he'd been working on in the vain hope that the singer might consider them passable to work up as B-sides for Rough Trade's final *Strangeways* singles. In the third week of August, Street received an unexpectedly enthusiastic letter of reply that would have far-reaching consequences. With The Smiths' 'Girlfriend In A Coma' only just entering the charts and the shockwaves of Marr's exit still ricocheting around the music press, Morrissey's sudden U-turn read loud and clear: 'I want The Smiths to be laid to rest. I want to record for EMI under my own name.'

Six weeks after Marr confirmed his 'resignation', in mid-September the *NME* finally pronounced that in spite of the past month's rumours of recruiting a substitute, The Smiths were officially finished. *Strangeways, Here We Come* was released the following week just one month before what had been intended as a celebratory documentary on ITV's *South Bank Show* was broadcast as an inadvertent memorial. The programme concluded with Morrissey mourning not just the death of The Smiths, but that of pop music itself: 'I think this is really more or less the end of the story. Ultimately popular music will end – that must be obvious to almost anybody. I think the ashes are already about us, if we could but notice them.'

'I watched that programme round Mike's house,' reveals Marr. 'We were sat there but there were these furtive glances back and forth because I think they were still working together. But I told Mike that he was better off without the situation. I felt like I'd bailed him out of a situation he wasn't happy with as well. Emotionally, I think I was bailing everybody out.'

Though it's true Morrissey did consider retaining Joyce and Rourke as his rhythm section, by the time the *South Bank Show* film was broadcast, he was already back in The Wool Hall studio near Bath undertaking his first solo recording session with Stephen Street and a specially assembled backing group. By far the most prolific member of his new entourage was venerated Mancunian guitar virtuoso Vini Reilly of The Durutti Column. 'I introduced Morrissey to Vini round my flat in Moorlake,' explains Street. 'I'd worked with both before so I knew neither of them make friends that easily. Fortunately they got on well. Vini was a better player than myself so I knew if I showed him the chords he'd be able to take the music to next level.'[136] Street himself volunteered to play bass, while the line-up was completed by session drummer Andrew Paresi, whom the producer had met at a recent demo session for CBS.

After familiarising himself with Street's first batch of instrumental designs, Morrissey visited the producer's flat in September to test his vocal on a handful of portastudio demos. The earliest Morrissey/Street efforts included the subtly homo-erotic 'Lifeguard On Duty' ('lifeguard, lifeguard, save me from life!'), which like the similarly shaky 'Safe Warm Lancashire Home' would eventually be scrapped early on during The Wool Hall sessions. Such false starts merely heightened Morrissey's understandable insecurity. 'What tends to happen with Morrissey is that if one song isn't working for him it'll cloud the entire session,' says Paresi. 'He was enormously vulnerable. Every day was a rather terrifying experience for all of us, but especially for him.'

'It was a huge risk,' admits Street. 'He must have been feeling incredibly nervous because it was so daunting. EMI had signed The Smiths, but before they could do anything the band had disintegrated in front of them. This was very much untested waters.' Morrissey's new label were concerned enough to visit The Wool Hall for an early playback of work in progress. Luckily, their apprehension rescinded upon hearing a rough mix of the impressively Smiths-esque 'Suedehead'. As the satisfied EMI delegation departed, Morrissey's relief was palpable. 'The label giving us the thumbs up was a major turning point,' says Street. 'After that, the pressure came off a bit and we could just enjoy making the album.'

Although there were occasional excursions sampling what night life Bath had to offer, compared with the nocturnal carousing during the making of *Strangeways, Here We Come*, the *Viva Hate* session at The Wool Hall was a far more sober affair, tempered by Trivial Pursuit, charades, visits to the gym and flapjacks with Sandie Shaw. 'She was around a lot,' says Street. 'Morrissey would be very excited about Sandie coming down, but then minutes after she arrived he'd be totally bored of her and couldn't wait for her to go again.'[137] Shaw would later offer her own highly perceptive observation on

136 Street had recently produced The Durutti Column's *The Guitar and Other Machines* (1987). Despite the Manchester connection, Morrissey and Reilly hadn't crossed paths until Street introduced them.

137 Shaw was invited down to record backing harmonies on the soon-to-be-abandoned 'Please Help The Cause Against Loneliness', later recording her own version of the song in 1988. Featured on her *Hello Angel* album, it was also released as a single, but failed to chart in the UK. A cardboard cut-out of Morrissey appeared in the accompanying video.

the interaction between Morrissey and his new cohorts in her 1991 autobiography, *The World at my Feet*: 'It was intriguing to observe each vying with the other for his attention, his laughter, his approval, or his admiration of their musical prowess. They tiptoed around in his presence as if on eggshells, not wanting to offend their maestro.'

The unspoken rivalry Shaw witnessed would worsen as time went on. As things were, Street already sensed brewing hostility from Vini Reilly. 'After a while I felt as though Vini was being a bit critical,' claims Street. 'He started to object to the tunes I'd written, criticising the chords as being too obvious because he was used to playing more way out stuff with The Durutti Column. That was understandable, but the way he went about it upset me. He refused outright to play the riff on 'Suedehead'. I ended up having to do that myself because he wouldn't. I just felt as though he was being a musical snob.'

Though perhaps 'obvious' to a classically trained jazz scholar like Reilly, Street's tunes displayed a rich melodic pop sensibility, with many of his compositions born of a deliberately playful sense of appropriation: the string-soaked 'Everyday Is Like Sunday' took its cue from Echo & The Bunnymen (specifically the bass line of 1984's 'Seven Seas'); 'Little Man, What Now?' pinched its chugging flamenco rhythm from Bowie's 'Andy Warhol'; 'I Don't Mind If You Forget Me' was Street's vision of 'Motown meets the Buzzcocks'; and 'Dial-A-Cliché' was a deliberate attempt to write 'something Lennon and McCartney-ish, like 'Norwegian Wood'. Other reference points were far more perverse. The opening 'Alsatian Cousin' was based upon Grandmaster & Melle Mel's 1983 rap classic 'White Lines (Don't Do It)', while the Joni Mitchell-esque 'Late Night, Maudlin Street' was perforated by a drum sample from Prince's 'Housequake'. As Paresi notes: 'Stephen Street is the underrated hero of that album. Not just the writing of it, but the marshalling of it, how he used all different styles.'

Although Morrissey was appreciative enough to tell the studio's cook that he regarded Street as 'his rock to cling to', even as the recording of *Viva Hate* commenced, he was privately hoping to make his peace with Marr. Between the initial album session in October and a second stint from November through to Christmas, Morrissey made provisional contact with his former partner to suggest they get together for one last Smiths concert. 'He suggested we play a farewell gig at the Albert Hall,' confirms Marr, 'which was obviously a no no.'

Marr's rejection of a sentimental Smiths send-off did little to help Morrissey's fragile morale. His pessimism increased when an intended John Peel session in December broke down halfway through recording at BBC's Maida Vale studios due to alleged insolence from the in-house engineers.

'The whole thing was a very sad experience,' remembers Street. 'I was getting uptight. Vini was in one of his moods. It was a fucking nightmare. Quite rightly we pulled the plug on it.' As Paresi notes, 'the worst thing about that whole BBC session experience was that, as far as Morrissey was concerned, it put an end to any hope of us ever going out as a live band.'

Originally titled *Education In Reverse*, the *Viva Hate* album was finally completed on 23 December 1987, less than a week after the final Smiths single, 'Last Night I Dreamt That Somebody Loved Me', entered the lower reaches of the UK singles chart. As the group dispersed for Christmas, the mood at The Wool Hall was a mixture of triumph, relief and bodily exhaustion. 'I was quite ill by the end,' Street confesses. 'Purely through the pressure of the session I'd given myself stomach ulcers. As we were finishing the last track, 'Break Up The Family', I physically couldn't get out of bed. Morrissey had to do his vocal without me.'

Considering the events preceding and during its creation, it was surely no surprise that the lyrics of Morrissey's first solo foray harked back to the recent demise of The Smiths. Specifically the wistful remorse of 'Break Up The Family' ('let me see all my old friends, let me put my arms around them'), the nostalgic soul-baring of 'Late Night, Maudlin Street' and the poignant chamber piece 'Angel, Angel, Down We Go Together' (which Morrissey later admitted was indeed 'written with Johnny Marr in mind'). Elsewhere were other remnants of previously discarded Smithsisms; 'Margaret On The Guillotine' had been an alternate suggestion for the group's third album prior to *The Queen Is Dead*, while the equally controversial 'Bengali In Platforms' was salvaged from that doomed Ivor Perry session and remodelled to fit one of Street's more understated melodies. Arguably the album's highlights were its two spin-off singles; the very British apocalypse of 'Everyday Is Like Sunday', which transposed the sentiment of John Betjeman's 'Slough' to an end-of-the-pier ghost town; and 'Suedehead', named after Richard Allen's 1972 'skinploitation' novel and boasting an impressively Marr-ish jangling guitar line.

Sadly, by the time the latter was released in February 1988 (charting at a euphoric number 5, higher than any previous Smiths single), Street's long-term future with Morrissey was already clouded in doubt. Still to negotiate a production royalty, Street spent the first two weeks of January trying to contact the singer to no avail. 'I was in utter confusion because there was no communication. I started to think that maybe he'd changed his mind and he didn't like the record. I didn't know what was going on.'

It was only when Street read Morrissey's first interview of the new year with the *NME* that the motives behind the singer's sudden detachment became clear. Asked about the likelihood of a Smiths reformation, he confessed 'I think about it all the time … I would be totally in favour of a reunion – which isn't to cast doubts on the album or the immediate future. If a reunion never occurs I'm sure I'll be quite happy as I am. But yes I do entertain those thoughts and as soon as anybody wants to come back to the fold and make records I will be there!'. Unluckily for Morrissey, at the time of his comment the three other ex-Smiths were all gainfully employed elsewhere; Johnny Marr had accepted Chrissie Hynde's offer to join The Pretenders, while both Andy Rourke and Mike Joyce were playing for Sinead O'Connor.

'I always thought they were gonna reform,' reasons Street. 'Even after *Viva Hate*. I thought it was just a tiff, that in six weeks, six months they'd sort it out and get back together. But as time went on it became more and more obvious that they weren't. What upset me about that *NME* piece though was the fact that the album wasn't even out yet and he was telling the press he wanted to reform The Smiths. It annoyed me at the time, but to be honest I don't think he was completely happy with *Viva Hate*.' At least the success of 'Suedehead' had a positive effect on Morrissey's mood, though his proud boast that month in a letter to Street that 'I believe Johnny has a copy of *Viva* and he considers it to be brilliant' hardly placated the producer's worries over the singer's immediate game plan.

It was therefore with justifiable trepidation that Street returned to The Wool Hall with Morrissey in March 1988 to record B-sides for the 'Everyday Is Like Sunday' single. 'It was a very different session compared with the making of *Viva Hate*,' he admits. 'There were still money issues because I still hadn't sorted out my production contract. My main problem was that myself and Morrissey were both being managed by Gail Colson at the time. I was happy with Gail, whereas Morrissey was starting to complain about her, so that made things very difficult for everybody. Vini and Andrew also seemed to change. I think they were trying to get more involved and push me aside. I felt that Vini especially was trying to undermine my confidence and be even more critical. He threw a wobbler while we were recording 'Sister I'm A Poet' and stormed out. So it was a very weird vibe.'[138]

The session ended dismally when a party intended as a celebration of *Viva Hate*'s entry in the UK album charts at number one turned sour. 'The studio organised a do at The Cactus Club in Bath,' explains Street, 'but it was cut

138 Other than 'Sister I'm A Poet', the session resulted in the tongue-in-cheek 'How Soon Is Now?' clone 'Disappointed' and the lush orchestral pop confessional 'Will Never Marry?', which featured an uncredited cameo from Street's wife, Sarah. 'It was Morrissey's idea,' explains Street, 'he said he wanted the sound of a playground with a mother calling out to her son. Sarah was the only woman in the studio at the time so we asked her to shout out "Steven!" and added it to this BBC sound effect track of children playing.'

short because Morrissey felt very awkward, like he was on display in a goldfish bowl. He went back to Manchester with Vini the next day. The night after they'd gone I wrote in my diary "I didn't feel any warmth towards them as they left, which put me in a bad mood for the rest of the day"! So yeah, that whole week ended on a real downer.'

Regardless of the unresolved finances and distressing band politics, Street continued to send Morrissey music over the summer of 1988. It was only later that the producer discovered he wasn't alone, since both Reilly, and even Paresi, had also begun submitting demos in the hope of being granted a co-writer credit. In June, 'Everyday Is Like Sunday' provided Morrissey with his second solo Top 10 hit, prompting his first post-Smiths appearance in the studios of *Top of the Pops*. Yet if the fact that he declined to invite Street, Reilly and Paresi to join him wasn't statement enough, then his attire left little misinterpretation; a symbolic hearing aid dangling from his belt and a simple blazer exposing an all-too-familiar *Queen Is Dead* T-shirt underneath. Barely ten months after writing to Street that he wished 'The Smiths to be laid to rest', his actions were those of somebody still mourning their fate.

Morrissey's ache for the days of old would intensify with his active supervision of *Rank*, Rough Trade's posthumous live Smiths album released that September.[139] It was perhaps inevitable that within the month Morrissey would not only resume contact with Andy Rourke and Mike Joyce but also secure their commitment to join him on his next recording session. While Joyce's return systematically excluded Paresi,[140] Vini Reilly fell victim to a contractual row between Factory Records and EMI, which similarly precluded his further involvement ('I think Tony Wilson was haggling for too much' claims Street). Instead, he would be replaced by Neil Taylor, a session player for Tears For Fears recommended by EMI, along with another much more familiar face.

Exactly two years after he'd been unceremoniously ousted from The Smiths, Craig Gannon found himself back in the company of Morrissey, Joyce and Rourke at The Wool Hall in November 1988. Bar one very

139 Originally titled *The Smiths In Heat*, Morrissey eventually insisted on 'Rank, as in J Arthur' – a reference to the British movie mogul but, typical of the singer's subversive wit, also a common English euphemism for masturbation. Early press reports indicated the album would include 'unusual live tracks' and 'very different versions of the songs' culled from a series of concerts rather than the straightforward edit of the October '86 Kilburn National Ballroom show recorded by the BBC that finally appeared.

140 Paresi would work with Morrissey again, from 1989's 'Ouija Board, Ouija Board' through to 1991's *Kill Uncle* album and the singles 'Pregnant For The Last Time' and 'My Love Life'. During that time he would continue to submit musical ideas in the hope of becoming a co-writer. Nothing transpired, though according to Paresi one of his tunes was provisionally given lyrics and a title: 'Angie' (the forename of Johnny Marr's wife).

obvious exception, this was a Smiths reunion in all but name. 'I'm sure they felt as if it *was* The Smiths all over again,' confirms Street. 'That's how it seemed to me because I wasn't able to get the same drive or respect out of them. Much as I enjoyed working with Mike, Andy and Craig again, it was very frustrating. I think they just saw me as 'Streety the engineer' when in fact I was there as producer and co-writer. I definitely felt pushed aside.'

Street's isolation was compounded when he unintentionally offended Morrissey during a visit from EMI press officer Murray Chalmers. 'Murray came down one Sunday and Morrissey spent the whole evening with him. I was in the studio trying new stuff but I sensed Morrissey was in a very weird mood. I found out later that he'd thought I'd snubbed Murray. I hadn't, I was just busy recording. I tried to explain but Morrissey felt as though I'd gone out of my way to make Murray feel uncomfortable. I knew then that I'd more or less put the signature on my death warrant as far as working with him ever again was concerned.'

As Street gloomily suspected, it was to be his last session with Morrissey. The breakdown in their working relationship seemed all the more ironic given the strength of the material completed during their final stint together: particularly the Fall-inspired stomp of 'The Last Of The Famous International Playboys', the sprightly 'Interesting Drug' and the elegant 'Such A Little Thing Makes Such A Big Difference' (the latter purposely modelled upon another of Morrissey's favourites, Sparks' 'Never Turn Your Back On Mother Earth').[141]

After escaping to Manchester for a necessary weekend break from the troubled atmosphere of The Wool Hall, Morrissey returned on 12 December in noticeably higher spirits. The cause of his new found enthusiasm was his announcement of a surprise gig at Wolverhampton Civic Hall three days before Christmas. Street's initial delight was swiftly crushed when he was told 'in no uncertain terms' that he wouldn't be joining the ex-Smiths on stage. 'Morrissey took me aside and told me he wanted it to be a Smiths gig. He felt it was time to move on and exorcise The Smiths so he saw it as a farewell. He even said he wasn't sure if he'd work with Mike and Andy again after this. But I was really pissed off.'

Morrissey's caution towards Rourke and Joyce was understandable, given that both had already started legal proceedings contesting their share of income from The Smiths, as had Craig Gannon. Consequently, the imminent Wolverhampton gig created the farcical scenario of a band whose guitarist,

141 Half a dozen tracks were completed in total. 'The Last Of The Famous International Playboys', 'Lucky Lisp', 'Michael's Bones', 'Interesting Drug' and 'Such A Little Thing Makes Such A Big Difference'. A sixth track, 'The Bed Took Fire', was shelved until 1990 when it was remixed by Clive Langer and Alan Winstanley and released as a B-side under the new title 'At Amber'.

bassist and drummer were all involved in separate legal writs against their frontman. 'It's something that just wasn't discussed,' says Joyce, 'or if the subject was brought up the conversation was quickly changed. Morrissey didn't seem bothered about it, put it that way.'

The gig was announced on Radio 1 just days prior to the event itself. Somewhere between a sincere gesture towards his fans and a shrewd publicity stunt, the fact that entry was free to anybody who turned up in a Smiths or Morrissey T-shirt instigated a mass pilgrimage of die-hard followers who began camping out three nights before to assure their place at the front of the queue. Come the morning of the concert, with several hundred fans now gathered, those who'd spent the past few nights shivering under polythene suddenly found themselves trampled under foot by eleventh-hour gate crashers. The queue system disintegrated into farce while further scenes of mass hysteria greeted that afternoon's arrival of Morrissey and the band in a vintage 1940s 'St Trinian's' bus.

With the venue's 7000 capacity reduced by safety officials to 1500, approximately 3000 people actually turned up hoping to gain admittance. Chaos reigned while the Midlands police struggled to control the bitterly disappointed majority, eventually having to arrest the irate hordes engaging in last-minute attempts to gain entry by breaking windows and smashing down fire doors. According to the *NME*'s James Brown: 'The excitement and atmosphere inside the hall was the most electric I have ever experienced at any public event. Sensible and intelligent fans were transformed into screaming Mozettes (male and female) at the return of their beloved rebel boy. Outside, the air of despondency, the mangled barriers, the police presence, and the silent vigil, could only remind me of the picket line communities of the battered British mineworkers of 1984.'

Playing before a backdrop of the 'That Joke Isn't Funny Anymore' sleeve and with entrance music by Klaus Nomi (as had been the case with The Smiths' 1982 live debut), Morrissey's half-hour set was a mixture of solo material and late period Smiths.[142] 'One of the conditions that we agreed upon,' explains Joyce, 'was that we weren't going to do any Smiths songs that we'd played live with Johnny. We were kind of mulling it over because we didn't want to pretend "this is The Smiths" because it wasn't without Johnny. So we thought if we don't play any song we played live before, some things off *Strangeways* for instance, coupled with Morrissey's solo stuff then what's wrong with that?'.

142 The full Wolverhampton set list ran: (Entrance music: Klaus Nomi's interpretation of Schumann's 'Der Nissbaum'); 'Stop Me If You Think You've Heard This One Before'; 'Disappointed'; 'Interesting Drug'; 'Suedehead'; 'The Last Of The Famous International Playboys'; 'Sister I'm A Poet'; 'Death At One's Elbow'; and 'Sweet And Tender Hooligan'.

As it turned out, the setlist took second place to the historic visual spectacle of Morrissey and three ex-Smiths playing their first concert in two years, marked by the kind of fanatical stage invasions that would later come to typify Morrissey's solo performances. 'The amount of fans getting on stage was ridiculous,' says Joyce. 'It had never been that bad with The Smiths. At one point all you could hear was drums and vocals because Andy had his pedals stood on and his leads had come out, Craig was mobbed so his strap had come off and Moz was cramped down with his mic feeding back next to the monitor with people diving on him. It was actually dangerous with all the electrics. Okay, it was a free gig and all, but I felt bad about how it must have sounded out front.' Gannon agrees: 'It was chaos. As soon as we hit the first note it was just people constantly diving on stage, leads constantly being pulled out, amps wobbling, me quiff falling. I mean it was a good laugh but musically it was frustrating.' Perhaps the only person who failed to enjoy the occasion was Stephen Street, not only barred from the stage but symbolically confined to an outside broadcast radio van.

The day after the concert, while Rourke and Joyce recovered in Wolverhampton, Gannon and Morrissey attempted to head back to Manchester in the same antiquated transport in which they'd arrived. 'It was just me and Morrissey in this St Trinian's bus with the driver,' laughs Gannon. 'It seemed a good idea but as soon as we got to the outskirts of Wolverhampton it broke down. So we were stranded. We had to go and find a telephone so me and Morrissey set off and eventually found this pub in the middle of nowhere. It was mid-morning, so it wasn't even open. The landlord heard us knocking so came down and opened the door. He was met with Morrissey stood there, me behind him, asking "Have you got 10p for the phone?". We managed to get hold of the tour manager who said he'd drive over and pick us up so we just waited for ages back in this bus by ourselves. This was two days before Christmas. We were freezing!'

Despite their collective summons against him, Morrissey would perform with Gannon, Rourke and Joyce one more time, miming to 'The Last Of The Famous International Playboys' on *Top of the Pops* on 9 February. Recognising that his relationship with Street was now probably beyond repair in view of a similar unresolved monetary quarrel, it was peculiar that Morrissey should turn to Craig Gannon, another of his legal plaintiffs, to replace Street as musical co-writer. 'He started asking me for song ideas so I started doing bits of writing. He really liked them and said that he wanted to start recording so I was hoping it was gonna be a continuous thing. In my mind things were going really well, he seemed really into it. Until I got a letter from him which said "Things are looking good and I'm looking forward to working with you. The only thing is if you want to keep on doing this with me then you've got to drop your court case." I mean I wanted to work with him but I wasn't going to drop the case out of principle. As far as I'm aware, Andy and Mike were told the same thing. I just think he knew I was going to win the case and that he didn't have a leg to stand on. But he had to say that really.' Gannon did, indeed, win his case, a decision Morrissey deemed 'an outrage of public justice'.

Stephen Street would also spend most of 1989 chasing due earnings from Morrissey. Still to receive a satisfactory royalty for his work on *Viva Hate*, the producer was forced to place an injunction on the release of April's 'Interesting Drug' single until a settlement was reached. Morrissey was equally incensed by the regrettable misinformation that Street had been conniving with Johnny Rogan, who was in the process of writing his Smiths biography *Morrissey & Marr: The Severed Alliance*. The singer was sufficiently paranoid to send a postcard with the sinister inscription; 'Oh Stephen – You shouldn't have done the Rogan thing.' The irony was that Street had actually refused Rogan's request for fear of upsetting Morrissey.[143]

'I was proud of the fact that I helped him through that initial dark period,' concludes Street. 'It was a very weird, intense period after The Smiths split up and in that time I suppose I'd grown to love him like a brother in a way. He's one of those people that you meet and you think "Jesus! He's fantastic." When things are going really well with a character like that it gives you a sense of immense power. I thought I was close to him. I thought we were getting on really well, so it was very sad how that whole chapter ended.'

It was minor consolation for Morrissey that Andy Rourke bowed to the request to drop his lawsuit and accepted an out-of-court settlement in the region of £80,000. 'I was broke,' he later explained. 'I'd just got married, I had no money and I was dangled a carrot.' Rourke hoped his acquiescence would secure his long-term future as Morrissey's full-time bass player. Sadly, he attended just one more session later that year, while Morrissey's alleged promise of a permanent co-writing arrangement went no further than three meagre B-sides.[144] Rourke's submission would also cause great offence to Mike Joyce, who refused to speak to Andy for the next two years (even forfeiting his invite to be best man at the bassist's wedding). In the interim, Joyce's own writ against Morrissey and Marr began its slow but steady journey through the corridors of power towards judgement day.

Marr himself had maintained a conspicuously low profile for most of 1988, save his cameo appearance on Talking Heads' *Naked* and a perky

143 Street finally agreed to speak with Johnny Rogan when he came to write a companion book, *The Smiths: The Visual Documentary*.

144 The three collaborations with Rourke were: 'Yes, I Am Blind'; 'Girl Least Likely To'; and 'Get Off The Stage', issued as B-sides to 'Ouija Board, Ouija Board', 'November Spawned A Monster' (12-inch/CD only) and 'Piccadilly Palare' respectively.

signature tune for Channel 4's Sunday afternoon music magazine programme *APB*. By contrast, 1989 witnessed his ubiquitous return courtesy of three Top 20 hits in three separate guises (it could very nearly have been four had his only record with The Pretenders, the 'Windows Of The World' single, not flopped). First came 'The Beat(en) Generation' in his new position as guitarist with Matt Johnson's The The (number 18 in April), followed by his part in Kirsty MacColl's cover of The Kinks' 'Days' (number 12 in July)[145] and finally Electronic's 'Getting Away With It', the first fruits of his collaboration with New Order's Bernard Sumner and co-written with guest vocalist Neil Tennant of the Pet Shop Boys. A glorious fusion of Sumner's Balearic beats with Marr's evocatively melancholic harmonies (even its opening line – 'I've been walking in the rain just to get wet on purpose' – seemed an unconsciously Smiths-esque sentiment), considering its release into the annual Christmas singles skirmish, 'Getting Away With It' did well to reach an admirable number 12.

In grim contrast, the previous month had seen Morrissey's solo career finally taking a nosedive with the Clive Langer/Alan Winstanley produced 'Ouija Board, Ouija Board'. Modelled on a leftover tune by Stephen Street (who for obvious reasons took no part in its recording), its critical drubbing and poor chart performance (the first solo Morrissey single not to go Top 10, stalling at number 18) marked the end of his post-Smiths honeymoon period.

As the 1980s came to an end, so too did the likelihood of The Smiths ever reforming. Seven years later, the High Court case of December 1996 eradicated any final suggestion of a reconciliation once and for all. Mike Joyce successfully won his longstanding claim for a quarter of all performance earnings; an estimated £1 million in back royalties. In summing up, Judge John Weeks offered his infamously damning character summary of Morrissey as 'devious, truculent and unreliable when his own interests were at stake.'

'It was like watching a plane crash,' the singer later reflected. 'I'd look down at Johnny's face and I would look at Mike and Andy and think "this is probably as sad as life would ever get."'

In May 1998, 18 months after that notorious court ruling, Morrissey was presented an Ivor Novello award for his 'Outstanding Contribution to

145 Marr played on the majority of MacColl's accompanying *Kite* album, including her cover of The Smiths' 'You Just Haven't Earned It Yet, Baby', which would be his only nostalgic concession to his immediate past following the break up. It was cryptic coincidence that the month of the album's release, MacColl could also be heard in the UK Top 10 singles chart providing backing vocals on Morrissey's 'Interesting Drug'.

British Music'. When accepting the trophy, he made a point of thanking 'John Maher of Wythenshawe. For getting me where I am today. Which begs the question, where am I?'

'We did see each other again,' says Marr. 'It was in the mid-Nineties, before the court case. I thought we needed to get back together in private because the relationship, something that was very important to the two of us, was unresolved. It had become public property. So we spoke a couple of times and got together quite a few times. I took him for a drive. We probably ended up in Duckingfield or somewhere appropriately glamorous. But after a couple of hours it seemed like there was no point in us getting together just to drive around and talk about the good old days. We came together to make music. We were the right people to make music together and then we formed an amazing and unique friendship. But without the music that friendship was kind of redundant really.'

'Amazing and unique'. As the last words on Morrissey and Marr's creative partnership and the music of The Smiths, these two adjectives encapsulate everything that needs to be said.

At the very outset of their career, Morrissey stated 'For the most part products are disposable, but just for that extra one song that changes your direction in life, the importance of popular music just cannot be stressed enough. Music is the most important thing in the world.' The Smiths more than proved this point. In the song 'Rubber Ring', Morrissey memorably beseeched the listener not to forget 'the songs that saved your life'. It's unlikely The Smiths will be so easily forgotten. So long as people are interested in hearing the sound of a life-affirming voice to a heavenly guitar melody, a killer bass line and an impassioned drum beat, theirs is a light that will never go out.

Appendix I

The Smiths Chronological Timeline

As a visual guide to the recording sessions, concerts and radio/TV appearances covered in this book, the following chart is a chronological overview, plotting these events simultaneously alongside their official record release schedule. NB – Only the main studio sessions relating to the individual song entries have been listed, excluding minor overdub work and mixing sessions. Similarly, only those major TV and radio appearances mentioned under the respective sub-sections within this book have been included below, omitting minor interviews and broadcasts of pop promos.

YEAR month	STUDIO [song no.]	IN CONCERT (day) Town, Venue	BBC Radio Session/Concert (first broadcast date)	UK TELEVISION (broadcast date) *Show*: song	ROUGH TRADE DISCOGRAPHY (*Format*) Catalogue number
1982					
May					
June					
July					
August	Decibel [1]				
September					
October		(4) Manchester, The Ritz			
November					
December	Drone [2]				
1983					
January		25) Manchester, Manhattan			

YEAR month	STUDIO [song no.]	IN CONCERT (day) Town, Venue	BBC Radio Session/Concert (first broadcast date)	UK TELEVISION (broadcast date) *Show:* song	ROUGH TRADE DISCOGRAPHY (*Format*) Catalogue number
February	Strawberry [4]	(4) Manchester, Hacienda [3] (21) Manchester, Rafters			
March		(23) London, Rock Garden			
April					
May		(6) London, ULU (21) London, Electric Ballroom	(31) **John Peel** #1 What Difference Does It Make?/ Handsome Devil/Reel Around The Fountain/Miserable Lie (Recorded 18/5/83)		**HAND IN GLOVE**/Handsome Devil *7-inch single* (RT131)
June		(2) Cannock Chase, Miner's Gala (3) Birmingham, Fighting Cocks (4) London, Brixton Ace (29) London, Brixton Ace (30) Coventry, Warwick Uni			
July	Elephant [5]	(1) Bournemouth, MEC (6) Manchester, Hacienda (7) London, Rock Garden	(4) **David Jensen** #1 You've Got Everything Now/These Things Take Time/Wonderful Woman (Recorded 26/6/83)		
August	Elephant [5]	(7) London, Lyceum (9) London, Dingwalls (11) Leeds, Warehouse (12) Hull, Dingwalls (19) Norwich, Gala Ballroom (30) London, Dingwalls			
September	Matrix [7-10]	(3) Colchester, Woods Leisure Centre (15) London, The Venue (16) Bath, Moles Club (24) Brighton, Escape Club (25) London, Lyceum Ballroom	(5) **David Jensen** #2 I Don't Owe You Anything/Pretty Girls Make Graves/Accept Yourself (+ Reel Around The Fountain, not broadcast, Recorded 25/8/83)		

YEAR month	STUDIO [song no.]	IN CONCERT (day) Town, Venue	BBC Radio Session/Concert (first broadcast date)	UK TELEVISION (broadcast date) *Show*: song	ROUGH TRADE DISCOGRAPHY (*Format*) Catalogue number
September (cont.)		(29) Blackburn, Gum Club (30) Birmingham, University	(21) **John Peel** #2 Still Ill/This Night Has Opened My Eyes [6]/ Back To The Old House/ This Charming Man (Recorded 14/9/83)		
October	Strawberry [7] Pluto [11-20]	(5) London, ICA (8) Liverpool, Polytechnic (12) Pontypridd, NWP (14) Bangor, University (17) Sheffield, University (21) London, NEL Polytechnic (22) Liverpool, Polytechnic (27) London, Kingston Polytechnic (28) London, King's College			
November	Eden [12,14,18]	(10) Portsmouth, Polytechnic (16) Leicester, Polytechnic (17) London, Westfield College (18) Liverpool, Edge Hill College (23) Huddersfield, Polytechnic (24) Manchester, Hacienda		(4) **The Tube**: This Charming Man (7) **Riverside**: This Charming Man (24) **Top Of The Pops**: This Charming Man	**THIS CHARMING MAN**/ Jeane *7-inch single* (RT136) **THIS CHARMING MAN** (Manchester)/This Charming Man (London)/Accept Yourself/ Wonderful Woman *12-inch single* (RTT136)
December		(7) Derby, Assembly Rooms (9) Dublin, SFX (19) London, Electric Ballroom (31) USA – New York, Danceteria		(9) **Whistle Test** – On The Road: Handsome Devil/ Still Ill /This Charming Man/Pretty Girls Make Graves/ Reel Around The Fountain/ What Difference Does It Make?/ Miserable Lie/This Night Has Opened My Eyes/Hand In Glove/ These Things Take Time/You've Got Everything Now (Recorded Live at Derby Assembly Rooms 7/12/83)	**THIS CHARMING MAN** (New York Vocal)/ This Charming Man (New York Instrumental) *12-inch single* (RTT136NY)

YEAR month	STUDIO [song no.]	IN CONCERT (day) Town, Venue	BBC Radio Session/Concert (first broadcast date)	UK TELEVISION (broadcast date) *Show*: song	ROUGH TRADE DISCOGRAPHY (*Format*) Catalogue number
1984					
January		(31) Sheffield, University		(26) **Top Of The Pops**: What Difference Does It Make? (27) **The Tube**: (Morrissey interview)	**WHAT DIFFERENCE DOES IT MAKE?/** Back To The Old House *7-inch single* (RT146) + These Things Take Time *12-inch single* (RTT146)
February	Matrix [21]	(1) Stoke On Trent, NSP (2) Coventry, Warwick University (12) London, Lyceum (14) Norwich, UEA (15) Nottingham, Rock City (16) Leicester, University (18) Colchester, Essex University (21) Bournemouth, Town Hall (22) Reading, University (23) Swansea, University (24) Bristol, University (25) Brighton, Polytechnic (27) Canterbury, Kent University (28) Hanley, Victoria Hall (29) Leeds, University		(6) **YES**: What Difference Does It Make?/This Night Has Opened My Eyes (9) **Top Of The Pops**: What Difference Does It Make? (10) **Oxford Road Show**: What Difference Does It Make?	**'THE SMITHS'** LP (ROUGH61) Side 1 – Reel Around The Fountain/You've Got Everything Now/Miserable Lie/ Pretty Girls Make Graves/ The Hand That Rocks The Cradle Side 2 – Still Ill/Hand In Glove/What Difference Does It Make?/I Don't Owe You Anything/Suffer Little Children (*Cassette* ROUGHC61+ This Charming Man at start of Side 2)
March	Island [21-23]	(2) Glasgow, QMU (3) Dundee, University (4) Aberdeen, Fusion Club (5) Edinburgh, Coaster's (7) Newcastle, Mayfair (8) Middlesbrough, Town Hall (9) Lancaster, University (10) Coventry, Polytechnic (12) London, Hammersmith Palais (13) Manchester, Free Trade Hall (14) Liverpool, University (15) Hull, University		(16) **The Tube**: Hand In Glove/Still Ill/Barbarism Begins At Home (31) **Earsay**: Heaven Knows I'm Miserable Now/(Morrissey and Sandie interview)/Hand In Glove (Sandie Shaw)	

YEAR month	STUDIO [song no.]	IN CONCERT (day) Town, Venue	BBC Radio Session/Concert (first broadcast date)	UK TELEVISION (broadcast date) *Show*: song	ROUGH TRADE DISCOGRAPHY (*Format*) Catalogue number
March (cont.)		(17) Loughborough, University (18) Leicester, De Montfort Hall (19) Sheffield, City Hall (20) Birmingham, Tower Ballroom			
April	Powerhouse [24]	(21) NETHERLANDS – Amsterdam, De Meervaart (22) BELGIUM – Bree, Brecon Festival (24) SWITZERLAND – Zurich, Rote Fabrik	(14) **Saturday Live** I Don't Owe You Anything (Sandie Shaw, Johnny Marr & Andy Rourke)/Jeane (Sandie Shaw & Johnny Marr) (live broadcast)	(7) **Datarun**: (Morrissey and Marr interview) (26) **Top Of The Pops**: Hand In Glove (Sandie Shaw)	**SANDIE SHAW** HAND IN GLOVE/ I Don't Owe You Anything *7-inch single* (RT130) + Jeane *12-inch single* (RTT130)
May		(4) GERMANY – Hamburg, Markthalle (9) FRANCE – Paris, El Dorado (17) Belfast, Ulster Hall (18) Dublin, SFX (19) Dublin, SFX (20) Cork, Savoy		(25) **Eight Days A Week**: (with Morrissey) (26) **Pop Quiz**: (with Morrissey) (31) **Top Of The Pops**: Heaven Knows I'm Miserable Now	**HEAVEN KNOWS I'M MISERABLE NOW/** Suffer Little Children *7-inch single* (RT156) + Girl Afraid *12-inch single* (RTT156)
June		(2) FINLAND – Seinajoki, Provinssi Rock Festival (10) London, GLC Jobs For A Change Festival (12) Carlisle, Market Hall (13) Glasgow, Barrowlands (14) Edinburgh, Caley Palais (15) Dundee, Caird Hall (16) Aberdeen, Capital Theatre (17) Inverness, Eden Court (20) Blackpool, Opera House (22) St Austell, Cornish Coliseum (23) Glastonbury Festival		(9) **Earsay**: Heaven Knows I'm Miserable Now (as 31/5/84)/ (Morrissey interview) (14) **Top Of The Pops**: Heaven Knows I'm Miserable Now (16) **SPLAT** (Charlie's Bus): (Morrissey and Marr interview)/Jeane (Sandie Shaw)	
July	Jam [25-28]				

YEAR month	STUDIO [song no.]	IN CONCERT (day) Town, Venue	BBC Radio Session/Concert (first broadcast date)	UK TELEVISION (broadcast date) *Show*: song	ROUGH TRADE DISCOGRAPHY (*Format*) Catalogue number
August			(9) **John Peel** #3 William, It Was Really Nothing/ Nowhere Fast/Rusholme Ruffians/How Soon Is Now? (Recorded 1 August 1984)	(30) **Top Of The Pops**: William, It Was Really Nothing	**WILLIAM, IT WAS REALLY NOTHING/** Please Please Please Let Me Get What I Want *7-inch single* (RT166) + How Soon Is Now? *12-inch single* (RTT166) Reissued in Nov 1987 with B-sides reversed and different sleeve
September		(24) Gloucester, Leisure Centre (25) Cardiff, University (26) Swansea, Mayfair			
October	Amazon & Ridge Farm [29-37]				
November	Amazon & Ridge Farm [29-37]	(11) Waterford, Savoy (12) Dublin, SFX (13) Dublin, SFX (16) Limerick, Savoy (17) Galway, Leisureland (18) Cork, Savoy (20) Letterkenny, Leisure Centre (21) Coleraine, University (22) Belfast, Ulster Hall			**'HATFUL OF HOLLOW'** compilation LP (ROUGH76) Side 1 – William, It Was Really Nothing/What Difference Does It Make?*/ These Things Take Time*/ This Charming Man*/How Soon Is Now?/ Handsome Devil*/ Hand In Glove/ Still Ill* Side 2 – Heaven Knows I'm Miserable Now/This Night Has Opened My Eyes*/ You've Got Everything Now*/Accept Yourself*/Girl Afraid/Back To The Old House*/Reel Around The Fountain*/ Please Please Please Let Me Get What I Want (* indicates BBC Session recording)
December	Island [38]	(1) FRANCE – Paris, Versailles			
1985					
January	Ridge Farm [39,40] Utopia [41]				

YEAR month	STUDIO [song no.]	IN CONCERT (day) Town, Venue	BBC Radio Session/Concert (first broadcast date)	UK TELEVISION (broadcast date) *Show*: song	ROUGH TRADE DISCOGRAPHY (*Format*) Catalogue number
February		(27) Chippenham, Golddiggers (28) Guildford, Civic Hall		(12) **Whistle Test**: (Making of Meat Is Murder)/Nowhere Fast (14) **Top Of The Pops**: How Soon Is Now? (21) **Pebble Mill At One**: (Morrissey interview) (21) **Granada Reports**: (Full band interviewed by Tony Wilson) (22) **Oxford Road Show**: Shakespeare's Sister/The Headmaster Ritual	**HOW SOON IS NOW?**/Well I Wonder *7-inch single* (RT176) + Oscillate Wildly *12-inch single* (RTT176) **'MEAT IS MURDER'** *LP* (ROUGH81) Side 1 – The Headmaster Ritual/Rusholme Ruffians/I Want The One I Can't Have/What She Said/That Joke Isn't Funny Anymore Side 2 – Nowhere Fast/Well I Wonder/ Barbarism Begins At Home/Meat Is Murder
March		(1) London, Brixton Academy (3) Portsmouth, Guildhall (4) Reading, Hexagon (6) Poole, Arts Centre (7) Brighton, Dome (8) Margate, Winter Gardens (11) Ipswich, Gaumont (12) Nottingham, Royal Centre (16) Hanley, Victoria Hall [42] (17) Birmingham, Hippodrome (18) Oxford, Apollo Theatre (22) Sheffield, City Hall (23) Middlesbrough, Town Hall (24) Newcastle, City Hall (27) Liverpool, Royal Court (28) Bradford, St George's Hall (29) Northampton, Derngate (31) Manchester, Palace Theatre			**SHAKESPEARE'S SISTER**/What She Said *7-inch single* (RT181) + Stretch Out And Wait *12-inch single* (RTT181)
April		(1) Leicester, De Montfort Hall (4) Bristol, Hippodrome (6) London, Royal Albert Hall			

YEAR month	**STUDIO** [song no.]	**IN CONCERT** (day) Town, Venue	**BBC Radio Session/Concert** (first broadcast date)	**UK TELEVISION** (broadcast date) *Show*: song	**ROUGH TRADE DISCOGRAPHY** (*Format*) Catalogue number
May		(14) ITALY – Rome, Tendetrisce (17) SPAIN – Barcelona, Studio 54 (18) SPAIN – Madrid, Paseo De Camoens	(9) **The Evening Show** (with Janice Long) William, It Was Really Nothing/ Nowhere Fast/What She Said/Hand In Glove/How Soon Is Now?/ Stretch Out And Wait/That Joke Isn't Funny Anymore/Barbarism Begins At Home/You've Got Everything Now/Shakespeare's Sister/The Headmaster Ritual/Still Ill/Meat Is Murder/Miserable Lie (Recorded at Oxford Apollo Theatre, 18 March 1985)	(24) **Studio One**: (Morrissey interview)	
June		(7) USA – Chicago, Aragon Ballroom (8) USA – Detroit, Royal Oak Theater (9) CANADA – Toronto, Kingswood Theater (11) USA – Washington, Warner Theater (12) USA – Philadelphia, Tower Theater (14) USA – Boston, Opera House (17) USA – New York, Beacon Theater (18) USA – New York, Beacon Theater (21) USA – Oakland, HJ Kaiser Auditorium (25) USA – San Diego, State University Open Air Theater (27) USA – Los Angeles, Palladium Theater (28) USA – Los Angeles, Palladium Theater (29) USA – Laguna Hills, Irving Meadows Amphitheater			

YEAR month	**STUDIO** [song no.]	**IN CONCERT** (day) Town, Venue	**BBC Radio Session/Concert** (first broadcast date)	**UK TELEVISION** (broadcast date) *Show*: song	**ROUGH TRADE DISCOGRAPHY** (*Format*) Catalogue number
July					**THAT JOKE ISN'T FUNNY ANYMORE/** Meat Is Murder (Live) *7-inch single* (RT186) + Nowhere Fast (Live)/ Shakespeare's Sister (Live)/ Stretch Out And Wait (Live) *12-inch single* (RTT186) (live tracks are BBC recordings from Janice Long Oxford Apollo concert 18/3/85)
August	Drone [43] RAK [43-45]				
September	RAK [46-48]	(22) Irvine, Magnum Leisure Centre (24) Edinburgh, Playhouse (25) Glasgow, Barrowlands [49] (26) Dundee, Caird Hall (28) Lerwick, Clickimin Centre (30) Aberdeen, Capital Theatre			**THE BOY WITH THE THORN IN HIS SIDE/** Asleep *7-inch single* (RT191) + Rubber Ring *12-inch single* (RTT191)
October	Jacobs [46-48, 50-55]	(1) Inverness, Eden Court		(10) **Top Of The Pops**: The Boy With The Thorn In His Side (25) **The Tube**: (Morrissey interviewed by Margi Clarke during Scottish Tour)/Hand In Glove (Recorded live in Glasgow 25/9/85)	
November	Jacobs [46-48, 50-55]				
December	Wessex [56,57]				
1986					
January		(31) Newcastle, City Hall (Red Wedge)			

YEAR month	STUDIO [song no.]	IN CONCERT (day) Town, Venue	BBC Radio Session/Concert (first broadcast date)	UK TELEVISION (broadcast date) *Show*: song	ROUGH TRADE DISCOGRAPHY (*Format*) Catalogue number
February		(8) Liverpool, Royal Court (10) Dublin, National Stadium (11) Dundalk, Fairways Hotel (12) Belfast, Queens University			
March					
April					
May	Livingston [58,59]			(20) **Whistle Test**: Bigmouth Strikes Again/ Vicar In A Tutu	**BIGMOUTH STRIKES AGAIN**/Money Changes Everything *7-inch single* (RT192) + Unloveable *12-inch single* (RTT192)
June	Jam [60,61]				**'THE QUEEN IS DEAD'** *LP* (ROUGH96) Side 1 – The Queen Is Dead/Frankly, Mr Shankly/I Know It's Over/Never Had No One Ever/Cemetry Gates Side 2 – Bigmouth Strikes Again/The Boy With The Thorn In His Side/Vicar In A Tutu/There Is A Light That Never Goes Out/Some Girls Are Bigger Than Others
July		(16) Glasgow, Barrowlands (17) Newcastle, Mayfair (19) Manchester, G-Mex (Festival Of The Tenth Summer) (20) Salford, University (30) CANADA – Ontario, Centennial Hall (31) CANADA – Toronto, Kingswood Music Theater		(5) **Eurotube** (The Tube Special): There Is A Light That Never Goes Out/ Panic	**PANIC**/Vicar In A Tutu *7-inch single* (RT193) + The Draize Train *12-inch single* (RTT193)

YEAR month	STUDIO [song no.]	IN CONCERT (day) Town, Venue	BBC Radio Session/Concert (first broadcast date)	UK TELEVISION (broadcast date) *Show*: song	ROUGH TRADE DISCOGRAPHY (*Format*) Catalogue number
August		(2) CANADA – Ottawa, Capital Congress Centre (3) CANADA – Montreal, University (5) USA – Mansfield, Great Woods Center (6) USA – New York, Pier 84 (8) USA – Washington, Smith Center (11) USA – Cleveland, Music Hall (12) USA – Pittsburg, Fulton Theater (14) USA – Detroit, Fox Theater (15) USA – Chicago, Aragon Ballroom (16) USA – Milwaukee, Performing Arts Center (22) USA – Santa Barbara, Arlington Theater (23) USA – San Francisco, Greek Theater (25) USA – Los Angeles, Universal Amphitheater (26) USA – Los Angeles, Universal Amphitheater (28) USA – Laguna Hills, Irving Meadows Amphitheater (29) USA – San Diego, Open Air Theater (31) USA – Phoenix, Mesa Amphitheater			
September		(3) USA – Boulder, Events Center (5) USA – Houston, Cullen Auditorium (6) USA – Dallas, Bronco Bowl (8) USA – New Orleans, McAlister Auditorium (10) USA – St Petersburg, Bayfront Arena			

YEAR month	STUDIO [song no.]	IN CONCERT (day) Town, Venue	BBC Radio Session/Concert (first broadcast date)	UK TELEVISION (broadcast date) *Show*: song	ROUGH TRADE DISCOGRAPHY (*Format*) Catalogue number
October	Mayfair [62-64]	(13) Carlisle, Sands Centre (14) Middlesbrough, Town Hall (15) Wolverhampton, Civic Hall (17) St Austell, Cornish Coliseum (18) Gloucester, Leisure Centre (19) Newport, Leisure Centre (21) Nottingham, Royal Concert Hall (23) London, Kilburn National Ballroom (24) London, Brixton Academy (26) London, Palladium (27) Preston, Guildhall (30) Manchester, Free Trade Hall			**ASK**/Cemetery Gates *7-inch single* (RT194) + Golden Lights *12-inch single* (RTT194)
November	Trident [65]				
December		(12) London, Brixton Academy	(17) **John Peel** #4 Is It Really So Strange?[66]/ London/Half A Person/Sweet And Tender Hooligan [67] (Recorded 2 December 1986)		
1987					
January	Good Earth [68,69]			(23) **The Tube**: (Morrissey interviewed by Shaun Duggan)	**SHOPLIFTERS OF THE WORLD UNITE/** Half A Person *7-inch single* (RT195) + London *12-inch single* (RTT195)
February		(7)The Smiths appear at the San Remo Festival in Italy – a mimed performance for Italian television		(5) **Top Of The Pops**: Shoplifters Of The World Unite	

YEAR month	STUDIO [song no.]	IN CONCERT (day) Town, Venue	BBC Radio Session/Concert (first broadcast date)	UK TELEVISION (broadcast date) *Show*: song	ROUGH TRADE DISCOGRAPHY (*Format*) Catalogue number
March	The Wool Hall [69-79]				**'THE WORLD WON'T LISTEN'** *compilation LP* (ROUGH101) Side 1 – Panic/Ask/London/ Bigmouth Strikes Again/ Shakespeare's Sister/ There Is A Light That Never Goes Out/Shoplifters Of The World Unite/The Boy With The Thorn In His Side Side 2 – Asleep/Unloveable/ Half A Person/ Stretch Out And Wait/That Joke Isn't Funny Anymore/Oscillate Wildly/You Just Haven't Earned It Yet, Baby/Rubber Ring (Cassette ROUGHC101 + Money Changes Everything at end of Side 1)
April	The Wool Hall [69-79]		(18) **In Concert** The Queen Is Dead/Panic/Vicar In A Tutu/ There Is A Light That Never Goes Out/ Ask/His Latest Flame-Rusholme Ruffians/ Frankly, Mr Shankly/The Boy With The Thorn In His Side/What She Said/Cemetry Gates/London/I Know It's Over/The Draize Train/How Soon Is Now?/ Bigmouth Strikes Again (Recorded at Kilburn National Ballroom, 23 October 1986)	(10) **The Tube**: Sheila Take A Bow/ Shoplifters Of The World Unite (23) **Top Of The Pops**: Sheila Take A Bow	**SHEILA TAKE A BOW**/ Is It Really So Strange* *7-inch single* (RT196) + Sweet And Tender Hooligan* *12-inch single* (RTT196) (* BBC session recording)
May	The Last Session: Firehouse [80-82]				**'LOUDER THAN BOMBS'** *compilation double LP* (US import on Sire Records 9255691, later issued as Rough Trade ROUGH255) Side 1 – Is It Really So Strange?*/Sheila Take A Bow/Shoplifters Of The World Unite/Sweet And Tender Hooligan*/Half A Person/London Side 2 – Panic/Girl Afraid/ Shakespeare's Sister/William, It Was Really Nothing/You Just Haven't Earned It Yet, Baby/Heaven

YEAR month	**STUDIO** [song no.]	**IN CONCERT** (day) Town, Venue	**BBC Radio Session/Concert** (first broadcast date)	**UK TELEVISION** (broadcast date) *Show*: song	**ROUGH TRADE DISCOGRAPHY** (*Format*) Catalogue number
May (cont.)					Knows I'm Miserable Now Side 3 – Ask/Golden Lights/ Oscillate Wildly/ These Things Take Time/Rubber Ring/Back To The Old House Side 4 – Hand In Glove/ Stretch Out And Wait/Please Please Please Let Me Get What I Want/This Night Has Opened My Eyes*/ Unloveable/Asleep (*BBC session recording)
June					
July					
August	The Smiths attempt to continue with new guitarist Ivor Perry atPowerhouse				**GIRLFRIEND IN A COMA/** Work Is A Four Letter Word *7-inch single* (RT197) + I Keep Mine Hidden *12-inch single* (RTT197), *Cassette single* (RTT197C)
September					**'STRANGEWAYS, HERE WE COME'** *LP* (ROUGH106) Side 1 – A Rush And A Push And The Land Is Ours/I Started Something I Couldn't Finish/ Death Of A Disco Dancer/Girlfriend In A Coma/Stop Me If You Think You've Heard This One Before Side 2 – Last Night I Dreamt That Somebody Loved Me/ Unhappy Birthday/Paint A Vulgar Picture/Death At One's Elbow/I Won't Share You
October	Morrissey starts to record Viva Hate at The Wool Hall			(13) Johnny Marr appears with Bryan Ferry on ITV's **The Roxy** (18) **The South Bank Show**: (Documentary)	Bryan Ferry releases 'The Right Stuff' single featuring Johnny Marr

YEAR month	STUDIO [song no.]	IN CONCERT (day) Town, Venue	BBC Radio Session/Concert (first broadcast date)	UK TELEVISION (broadcast date) *Show*: song	ROUGH TRADE DISCOGRAPHY (*Format*) Catalogue number
October (cont.)					**I STARTED SOMETHING I COULDN'T FINISH**/Pretty Girls Make Graves (Troy Tate) *7-inch single* (RT198) + Some Girls Are Bigger Than Others (Live at Brixton Academy 12/12/86) *12-inch single* (RTT198) + What's The World? (Live at Glasgow Barrowlands 25/9/85) *Cassette single* (RTT198C)
November					
December	Morrissey completes Viva Hate at The Wool Hall		Morrissey records solo session for John Peel at BBC Maida Vale with Vini Reilly, Andrew Paresi and Stephen Street. The tracks are never broadcast		**LAST NIGHT I DREAMT THAT SOMEBODY LOVED ME**/Rusholme Ruffians* *7-inch single* (RT200) + Nowhere Fast* *12-inch single* (RTT200) + William, It Was Really Nothing* *CD single* (RTT200CD) (* BBC session recording)
1988					
January					
February					Morrissey releases debut solo single 'Suedehead'
March	Morrissey records B-sides for 'Everyday Is Like Sunday' at The Wool Hall				Morrissey releases debut solo album **'VIVA HATE'**
April					

YEAR month	**STUDIO** [song no.]	**IN CONCERT** (day) Town, Venue	**BBC Radio Session/Concert** (first broadcast date)	**UK TELEVISION** (broadcast date) *Show*: song	**ROUGH TRADE DISCOGRAPHY** (*Format*) Catalogue number
May					
June					Morrissey releases second solo single 'Everyday Is Like Sunday'
July					
August					
September					**'RANK'** *live LP* (ROUGH126) Side 1 – The Queen Is Dead/Panic/Vicar In A Tutu/ Ask/(Marie's The Name) His Latest Flame – Rusholme Ruffians/The Boy With The Thorn In His Side/What She Said Side 2 – Is It Really So Strange?/Cemetry Gates/ London/I Know It's Over/The Draize Train/Still Ill/ Bigmouth Strikes Again (Adapted from BBC In Concert recording of Kilburn National Ballroom 23/10/86)
October					**THE PEEL SESSION EP** (Strange Fruit Records) What Difference Does It Make?/Miserable Lie/Reel Around The Fountain/Handsome Devil *12-inch EP* (SFPS055) (Complete first BBC John Peel session, May 1983)
November					
December	Morrissey records his next two singles at The Wool Hall with Joyce, Rourke and Gannon	(22) Wolverhampton, Civic Hall Morrissey solo live debut backed by Mike Joyce, Andy Rourke and Craig Gannon			

Appendix II
Cover Stars & Matrix Messages

Integral to The Smiths, their public image and their aesthetic agenda was their distinctive cover art, designed by Morrissey to parade and promote his celluloid heroes, style icons and visual influences.

Whether reasserting their northern roots with emblematic kitchen-sink stills of Shelagh Delaney, Pat Phoenix and Viv Nicholson or celebrating masculine beauty via the poise of Jean Marais, Terence Stamp and Elvis Presley, the cultural content and specific graphic sensibilities of The Smiths' artwork were such that, even to look at, their records could never be confused with those of any other contemporary band. According to Morrissey, 'it really emerged from all the photographs I'd collected and all the books I'd found and kept and taken back to my bedroom for many years. All of those Smiths sleeves had literally been stuck on my bedroom walls during the Seventies.'

Just as indicative of the band's mindset were the unfathomable private jokes and public slogans etched into the run-out groove (or 'matrix') of the original vinyl releases. What follows is a complete list detailing the cover stars and matrix messages from their original UK Rough Trade discography. For further insight into the creative process behind The Smiths' sleeves, refer to Jo Slee's indispensable *Peepholism: Into the Art of Morrissey* (Sidgwick & Jackson, 1994).

SINGLES

'Hand In Glove'

Cover star: An unknown nude model photographed by Jim French and taken from Margaret Walters' 1978 study of *The Nude Male.* According to Walters, French's photographs 'are a protest, and an important and valid one, against the unthinking assumption that beauty belongs only to women; against the kind of old-fashioned bias that allowed, for example, a London Sunday supplement to have a whole series on Beauty, hardly mentioning men except as observers and judges. We need to be reminded, for all our sakes, that men are beautiful too.' Curiously, what appears to be a large mole at the bottom of the model's right shoulder blade is actually a stain or blemish on the copy of the photo provided for the sleeve, since it's absent from the original print as reproduced in Walters' book. 'Hand In Glove' would be the only UK Smiths single to feature the song title on the front cover.

Matrix messages: A – 'Kiss my shades' (lyric from 'Hand In Glove', as sung by Morrissey during the bridge section); B – 'Kiss my shades too' (Marr's response to Morrissey's inscription on side A).

'This Charming Man'

Cover star: French actor Jean Marais, in the title role of 1949's *Orphée,* directed by Jean Cocteau (whom Morrissey would reference again with the sleeve for *Hatful Of Hollow,* as well as his wry 'Poppycocteau' poem printed on the reverse of the live 'London' flexi-disc given away with *The Catalogue* in 1988). The 12-inch, and its New York remix version, featured just the image and no text. The 'This Charming Man' 12-inch was also the first time Morrissey's lyrics were printed on a Smiths sleeve.

Matrix messages: 12-inch A – 'Will nature make a man of me yet?' (lyric from 'This Charming Man'); 7-inch B – 'Slap me on the patio' (lyric from 'Reel Around The Fountain', the original choice of A-side, which 'This Charming Man' later replaced).

'What Difference Does It Make?'

Cover star: Terence Stamp, maniacally grinning whilst brandishing a chloroform pad in a publicity shot from William Wyler's 1965 chiller *The Collector* (later cited by Marr as his favourite movie). Based upon John Fowles' extraordinary novel, Stamp plays inadequate bank clerk and butterfly collector Freddie Clegg who, after winning the pools, purchases a secluded country mansion where he later kidnaps and 'keeps' a beautiful art student whom he has obsessively stalked (Samantha Eggar). It may be pure coincidence, but during the film Stamp actually says the line 'What difference does it make?'.

Within weeks of the record's release and much to Morrissey's 'indescribable unhappiness', Stamp famously objected to the use of his picture, instigating a replacement sleeve to avoid legal action: a comical homage of the original *Collector* pose featuring Morrissey bearing a glass of milk. Mutual acquaintance Sandie Shaw later apologised to Stamp on The Smiths' behalf, resulting in his image eventually being restored by permission on future pressings. At any rate, the incident did little to quell

Morrissey's fascination with the actor. Describing his idea of happiness as 'being Terence Stamp' in 1991, he used the pseudonym 'Terrace Stomp' on the credits of that year's *Kill Uncle* album and also borrowed the title of Stamp's 1962 feature debut *Billy Budd* for a track on 1994's *Vauxhall & I*. Like 'This Charming Man', the 12-inch cover of 'What Difference Does It Make?' was text-free.
No matrix messages

'Hand In Glove' by Sandie Shaw

Cover star: Rita Tushingham as Jo in Tony Richardson's 1961 film adaptation of Shelagh Delaney's *A Taste of Honey*.
Matrix messages: A – 'Kiss my shades' (A repeat of the inscription featured on the matrix of The Smiths' original 'Hand In Glove' single; see above); B – 'J.M.' (Johnny Marr)

'Heaven Knows I'm Miserable Now'

Cover star: A suitably despondent Viv Nicholson, sourced from her 1977 autobiography *Spend, Spend, Spend* (the photo's original accompanying caption read 'Viv returns to her childhood home after Keith's death'). In 1961 Nicholson was a married 21-year-old mother of three, trying to survive on her husband's £7 a week miner's wage in an impoverished Yorkshire working-class terrace when a pools win spectacularly changed her life. Far from a rags to riches fairy tale, Nicholson's fate was that of a modern tragedy. After her second husband died in a car crash, her life collapsed in spite of her nest egg, which had already been idly frittered away. A succession of bad, abusive relationships, four further failed marriages (her fifth husband committed suicide), alcoholism and depression left her bankrupt, eventually finding succour as a Jehovah's Witness. As part of the posthumous 1987 *South Bank Show* documentary, Morrissey and Nicholson were united for the benefit of the cameras. The singer would later write off their meeting as 'very awkward' and 'like some curious Polish play'.
Matrix messages: 7-inch A – 'Smiths indeed' (This would later be used as the title of the first specifically dedicated Smiths fanzine, which ran between 1986 and 1989); 7-inch B – 'Ill forever'; 12-inch A – 'Smiths presumably'; 12-inch B – 'Forever ill'.

'William, It Was Really Nothing'

Cover star: Unknown model taken from a US hi-fi advertisement for ADS Speakers, sourced from a Seventies edition of American GQ magazine. Morrissey later referred to this image as 'an example of how much of an

impact fashion photography and fashion magazines had on me.' Sadly, Rough Trade were eventually forced to delete the single and its original sleeve for copyright reasons. In November 1987, 'William... ' was reissued in a new cover featuring actress Billie Whitelaw in a still from 1967's *Charlie Bubbles* (directed by Albert Finney, scripted by Shelagh Delaney).
Matrix messages: A – 'The impotence of Ernest' (A pun on Oscar Wilde's *The Importance of Being Earnest,* also serving as a reference to author Ernest Hemingway, who in later years suffered from impotence); B – 'Romantic and square is hip 'n' aware' (one of several matrix messages coined by Johnny Marr rather than Morrissey); Re-issued B – 'We hates bad grammer'.

'Barbarism Begins At Home' (Promo Single)

Cover star: Viv Nicholson, again, in another photo sourced from her autobiography *Spend, Spend, Spend*. The caption on the back sleeve read: 'Here is Viv with suitcase before going to Malta on a later spending spree after tragedy had almost robbed her of what remained of her fortune'
Matrix messages: A – 'These are the good times' (The back cover also contained a separate message, 'All god's children got wings').

'How Soon Is Now?'

Cover star: Sean Barrett as Frankie in the 1958 World War II Ealing drama *Dunkirk*.
Matrix messages: A – 'The tatty truth'.

'Shakespeare's Sister'

Cover star: *Coronation Street*'s Elsie Tanner, alias actress Pat Phoenix. Morrissey and Phoenix were later paired together for a 1985 interview in *Blitz* magazine, in which she coincidentally revealed that her novels were 'certainly no threat to Shakespeare'. The actress also appears in 1963's *The L-Shaped Room* (the source of the 'Take Me Back To Dear Old Blighty' sample on 'The Queen Is Dead'). Phoenix died of lung cancer in September 1986.
Matrix messages: A – 'Home is where the art is'.

'That Joke Isn't Funny Anymore'

Cover star: A detail of a child actor in a still from the 1964 Russian movie *Zacharovannaya Desna* (*The Enchanted Desna*), directed by Yuliya Solntseva and sourced from the February 1965 issue of *Film and Filmmaking* magazine. Morrissey would later use the same image as the backdrop for his live solo debut at Wolverhampton Civic Hall on 22 December 1988.
Matrix messages: A – 'Oursouls, oursouls, oursouls'.

'The Boy With The Thorn In His Side'

Cover star: Truman Capote, the American author and wit best known for writing *Breakfast at Tiffany's* (the 1961 film version of which featured Henry Mancini's 'Moon River', later covered by Morrissey on the B-side of his 1994 single 'Hold On To Your Friends'). Capote died of a drug overdose in August 1984. The photo was taken by Cecil Beaton.
Matrix messages: A – 'Arty bloody farty'; B – '"Is that clever"... J.M.' ('Is that clever?' is a line from Oscar Wilde's *The Importance of Being Earnest* which, as spoken by John Gielgud, can be faintly heard on this single's 12-inch B-side, 'Rubber Ring' prior to the more audible 'Everybody's clever nowadays'. 'J.M.' is Johnny Marr).

'Bigmouth Strikes Again'

Cover star: James Dean, astride his first motorbike aged 17, photographed by his school friend Nelva Jean Thomas. Born 8 February 1931, Dean would play just three leading film roles – *East of Eden, Rebel Without a Cause* and *Giant* – before his violent death in a car crash at the age of 24 on 30 September 1955. Though Morrissey would famously write a book on him – *James Dean Is Not Dead* (apparently it was supposed to be titled *James Dead Is Not Dean*) – as early as 1984 the singer admitted that 'what he did on film didn't stir me much'. Twenty years later, Morrissey was even more frank, describing the actor as 'reasonably unpleasant' and confessing his interest in Dean as being 'purely a physical obsession'. Nonetheless, for his debut solo video, 1988's 'Suedehead', Morrissey made a pilgrimage to Dean's hometown of Fairmount, Indiana, an experience he'd recall as being 'very, very moving'. The sleeve of 'Bigmouth Strikes Again' was the first of just two singles to feature only the word 'Smiths' on the cover.
Matrix messages: A – 'Beware the wrath to come'(A reference to the 1954 David Lean film *Hobson's Choice*. This slogan appears on a banner being carried by the Salvation Army band during the same scene from which the intro for 'Sheila Take A Bow' was sampled); B – 'Talent borrows, genius steals' (A maxim frequently attributed to Oscar Wilde).

'Panic'

Cover star: Richard Bradford in a still from the 1967 UK espionage series *Man In A Suitcase.* Texan-born Bradford played a disgraced ex-CIA agent working as a freelance troubleshooter in London, who was known only by his surname, McGill. Just 30 episodes of this superlative, yet often unsung, 'existential spy drama' were made. Morrissey would later list *Man In A Suitcase* as one of his 'Cathode Raves' (favourite TV shows) in the *NME.*

Like 'Bigmouth Strikes Again', the sleeve of 'Panic' bore only the word 'Smiths'.
Matrix messages: B – 'I dreamt about stew last night' (Pun on the Shelagh Delaney-inspired lyric 'I dreamt about you last night' from 'Reel Around The Fountain').

'Ask'

Cover star: Yootha Joyce on the set of The Dave Clark Five's 1965 musical comedy *Catch Us If You Can*. Joyce was best known for the Seventies British sitcom *George & Mildred* (a spin-off of *Man About the House*) and also played a minor role in another of Morrissey's favourite films, *Charlie Bubbles*. She died of hepatitis in 1980.
Matrix messages: A – 'Are you loathsome tonight?' (Pun on the 1960 Elvis Presley hit 'Are You Lonesome Tonight?'); B – 'Tomb it may concern' (A *possible* pun on Chris Andrew's 1965 hit 'To Whom It Concerns').

'Shoplifters Of The World Unite'

Cover star: Elvis Presley, in what was allegedly his first publicity still from 1954, having just signed with Sam Phillips' Sun Records. In a disastrous photo session for *Record Mirror* circa the single's release, Morrissey attempted to emulate the same dark-eyed Elvis pose but ended up, as he later lamented, overdoing the Max Factor and looking 'like a ponce.' The back cover carried a dedication in memory of Ruth Polsky, The Smiths' New York promoter and former caretaker-manager who was killed when a taxi ran over her outside a nightclub on 7 September 1986.
Matrix messages: A – 'Alf Ramsey's revenge' (Ramsey was the legendary football manager who took the England team to World Cup victory in 1966).

'Sheila Take A Bow'

Cover star: Warhol Superstar and New York transvestite Candy Darling, from the 1971 Paul Morrissey movie *Women In Revolt.* Born James Lawrence Slattery, Darling was the alleged inspiration behind The Velvet Underground's 'Candy Says' and Lou Reed's 'Walk On The Wild Side'. She died of leukaemia in March 1974, leaving a letter to her friends in which she wrote 'You know I couldn't last', a phrase later appropriated by Morrissey as the closing track on his 2004 album *You Are The Quarry*.
Matrix messages: A – 'Cook Bernard Mathews' (During the Eighties, Norfolk poultry farmer Matthews was a ubiquitous figure during UK television commercial breaks, peddling a variety of patented frozen meat products with carnivorous glee and his trademark catchphrase 'They're bootiful, really boo-tiful!').

'Girlfriend In A Coma'

Cover star: Playwright Shelagh Delaney, author of *A Taste of Honey.* Born in Salford in 1939, Delaney failed her 11-plus exam and later left school at 16 with no academic qualifications. At 17 she was working in an engineering factory when she went to see a performance of Rattigan's play *Variation on a Theme*. Legend has it she thought it was so poor and unrealistic that she decided to write a drama of her own, resulting in 1959's *A Taste of Honey*. As discussed within this book, Morrissey drew enormous lyrical influences from both *Honey* and Delaney's next play, *The Lion in Love*. A different Delaney portrait was also used for the sleeve of *Louder Than Bombs*.
Matrix messages: 12-inch A – 'Everybody is a flasher at heart'; 12-inch B and 7-inch A – 'And never more shall be so'; 7-inch B – 'So far, so bad'.

'I Started Something I Couldn't Finish'

Cover star: Avril Angers in a still from Roy Boulting's 1966 movie *The Family Way* – a kitchen-sink sex comedy based upon Bill Naughton's stage play *Honeymoon Deferred.* Hayley Mills and Hywel Bennett starred as northern working-class newly-weds experiencing difficulties consummating their marriage. Another still from the film featuring actor/singer Murray Head was also used on the sleeve of an import single of 'Stop Me If You Think You've Heard This One Before'.
Matrix messages: A – '"Murder at the Wool Hall" (X) starring Sheridan Whiteside' (The Wool Hall was the recording studio near Bath where The Smiths recorded this single and where, at the time of its release, Morrissey was also making *Viva Hate.* For a full explanation of Sheridan Whiteside see **[53]** 'Cemetry Gates'); B – 'You are believing, you do not want to sleep' (A reverse of the sample featured on 'Rubber Ring' – 'you are sleeping, you do not want to believe').

'Last Night I Dreamt That Somebody Loved Me'

Cover star: British Fifties rocker Billy Fury. Born Ronald Wycherley, the Liverpudlian singer was by far the best homegrown rock 'n' roller to emerge from England in response to Elvis, though by the early Sixties he'd progressed to broken-hearted pop ballads. Other than his musical and aesthetic appeal, Fury's love of animals combined with his sickly disposition (battling with heart problems since childhood) made him classic Morrissey fodder. 'He was entirely doomed and I find that quite affectionate,' the singer would tell *Smash Hits* in 1984. 'He was persistently unhappy and yet had a string of hit records. He always wanted to make very emotionally over-blown ballads but he found himself in the midst of the popular arena. He despised almost every aspect of the music industry and was very, very ill from an early age ... Billy's singles are totally treasurable.'

The choice of this, their last, 45's cover star roused valid comparisons that the title may owe a debt to Fury's 1962 single 'Last Night Was Made For Love'. However, in sentiment and orchestral angst it was much closer to a later Fury disc, 1966's emotionally torrid 'I'll Never Quite Get Over You', which Morrissey named as one of his favourite records in an *NME* survey a few years earlier.

This single's original 12-inch sleeve design, eventually scrapped, was to feature details of the same Fury cover portrait accompanied by two separate quotations; 'Please keep me in mind' (from 'Well I Wonder' **[see 31]**) and 'When I sleep with that picture beside me ... I really think it's you' (a phrase that would eventually appear on 'Late Night Maudlin Street' from Morrissey's 1988 solo debut *Viva Hate*).

Matrix messages: A – '"The Return of the Submissive Society" (X) starring Sheridan Whiteside'; B – '"The Bizarre Oriental Vibrating Palm Death" (X) Starring Sheridan Whiteside' (For an explanation of Sheridan Whiteside see **[53]** 'Cemetry Gates'). Originally the etched matrixes were to be: 'Attention Stalybridge!'; 'Linder Found A Cobra' – a pun on 'Girlfriend In A Coma' referencing Morrissey's friend Linder Sterling; 'Smiths = Peepholism', which would later be adapted as the matrix message on *Rank*; and two alternatives acknowledging Fifties UK rock 'n' roll idol Vince Eager – 'Eaten by Vince Eager' and 'Vince Eager, Come And Get Me'.

ALBUMS

The Smiths

Cover star: Joe Dallesandro as featured in 1968's *Flesh*, directed by Paul Morrissey and 'produced' by Andy Warhol (who, during filming, was actually recovering in hospital after being shot by Valerie Solanas). Dallesandro played a junkie who turns to male prostitution in order to support his habit along with that of his lesbian wife. Apparently, the film was Warhol's response to John Schlesinger's *Midnight Cowboy*, which was being made in New York at the time. The sleeve was actually a mischievous crop of a larger image in which Dallesandro is engaged in homosexual foreplay with Louis Waldon. Morrissey later expressed regret that in choosing this image he'd 'succumbed to the whole Warhol thing – like those modernites who crave the Factory thing and everything from

late-Sixties New York, which surely was a depressing waste of time.' Nevertheless, he'd return to Warholia again on 1987's 'Sheila Take A Bow' single featuring Candy Darling (who also starred in *Flesh*).
No matrix messages

Hatful Of Hollow

Cover star: 'Unknown Cocteau model'. The image was culled by Morrissey from a '1960s French magazine'. The giveaway Jean Cocteau reference is the drawing/tattoo that can be seen on the model's shoulder. The original gatefold album sleeve set this image within a blue border. It was later reissued in a less effective, full-bleed cropped version.
Matrix messages: A – 'The impotence of Ernest' (the same message etched on the 'William, It Was Really Nothing' single) B – 'Ian [Eire]' (Marr's tribute to his younger brother, Ian, and his family roots in Ireland).

Meat Is Murder

Cover star: Four repeated images of an unknown soldier from Emile de Antonio's 1968 Vietnam documentary *In The Year of the Pig*. The image is actually doctored; the original helmet inscription being 'Make war, not peace'.
Matrix messages: A – 'Illness as art'; B – 'Doing the Wythenshawe Waltz' (pun on the Cockney music hall song 'Doing the Lambeth Walk', Wynthenshawe being Marr's native area of Manchester).

The Queen Is Dead

Cover star: Alain Delon from the 1964 French movie *L'Insoumis* (*The Unvanquished*). Delon was also the father of Nico's son, Ari (though he denied paternity), who can be heard singing 'Le Petit Chevalier' on Nico's 1970 LP *Desertshore*, one of Morrissey's favourite records.
Matrix messages: A – 'Fear of Manchester'; B – 'Them was rotten days' (a line from the 1960 movie *Saturday Night and Sunday Morning*, as spoken by Hylda Baker).

The World Won't Listen

Cover star: Unknown group of boys photographed by Jurgen Vollmer. Front, rear and inner sleeve pictures were all sourced from Vollmer's 1981 book *Rock 'n' roll Times: The Style and Spirit of the Early Beatles and Their First Fans*, documenting Hamburg and Paris between 1961 and 1964. Johnny Marr later revealed that the back cover was Morrissey's intentional visual joke; a portrait of four teenage girls whose faces bore an uncanny resemblance to the individual members of The Smiths. Left to right, the

girls supposedly represent Joyce, Rourke, Marr and Morrissey. 'We didn't discuss it,' said Marr, 'but I understood.'
No matrix messages

Louder Than Bombs

Cover star: Shelagh Delaney (see 'Girlfriend In A Coma').
No matrix messages

Strangeways, Here We Come

Cover star: Richard Davalos, on the set of the 1955 James Dean movie *East of Eden.* Prior to The Smiths, in December 1981 Morrissey wrote to his Scottish pen friend Robert Mackie stating; '*East of Eden* is a wonderful film. My ambition is to track down Richard Davalos (who played Aron, the angelic brother) and interview him.' However, Davalos was actually Morrissey's hasty second choice. Originally a young Harvey Keitel, laughing hysterically, cigarette in hand from 1967's *Who's That Knocking On My Door* was to grace the cover, but when Rough Trade sought the actor's permission Keitel – oblivious to the existence of the group – declined. Four years later, Keitel relented and allowed Morrissey to use the same photo as a backdrop on his solo 1991 *Kill Uncle* tour.

Visitors to Manchester today are advised not to waste their time searching for the back sleeve road sign directing traffic to *Strangeways* prison either – the plaque in question was stolen by a maniacal Smiths devotee shortly after the album's release.
Matrix messages: A – 'Guy Fawkes was a genius'.

Rank

Cover star: British actress Alexandra Bastedo, best known for her role in the Sixties action drama series *The Champions*, taken from John D Green's best-selling 1967 photo book *Birds of Britain*.
Matrix messages: A – 'Peepholism'.

Appendix III
Select Bibliography

All works published in London unless otherwise stated.

Bockris, Victor with Gerard Malanga, *Up-tight: The Velvet Underground Story* (Omnibus Press, 1983)

Bockris, Victor, *Patti Smith* (Fourth Estate, 1998)

Bracewell, Michael, *England is Mine* (Flamingo, 1998)

Bret, David, *Morrissey: Landscapes of the Mind* (Robson, 1994)

Burke, John, *Privilege* (Pan, 1967)

Collins, Andrew, *Billy Bragg: Still Suitable for Miners* (Virgin, 1998)

Cummins, Kevin, *The Smiths and Beyond* (Vision On, 2002)

Dawson, Jim and Steve Propes, *What Was the First Rock 'n' Roll Record?* (Faber & Faber, 1992)

Delaney, Shelagh, *A Taste of Honey* (Methuen, 1982)

Delaney, Shelagh, *The Lion in Love* (Methuen, 1962)

Delaney, Shelagh, *Sweetly Sings the Donkey* (Methuen, 1964)

Doyle, Tom, *The Glamour Chase: The Maverick Life of Billy MacKezie* (Bloomsbury, 1999)

Farrell, Warren, *The Liberated Man* (revised edition) (New York: Berkley, 1993)

Fowles, John, *The Collector* (Vintage, 1988)

Garner, Ken, *In Session Tonight* (BBC Books, 1993)

Gatenby, Phill, *Morrissey's Manchester* (Manchester: Empire Publications, 2002)

Goodman, Jonathan, *The Moors Murderers* (Magpie, 1994)

Greig, Charlotte, *Will You Still Love Me Tomorrow: Girl Groups from the 50s on…* (Virago, 1989)

Hart, Moss and George S Kaufman, *Three Plays* (Methuen, 1981)

Haskel, Molly, *From Reverence to Rape* (second edition) (Chicago: University of Chicago, 1987)

Haslam, Dave, *Manchester, England* (Fourth Estate, 1999)

Kerouac, Jack, *The Dharma Bums* (Penguin, 2000)

MacDonald, Ian, *Revolution in the Head: The Beatles' Records and The Sixties* (revised edition) (Pimlico, 1997)

Middles, Mick, *The Smiths* (Omnibus Press, 1985)

Morrissey, *The New York Dolls* (Manchester: Babylon Books, 1981)

Morrissey, *James Dean is Not Dead* (Manchester: Babylon Books,1983)

Nichols, Jack, *Men's Liberation: A New Definition of Masculinity* (New York: Penguin, 1975)

Nicholson, Viv and Stephen Smith, *Spend, Spend, Spend* (Fontana, 1978)

Orton, Joe, *The Orton Diaries* (Methuen, 1986)
Pegg, Nicholas, *The Complete David Bowie* (revised edition) (Reynolds & Hearn, 2002)
Pernice, Joe, *33 1/3: Meat Is Murder* (New York: Continuum, 2003)
Raudive, Konstantin, *Breakthrough: An Amazing Experiment in Electronic Communication with the Dead* (Colin Smythe, 1971)
Reid, Pat, *Bigmouth: Morrissey 1983-1993* (The Dunce Directive, 1993)
Reid, Pat, *Morrissey (Outlines)* (Bath: Absolute Press, 2004)
Rogan, Johnny, *Morrissey & Marr: The Severed Alliance* (revised edition) (Omnibus Press, 1993)
Rogan, Johnny, *The Smiths: The Visual Documentary* (Omnibus Press, 1994)
Rogan, Johnny, *The Complete Guide to the Music of the Smiths and Morrissey/Marr* (Omnibus Press, 1995)
Russell, Willy, *The Wrong Boy* (Doubleday, 2000)
Savage, Jon, *Time Travel* (Chatto & Windus, 1996)
Selby Jnr, Hubert, *Last Exit to Brooklyn* (Paladin,1987)
Shakespeare, William, *The Complete Works of William Shakespeare* (HarperCollins, 1994)
Shaw, Sandie, *The World at my Feet* (Fontana, 1992)
Sitwell, Edith, *English Eccentrics* (Penguin, 1978)
Slee, Jo, *Peepholism: Into the Art of Morrissey* (Sidgwick & Jackson, 1994)
Smart, Elizabeth, *By Grand Central Station I Sat Down and Wept* (Paladin, 1991)
Smith, Patti, *Complete: Lyrics, Reflections and Notes for the Future* (Bloomsbury, 1998)
Sterling, Linder, *Morrissey Shot* (Secker & Warburg, 1992)
Taylor, John Russell, *Anger and After: A Guide to the New British Drama* (Methuen, 1962)
Vonnegut, Kurt, *Slaughterhouse 5* (Jonathan Cape, 1970)
Walters, Margaret, *The Nude Male* (Paddington Press, 1978)
Whiteside, Johnny, *Cry: The Johnnie Ray Story* (Barricade Books, 1997)
Wilde, Oscar, *The Complete Works of Oscar Wilde* (Collins, 1983)
Williams, Emlyn, *Beyond Belief* (Pan, 1968)
Wilson, Tony, *24 Hour Party People* (Channel 4 Books, 2002)
Woolf, Virginia, *A Room of One's Own* (Penguin, 1970)

Further information and quotations were sourced from the author's own collection of press cuttings as well as original periodicals stored at The British Newspaper Library in Colindale, North London. These include: *Melody Maker, Sounds, Record Mirror, Jamming!, Uncut, Record Collector, Q, Select, Mojo, Vox, Time Out, Guitar, Guitar Player, i-D, The Face, Blitz, The Hit, Smash Hits, No 1, NME, Rolling Stone, Creem, Hot Press, Zig Zag* and *The Catalogue*. Mention must also be made of Robert Mackie's correspondence with Morrissey from 1980-81, reproduced in fanzine form as *Words by Morrissey* in the early Nineties.

Special thanks to Catherine Hurley for providing issues of the original fanzine *Smiths Indeed*.

At the time of publishing, the author also acknowledges the following websites: *The Arcane Old Wardrobe* (an excellent on-line library of press cuttings at www.arcaneoldwardrobe.com); *Passions Just Like Mine* (a meticulous discography and concert chronology at www.passionsjustlikemine.com); and the network of Smiths-related sites accessible via the *Shoplifters Union* (http://shoplifters.morrissey-solo.com), an affiliate of the California-based *Morrissey Solo* site, the primary Smiths news resource on the web (www.morrissey-solo.com). Thanks also to Johnny Marr's official web forum (www.jmarr.com) and the *Morrissey Tour* site (www.morrisseytour.com).

Song Index